The Rough Guide to
The Ionian Islands

There are more than one hundred and fifty Rough Guide titles
covering destinations from Amsterdam to Zimbabwe

Forthcoming titles include
Argentina • Croatia • Ecuador • Southeast Asia

Rough Guide Reference Series
Classical Music • Country Music • Drum 'n' Bass • English Football
European Football • House • The Internet • Jazz • Music USA • Opera
Reggae • Rock Music • Techno • Unexplained Phenomena • World Music

Rough Guide Phrasebooks
Czech • Dutch • Egyptian Arabic • European Languages • French
German • Greek • Hindi & Urdu • Hungarian • Indonesian • Italian
Mandarin Chinese • Mexican Spanish • Polish • Portuguese • Russian
Spanish • Swahili • Thai • Turkish • Vietnamese

Rough Guides on the Internet
www.roughguides.com

Rough Guide Credits

Text Editor:	Chris Schüler
Series Editor:	Mark Ellingham
Editorial:	Martin Dunford, Jonathan Buckley, Jo Mead, Kate Berens, Amanda Tomlin, Ann-Marie Shaw, Paul Gray, Helena Smith, Judith Bamber, Orla Duane, Olivia Eccleshall, Ruth Blackmore, Sophie Martin, Geoff Howard, Claire Saunders, Gavin Thomas, Alexander Mark Rogers, Polly Thomas, Joe Staines, Lisa Nellis, Andrew Tomičíc, Richard Lim, Claire Fogg, Duncan Clark, Peter Buckley (UK); Andrew Rosenberg, Mary Beth Maioli, Don Bapst, Stephen Timblin (US)
Online Editors:	Kelly Cross (US)
Production:	Susanne Hillen, Andy Hilliard, Link Hall, Helen Ostick, Julia Bovis, Michelle Draycott, Katie Pringle, Robert Evers, Niamh Hatton, Mike Hancock
Cartography:	Melissa Baker, Maxine Repath, Nichola Goodliffe, Ed Wright
Picture Research:	Louise Boulton, Sharon Martins
Finance:	John Fisher, Gary Singh, Edward Downey, Mark Hall, Tim Bill
Marketing & Publicity:	Richard Trillo, Niki Smith, David Wearn, Jemima Broadbridge (UK); Jean-Marie Kelly, Myra Campolo, Simon Carloss (US)
Administration:	Tania Hummel, Charlotte Marriott, Demelza Dallow

Acknowledgements

Nick Edwards: I would like to say *efharistó polý* to all the folk who helped out during the course of a hot summer. Special thanks to Mariana, Petros, Orestis and Orpheas Zoupanos, Spyros Hytiris and Hilary Whetton-Paipeti for hospitality and invaluable help in Corfu; an extra helping of gratitude to Mariana and Spyros for rallying round during the lost notebook crisis. Also thanks to Efi and Antonio for introducing me to the Pérdika turtle; Captain Elias Vernikos for making me first mate in Lefkádha and the Kálamos trip; Panayiotis of *Hotel Chara*, Argostóli; Christina and Fotis for trips, company and Scrabble on Kefalloniá; Yiannis Karapapas, Spyros Kouvaras and Telemachus & family for *paniyíri* nights on Itháki; June and Angie Kalogeratou for hospitality in Zákynthos. Back in London, thanks to all the Rough Guide staff for the constantly friendly welcome on my sporadic visits and to Chris Schüler for skilful editing; also to Auntie Dos for multiple cups of tea. Finally, heart-felt thanks to Maria for inspiration from afar during research and closer at hand while writing up and beyond.

The editor would like to thank Stephen Townshend and Charles Hebbert for Oz and UK Basics research; Jennifer Speake for proofreading; and Stratigraphics for cartography.

The publishers and authors have done their best to ensure the accuracy and currency of all information in *The Rough Guide to The Ionian Islands*; however, they can accept no responsibility for any loss, injury, or inconvenience sustained by any traveller as a result of information or advice contained in the guide.

This second edition published May 2000 by Rough Guides Ltd, 62–70 Shorts Gardens, London WC2H 9AB. Distributed by the Penguin Group:

Penguin Books Ltd, 27 Wrights Lane, London W8 5TZ.
Penguin Putnam, Inc. 375 Hudson Street, New York, NY 10014.
Penguin Books Australia Ltd, 487 Maroondah Highway, PO Box 257, Ringwood, Victoria 3134, Australia.
Penguin Books Canada Ltd, 10 Alcorn Avenue, Toronto, Ontario M4V 1E4, Canada.
Penguin Books (NZ) Ltd, 182–190 Wairau Road, Auckland 10, New Zealand.
Printed in England by Clays Ltd, St Ives PLC.
Typography and original design by Jonathan Dear and The Crowd Roars.
Illustrations throughout by Edward Briant.

The Rough Guide to

The Ionian Islands

Written and researched by
John Gill

This edition revised and updated by
Nick Edwards

ROUGH GUIDES

Help us update

We've gone to a lot of trouble to ensure that this second edition of *The Rough Guide to The Ionian Islands* is accurate and up-to-date. However, things inevitably change, and if you feel we've got it wrong or left something out, we'd like to know: any suggestions, comments or corrections would be much appreciated. We'll credit all contributions and send a copy of the next edition – or any other Rough Guide if you prefer – for the best correspondence.

Please mark letters "Rough Guide to The Ionian Islands" and send to: Rough Guides, 62–70 Shorts Gardens, London WC2H 9AB or Rough Guides, 4th Floor, 345 Hudson St, New York, NY 10014.

Email should be sent to:
mail@roughguides.co.uk

Online updates about Rough Guide titles can be found on our Web site at *www.roughguides.com*

The Author

John Gill has been a regular visitor to the Ionian Islands for the last fifteen years, and published a book about one, *The Stars over Paxos*, in 1995. He has published several other books and works as a journalist in London.

Rough Guides

Travel Guides • Phrasebooks • Music and Reference Guides

We set out to do something different when the first Rough Guide was published in 1982. Mark Ellingham, just out of University, was travelling in Greece. He brought along the popular guides of the day, but found they were all lacking in some way. They were either strong on ruins and museums but went on for pages without mentioning a beach or taverna. Or they were so conscious of the need to save money that they lost sight of Greece's cultural and historical significance. Also, none of the books told him anything about Greece's contemporary life – its politics, its culture, its people, and how they lived.

So with no job in prospect, Mark decided to write his own guidebook, one which aimed to provide practical information that was second to none, detailing the best beaches and the hottest clubs and restaurants, while also giving hard-hitting accounts of every sight, both famous and obscure, and providing up-to-the-minute information on contemporary culture. It was a guide that encouraged independent travellers to find the best of Greece, and was a great success, getting shortlisted for the Thomas Cook travel guide award, and encouraging Mark, along with three friends, to expand the series.

The Rough Guide list grew rapidly and the letters flooded in, indicating a much broader readership than had been anticipated, but one which uniformly appreciated the Rough Guides' mix of practical detail and humour, irreverence and enthusiasm. Things haven't changed. The same four friends who began the series are still the caretakers of the Rough Guide mission today: to provide the most reliable, up-to-date and entertaining information to independent-minded travellers of all ages, on all budgets.

We now publish 150 titles and have offices in London and New York. The travel guides are written and researched by a dedicated team of more than 100 authors, based in Britain, Europe, the USA and Australia. We have also created a unique series of phrasebooks to accompany the travel series, along with the acclaimed series of music guides, and a best-selling pocket guide to the Internet and World Wide Web. We also publish comprehensive travel information on our Web site: *www.roughguides.com*

Contents

Part Three   Contexts   257

Index   290

List of maps

MAP SYMBOLS

▪▪▪▪▪	National border	Ⓓ	Monastery (regional maps)
═══	Major road	♜	Castle
══	Minor road	∴	Ruins
- - - -	Path	◠	Cave
▬▬▬	Railway	▲	Mountain peak
— —	Ferry route	⌁	Lighthouse
··········	Waterway	ⓘ	Tourist office
▬▬▬	Wall	⊠	Post office
✗	Airport	Ⓗ	Hospital
★	Bus stop	▮	Building
◉	Hotel	➕	Church/cathedral (town maps)
Ⓧ	Campsite	†₊†	Cemetery
▣	Restaurant	▦	Park
◆	Point of interest	▒	Sand/beach
‡	Church (regional maps)		

Introduction

T he **Ionian islands** comprise a core group of six – Corfu (Kérkyra), Paxí (Paxos), Lefkádha (Lefkas), Itháki (Ithaca), Kefalloniá (Cephallonia) and Zákynthos (Zante) – which trace a ragged line down the west coast of Greece*. None is more than 30km from the mainland, yet this has been far enough to exclude the Ionians from many of the key events in Greek history, most notably occupation by the Ottoman Turks. However, their position at the south of the Adriatic instead put them at the mercy of northerly invaders, primarily the **Venetians** and, later, the **British**, whose cultures fused with those of the islands. The Venetians, who first arrived in the archipelago in the late fourteenth century, imported language, art, music, law and architecture; the British turned up in the eighteenth century and unpacked local government, education, civil engineering, cricket and ginger beer. To a lesser or greater degree, all these things can still be found in the islands, and the Italians and British remain the region's main summer invaders.

As the big narrative happened elsewhere, the Ionian has no major archeological sites – though Olympia, just two hours' drive from Pátra on the Peloponnese mainland, is accessible from the southern islands. However, there are some spectacular medieval fortresses, and museums on the larger islands trace the archipelago's cultures back to the Paleolithic era. Itháki is still the favourite for the disputed site of Odysseus' Homeric home and has some scattered remains as proof, with neighbouring islands laying claim to particular settings and events from the *Odyssey*.

But the major feature that distinguishes the Ionians from the mainland and the central swarm of Greek islands in the Aegean is climatic: a reliable rainfall pattern has allowed centuries of fairly stable agriculture and has nurtured olive trees, vineyards, rich fruit and

---

* Kýthira, isolated at the foot of the Peloponnese along with its satellite Andikýthira, is officially part of the Ionian group, completing the seven islands of the Heptanese. We haven't covered them in this Guide, as they bear few similarities to the core group of islands, share no transport connections with them and would not be visited on the same trip.

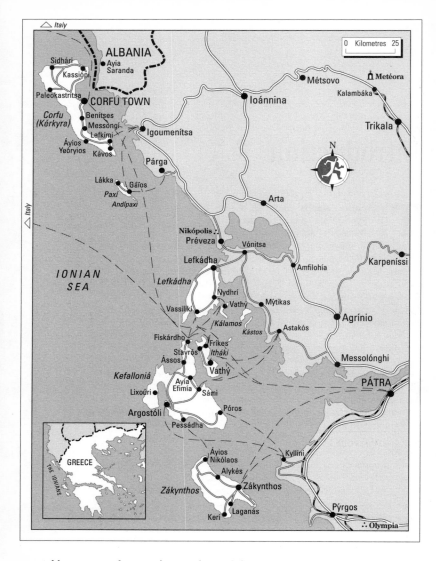

vegetable crops, and even wheat and cereal farming on some islands. The Ionian islands display similar geographical characteristics, too: all are mountainous (even tiny Paxí has a small mountain of sorts), with their east coasts tending to be gentle dip slopes above flat, sometimes reclaimed, farm land. The west coasts are often rocky, with cliffs up to 200 metres high. This geology conspires against tourism, placing most of the best beaches on the less accessible west coasts, and the worst on the handy east coasts – where lazy developers have tended to concentrate their attentions. With the exception of Corfu's southwest and north coasts, the south coast of Kefalloniá, southern Zákynthos and pockets of western Lefkádha, most beaches are pebbly, usually shelving into sand.

Island-hopping through the Ionian is not as tricky as some people imagine and, with a month on your hands, you could easily get a taster of all six major islands, though you would be unlikely to see any of them in depth. There is certainly not the abundance of ferry and hydrofoil lines weaving through the group that the Aegean is blessed with, but most of the islands are connected to their nearest neighbour or two at some point. The only really broken link in the chain, with the exception of a very infrequent service between Corfu and Kefalloniá, is that the northern duo, Corfu and Paxí, have no direct boats to the southern quartet, forcing you to travel via the mainland, though that in itself can be a pleasurable experience and allows you to glimpse a different side of Greece. Full details of all the possible inter-island connections are given throughout the Guide.

For those with less time to play, **Corfu** and **Zákynthos** are the easiest of the islands to visit: both have busy international airports, and a developed structure of package and independent tourism. Over the years, however, they have acquired a not entirely undeserved reputation as sleazepits, the blame for which can be laid at the door of unscrupulous Greek and British tourism operators. The tackier resorts on Corfu tend to be on its east coast – Ípsos and Kávos are given over to booze, bonking and bungee-jumping, although an earlier slump in tourism has had the effect of once-notorious Benítses reinventing itself as more of a family venue. On Zákynthos, Laganás is set on one of the island's finest beaches, but has reached levels of excess to rival anything on Corfu. However, such large-scale tourist

---

Transliteration

Because there's no standard system of transliterating Greek script into Roman, you're sure to find that the Greek words and proper names in this book do not always match the versions written elsewhere. Place names are the biggest source of confusion, varying from map to map, and often sign to sign. The word for "saint", for instance, one of the commonest prefixes, can be rendered Áyios, Ágios, or Ághios. To make matters worse, there are often two forms of a name in Greek – the modern, popularly used *dhimotikí* and the older, elitist *katharévoussa*. Thus, for example, you will come across the older Paxoí and the newer Paxí, as well as Anglicized Paxos. Throw in inherited Italian and English names, a boggling array of island dialects with their own variants on pronunciation, and haphazard spelling, and you have a real mare's nest.

In this book, we've used a modern, largely phonetic system in the spelling of modern Greek place names. We have, however, retained the accepted "English" spelling for familiar places like Corfu and Athens. We have also accented (with an acute) the stressed letter of each word; getting this right in pronunciation is vital in order to be understood.

developments take up only a small proportion of either island, and most locals and visitors remain quite undisturbed by such overblown commerce and razzmatazz.

Kefaloniá's relatively new airport has yet to attract the volume of traffic of either Corfu or Zákynthos, but the island boasts some of the best unspoilt beaches and wildest mountainscapes in the Ionian. It remains a reasonably well-kept secret: chic resorts like Fiskárdho are very busy throughout the season, but others, such as Ayía Efimía, never seem to fill. Its northerly neighbour **Lefkádha** has two notable pockets of development – Nydhrí and the windsurfers' paradise, Vassilikí – but the rest of the heavily indented coastline and the handsome, mountainous interior are largely untouched by tourism. It goes without saying that the further you travel from an airport, or an island with an airport, the more you'll distance yourself from the crowds. Many landing at Corfu head at great speed for **Paxí**, those at Kefaloniá for **Itháki**. The former, barely 12km long and covered in olive trees, supports just three busy fishing village resorts, two of them tiny; small and mountainous, the latter is the most unspoilt of the core islands.

The **satellite islands**, such as the Dhiapóndia islets off northwest Corfu, Meganíssi off Lefkádha, and even Andípaxi south of Paxí, are becoming more accessible to adventurous travellers each year. Committed loners and misanthropes might also consider the areas around Korissíon lagoon or Mount Pandokrátor on Corfu; the hills around Karyá or the little-visited southwest coast, especially Atháni, on Lefkádha; the quieter parts of Kefaloniá, such as the Lixoúri peninsula or Ássos; or the northeast of Zákynthos. If you want to live as the Greeks live away from the tourism racket, try the island capitals: Corfu Town has transformed itself in recent years, Lefkádha Town has a lively buzz to it, and Argostóli retains a spacious charm despite being razed by the 1953 earthquake. The other seismic victim, Zákynthos Town, also has a certain class and lovely setting, despite busy traffic detracting from its charm at times. The latter two are particularly authentic, and secondary towns like Lefkími on Corfu or Lixoúri on Kefaloniá are even less influenced by tourism. Of course, some mountain villages still see hardly any outsiders at all.

It's worth noting that nobody ever came to the Ionian islands looking for cordon bleu food or Scandinavian plumbing, but that applies to just about the whole of the country. In all but the smartest accommodation, bathrooms are haphazard, though rarely insanitary. And while there are excellent tavernas on many islands, most, over the decades, have been content to reach a happy medium with their foreign customers. They generally serve meals lukewarm, following the Greek nostrum that hot food is bad for the system, and on the smaller islands certain vegetables can be difficult to obtain (you could launch a career as a comedian on Paxí by asking for lettuce). Yet these shortcomings have actually entered the mythology of the thousands who return regardless to the islands year after year. One of the reasons they return – beyond some of the finest swimming and watersports in the Mediterranean, the landscape, sunshine and balmy nights out under the Milky Way – is the welcome that all but the largest resorts still manage to extend. Despite the pressure of tourism, the islanders remain a disarmingly friendly people, and reserved Britons are often embarrassed by their astonishing kindness. The traditional quality of *filoxenía*, kindness to strangers, survives, and can take the form of anything from an orange offered from someone's garden to a meal, a lift or a room for the night. And after decades of handling tourists who insist on speaking their own tongue, islanders are genuinely charmed by attempts to speak their language, even if it's just a *yiá sou* or *kalí méra*.

When to go

If you can, it's best to avoid the islands in late July and most of August, when holidaying Greeks and Italians descend en masse, accommodation is scarce, and temperatures and prices soar. June and early September are just as good for those concerned about fine weather (in fact, the 1990s have seen a number of fairly unstable high summers, with rainy Augusts followed by stunning Septembers and Octobers). In June, the sea is usually warm enough for swimming; in September it can be as warm as a bath.

May, September and October are the times for bargain flights and packages, and, though you may risk short spells of inclement weather, are probably the best times to visit. In May many spring flowers are still in bloom, and villages and villagers are fresh from the winter. In late September and early October you can be blessed with fine weather, warm seas and almost no other visitors. However, bargain package deals in these low-season periods should be carefully scrutinized: some remote resorts (noted in the Guide) close early, often stranding those without the wherewithal to hire transport.

Early May and late October mark the beginning and end of charter flights to the islands, although there's a mini winter season around Christmas and New Year. Outside these times you have to fly via Athens, but, with the exception of Paxí, every island capital has hotels open year-round, and most local accommodation companies can rustle up some suitable accommodation. When the rafts of knick-knacks are packed away until next season, even the most developed resorts resume their prelapsarian charm, and major towns – in particular, Corfu Town – are to be seen at their best. The only bars or tavernas will be those the Greeks themselves use, which is usually the best recommendation at any time of the year. The winter months, November especially, see spectacular storms in the Ionian, yet it is possible to get sunburnt on Christmas Day. Off-season travel is also the only way to catch the two biggest festivals of the year: pre-Lenten carnival, a Venetian tradition maintained with parades, parties and mischief; and Orthodox Easter, which is celebrated for a full week and can be an extremely moving experience.

Prevailing northwesterly winds affect all the Ionian islands, commonly rising in the afternoon, occasionally developing into the *maéstro* – the Ionian equivalent of the Aegean *meltémi* – which can blow for three days or more. These winds make the Ionians ideal for yachting holidays and watersports, but can make beaches at exposed resorts hellish. The climate figures given below are averages for Corfu – if any generalizations about Ionian weather can be made in advance, they can be made only about the region as a whole. The archipelago has any number of micro-climates: Lefkádha's valleys are like little lost Shangri-Las of meteorology, and Paxí gets only a fraction of the storms that gang up on nearby Corfu's Mount Pandokrátor.

CORFU CLIMATE TABLE

	Jan	Feb	Mar	Apr	May	Jun	Jul	Aug	Sep	Oct	Nov	Dec
Daily temperatures (°C)	13	14	16	19	23	28	30	31	28	23	18	15
Average rainfall (cm)	15	14	10	6	4	1	0	0	1	15	20	18

The Basics

Getting there from Britain

At roughly 2000km and three hours by air from London, Corfu is the nearest Greek island to Britain; its southerly siblings Kefalloniá and Zákynthos are barely half an hour's flight further. For most visitors, flying is the only viable option for getting to the Ionians: buses and trains can take up to four days, and are no bargain unless you're planning to work your way slowly through Europe (see pp.15–17 for information about getting to the islands from mainland Greece and Italy).

Corfu was one of the earliest destinations for British tourism in Greece. There are no direct scheduled flights to the Ionian islands, but Corfu is well connected by **summer charter flights** with British airports: Gatwick, Manchester, Birmingham, Belfast, Bristol, Cardiff, Edinburgh, Glasgow, Luton, Newcastle, Norwich and Stansted all have charter flights to Corfu at least once a week in summer. More and more British airports are also developing seasonal charter connections with the region's three other airports: **Zákynthos** (the busiest and most accessible after Corfu), **Kefalloniá** and **Préveza**. Island-hoppers aiming for the hopper-friendly triangle of Lefkádha, Itháki and Kefalloniá should consider either Préveza or Kefalloniá airports: both offer good access to the islands, and Préveza, though on the mainland, is

only thirty minutes by regular bus from Lefkádha Town. **Routing via Athens** is generally only a useful option if you're travelling **out of season** (when there are only a few obscure charters into the Ionians around Christmas or Easter), if you're planning to stay longer than a charter would allow and need a **scheduled ticket**, or as a last resort in season.

Classified ads in national papers – the *Guardian, Independent, Observer, Sunday Times* – as well as Teletext and, increasingly, a number of Internet addresses (*www.usitcampus.co.uk*, the Web site of Usit CAMPUS, *www.cheapflights.co.uk* for flight deals and travel agents, and *www.lastminute.co.uk* for holiday deals), are useful sources when shopping around for flights. Local newspapers and listings magazines also carry ads for companies selling budget flights. Among travel agents, high-street branches of the major chains tend to be geared to selling you a package holiday rather than a bargain flight, but this can be an extremely cheap way of getting to the destination of your choice if you don't mind being restricted to staying in the busy resorts.

Charter flights

Most British travellers to the Ionian islands will arrive by direct **charter flight**, either with a package holiday or on a flight-only deal. These flights have fixed and unchangeable outward and return dates, and are usually for one or two weeks, although most operators can offer three- or four-week flights for a nominal extra fee. Some may even agree longer periods, although these tend to be low-season deals or dependent on how busy the season is. The cheapest charter flights tend to be those into Corfu (it doesn't make much difference which mainland British airport you fly from). A charter flight to Corfu in July costs around £200.

The cheapest charter flights to Greece are usually weekday flights leaving late at night or early in the morning. However, the days of ultra-cheap last-minute deals are – for the time being, at least – over. Sophisticated computer systems (and not a little commercial ruthlessness) have largely eliminated the situation where seats on half-empty flights were available for a song. The mid-1990s have seen a return to early booking to secure flights or holidays, but if you can be flexible, then it is worth checking the Internet for cheap and last-minute deals (see box on p.5).

Flight-only deals from Gatwick to Corfu generally **cost** between £150 and £200, although "red-eye" flights, which typically leave Britain around 11pm and arrive around 4am local time, can cost as little as £120. Flights from major provincial airports such as Manchester and Birmingham tend to be £10–20 higher, those from Glasgow and smaller airports like Bristol £30–40 higher. Flights to Zákynthos and Kefalloniá are limited to Gatwick and the major provincial airports and are more expensive, costing between £170 and £220 depending on season. Préveza's small, semi-military airport is the worst served, with only one or two flights from the major airports per week, at prices starting from around £170. Charter flights to Athens are worth investigating in low season (for example, £99 for a week in March through *www.cheapflights.co.uk*).

Different regulations concerning charter tickets apply to EU nationals and those from outside the EU. **Non-EU nationals** flying charter must purchase a return ticket, valid for no fewer than three days and no more than four weeks. They should also have an accommodation voucher – a hangover from the days when flight-only deals were not meant to be issued – which should be issued by the ticketing agency but which will not actually get you accommodation. The accommodation voucher system applies to **EU nationals** too, in theory, but recent relaxation in airport practices means that few (if any) EU nationals are checked by customs and immigration.

Student/youth charters are sold as one-way flights only and are available to both EU and non-EU nationals. By combining two one-way charters you can stay for over a month. Student/youth charter tickets are available to anyone under 26, and to all card-carrying full-time students under 32.

Finally, while some carriers now regard it as a formality, **reconfirmation** of your return flight is still strongly recommended, at least 48 hours before departure. It's most common to telephone to confirm, but allow plenty of time, as the local agents who usually handle these services are often engaged. Try visiting the agent in person, or

if the worst comes to the worst, contact the head office of the company you flew with. Problems are rare, but failure to reconfirm could allow the carrier to bounce you off a flight if there's a problem with overbooking.

Scheduled flights

Getting from Britain to the Ionian islands using **scheduled flights** is a roundabout process. The Greek national carrier Olympic Airways (1–2 daily), British Airways (2 daily) and Virgin Atlantic (1 daily) have direct flights from London Heathrow to Athens, which with advance booking can cost under £200, even in August. Flights also leave from Gatwick: British Airways one daily, Virgin one daily (except Tues) March to October. From Athens, there are daily internal flights on Olympic to Préveza and the Ionian island airports, costing from around £25 one way (20,000 drachmas there, 26,000 for pre-booked return) and averaging 45 minutes' flying time. Bus and ferry connections from Athens are cheaper and more frequent, but take over eight hours to reach even Corfu. Scheduled flights from British regional airports route via Heathrow in the first instance.

Consolidators for London–Athens flights on eastern European airlines such as Balkan may have cheaper discount flights than Olympic, BA and Virgin (for example £178 with CSA Czech Airlines), but flights are routed via the airlines' capital cities, where you may have to spend several hours.

The advantages of scheduled flights are that they can be booked well in advance, have long ticket validities and tend to leave at more sociable hours than charter flights. Many cheaper APEX and SuperAPEX fares, however, do have advance-purchase (usually fourteen days) and/or minimum-stay requirements, as well as

---

Scheduled airlines

Balkan Airlines Tradewinds ☎020/7631 1840.
British Airways ☎0345/222111.
CSA Czech Airlines Collets ☎020/8202 8101.
LOT Polish Airlines Orbis ☎020/7636 4701.
Malev Hungarian Airlines Danube Travel ☎020/7724 7577.
Olympic Airways ☎020/7409 3400.
Virgin Atlantic Airways ☎01293/747747.

FLIGHT AGENTS

Alecos Tours, 3a Camden Rd, London NW1 ☎020/7267 2092. Regular Olympic Airways consolidator, plus charter flights to Corfu.

Andrews, 132 Green Lanes, London N13 5UN ☎020/8882 7153. Consolidator for CSA. Also handles flights to all the Ionian airports.

Argo Holidays, 100 Wigmore St, London W1H 9DR ☎020/7331 7000; *www.argo-holidays.com*. Consolidator for Olympic, BA and Virgin Atlantic. Charter flights and packages to Corfu, Zákynthos and Kefalloniá.

Council Travel, 28a Poland St, London W1V 3DD ☎020/7437 7767. Flights with student discounts to Athens and charters to the Ionians.

Eclipse Direct ☎0990 010203. Probably the largest range of flights to the Ionians.

Springways Travel, 46 Victoria Rd, Surbiton, Surrey KT6 4JL ☎020/8339 9929. Scheduled and charter flights to Athens, and charters to Corfu, Zákynthos, Kefalloniá and Préveza.

STA Travel, 86 Old Brompton Rd, London SW7 3LH; 117 Euston Rd, London NW1 2SX; 38 Store St, London WC1E 7BZ; 11 Goodge St, London W1P 1FE ☎020/7 361 6161 (Europe), ☎020/7361 6262 (worldwide); 38 North St, Brighton ☎01273/728 282; 25 Queens Rd, Bristol BS8 1QE ☎0117/929 4399; 38 Sidney St, Cambridge CB2 3HX ☎01223/366 966; 75 Deansgate, Manchester M3 2BW ☎0161/834 0668; 88 Vicar Lane, Leeds LS1 7JH ☎0113/244 9212; 78 Bold St, Liverpool L1 4HR ☎0151/707 1123; 9 St Mary's Place, Newcastle-upon-Tyne NE1 7PG ☎0191/233 2111; 36 George St, Oxford OX1 2OJ ☎01865/792 800; 27 Forrest Rd, Edinburgh ☎0131/226 7747; 184 Byres Rd, Glasgow G1 1JH ☎0141/338 6000; 30 Upper Kirkgate, Aberdeen ☎0122/465 8222; and branches on university campuses; *www.statravel.co.uk*. Very good rates with Virgin and Olympic via

Athens to the Ionian islands, eg £105 return in low season to Athens (Virgin) plus £25 one way to any Ionian airport.

Trailfinders, 1 Threadneedle St, London EC2R 8JX (all destinations) ☎020/7628 7628; 42–50 Earls Court Rd, London W8 6FT ☎020/7938 3366 (long-haul flights); 194 Kensington High St, London, W8 7RG ☎020/7938 3939 (long-haul flights); 215 Kensington High St, London W6 6BD ☎020/7937 5400 (transatlantic and European); 58 Deansgate, Manchester M3 2FF ☎0161/839 6969; 254–284 Sauchiehall St, Glasgow G2 3EH ☎0141/353 2224; 22–24 The Priory, Queensway, Birmingham B4 6BS ☎0121/236 1234; 48 Corn St, Bristol BS1 1HQ ☎0117/929 9000; *www.trailfinders.co.uk*. One of the best-informed and most efficient agents for independent travellers; all branches open daily until 6pm, Thurs until 7pm. Arranges scheduled flights to Athens with Olympic, eg £225 in May.

Usit CAMPUS, national call centre ☎0870/240 1010; 52 Grosvenor Gardens, London SW1W 0AG ☎020/7730 3402 (Europe); 51 branches in Britain, including 541 Bristol Rd, Selly Oak, Birmingham B29 6AU ☎0121/414 1848; 61 Ditchling Rd, Brighton BN1 4SD ☎01273/570 226; 37–39 Queen's Rd, Clifton, Bristol BS8 1QE ☎0117/929 2494; 5 Emmanuel St, Cambridge CB1 1NE ☎01223/324 283; 53 Forest Rd, Edinburgh EH1 2QP ☎0131/225 6111, (telesales) 668 3303; 122 George St, Glasgow G1 1RF ☎0141/553 1818; 166 Deansgate, Manchester M3 3FE ☎0161/833 2046, (telesales) 273 1721; 105–106 St Aldates, Oxford OX1 1DO ☎01865/242 067; *www.usitcampus.co.uk*. Charter flights to Athens and Corfu in summer.

Usit COUNCIL, 28a Poland St, London W1V 3DB ☎020/7287 3337 or 437 7767. Flights and student discounts (part of Usit CAMPUS).

restrictions on date changes and refunds, so check conditions carefully. As with charters, discount fares on scheduled flights are available from most high-street travel agents, as well as from a number of specialist flight and student/youth agencies.

If the preferred ticket is hard to find, and you have the time and money to improvise, it is also worthwhile considering flying on separate **one-way tickets** (but check p.20 regarding any visa restrictions that might affect you). Outside high season, island travel agents can often find bargain

SPECIALIST TOUR OPERATORS

Argo Holidays, 100 Wigmore St, London W1H 9DR ☎ 020/7331 7070. Package operator specializing in the larger hotel complexes of Corfu and Zákynthos, plus the *Paxos Beach Hotel*.

Club Vassilikí, Bridgefoot House, 2a Star St, Ware, Herts SG12 7AA ☎ 01920 484121. Windsurfing packages to Vassilikí on Lefkádha, including flights, accommodation, beginner instruction and insurance.

Corfu à la Carte, 1st floor, 32 High St, Thatcham, Berks RG19 3JD ☎ 01635/863030; *www.travelalacarte.co.uk*. Traditional villas on Corfu (the quieter northeast coast) and at Longós and Gáïos on Paxí.

CV Travel, 43 Cadogan St, London SW3 2PR ☎ 0870 606 0013; email: *cv.travel@dial.pipex.com*. One of the big three (along with Greek Islands Club and Simply Ionian), and *the* exclusive villa company on Corfu and Paxí, with some of the islands' most luxurious (and expensive) properties on its books.

Direct Greece, Granite House, 31–33 Stockwell St, Glasgow G1 4RY ☎ 0141/559 7111. Villas and apartments on Corfu, Lefkádha and Zákynthos (and at Párga on the mainland).

Explore Worldwide, 1 Frederick St, Aldershot, Hants GU11 1LQ ☎ 01252/760000; *www.explore.co.uk*. Offers a guided trekking tour of the Peloponnese, Kefalloniá and Itháki among its Greek itineraries.

Grecofile/Filoxenia, Sourdock Hill, Barkisland, Halifax, West Yorks HX4 0AG ☎ 01422/375999. Villa and apartment holidays all over the Ionian islands, including some self-catering and small hotels on Corfu and apartments and cottages on Paxos.

Greek Island Club, 10–12 Upper Square, Old Isleworth, Middlesex, TW7 7BJ ☎ 020/8232 9780; *www.vch.co.uk/villas*. One of the longest-established villa and apartment companies in the Ionian, with prime properties on Corfu, Paxí, Itháki, Kefalloniá and Zákynthos. Also offers specialist holidays, such as painting and cultural tours.

Island Wandering, 51a London Rd, Hurst Green, East Sussex TN19 7QP ☎ 01580/860733. Tailor-made holidays (island-wandering or one or two centres) to Corfu, Lefkádha, Itháki

(including the *Nostos* in Fríkes), Kefalloniá (including the *Mouikis* in Argostóli), Zákynthos and on the mainland.

Kosmar Villa Holidays, The Grange, 100 High St, Southgate, London N14 6FS ☎ 0870/7000 747. Hotels and apartments in Corfu, Lefkádha, Kefalloniá, Paxí, Párga and Zákynthos.

Manos Holidays, 168–172 Old St, London EC1V 9RE ☎ 020/7216 8000; *www.manos.co.uk*. One of the biggest package companies specializing in the Ionian, with a wide range of apartments and hotels on Corfu, Lefkádha, Kefalloniá, Zákynthos, Paxí, Meganíssi and Párga.

Neilson, 120 St George's Rd, Brighton BN2 1EA ☎ 01273/626284. Watersport and flotilla holidays based in Nidhrí and Vassilikí on Lefkádha.

Planos Holidays, Whatley Farm, Whatley, Frome, Somerset BA11 3LA ☎ 01373 836000. Now the biggest single operator on Paxí, Planos offers bonded flight–transfer–accommodation package deals, using some of the best properties on the island, many of them in and around Lákka.

Routsis Holidays, c/o Greek Options, 4th Floor, Abford House, 15 Wilton Rd, London SW1V 1LT ☎ 020/7233 5233. The Lákka-based travel company now also offers bonded package deals to the island, mainly in and around Lákka, plus sailing and diving options.

Simply Ionian, Kings House, Wood St, Kingston-upon-Thames, Ssurrey KT1 1UG ☎ 020/8995 1121, *www.simply-travel.com*. Fastest-growing of the big three, with select properties on Corfu, Paxí, Kefalloniá, Itháki, Lefkádha, Meganíssi and Zákynthos. Specializes in village and country villas, as well as specialist interest holidays, including sailing, painting and walking.

Something Special, 10 Bull Plain, Hertford SG14 1DT ☎ 01992/552231. Specializes in upmarket villas, many with pools, on the north coast of Corfu, particularly Nissáki, Áyios Stéfanos and Kalámi.

Sunvil Holidays, Sunvil House, 7–8 Upper Square, Old Isleworth, Middlesex TW7 7BJ ☎ 020/8568 4499. Specializes in upmarket, out-of-the-way villas and apartments on Corfu and Lefkádha (including the *Pension Ostria* in Áyios Nikítas). Also activity holidays: walking, painting, cycling and watersports.

one-way tickets back to Britain (many advertise them). However, avoid coming back on national holidays and, crucially, at the end of the season, when travel companies are looking for the cheapest way to get their guest workers home.

Packages and specialist tours

The vast majority of British people visiting the Ionian islands do so on **package holidays**, comprising flights, transfers and accommodation. Corfu and Zákynthos are the most developed, and so will probably have the cheapest deals, but comparing like with like, there is little difference between the islands. The other islands are less developed and can offer some surprisingly good-value package deals, especially if you shop around. Some package bargains are even worth

taking for the flight alone, leaving you to use the accommodation as you see fit.

For a more low-key and genuinely "Greek" holiday, it's best to travel with one of the smaller **specialist agencies** listed opposite. Most of these are more expensive than the mainstream package companies, but they tend to have found the best accommodation in the best areas, and you're also paying for a much higher standard of attention from resort staff. Best of all, however, is to contact a **local accommodation agency**, some of whom can arrange flights and even transfers. As well as plugging you straight into the local community, it also plugs your money into the local economy. Ask the Greek Tourist Office for a copy of their monthly *GTP Travel-Tourism Guide* and look in the travel agencies section (see p.6), or consult the guide on *www.gtpnet.com*.

Getting there from Ireland

Travelling to Greece from Ireland is more expensive than from Britain, though a number of companies do offer packages to the Ionian islands and direct charter flights to Athens and

Corfu. In high season, a charter flight from Dublin to Corfu currently costs around IR£330, including taxes, while a two-week package to the same island starts at IR£435, also including taxes. A charter flight from Belfast to Corfu costs around £310 in high season.

A more cumbersome, though possibly cheaper, alternative is to buy a **flight to London** and a charter ticket or package from there to the Ionians (see "Getting there from Britain" above). Companies such as Ryanair offer high-season returns from IR£69 to Gatwick, Luton or Stansted, which all have charter connections to the Ionian islands.

British Airways has numerous flights daily from both Belfast and Dublin to London Heathrow. Low-season prices from Belfast via Heathrow to Athens start at £234, from Dublin at IR£413. Aer Lingus quotes a routing via Frankfurt at IR£497 in high season. Olympic has high-season flights to Athens from Dublin via London, starting at around IR£345 return; daily internal flights to

AIRLINES IN IRELAND

Aer Lingus, Northern Ireland reservations ☎0645/737 747; 40–41 O'Connell St, Dublin 1; 13 St Stephen's Green, Dublin 2; 12 Upper St George's St, Dun Laoghaire; centralized reservations at Dublin airport ☎01/705 3333 or 844 4777; 2 Academy St, Cork ☎021/327 155; 136 O'Connell St, Limerick ☎061/474 239; Minicom/Text telephone ☎01/705 3994; *www.aerlingus.ie*.

British Airways, 1 Fountain Centre, College St, Belfast BT1 6ET ☎0345/222 111 (reservations), ☎0345/326 566 (bookings and travel agency services). BA doesn't have a Dublin office; for reservations from Eire, call ☎0141 /2222345.

Olympic Airways, Franklin House, 140/142 Pembroke Rd, Ballsbridge, Dublin 4 ☎01/608 0090.

Ryanair, Phoenix House, Conyngham Rd, Dublin 8 ☎01/609 7800; *www.ryanair.com*

TRAVEL AGENTS IN IRELAND

Budget Travel, 134 Lower Baggot St, Dublin 2 ☎01/661 3122. Discount flights and package tours to Corfu.

Co-op Travel Care, 35 Belmont Rd, Belfast 4 ☎01232/471 717, fax 471 339. Package holidays to Corfu and Zakynthos, charter flights to all Ionian airports.

John Cassidy, 103 Talbot St, Dublin 1 ☎01/878 6888. Agents for Falcon and Budget, offering holidays and charter flights.

Link Travel, 28 Capel St, Dublin 1 ☎01/872 1444. Charter flights and package holidays to Corfu.

Sky Tours, 75 Talbot St, Dublin 1 ☎01/836 6677. Charter flights and package tours.

Thomas Cook, 11 Donegall Place, Belfast ☎01232/550232/554455; 18 Grafton St, Dublin 2 ☎01/677 0469. Package holiday and charter flight agent, covering all the Ionian islands from both Belfast and Dublin.

Usit NOW, Fountain Centre, Belfast BT1 6ET ☎01232/324073; 10–11 Market Parade, Patrick St, Cork ☎021/270900; 33 Ferryquay St, Derry ☎01504/371888; 19–21 Aston Quay, O'Connell Bridge, Dublin 2 ☎01/602 1777, telesales ☎01/602 1600; Victoria Place, Eyre Square, Galway ☎091/565177; Central Buildings, O'Connell St, Limerick ☎061/415064; 36–37 Georges St, Waterford ☎051/872601. Student and youth specialists.

Williames, 18–20 Howard St, Belfast BT1 6FQ ☎01232/230 714, fax 439 637. Packages and tailor-made holidays to Corfu and the other islands.

Préveza, Corfu, Kefalloniá and Zákynthos can be booked in advance through their Dublin office. BA currently offers a Belfast–Heathrow–Athens flight from £232 low season. For **students and young people**, the picture is generally rosier: Usit NOW has, for example, returns from Dublin to Athens, valid for stays of up to three months, from IR£189.

Getting there from North America

Only a few carriers fly directly to Greece from North America, and none offers direct flights to Corfu and the Ionians, so all arrangements are routed at least through Athens. If you have time, you may discover it cheaper to arrange your final Greece-bound leg of the journey in the UK, in which case your only criterion will be finding a suitable and good-value North America–Europe flight. For details of onward flights from the UK, see "Getting there from Britain".

In general there just isn't enough traffic between North America and Athens to make for very cheap fares. The Greek national airline, Olympic Airways, only flies out of New York (JFK), Boston, Montréal and Toronto, but offers reasonably priced add-on flights from Athens to Corfu and the other islands.

Shopping for tickets

Barring special offers, the cheapest of the airlines' published fares is usually an **APEX** (Advance Purchase Excursion) ticket, although this will carry certain restrictions: you have to book – and pay – at least 21 days before departure, spend at least seven days abroad (maximum stay three months), and you tend to get penalized if you change your schedule. On transatlantic routes, there are also winter **Super APEX** tickets, sometimes known as "Eurosavers" – slightly cheaper than an ordinary APEX, but limiting your stay to between seven and

---

AIRLINES IN THE US AND CANADA

Air Canada in Canada, ☎1-888/247-2262; in US, ☎1-800/776-3000; *www.aircanada.ca*

Air France in US, ☎1-800/237-2747; in Canada, ☎1-800/667-2747; *www.airfrance.fr*

Alitalia in US, ☎1-800/223-5730 except in New York ☎1-800/442-5860; in Canada, ☎1-800/361-8336; *www.alitalia.com*

American Airlines ☎1-800/433-7300; *www.americanair.com*

British Airways in US, ☎1-800/247-9297; in Canada, ☎1-800/668-1059; *www.british-airways.com*

Canadian Airlines in Canada, ☎1-800/665-1177; in US, ☎1-800/426-7000; *www.cdnair.ca*

Czech Airlines ☎1-800/223-2365; *www.csa.cz*

Delta Airlines in US, ☎1-800/241-4141; in Canada, ☎1-800/221-1212; *www.delta-air.com*

Iberia ☎1-800/772-4642; *www.iberia.com/ingles/home.html*

KLM/Northwest in US, ☎1-800/447-4747; in Canada, ☎1-800/361-5073; *www.klm.com*

LOT Polish Airlines in US, ☎1-800/223-0593; in Canada, ☎1-800/361-1017; *www.lot.com*

Lufthansa in US, ☎1-800/645-3880; in Canada, ☎1-800/563-5954; *www.lufthansa.com*

Olympic Airways ☎1-800/223-1226; *agn.hol.gr/info/olympic1.htm*

TWA ☎1-800/892-4141; *www.twa.com*

US Airways ☎1-800/622-1015; *www.usairways.com*

DISCOUNT TRAVEL AGENCIES IN THE US AND CANADA

Air Brokers International, 323 Geary St, Suite 411, San Francisco, CA 94102 ☎ 1-800/883-3273 or 415/397-1383. Consolidator.

Airhitch, 2641 Broadway, New York, NY 10025 ☎ 1-800/326-2009 or 212/864-2000; *www.airhitch.org*. Standby seat broker; guarantees to get you as close as possible to preferred destination within a week.

Council Travel, 205 E 42nd St, New York, NY 10017 ☎ 1-888/COUNCIL; *www.counciltravel.com* and branches in many other US cities. Student/budget travel agency.

Educational Travel Center, 438 N Frances St, Madison, WI 53703 ☎ 1-800/747-5551 or 608/256-5551; *www.edtrav.com*. Student/youth and consolidator fares.

International Travel Network, *www.itn.net/airlines*. Online air travel info and reservations site.

New Frontiers/Nouvelles Frontières, 12 E 33rd St, New York, NY 10016 ☎ 1-800/366-6387; *www.new-frontiers.com*, and other branches in LA, Montréal, Québec City and San Francisco. French discount travel firm for Europe.

Skylink, 265 Madison Ave, 5th Floor, New York, NY 10016 ☎ 1-800/AIR-ONLY or 212/573-8980, with branches in Chicago, Los Angeles, Montréal, Toronto and Washington DC. Consolidator.

STA Travel, Head Office: 5900 Wiltshire Blvd, Suite 2110, Los Angeles, CA 90036 ☎ 1-800/777-0112 or 212/627-3111, and other branches in the New York, San Francisco, Washington DC, Chicago, Philadelphia, Miami and Boston areas. Worldwide discount travel firm specializing in student/youth fares.

Student Flights, 5010 E Shea Blvd, Suite 104A, Scottsdale, AZ 85254 ☎ 1-800/255-8000 or 602/951-1177; *www.isecard.com*. Specialist in student/youth fares.

TFI Tours International, 34 W 32nd St, New York, NY 10001 ☎ 1-800/745-8000 or 212/736-1140. Consolidator.

Travac Tours, 989 6th Ave, New York, NY 10018 ☎ 1-800/872-8800 or 212/563-3303; *www.travac.com*. Consolidator and charter broker. Current fares on fax line ☎ 1-888/872-8327.

Travel Avenue, 10 S Riverside, Suite 1404, Chicago, IL 60606 ☎ 1-800/333-3335 or 312/876-6866; *www.tipc.com*. Full-service travel agent that offers discounts in the form of rebates.

Travel CUTS, 187 College St, Toronto, ON M5T 1P7 ☎ 1-800/667-2887 in Canada only or 416/979-2406; *www.travelcuts.com*. Organization specializing in student fares, with branches all over Canada.

UniTravel, 11737 Administration Dr, Suite 120, St Louis, MO 63146 ☎ 1-800/325-2222 or 314/569-2501; *www.unitravel.com*. Consolidator.

21 days. Some airlines also issue **Special APEX** tickets to people younger than 24, often extending the maximum stay to a year. Many airlines offer youth or student fares to **under-26s**; a passport or driving licence is sufficient proof of age, though these tickets are subject to availability and can have eccentric booking conditions.

You can normally cut costs further by going through a **specialist flight agent** – either a **consolidator**, who buys up blocks of tickets from the airlines and sells them at a discount, or a **discount agent**, who, in addition to dealing with discounted flights, may also offer special student and youth fares and a range of other travel-related services such as travel insurance, rail passes, car rental, tours and the like. Some agents specialize in **charter flights**, which may be cheaper than anything available on a scheduled flight, but again depar-

ture dates are fixed and withdrawal penalties are high (check the refund policy). If you travel a lot, **discount travel clubs** are another option – the annual membership fee may be worth it for benefits such as cut-price air tickets and car rental.

Don't automatically assume that tickets purchased through a travel specialist will be cheapest – once you get a quote, check with the airlines and you may turn up an even better deal. Be advised also that the pool of travel companies is swimming with sharks – exercise caution and never deal with a company that demands cash up front or refuses to accept payment by credit card.

Regardless of where you buy your ticket, fares will depend on the **season** and are highest from May to September, when the weather is best; they drop during the "shoulder" seasons – September/October and March/April – and you'll

SPECIALIST TOUR OPERATORS IN THE US AND CANADA

Very few North American operators book group tours specifically for Corfu and the Ionians; at most, they might include one or two nights on Corfu. You can, however, get a tour operator to book you a tailor-made, independent package trip.

Adventures Abroad, 20800 Westminster Highway, Suite 2148, Richmond, BC V6V 2W3 ☎ 1-800/665-3998 or 604/303-1099. General operator, offering group and individual tours and cruises.

Auratours, 1470 Peel St, Suite 252, Montréal, Québec H3A 1TL ☎ 1-800/363-0323 or 514/282-9056. General operator, offering group and individual tours and cruises.

Chat Tours, 241 Bedford Rd, Toronto, Ontario M5R 2K9 ☎ 1-800/268-1180. Motorcoach and sea tours, and cruises.

Cloud Tours, 645 Fifth Ave, New York, NY 10022 ☎ 1-800/223-7880. Customized itineraries and honeymoon specials.

Educational Tours and Cruises, 9 Irving St, Medford, MA 02155 ☎ 1-800/275-4109. Custom-designed tours to Greece and the islands, specializing in art, history, food and wine, ancient drama, painting and birdwatching.

Guaranteed Travel, 83 South St, Morristown, NJ 07963 ☎ 201/540-1770. "Greece-your-way" independent travel.

Hellenic Adventures, 4150 Harriet Ave South, Minneapolis, MN 55409 ☎ 1-800/851-6349 or 612/827-0937. A vast range of small group and independent tours: cultural, historical, horseback riding, hiking, wilderness, culinary and family-oriented.

Homeric Tours, 55 East 59th St, New York, NY 10017 ☎ 1-800/223-5570. General Hellenic tour operator, with packages to Corfu via Athens.

ST Cultural Tours, 225 West 34th St, New York, NY 10122 ☎ 1-800/833-2111 or 212/563-1202. A wide range of package and independent educational tours.

Valef Yachts, Box 391, Ambler, PA 19002 ☎ 1-800/223-3845 or 215/641-1624. Yachting trips and charters.

---

get the best prices during the low season, November to March (excluding Christmas and New Year, when prices are hiked up and seats are at a premium). Note also that flying on weekends ordinarily adds at least $50 to the round-trip fare; price ranges quoted below assume **midweek travel**.

From the US

Nonstop Olympic Airways flights **from New York** to Athens (daily) start at around $650 return in winter and rise to $1000 during the summer for a maximum thirty-day stay; tickets must be bought at least seven days in advance. For a similar price, Olympic flies from **Boston** twice a week. Delta has five flights weekly from New York to Athens, round trips comparing favourably with Olympic off season at around $600, also around $1000 in summer with the same purchase and stay conditions.

European connections

There are direct scheduled flights to **Corfu** from Amsterdam, Dusseldorf, Frankfurt, Geneva, London, Milan and Stuttgart.

Delta also has four direct flights a week from **Atlanta**, even cheaper in winter at $540 return.

Other American and all European carriers require you to change planes in a gateway city. Somewhat surprisingly, LOT Polish Airlines has cheap flights from New York to Athens, via Warsaw, three times a week, beginning at $500 in winter. Other companies such as American, British Airways, Air France, KLM, Lufthansa, Swissair, Sabena and United also all fly indirectly from **East Coast** cities for around $600 to $1100 return, depending on the season. In the case of the European airlines, you should check carefully how long the layover between flights is. Flights from Chicago or the **Midwest** should not cost substantially more than East Coast prices. You are unlikely to find many discounts from anywhere in summer but sales and special fares often crop up during the shoulder and low seasons, meaning you could travel for even less than the lowest prices quoted above.

Since all scheduled flights to Athens from the **West Coast** go via New York or another eastern city (such as Atlanta), you basically end up paying for a transcontinental flight on top of the transatlantic fare: round-trip APEX tickets from

Seattle, San Francisco or Los Angeles on all airlines start at just over $1000 in winter and exceed $1300 in the summer.

From Canada

As with the US, air fares **from Canada** to Athens vary depending on where you start your journey but are generally more expensive than south of the border. The scheduled round-trip fare on Olympic, which flies nonstop out of Montréal and Toronto twice a week, is CDN$1380 (winter) up to CDN$1540 (summer). Air Canada flying in conjunction with Lufthansa, quote the following low/high season fares to Athens: from Toronto/Montréal around CDN$1360/CDN$1540, and from Vancouver around CDN$1740/CDN$1970. Canadian Airlines offers a much cheaper option from Toronto at about CDN$950/CDN$1320.

Northwest/KLM operates several flights a week to Athens via Amsterdam, from Toronto, Montréal, Vancouver and Edmonton. From Toronto, expect to pay around CDN$1550 in low season, CDN$1850 in high season; and from Vancouver CDN$1900 (low) or CDN$2300 (high). Numerous European carriers – Air France, Alitalia, British Airways, Iberia and Swissair – fly out of Montréal several times a week to Athens via major European cities, most starting at CDN$1450 in low season, some going up to as much as CDN$1800 during the summer. One unlikely source for good deals is Czech Airlines, which flies out of Montréal to Athens via Prague for CDN$880 (low) or CDN$1285 (high). Keep in mind that these stopovers range from a few hours to an entire night.

Getting there from Australia and New Zealand

There are no direct flights from Australia and New Zealand to the Ionian islands, so your best options are either to fly to Athens, where you can get a connecting flight with Olympic Airways (around A$100/NZ$125 one way) or continue your journey overland, or to fly to London where it's possible to pick up a cheap charter flight or package holiday (see "Getting there from Britain").

For both Greece and London, most airlines operate the following fare **seasons** (with some slight variations): **low** January 16–end February; **high** May 16–31, June 1–July 31 and December 11–23; and **shoulder** the rest of the year. Fares from the major Australian cities are common-rated, and A$200–400 more if you go via Canada or the US. Flying from Christchurch and Wellington costs NZ$150–300 more than from Auckland.

Tickets purchased direct from the airlines tend to be expensive, so it's best to head for a **travel agent**, who as well as offering better deals on fares, should have the latest information on limited special deals such as free stopovers en route and on fly-drive-accommodation packages. STA, which offers fare reductions for ISIC card holders and those under 26, and Flight Centres generally offer the lowest fares.

Olympic Airways in conjunction with Qantas and Air New Zealand have a good connecting service from Australian and New Zealand cities **to Athens** and then on to Corfu, available from travel agents for around A$1950 in low season/2099 shoulder season/2199 high season (common-rated), NZ$2440/2625/2750 (from Auckland). Flights to Athens with Alitalia-KLM or Thai cost A$1600/1800/2200, NZ$2000/ 2250/2750. More expensive, at A$2099/2299/ 2499, NZ$2625/ 2875/3125, but a little more comfortable are Qantas and British Airways.

The lowest fares **to London** are with Britannia during their charter season from November to

---

Alitalia-KLM, Level 13, 115 Pitt St, Sydney ☎ 02/9233-6355; Level 2, Salvation Army Building, 369 Queen St, Auckland ☎ 09/309-1782; *www.alitalia.it; www.klm.com*. New airline alliance flying six times a week to Athens via Amsterdam/Milan from Sydney.

Britannia Airways, c/o UK Flight Shop, 7 Macquarie Place, Sydney ☎ 02/9247-4833; 6/229 Queen St, Auckland ☎ 09/308-3360; *www.ukflightshop.com.au*. Charter flights to London, via Bangkok and Abu Dhabi, from major Australian cities and Auckland.

British Airways, Level 19, AAP Centre, 259 George St, Sydney ☎ 02/9258-3200; 154 Queen St, Auckland ☎ 09/356-8690; *www.british-airways.com*. Daily flights to London via Bangkok/Singapore from major Australian cities and via LA from Auckland.

Garuda Indonesia, 55 Hunter St, Sydney ☎ 02/9334-9900; Level 10, Westpac Tower, 120 Albert St, Auckland ☎ 09/366-1855. Several flights a week to London, with either a transfer or stopover in Denpasar, from major Australasian cities.

Olympic Airways, 37–49 Pitt St, Sydney ☎ 02/9251-2044; no NZ number; *www. olympic-airways.gr*. Three flights weekly to Athens, with connections to Corfu, via Sydney and Bangkok from major eastern Australian cities.

Qantas, Chifley Square, 70 Hunter St, Sydney ☎ 02/9691-3636; 191 Queen St, Auckland ☎ 09/357-8900; *www.qantas.com.au*. Flies to London via Bangkok/Singapore from major Australasian cities.

Thai Airways, 75–77 Pitt St, Sydney ☎ 02/9844-0999; Level 1, Kensington Swan Building, 22 Fanshawe St, Auckland ☎ 09/377-3886; *www.thaiair.com*. Twice-weekly flights to Athens, with a transfer in Bangkok, from major Australasian cities.

TRAVEL AGENTS AND CONSOLIDATORS IN AUSTRALIA AND NEW ZEALAND

Accent on Travel, 545 Queen St, Brisbane ☎07/3832-1777.

Anywhere Travel, 345 Anzac Parade, Kingsford, Sydney ☎02/9663-0411; email: *anywhere@ozemail.com.au*.

Budget Travel, 16 Fort St, Auckland; other branches around the city ☎09/366-0061; ☎0-800/808-040.

Destinations Unlimited, Level 7, FAI Building, 220 Queen St, Auckland ☎09/373-4033.

Flight Centres, Gateway Quayside, 1 Macquarie Place, Sydney ☎02/9241-2422; 19 Bourke St, Melbourne ☎03/9650-2899; plus other branches nationwide ☎13-1600; National Bank Towers, 205-225 Queen St, Auckland ☎09/309-6171, and other branches countrywide; *www.flightcentre.com.au*.

Harvey World Travel, 631 Princes Highway, Kogarah, Sydney (☎02/9567-6099); branches nationwide.

Northern Gateway, 22 Cavenagh St, Darwin ☎08/8941-1394; email: *oztravel@norgate.com.au*.

Passport Travel, Suite 11a/401 St Kilda Rd, Melbourne ☎03/9867-3888; *www.travelcentre. com.au*; email: *passport@travelcentre.com.au*.

STA Travel, 855 George St, Sydney ☎02/9212-1255; 208 Swanston St, Melbourne ☎03/9639-0599; other offices in state capitals and major universities ☎13-1776; fastfare telesales ☎1-300/360 960; Travellers' Centre, 10 High St, Auckland ☎09/309-0458; fastfare telesales ☎09/366-6673; toll-free ☎0800/874-773, plus branches in Wellington, Christchurch, Dunedin, Palmerston North, Hamilton and at major universities; *www.statravel.com.au*; email: *traveller@statravelaus.com.au*.

Thomas Cook, 175 Pitt St, Sydney ☎02/9231-2877; 257 Collins St, Melbourne ☎03/9282-0222; branches in other state capitals ☎13-1771 or toll-free ☎1-800/063-913); 191 Queen St, Auckland ☎09/379-3920; *www. thomascook.com.au*.

Topdeck Travel, 65 Grenfell St, Adelaide ☎08/8232-7222.

Travel Direct Pty Ltd, Level 3, 349 Queen Street, Brisbane ☎07/3221-4933.

Travel Shop, Suite 13, 890 Canning Highway, Perth ☎08/9316-3888 or 1-800/108-108.

Tymtro Travel, Level 3, 355 Bulwara Rd, Sydney ☎1-300/652-969.

March (from A$1289; NZ$1799−2049). Failing that, try Garuda, who operates only two seasonal bands, and at the time of writing is offering fares of A$1350 low season/1750 high season, NZ$1690/2190.

Among **round-the-world (RTW)** tickets that include Athens (all valid for one year) are the BA-Qantas "Explorer Plus" (A$2099 if you depart in low season/2599 if you depart in high season;

NZ$2625/3250) and the Cathay-United Airlines "Globetrotter" (A$2469/$3079; NZ$3085/$3850), both of which allow limited backtracking and six free stopovers; additional stopovers cost A$100/NZ$110. Thai in conjunction with Air New Zealand and Varig offer an RTW ticket ("Star Alliance" fare) with unlimited stopovers − except within the US and Canada − starting at A$2799/NZ$3500.

SPECIALIST TOUR OPERATORS IN AUSTRALIA AND NEW ZEALAND

Since the Ionians are not a major destination for Australians and New Zealanders, there are no prepackaged holidays, but the following agents can put together a holiday to suit your needs.

Eurolynx, Level 3, 20 Fort St, Auckland ☎09/379-9716. Individually tailored travel itineraries.

Grecian Travel, 237a Lonsdale St, Melbourne ☎03/9663-3711. Accommodation, sailing and land tours.

Kyrenia Travel Services, 92 Golburn St, Sydney ☎02/9283-2144. Greek holidays, accommodation, tours and cruises.

Sun Island Tours, 92 Goulburn St, Sydney ☎02/9283-3840. Accommodation, cruise and land tours.

Travel Market, 243 Edward St, Brisbane ☎07/3210-0323. Custom-made holidays, accommodation, car rental, yacht charter.

Getting there from mainland Greece and Italy

The Ionian islands have a wide choice of ferry connections with mainland Greek and Italian ports, as well as scheduled flights between Athens and Corfu, Préveza (for Lefkádha), Kefaloniá and Zákynthos. These links are particularly useful if you're working your way slowly around Europe and want to bypass the former Yugoslavia.

Besides the long-distance sea connections with Italy and the larger Greek ports described below, the Ionian islands are served by a variety of **local ferries** from the Greek mainland (Lefkádha, which has a land link and direct bus connections with the mainland, is the exception). Full details of each island's local ferry services are given in the "Travel details" at the end of the relevant chapter, and the more significant mainland ports are described in the Guide – **Igoumenítsa** on p.66, **Párga** on p.120, **Préveza** on p.140 and **Pátra** on p.190. Information about routes between the islands and general advice on Greek ferries can be found on pp.31–2. If you're travelling direct to the Ionians **from Athens**, flying is the most convenient mode of transport, given the length of the bus and train journeys to the ports (8hr, for example, to Igoumenítsa), and is relatively cheap.

Flights from Athens

Olympic Airways operates daily **flights from Athens** to all the Ionian island airports: Corfu (3–5 daily), Kefaloniá (1–2 daily) and Zákynthos (2–3 daily), as well as Préveza (1 daily) on the mainland (for Lefkádha bus connections). Current standard one-way **prices** are Corfu 19,500dr, Kefaloniá 16,800dr, Zákynthos 16,500dr and Préveza 13,200dr. Return prices are exactly double those of single tickets. Air Greece runs a marginally cheaper daily flight to Corfu only from Athens.

Olympic **schedules** can be picked up at their offices abroad (see "Getting there" sections) or through their branch offices and representatives in Greece, which are maintained in almost every town or island of any size; Greek-only small booklets, which include prices for domestic routes, appear three times yearly (March, June and Oct) while English-language books geared more for an international readership are published twice yearly (March and Oct).

Island flights are often full in peak season; if they're an essential part of your plans, it is worth trying to make a **reservation** at least a week in advance. Domestic air tickets are non-refundable, but you can change your flight, space permitting, without penalty up to a few hours before your original departure.

Size restrictions mean that the 15-kilo **baggage weight limit** is fairly strictly enforced; if, however, you've just arrived from overseas or purchased your ticket outside Greece, you are allowed the 23-kilo standard international limit. All services operated on the domestic network are non-smoking.

Ferries from Italy

Ferries operated by a variety of companies connect five of Italy's Adriatic ports – frequently from **Ancona**, **Bari** and **Brindisi** with fewer from **Venice** and **Trieste** – to some or all of Greece's main Ionian Sea ports (Igoumenítsa, Corfu, Sámi on Kefalloniá, and Pátra). Some of these ferries call at more than one port en route; you can stop

FERRIES FROM ITALY TO THE IONIANS AND MAINLAND GREECE

ROUTES

From the Italian ports, most ferries depart between 8pm and 10pm, though there are a number of afternoon and occasional high-season morning departures. All voyage durations given are approximate. Superfast, Minoan and Hellenic Mediterranean have the fastest crossings. The companies with the most frequent crossings are given.

From Ancona Strintzis, ANEK and Minoan go via Igoumenítsa (15–22hr) to Pátra (24–25hr); Minoan goes 6 days a week. Strintzis sails via Corfu (24hr) twice a week. Also Superfast goes direct to Pátra in 20hr daily.

From Bari Superfast (daily) amd Marlines to Igoumenítsa (10–12hr). Superfast goes on to Pátra (16hr 30 mins).

From Brindisi Medlink (May–Sept, almost daily) and Hellenic Mediterranean goes direct to Pátra (14hr). Hellenic Mediterranean also goes via Corfu (8hr) and Igoumenítsa (10hr); Fragline and Strintzis go via Corfu (8–9hr) to Igoumenítsa (10–12hr) about six days a week

March to October; Strintzis daily June to September. In July and August Hellenic Mediterranean also goes via Paxí, Kefalloniá, Itháki, Lefkádha and Zákynthos. Medlink goes via Kefalloniá in July and August.

From Trieste: ANEK goes via Igoumenítsa (29hr) to Pátra (39hr) about twice a week January to October, five times a week July to September. Ferries call at Corfu (27 hours) once or twice a week in summer.

From Venice: Minoan and Strintzis go via Igoumenítsa (26–29hr) and Corfu (28–30hr) to Pátra (34–37hr); Minoan goes at least five times a week (not all ferries stop at Corfu) and daily March to October.

SAMPLE FARES

Prices below are one-way high/low season fares; port taxes ($3–5/$5–8 per person in each direction) are not included.

Corfu/Igoumenítsa from Ancona: deck class $32–52/$20–36 ($51–83/$32–58); vehicle from $55–74/$28–40 ($88–118/$45–64).

Corfu/Igoumenítsa from Bari or Brindisi: deck class $18–24/$12–20 ($30–40/$20–32); vehicle from $24–32/$13–20 ($38–51/$21-32).

Corfu/Igoumenítsa from Trieste: deck class $30/$20 ($48/$32); vehicle from $68/$40 ($109/$64).

Corfu/Igoumenítsa from Venice: deck class $33/$22 ($53/$35); vehicle from $75/$40 ($120/$64).

Pátra from Ancona: deck class $42–52/$28–36 ($67–83/$45–58); car from $65–74/$35–40 ($104–118/$56–64).

Pátra from Bari or Brindisi: deck class $25–35/$15–$24 ($40–56/$24–38); car from $28–46/$18–25 ($45–74/$29–40).

Pátra from Trieste: deck class $39/$29 ($62/$46); car from $79/$39 ($126/$62).

Pátra from Venice: deck class $43/$32 ($69/$51); car from $86/$43 ($138/$69).

over at no extra charge if you get these stops specified on your ticket. All the ferries detailed in the box above also run in the opposite direction, with similar frequencies and durations.

Ferries have several classes of ticket, from deck through aircraft-style seats and shared cabins to deluxe. In summer, it's essential to **book tickets** a

few days ahead, especially in the peak July–August period – and certainly if you are taking a car across. During the winter you can usually just turn up at the ports, but it's still wise to book in advance if possible. Substantial reductions apply on many lines for both InterRail or Eurail pass holders, and for those under 26. Rail

AGENTS IN ITALY

The dialling code for Italy is ☎ 39. Omit the initial "0" when dialling local numbers from overseas.

Adriatica, c/o Adria Shipping, Corso Garibaldi 85/87, Brindisi ☎ 0831/523825, fax 590758.

Agoudimos, c/o Hellas Ferry Lines, Corso Garibaldi 81, Brindisi ☎ 0831/529091, fax 529217.

ANEK, Ancona: Stazione Marittima ☎ 071/205959; Trieste, Stazione Marittima ☎ 040/302888, fax 311881.

Diler, c/o Italian Ferries, Corso Garibaldi 96/98, Brindisi ☎ 0831/590305, fax 590191.

European Seaways, c/o Adriatico, Corso Garibaldi 54, Brindisi ☎ 0831/523355, fax 561014.

Fraglines, Corso Garibaldi 88, Brindisi ☎ 0831/590196, fax 590181.

Hellenic Mediterranean Lines, Corso Garibaldi 8, Brindisi ☎ 0831/528531, fax 526872.

Marlines, c/o Pier Paolo Santelia, Stazione Marittima, Bari ☎ 080/5231824, fax 5230287.

Med Link Lines, c/o Discovery Shipping, Corso Garibaldi 49, Brindisi ☎ 0831/527667, fax 564070.

Minoan Lines, Ancona: Via Astagno 1 ☎ 071/201708, fax 201933; Venice, Santa Marta (San Basilio) Magazzino 17 ☎ 041/2712345, fax 5212929.

Strintzis Lines, Brindisi: Corso Garibaldi 65 ☎ 0831/562200, fax 568300; Ancona: Stazione Marittima ☎ 071/2071068, fax 2070874; Venice: Stazione Marittima 103 ☎ 041/2770559, fax 2770367.

Superfast Ferries, Ancona: Morandi & Co, Via XXIX Settembre 2/0 ☎ 071/202033, fax 202219; Bari, c/o Portrans, Corso A. de Tullio 6 ☎ 080/5211416, fax 5720427.

Ventouris, Bari: c/o P. Lorusso & Co, Stazione Marittima Booths 3–4 ☎ 080/5217118, fax 5217734; Brindisi, c/o Venmare, Corso Garibaldi 56 ☎ 0831/5212614, fax 521654.

ONLINE BOOKING

Most of the more durable shipping companies have Web sites, or emails for making bookings. They include:

Adriatica *www.adriatica.it;*
adrnav@interbusiness.it

ANEK *www.anek.gr*

Hellenic Mediterranean Lines
hml@mail.otenet.gr

Marlines *www.marlines.gr;*
info@marlines.gr

Minoan Lines *www.minoan.gr;*
booking-eta@minoan.gr

Strintzis Lines *www.strintzis.gr;*
sales@strintzis.gr

Superfast *www.superfast.com;*
superfast@superfast.com

UK AGENTS

Serena Holidays, 40 Kenway Rd, London SW5 ☎ 020/7244 8422. For Adriatica Lines.

Viamare Travel, Graphic House, 2 Sumatra Rd, London NW6 ☎ 020/7431 4560. Agents for ANEK, Arkadia, Fragline, Marlines, Strintzis and Ventouris.

pass holders should check if there are free crossings on particular lines in any given year. Slight discounts are usually available on return fares for all travellers. For those with camper vans, many companies allow you to sleep in your van on board, sparing you the cost of a cabin berth; ask about reduced "camping" fares. Bicycles go free, motorbikes cost £10-40, but are free from Brindisi.

Travellers with disabilities

Lightweight wheelchairs are not an uncommon sight on beaches in the Ionian, proving that wheelchair users, at least, do holiday here. With planning, wheelchair users and those with sight, ambulatory or other disabilities can enjoy an inexpensive and trauma-free holiday in even the smallest island resorts (see the box below for a list of useful contacts).

It has to be admitted, though, that little in Greece, from the roads and buses to public and private buildings, is designed with the disabled in mind. There is only one public building in the Ionian designed for the disabled visitor – Corfu's excellent Archeological Museum – and the archi-pelago's sole public toilet with disabled access, on Corfu's Spianádha, was vandalized and out of order when last checked.

The first thing to do is spend some time gathering **information** about your choice of destination, and options for travel and accommodation. Addresses of contact organizations are published below, and the Greek National Tourist Organization is a good first step, as long as you have specific questions to put to them; they publish a useful questionnaire which you can send to hotels or apartment/villa owners. Where possible, try to double-check all information, as things in Greece have a habit of changing without warning.

USEFUL CONTACTS FOR TRAVELLERS WITH DISABILITIES

National Tourist Organization of Greece (see box on p.30 for addresses). Offers general advice on terrain and climate. They have nothing specific for disabled visitors except a brief list of hotels which may be suitable.

AUSTRALIA

ACROD (Australian Council for Rehabilitation of the Disabled), PO Box 60, Curtin ACT 2605

☎06/682 4333; 55 Charles St, Ryde ☎02/9809 4488.

CANADA

Jewish Rehabilitation Hospital, 3205 Place Alton Goldbloom, Montréal, PQ H7V 1R2 ☎514/ 688-9550 ext 226. Guidebooks and travel information.

Twin Peaks Press, Box 129, Vancouver, WA 98666 ☎206/694-2462 or 1-800/637-2256.

Publisher of the *Directory of Travel Agencies for the Disabled* ($19.95), listing more than 370 agencies worldwide; *Travel for the Disabled* ($14.95); and the *Directory of Accessible Van Rentals and Wheelchair Vagabond* ($9.95), loaded with personal tips.

GREECE

Association Hermes, Patriárhou 13, Grigoríou E, 16542 Aryiroúpoli, Athens ☎01/996 1887. Can advise disabled visitors to Greece.

Lavinia Tours, Egnatía 101, 54110

Thessaloníki ☎031/232 828. Evyenia Stavropoulou will advise disabled visitors and has tested many parts of Greece in her wheel-chair. She also organizes tours within Greece.

IRELAND

Disability Action Group, 2 Annadale Ave, Belfast BT7 3JH ☎01232/491011. Information and advice group.

Irish Wheelchair Association, Blackheath

Drive, Clontarf, Dublin 3 ☎01/833 8241, fax 833 3873; email *iwa@iol.ie* . A national voluntary organization working with people with disabili-ties, with related services for holidaymakers.

Planning a holiday

There are **organized tours and holidays** specifically for people with disabilities, and both Thomson and Horizon in Britain will advise on the suitability of holidays advertised in their brochures. Travelling more independently is also perfectly possible, provided you establish your parameters of ability as a traveller, plan for the worst and don't automatically expect that assistance will always be immediately at hand. If you're not entirely confident you can manage alone, try to travel with an able-bodied friend (or two). Greek airports, in particular, can resemble rugby scrums, are not always fitted with access ramps or other aids and airport staff may not always be able to help.

Read your travel **insurance** small print carefully to make sure that people with a pre-existing medical condition are not excluded. And use your travel agent to make your journey simpler:

airlines can cope better if they are expecting you, with a wheelchair provided at airports and staff primed to help. A medical certificate of your fitness to travel, provided by your doctor, is also extremely useful; some airlines or insurance companies may insist on it.

Make a **list** of all the facilities that will make your life easier while you are away. You may want a ground-floor room, or access to a large elevator; you may have special dietary requirements, or need level ground to enable you to reach shops, beaches, bars and places of interest. You should also keep track of all your other special needs, making sure, for example, that you have extra supplies of drugs – carried with you if you fly – and a prescription including the generic name in case of emergency. Carry spares of any kind of clothing or equipment that might be hard to find in Greece.

NEW ZEALAND

Disabled Persons Assembly, 173–175 Victoria St, Wellington ☎04/811 9100.

UK

Holiday Care, 2nd Floor, Imperial Building, Victoria Rd, Horley, Surrey RH6 7PZ ☎01293/774 535; fax 784 647; *www.freespace.virgin.net/hol-care*. Provides free lists of accessible accommodation abroad and information on financial help for holidays.

RADAR (Royal Association for Disability and Rehabilitation), 12 City Forum, 250 City Rd, London EC1V 8AF ☎020/7250 3222; Minicom ☎020/7250 4119. A good source of advice on travel abroad; they produce an

annual holiday guide for Europe (£7.50 inc. p&p) and *Getting There* transport guide (£5 inc. p&p). Well-organized website: *www.radar.org.uk*.

Tripscope, Alexandra House, Brentford High Street, Brentford, Middlesex, TW8 0NE, ☎08457 585641; *www.justmobility.co.uk/tripscope*. This registered charity provides a national telephone information service offering free advice on international transport and travel for those with a mobility problem.

USA

AccessAbility Travel, 186 Alewife Brook Parkway, Cambridge. MA 02138–1102 ☎1-800/610-5640. A division of FPT Travel Management Group with travel information and tips for disabled travellers.

Access First, 45A Pleasant St, Malden, MA 02148 ☎1–800/557–2047. Current information for disabled travellers.

Mobility International USA, PO Box 10767, Eugene, OR 97440 (Voice and TDD: ☎541/343-1284). Information and referral services, access

guides, tours and exchange programmes. Annual membership $35 (includes quarterly newsletter).

Society for the Advancement of Travel for the Handicapped (SATH), 347 5th Ave, Suite 610, New York, NY 10016 ☎212/447-7284. Non-profit travel-industry referral service that passes queries on to its members as appropriate; allow plenty of time for a response. Website: *www.sittravel.com*.

Travel Information Service, ☎215/456-9603. Telephone-only information and referral service.

Visas and red tape

UK, Irish and all other EU nationals need only a valid passport for entry to Greece; you are no longer stamped in on arrival or out upon departure, and in theory enjoy the same civil rights as Greek citizens (see "Work", p.56). US, Australian, New Zealand, Canadian and most non-EU Europeans receive entry and exit stamps, effectively a "tourist visa", in their passports and can stay, as tourists, for ninety days. If you are a non-EU citizen arriving on a busy charter from an EU country, especially in the dead of night, make sure your passport does get stamped to avoid awkward questions on departure.

Extensions

If you wish to remain in Greece for longer than three months, you should officially apply for an **extension**. This can be done in Corfu Town at the *Ipiresía Allodhapón* (Aliens' Bureau) at Alexandhrás 19 (☎0661/39 277); brace yourself for concerted bureaucracy. In other locations you visit the local police station, where staff are usually more co-operative.

In theory, if you are an **EU national**, you can stay indefinitely and have the same employment rights as any Greek; as your passport is never stamped, nobody knows or cares how long you have been in the country, and the equal rights theory is only likely to be tested if you fall foul of the authorities. Unless of Greek descent, visitors from **non-EU countries** are currently allowed only a three-month extension to the basic tourist visa, and this costs 11,000dr but for a non-employment resident visa you will still have to present yourself every six months to the relevant authorities; only the first extension is free. In all cases, the procedure should be set in motion a couple of weeks before your time runs out. If you don't have a work permit, you will be required to present pink, personalized **bank exchange receipts** (see p.23) totalling at least 500,000dr for the preceding three months, as proof that you have sufficient funds to support yourself without working. Possession of unexpired credit cards, a Greek savings account passbook or travellers' cheques can to some extent substitute for this requirement.

Some non-EU resident individuals get around the law by leaving Greece every three months and re-entering a few days later to get a new, ninety-day tourist stamp. However, with the recent flood of refugees from Albania and former Yugoslavia, plus a smaller influx of east Europeans looking for work, immigration personnel don't always look very kindly on this practice.

If you **overstay** your time and then leave under your own steam – ie are not detected within the country and deported – you'll be given a 22,000dr spot fine upon departure, effectively a double-priced retroactive visa extension; no excuses will be entertained except perhaps a

---

Greek embassies and consulates abroad

Australia 9 Turrana St, Yarralumla, Canberra, ACT 2600 ☎02/6273-3011.

Britain 1a Holland Park, London W11 ☎020/7221 6467.

Canada 76–80 Maclaren St, Ottawa, ON K2P 0K6 ☎613/238-6271.

Ireland 1 Upper Pembroke St, Dublin 2 ☎01/676 7254.

New Zealand 5–7 Willeston St, Wellington ☎04/473-7775.

USA 2221 Massachusetts Ave NW, Washington, DC 20008 ☎202/939-5800.

---

doctor's certificate stating that you were immobilized in hospital. It cannot be overemphasized just how exigent Greek immigration officials often are on these issues.

Customs regulations

For EU citizens travelling between EU countries, the limits on goods already taxed have been relaxed enormously, effectively meaning anything you can carry is fine. However, **duty-free allowances** (for as long as they still exist) are as follows: 200 cigarettes or 50 cigars, two litres of still table wine, one litre of spirits and 60ml of perfume. Exporting **antiquities** without a permit is a serious offence; **drug smuggling**, not surprisingly, incurs severe penalties.

Costs, money and banks

The cost of living in Greece has spiralled during the years of EU membership: the days of renting an island house for a pittance are gone forever, and food prices now differ little from those of other member countries. However, outside the established resorts, travel between and around the islands remains reasonably priced, with the cost of restaurant meals, short-term accommodation and public transport still cheaper than anywhere in northern or western Europe except Portugal.

Prices depend on where and when you go. The towns and larger tourist resorts are more expensive, and costs everywhere increase sharply in July, August and at Easter. **Students** with an International Student Identity Card (ISIC) can get discounted admission fees at many museums, though these, and other occasional discounts, are sometimes limited to EU students.

Some basic costs

In most parts of the Ionian islands a **daily budget** of £20–25/US$32–40 per person will get you basic accommodation, breakfast, picnic lunch and a simple evening meal, if you're one of a couple. Camping would cut costs considerably. On £30–40/US$48–64 a day you could be living quite well, plus treating yourself and sharing vehicle rental.

Inter-island **ferries**, one of the main expenses, are reasonably priced, subsidized by the government in an effort to preserve island communities. A deck-class ticket between any of the southerly islands and the mainland costs about £5/US$8, while between Corfu and the mainland or Paxí the ticket can be as little as £3/US$4.80. Long-distance journeys, such as between Corfu and Pátra, start at around £15/US$24.

The simplest double **room** generally costs around £12–15/US$18–23 a night, depending on the location and the plumbing arrangements. Organized **campsites** are little more than £2/US$3.20 per person, with similar charges per tent and perhaps 25 percent more for a camper van. With discretion you can camp for free in the more remote, rural areas and close to the smaller resorts.

A basic taverna **meal** with local wine can be had for around £6/US$10 a head. Add a pricier bottle of wine, seafood or more careful cooking, and it could be up to £10/US$16 a head – but you'll rarely pay more than that, except in Corfu

Town or the smarter island restaurants. Sharing seafood, Greek salads and dips is a good way to keep costs down in the better restaurants, and sharing is quite common, as is sticking to just one or two starters. Even in the most developed of resorts, with inflated "international" menus, you'll often be able to find a more earthy but decent taverna where the locals eat.

Currency

Greek currency is the **drachma** (*dhrakhmí*), and the exchange rate in the islands is currently around 500dr to the pound sterling, 310dr to the US dollar. The most common **notes** in circulation are those of 200, 500, 1000, 5000 and 10,000 drachmae (*dhrakhmés*), while coins come in denominations of 5, 10, 20, 50 and 100dr; you might come across 1-drachma and 2-drachma coins and 50-drachma bills too, though they're rarely used these days. Shopkeepers rarely bother with differences of less than 10dr.

Banks and exchange

Greek **banks** are normally open Monday–Thursday 8.30am–2pm, Friday 8.30am–1.30pm. Certain branches in larger island towns or tourist centres are open extra hours in the evenings and on Saturday mornings for **exchanging money**. Outside these times, the larger hotels and travel agencies can often provide this service – though often with hefty commission. In the busier centres **exchange bureaus** with low (sometimes no) commisson and longer hours are cropping up in increasing numbers. Unfortunately, the post office exchange service, once very useful in remote locations especially, has been discontinued. Always take your passport with you as proof of identity, and be prepared for a bit of a wait, although exchange procedures have been streamlined and the old method of having to go to a separate counter to pick up the cash is a rare annoyance these days.

The safest way to carry money is in **travellers' cheques**. These can be obtained from banks (even if you don't have an account) or from offices of Thomas Cook and American Express; you'll pay a commission of between one and two percent. You can cash the cheques at most banks, and (often at poorer rates) at quite a number of hotels, travel agencies and tourist shops. Each transaction in Greece will incur a **commission** charge of 400–800dr, so you won't want to change too many small amounts.

Small-denomination **foreign banknotes** are also extremely useful, and relatively unlikely to be stolen in Greece (see "Police and trouble", p.55). Since the lifting of all remaining currency controls for Greek residents in early 1994, a number of authorized brokers for exchanging foreign cash have emerged in Athens and major tourist centres. Choose those that charge a flat percentage commission (usually one percent) rather than a high minimum when you're changing small amounts. Automatic foreign banknote-changing machines can also be found in the larger resorts but tend to deduct a high minimum fee.

Most British banks can issue current-account holders with a **Eurocheque** card and chequebook; these are accepted in some shops in the larger towns and resorts and, if you know your PIN number, they can also be used for withdrawing drachmae from cash machines or Greek banks. An annual card fee is payable for this service, plus a two percent processing charge on the debit facility subject to a minimum of about £1.75, but there's no on-the-spot commission levied on straightforward transactions. The current limit is 50,000dr per cheque, and the bank or merchant does not need to know the prevailing exchange rate – useful if bank computers have gone down.

Finally, there is no need to purchase large amounts of drachmae **before arrival**. Airport arrival lounges will usually – though not always – have an exchange booth open for passengers on incoming international flights. If travelling independently, it's wise to bring a small stash of drachmae with you, for taxis, drinks or meals. If you're stuck, remember that hotel-owners rarely expect payment up front and will usually accept your passport as surety.

Credit cards and cash dispensers

Major **credit cards**, though still not as widely used as in many countries, are gradually being accepted by an increasing number of the more upmarhet hotels, and to a lesser extent, tavernas. However, credit cards are useful – indeed almost essential – for renting cars, for example. If you run short of money, you can get a **cash advance** on a credit card, but be warned that the minimum amount is 15,000dr. The Emboriki Trapeza (Commercial Bank) handles Visa, and the Ethniki Trapeza (National Bank) services Access/Mastercard customers. However, there is usually a two-percent credit-card charge, often unfavourable rates and always interminable delays while transaction approval is sought by telex.

It is far simpler to use the growing network of Greek **cash dispensers (ATMs)** that are now found in most large ports, resorts and island capitals, though not yet on any of the satellite islands. The best distributed are those of the National Bank (Ethniki Trapeza) and the Commercial Bank (Emboriki Trapeza), which happily and interchangeably accept Visa, Mastercard, Plus, Cirrus and Eurocheque cards; those of the Alpha Credit Bank (Alfa Trapeza Pisteos) and its subsidiary the Ionian Bank (Ioniki Trapeza) are less widespread and somewhat more restrictive – for example, Alpha Credit cash dispensers accept only American Express and Visa cards. Note that transactions using **debit cards** linked to current accounts via the Cirrus/Plus system work out far more economical than using credit cards in these cash dispensers.

Emergency cash

All told, learning and using the **PIN** numbers for any debit or credit cards you have will be the quickest and least expensive way of securing moderate amounts of emergency funds from abroad. In an emergency, however, you can arrange to have **money sent** from home to a bank in Greece. Receiving funds via telex takes a minimum of three days and often up to six days, so be prepared for delays. **From the UK**, a bank charge of three percent, or minimum £17, maximum £35, is levied. Bank drafts can also be sent, with higher commission rates. You can retrieve the amount in foreign currency, or even as travellers' cheques, but heavy commissions apply.

Funds can also be sent via **Western Union Money Transfer** (see box below) ,which is represented by the Ergo Bank, Alexándhras 31, in Corfu Town (Mon–Fri 8am–2pm; ☎0661/25 449). Fees depend on the amount being transferred, but as examples, wiring £400–500 should cost around £37, wiring $1000 should cost around $75; the funds should be available for collection within minutes of being sent. American Express'

MoneyGram facility is now only available to Amex card holders; the American Express Bureau de Change is at Kapodhístriou 20a, Corfu Town (Mon–Fri 8am–2pm; ☎0661/30 883).

From Australia and **New Zealand**, funds can be sent via International Money Transfers. These can be made from any bank in Australia and New Zealand to a nominated bank abroad and cost around A$25/NZ$30, but be warned – the whole process can take anywhere between a couple of days and several months. If you desperately need money, wire services (see box below) are faster, but about twice as expensive.

Currency regulations

Since 1994, Greek **currency restrictions** no longer apply to Greek nationals and other EU member citizens, and the drachma is freely convertible. Arcane rules may still apply to arrivals from North America, Australia or non-EU nations, but you would have to be extremely unlucky to run foul of them.

If you have any reason to believe that you'll be acquiring large quantities of drachmae – from work or sale of goods (the latter illegal, incidentally) – declare everything on arrival, then request (and save) pink, personalized receipts for all **exchange transactions**. Otherwise you may find that you can only re-exchange a limited sum of drachmae on departure; even at the best of times many banks stock a limited range of foreign notes, though you can usually strike lucky at airport exchange booths. These pink receipts are also essential for obtaining a non-employment resident visa (see p.20).

Australia American Express Moneygram ☎1-800/230-100; Western Union ☎1-800/649-565.
New Zealand American Express Moneygram ☎09/379-8243 & 0800/262-263; Western Union ☎09/270-0050.
UK Western Union ☎0800/833 833.
US and Canada Western Union ☎1-800/325-6000.

Health matters

There are no required inoculations for Greece, though it's wise to ensure that you are up to date on tetanus and polio. Don't forget to take out travel insurance (see p.26), so that you're covered in case of serious illness or accidents.

Water quality is variable in the Ionian islands and, although the larger hotels have a good drinking water supply, that cannot be said of smaller and more out-of-the-way places. In such cases, it is invariably a matter of taste rather than safety, although some villa and apartment companies warn you to boil tap water before drinking it. On smaller islands such as Paxí, many properties use undrinkable *glýpha*, desalinated seawater, in bathrooms. Bottled water is widely available if you're uncertain. On the other hand, in some places, especially in the mountains, you will find springs with cool, clear water, high in mineral content.

Specific hazards

The main health problems experienced by visitors have to do with **overexposure to the sun** and the odd nasty from the sea. To combat the former, don't spend too long in the sun, cover up and wear a hat, use high-factor sunblock (preferably not the waterproof variety: this simply bastes you) and drink plenty of fluids in the hot months to avoid any danger of sunstroke. Remember that even a hazy sun can burn. For sea wear, goggles or a diving mask are useful, as well as footwear for walking over slippery rocks.

Hazards of the deep

In the sea, you may have the bad luck to meet an armada of **jellyfish** (*tsoúkhtres*), especially in late summer; they come in various colours and sizes, from tiny purple ones to some the size of a large pizza. Various over-the-counter remedies are sold in resort pharmacies; baking soda or diluted ammonia also help to lessen the sting. The welts and burning usually subside of their own accord within a few hours; there are no deadly man-of-war species in Greek waters.

Less venomous but more common are black, spiky **sea urchins** (*ahiní*), which infest rocky shorelines year-round; if you step on or graze

one, a sewing needle (you can crudely sterilize it by heat from a cigarette lighter) and olive oil are effective for removing spines from your anatomy; if you don't extract them, they'll fester.

The worst maritime danger – fortunately very rare – is the **weever fish** (*dhrákena*), which buries itself in tidal zone sand with just its poisonous dorsal and gill spines protruding. If you tread on one, the sudden pain is excruciating, and the exceptionally potent venom can cause permanent paralysis of the affected area. The imperative first aid is to immerse your foot in water as hot as you can stand, which degrades the toxin and relieves the swelling of joints and attendant pain, but you should still seek medical attention as soon as possible.

Somewhat more common are **stingrays** (Greek names include *platý*, *seláhi*, *vátos* or *trígona*), who mainly frequent bays with sandy bottoms, against which they can camouflage themselves. Though shy, they can give you a nasty lash with their tail if trodden on, so shuffle your feet a bit on entering the water.

Sandflies, mosquitoes, snakes, scorpions

If you are sleeping on or near a beach, a wise precaution is to use insect repellent, either lotion or wrist/ankle bands, and/or a tent with a screen to guard against **sandflies**. Their bites are potentially dangerous, as the flies spread visceral leishmaniasis, a rare parasitic infection characterized by chronic fever, listlessness and weight loss.

Mosquitoes (*kounóupia*) in Greece carry nothing worse than a vicious bite, but they can be infuriating. The best solution is to burn pyrethrum incense coils (*spíres* or *fidhákia*), which are widely and cheaply available. Better, if you can get them, are the small electrical devices (trade name *Vape-Net*) that vaporize an odourless insecticide tablet; many "rooms" proprietors supply them routinely. Insect repellents, such as Autan, are available from most general stores and kiosks on the islands.

Adders (*ohiés*) and **scorpions** (*skorpií*) are found throughout the Ionian; both species are shy, and the latter usually quite small and harmless, but take care when climbing over dry-stone walls where snakes like to sun themselves, and don't put hands or feet in places (eg shoes) where you haven't looked first.

Pharmacies and drugs

For **minor complaints** it's easiest to go to the local **farmakío**. Greek pharmacists are highly trained and dispense a number of medicines that elsewhere could only be prescribed by a doctor. In the larger towns and resorts there'll usually be one who speaks good English. Pharmacies are usually closed evenings and Saturday mornings, but are supposed to have a sign on their door referring you to the nearest one that's open. **Homeopathic and herbal remedies** are quite widely available, too, and the larger island towns have dedicated homeopathic pharmacies, delineated by the green cross sign.

If you regularly use any form of **prescription drug**, you should take a copy of the prescription together with the generic name of the drug – this will help should you need to replace it and also avoid possible problems with customs officials. In this regard, it's worth pointing out that codeine is banned in Greece. If you import any you might find yourself in serious trouble, so check labels carefully; it's the core ingredient of Panadeine, Veganin, Solpadeine, Codis and Empirin-Codeine, to name just a few compounds.

Contraceptive pills are more readily available every year, but don't count on getting them outside of a few large island towns (over the counter from *farmakía*). **Condoms**, however, are inexpensive and ubiquitous – just ask for *profylaktiká* (the vulgar term *kapótes* is equally understood but not recommended) at any pharmacy or corner *períptero* (kiosk). It's also quite common to find them prominently displayed in supermarkets, sometimes with the blunt legend "Anti-AIDS".

Lastly, **hay fever** sufferers should be prepared for the early Greek pollen season, at its height from April to June. If you are taken by surprise, pharmacists stock tablets and creams, but it's cheaper to travel prepared: commercial antihistamines such as Triludan are difficult if not impossible to find in the islands, and local brands can cost around £10/US$16 for a pack of ten.

Doctors and hospitals

For **serious medical attention**, phone ☎ 166 for an ambulance. You'll find English-speaking doctors in any of the bigger towns or resorts; travel agencies or hotel staff should be able to come up with some names if you have any difficulty.

In **emergencies** – for cuts, broken bones etc – treatment is given free in **state hospitals**, though you will only get the most basic level of nursing care. Greek hospitals expect patients' families to feed and care for them in hospital, so as a tourist you'll be at a severe disadvantage. Somewhat better are the ordinary state-run **out-patient clinics** (*iatría*) attached to most public hospitals and also found in rural locales; these operate on a first-come, first-served basis, so go early – hours are usually 8am to noon.

Don't forget to obtain **receipts** for the cost of all drugs and medical treatment; without them you won't be able to claim back the money on your travel insurance.

Insurance

UK and other EU nationals are, officially at least, entitled to free medical care in Greece (see "Health matters", p.24), upon presentation of an E111 form, available from most post offices. In practice, the E111 is rarely demanded, nor is proof of nationality. "Free", however, means just admittance to the lowest grade of state hospital (known as a *yenikó nosokomío*), and does not include nursing care or the cost of medication.

Sometimes hospital staff tend to greet E111s with uncomprehending looks, and you may have to pay and request reimbursement by the NHS upon return home, though this is rare. It can also be the case that tests are conducted free in the case of admission but not for out-patients. In any case, if you need prolonged medical care, you're better off using private treatment, which is expensive – 8000dr minimum for a brief clinic consultation. Costs of prescription drugs and anything beyond basic medical equipment – bandages, splints, etc – escalate from there.

Some form of **travel insurance** is therefore advisable – indeed essential for **North Americans,**

TRAVEL INSURANCE COMPANIES AND AGENCIES

BRITAIN AND IRELAND

Columbus Direct ☎020/7375 0011; *www.columbusdirect.co.uk.*

Endsleigh Insurance ☎020/7436 4451.

Marcus Hearne & Co Ltd ☎ 020/7739 3444.

STA Travel ☎020/7361 6161.

Trailfinders ☎020/7628 7628; *www.trailfinders.co.uk.*

Usit CAMPUS ☎0870/240 1010 (national call centre); *www.usitcampus.co.uk.*

Usit NOW Belfast ☎01232/324073; Dublin ☎01/602 1777.

Worldwide Travel Insurance Services Ltd ☎01892/833 338.

NORTH AMERICA

Access America ☎1-800/284-8300; Canada ☎1-800/654-1908.

Carefree Travel Insurance ☎1-800/323-3149.

STA Travel ☎1-800/777-0112.

Travel Assistance International ☎1-800/821-2828.

Travel Guard ☎1-800/826-1300; Canada ☎715/345-0505.

Travel Insurance Services ☎1-800/937-1387.

Worldwide Assistance ☎1-800/821 2828.

AUSTRALIA AND NEW ZEALAND

Cover More, Level 3, 60 Miller St, North Sydney ☎02/9202-8000; email: *email@covermore.com.*

Ready Plan, Level 7, 333 Kent St, Sydney ☎02/9650-5700; 141–147 Walker St, Dandenong, Victoria ☎03/9771-4000; Level 10, 63 Albert St, Auckland ☎09/300-5333.

Australians and New Zealanders, whose countries have no formal healthcare agreements with Greece (other than allowing for free emergency treatment). For **medical claims**, keep receipts, including those from pharmacies. You will have to pay for all private medical care on the spot (insurance claims can be processed if you have hospital treatment), but it can all be claimed back eventually. Travel insurance usually provides cover for the **loss of baggage, money and tickets**, too. If you're thinking of **renting a moped** or motorbike on the islands (many people do), make sure the policy covers motorbike accidents. Some policies exclude hired bike or car accidents, others will cover such events but only if you were acting within local traffic laws when the accident happened. Check whether any policy excludes **"risk" pastimes**, which may include hang gliding, mountaineering, scuba-diving and even trekking.

Britain and Ireland

In **Britain and Ireland**, travel insurance schemes (from around £26 a month) are sold by almost every travel agent or bank, as well as by specialist insurance companies. Policies issued through the companies listed in the box opposite are all good value. Columbus also does an annual multi-trip policy (each trip up to 60 days) which offers twelve months' cover for £49.

Most **banks** and **credit card** issuers also offer some sort of vacation insurance, often automatic if you pay for the holiday with a card. Travel agents and tour operators are also likely to recommend insurance when you book; indeed some will insist you take it for package holidays. These policies are usually reasonable value, though as ever you should check the small print. If you have a good "all-risks" **home insurance** policy it may well cover your possessions against loss or theft even when overseas, and many **private medical schemes** also cover you when abroad – make sure you know the procedure and the helpline number.

US and Canada

Before buying an insurance policy, check that you're not already covered. **Canadians** are usually covered for medical mishaps overseas by their provincial health plans. Holders of official **student/teacher/youth cards** are entitled to accident coverage and hospital inpatient benefits. Students will often find that their student health coverage extends during the vacations and for

one term beyond the date of last enrolment. **Bank and credit cards** (particularly American Express) often have certain levels of medical or other insurance included, and you may automatically get travel insurance if you use a major credit or charge card to pay for your trip. **Home-owners' or renters' insurance** often covers theft or loss of documents, money and valuables while overseas, though conditions and maximum amounts vary from company to company.

After exhausting the possibilities above, you might want to contact a specialist **travel insurance company** (see box on p.26); your travel agent can also usually recommend one, though most can arrange the insurance themselves at no extra charge. Policies are comprehensive (accidents, illnesses, delayed or lost luggage, cancelled flights etc), but maximum payouts tend to be meagre. Premiums vary, so shop around. The best deals are usually to be had through student travel agencies – STA (ISIS) policies, for example, cost $115 for a month. If you're passing through Britain in transit, you may prefer to buy a British policy (see above), which is usually cheaper and wider in scope, though some British insurers may require a permanent UK address.

Most North American travel policies apply only to items lost, stolen or damaged while in the custody of an identifiable, responsible third party such as a hotel porter, an airline or a luggage consignment. In all cases of theft or loss of goods, you must contact the local police – often within a certain time limit – to have a complete report made out so that your insurer can process the claim. This can occasionally prove tricky in Greece, since many officials simply won't accept that anything could be stolen on their turf, or at least don't want to take responsibility for it. Be persistent, and if necessary enlist the support of the local tourist police or tourist office. Note that very few insurers will arrange on-the-spot payments in the event of a major expense or loss; you will usually be reimbursed once you're home.

Australia and New Zealand

Travel insurance is put together by airlines and travel agent groups in conjunction with insurance companies, and are all comparable in premium and coverage. A typical policy for the Ionians will cost around A$189/NZ$235 for one month, A$295/NZ$370 for two and A$382/NZ$475 for three. Certain adventure sports such as hang gliding and mountaineering with ropes are not covered; always check the policy first.

Information and maps

The National Tourist Organization of Greece (*Ellinikós Organismós Tourismoú* or EOT; GNTO abroad) has offices in most European capitals, and major cities in Australia and North America (see box on p.30 for details). It publishes an impressive array of free, glossy, regional pamphlets that are good for getting an idea of where you want to go, even if the text is usually in brochure-speak. The EOT also has a reasonable map of Greece, and brochures on special interests and festivals.

MAP OUTLETS

AUSTRALIA

Brisbane Worldwide Maps and Guides, 187 George St, Brisbane ☎ 07/3221-4330.

Foreign Language Bookshop, 259 Collins St, Melbourne ☎ 03/9654-2883; *www.languages.com.au*.

Mapland, 372 Little Bourke St, Melbourne ☎ 03/9670-4383; *www.mapland.com*.

The Map Shop, 6 Peel St, Adelaide ☎ 08/8231-2033.

Perth Map Centre, 884 Hay St, Perth ☎ 08/9322-5733; *www.perthmap.com.au*.

Travel Bookshop, 175 Liverpool St, Sydney ☎ 02/9261-8200.

CANADA

Open Air Books and Maps, 25 Toronto St, Toronto, ON M5R 2C1 ☎ 416/363-0719.

Ulysses Travel Bookshop, 4176 St-Denis, Montréal ☎ 514/289-0993.

World Wide Books and Maps, 1247 Granville St, Vancouver, BC V6Z 1E4 ☎ 604/687-3320.

IRELAND

Easons Bookshop, 40 O'Connell St, Dublin 1 ☎ 01/873 3811.

Fred Hanna's Bookshop, 27–29 Nassau St, Dublin 2 ☎ 01/677 1255.

Hodges Figgis Bookshop, 56–58 Dawson St, Dublin 2 ☎ 01/677 4754.

Waterstone's, Queens Building, 8 Royal Ave, Belfast BT1 1DA ☎ 01232/247 355.

NEW ZEALAND

Mapworld, 173 Gloucester Street, Christchurch ☎ 03/374 5399, fax 03/374 5633; *www.mapworld.co.nz*; email: *maps@mapworld.co.nz*.

Specialty Maps, 58 Albert St, Auckland ☎ 09/307-2217.

UK

Blackwell's Map and Travel Shop, 53 Broad St, Oxford OX1 3BQ ☎ 01865/792792; *bookshop.blackwell.co.uk*. Specialist outlet.

Daunt Books, 83 Marylebone High St, W1M 3DE ☎ 020/7224 2295; fax: 020/7224 6893; 193 Haverstock Hill, NW3 4QL ☎ 020/7794 4006.

Heffers Map and Travel, 3rd Floor, in Heffers Stationery Department, 19 Sidney St, Cambridge, CB2 3HL ☎ 01223/568467; *www.heffers.co.uk*. Mail order available from here; more maps and travel literature at their excellent bookshop at 20 Trinity Street.

Tourist offices

EOT offices in the Ionian are actually in very short supply; only Corfu and Argostóli now have offices, though both are friendly and keen to help. They keep lists of rooms and other accommodation, can advise on trips to island sights, and may know certain tricks about buses and ferries that don't appear on the timetables. Elsewhere, local travel companies, hotels and other businesses are usually happy to help with information.

Maps

The reliability of maps in the Ionian has improved no end since the Athens-based *Road Editions* mapped the area; their individual island maps (Kefaloniá and Itháki are together) are well worth seeking out and paying a bit extra for, as older and more common rivals such as *Toubi's* are nothing like as accurate. *Road* maps are fine for finding your way around by vehicle and even for walking main footpaths, but still not much good for serious country trekking.

John Smith and Sons, 57–61 St Vincent St, Glasgow, G2 5TB ☎0141/221 7472; fax: 0141/248 4412; *www.johnsmith.co.uk*; email: *malcolm.heroine@jthin.co.uk*. Specialist map department in long-established booksellers; full range of foreign maps; mail order service.

James Thin Melven's Bookshop, 29 Union St, Inverness, IV1 1QA ☎01463/233500; *www.jthin.co.uk*. Established 1849; map department with all foreign maps; mail order specialist.

National Map Centre, 22–24 Caxton St, London SW1H 0QU ☎020/7222 2466; *www.mapsworld.com*.

Newcastle Map Centre, 55 Grey St, Newcastle upon Tyne, NE1 6EF ☎0191/261 5622; email: *nmc@enterprise.net*. Ordnance survey stockists also keep a good range of foreign maps.

Stanfords, 12–14 Long Acre, London WC2E 9LP ☎020/7836 1321. Maps by mail or phone order are available on this number and via email: *sales@stanfords.co.uk*. Other London branches at Campus Travel, 52 Grosvenor Gardens, SW1W 0AG ☎020/7730 1314, and in the British Airways offices at 156 Regent St, W1R 5TA ☎020/7434 4744. Also at 29 Corn Street, Bristol BS1 1HT ☎0117/929 9966.

The Map Shop, 30a Belvoir St, Leicester, LE1 6QH ☎0116/2471400. Domestic and foreign maps; mail order available.

The Travel Bookshop, 13–15 Blenheim Crescent, London W11 2EE ☎020/7229 5260; *www.thetravelbookshop.co.uk*.

Waterstone's, 91 Deansgate, Manchester, M3 2BW ☎0161/837 3000; fax: 0161/835 1534; *www.waterstones-manchester-deansgate.co.uk*; email: *enquiries@waterstones-manchester-deansgate.co.uk*. Particularly good map department in this branch of the UK-wide chain of bookshops; mail order service.

US

The Complete Traveler Bookstore, 199 Madison Ave, New York, NY 10016 ☎212/685 - 9007. 3207 Fillmore St, San Francisco, CA 92123 ☎415/923-1511.

Map Link Inc, 30 S La Patera Lane, Unit 5, Santa Barbara, CA 93117 ☎805/692-6777.

Phileas Fogg's Books & Maps, #87 Stanford Shopping Center, Palo Alto, CA 94304 ☎1-800/533-FOGG.

Rand McNally, 444 N Michigan Ave, Chicago, IL 60611 ☎312/321-1751; 150 E 52nd St, New York, NY 10022 ☎212/758-7488; 595 Market St, San Francisco, CA 94105 ☎415/777-3131; 1201 Connecticut Ave NW, Washington, DC 20003 ☎202/223-6751. For maps by mail order or other locations, call ☎1-800/333-0136, ext 2111.

Sierra Club Bookstore, 6014 College Ave, Oakland, CA 94618 ☎510/658-7470.

Travel Books & Language Center, 4437 Wisconsin Ave NW, Washington, DC 20016 ☎1-800/220-2665.

Traveler's Choice Bookstore, 22 W 52nd St, New York, NY 10019 ☎ 212/664-0995.

Town maps, usually only available for the island capitals, are also limited in detail and accuracy.

Maps on a par with Britain's Ordnance Survey do exist in Greece, from the **Yeografikí Ipiresía Stratoú** (Army Geographical Service, or YIS), based in Athens. Unfortunately, you have to go there to get them, and those that cover any sensitive border areas are regarded as a military secret. This includes great chunks of Corfu, due to its proximity of Albania, and even parts of other Ionian islands – pretty amusing when you consider the border in question is with EU partner Italy, hundreds of kilometres away across the Adriatic. Consequently, these YIS master-

pieces are redundant for the Ionian until such a time as restrictions are relaxed, and the only printed help you are likely to find is in locally produced walking guides and maps, such as those by Friends of the Ionian and various enterprising individuals; such orientation aids not referred to below are mentioned in the relevant chapters of the Guide.

The most reliable general map of the Ionian region is the *Bartholomew Corfu & Ionian Islands Holiday Map* (1:100,000), which is as geographically accurate as possible at this scale, even on the smaller islands. Also serviceable are the AA-MacMillan and Globetrotter maps at a similar scale.

On **Corfu**, an independent mapmaker, Stephan Jaskulowski, has produced a beautiful set of hand-drawn maps to sections of the island, which should soon be available in book form. The maps detail all roads, tracks and main paths, with lines of elevation and navigational features. At the moment, each island section map costs 800dr in the form of a colour photocopy. A map of the whole island, the *Precise Road Map of Kérkyra*, costing around 1500dr, is expected to be published under the aegis of the *Corfiot* monthly English-language magazine.

A similar island map is available on **Paxí**. Produced in recent years by cartographers Elizabeth and Ian Bleasdale and sold by most tourism businesses on the island, it is chiefly a detailed walking map, but is the best, and certainly the most accurate, of any of the maps of Paxí.

Walkers should also check out Noel Rochford's two books, *Landscapes of Paxos* and *Landscapes of Corfu* (Sunflower), which detail walks around both islands. Available on Corfu, at least in the better bookshops, Hilary Whitton Paipeti's *Second Book of Corfu Walks* (Hermes Press) details more than thirty island walks researched by the author, a long-term resident on the island. As yet, there are no such guides covering the other Ionian islands.

Getting around

Island-hopping isn't as easy in the Ionian as it is in parts of the Aegean, although there are ferry connections throughout the archipelago. Particularly well served are Lefkádha, Itháki and Kefalloniá, within an hour's voyage of each other and with regular ferries to a choice of destinations on each island daily. Zákynthos is also connected to Kefalloniá, and to Kyllíni on the mainland.

There are now no inter-island flights in the Ionian region, although Corfu, Kefalloniá, Zákynthos and Préveza (on the mainland near Lefkádha) have daily connections to Athens. However, sheer expense and poor connections make this an unfeasible way to travel between islands. For getting around the islands themselves, there are basic bus services, which many tourists choose to supplement at some stage with moped, motorbike or car rental.

Ferries

Shuttle **ferries** from the islands **to the nearest mainland ports** – which, except in the case of Lefkádha, are the islands' primary links with the outside world – are usually relatively stable (see "Travel details" at the end of each island chapter in the Guide). However, apart from the Four Islands line services between Lefkádha, Itháki, Kefalloniá and Zákynthos, **inter-island ferries** cannot be trusted from one year to the next. The high-speed catamaran between Brindisi, Corfu, Paxí and Lefkádha has been discontinued; Corfu–Itháki links were cut a few years ago; and the Corfu–Kefalloniá Minoan sailing may not be continued. As a result, most people wanting to travel between Corfu or Paxí and the southern Ionian islands go via the mainland and bus.

Ferry services are drastically reduced in the **off season**, but with the exception of Paxí each island has at least a daily connection to a neighbouring island or mainland port. Only the worst weather conditions – a force six upwards, which

Inter-island ferry routes

All the ferries detailed below also run in the opposite direction, with similar frequencies and durations. See box on p.16 for details of Corfu–Pátra and Kefalloniá–Pátra ferries which begin their voyages in Italy.

From Corfu: To Paxí 2–3 daily (2–4hr; deck ticket 1500dr; vehicle 5000dr). Strintzis to Sámi on **Kefalloniá** weekly (6hr; deck ticket 5000dr; vehicle 18,000dr).

From Lefkádha (Nydhrí or Vassilikí): To **Meganíssi** 7 daily (20min; deck ticket 435dr; vehicle 1000dr). To Fríkes on **Itháki** 1 daily April–October (1hr 30min; deck ticket 1200dr; vehicle 2300dr). To Sámi on **Kefalloniá** 2 daily April–October (2hr; deck ticket 1500dr; vehicle 2500dr); to Fiskárdho on **Kefalloniá** 3 daily

(1hr; deck ticket 1000dr; vehicle 2000dr).

From Itháki (Fríkes): To Fiskárdho on **Kefalloniá** 1 daily (1hr; deck ticket 1000dr; vehicle 2000dr).

From Kefalloniá (Sámi): To Váthý on **Itháki** 2 daily (1hr; deck ticket 1000dr; vehicle 2000dr); to Pisaetós on **Itháki** 5 daily (40min; deck ticket 800dr; vehicle 1500dr).

From Zákynthos: To Pessádha on **Kefalloniá** daily (1hr 30min; deck ticket 1500dr; vehicle 2500dr).

---

few would want to sail in anyway – prevent large ships leaving. The **types of ferries** you'll encounter vary enormously, from the landing-craft lookalikes that shuttle between Corfu and Igoumenítsa, or Argostóli and Lixoúri, which have little more than a cabin, snack bar, toilet and open upper decks, to the comparatively luxurious vessels that ply international routes, and between the southerly islands and mainland, which have restaurants, shops and cinemas.

If planning to travel on any of the long-distance ferries, it is advisable to check availability with more than one ferry company – some agents will tell you theirs is the only ferry available, despite the fairly sizeable evidence to the contrary moored perhaps only a few metres from their office. Tickets are **deck class** unless you request otherwise, and on the larger ferries also allow use of bars, restaurants and public seating areas. Pullman or aeroplane-type seating, allowing you to sleep, costs slightly more. **Cabins**, worth considering in high season, bad weather or particularly if travelling in a group of two to four people, cost between double and quadruple the price of a basic ticket. **Motorbikes and cars** are issued extra tickets; slightly less than the cost of a deck ticket for the former, up to three or four times that for the latter. Pets and bicycles commonly travel free. Technically, written permission is required to take rental vehicles on ferries, although this is rarely if ever policed.

It's common to pay on board most inter-island ferries, although the larger ferries and lines have recently introduced computerized **ticketing**, which often requires pre-purchase at a quayside ticket agency. Most ferries run their own ticketing sys-

tems, and your ticket will probably commit you to a specific sailing on a named vessel, although on journeys such as Igoumenítsa–Corfu, it's easy to transfer tickets at the dockside ticket offices. If you're uncertain whether you'll make a specified departure, check if the ticket is transferable.

As independent fishing is gradually elbowed out by factory fishing, so the romantic notion of hiring a **kaïki** also sails off into the sunset. As with sea taxis, which command around £70-90 for an hour's journey one-way between islands, *kaïkia*, when available, tend to be very expensive. It is still possible, however, especially in smaller ports and at quieter times of the season, so ask around.

Buses

The mythical boneshakers you had to share with livestock have for the most part been replaced by the modern cream and green **buses** of the national company, KTEL (Kratíko Tamío Elliníkon Leoforíon). On small islands like Itháki, one island bus trundles back and forth from end to end; larger islands such as Corfu and Kefalloniá are served by fleets of buses based in the capital. Note that almost all routes radiate out from the capital, and there are few if any connections between outlying towns and villages except along the radial routes. In some places, however, there are weekday early morning and early afternoon services connecting outlying communities to collect or drop off students attending schools and colleges in larger towns. These are not always advertised on timetables, so it's worth asking, particularly if you've spotted a bus where the timetable said there wasn't a service.

Bus services on the islands are not as unreliable as popular myth would have it, and when printed **timetables** are available, they are usually adhered to surprisingly well, at least from the originating terminal. Most buses turn round immediately or after a short break, and can often be flagged down anywhere along the road, although on busy built-up stretches they will only pull up at designated stops. Bear in mind that KTEL also has buses in its fleet with livery other than the cream and green, normally for private hire, but sometimes used on normal routes. If in doubt, stick your hand out at anything that has your destination on the front.

You **pay** on board nearly all buses in the Ionians. Exceptions include those originating in Lefkádha Town which, like the mainland bus stations, has a computerized ticketing system, with numbered seats. Corfu's suburban blue bus system is a confusing mix of pay-on-board and pre-pay (from the ticket kiosk by the bus ranks in Platía San Rócco). Pre-pay buses are those with "*horís eíspraktor*" (without conductor) signs in the driver's window. **Prices** on island buses are good value – an hour's journey the length of an island will probably cost less than £2/US$3.20 – although mainland bus journeys are slightly more expensive.

There are no **airport bus** services in the Ionian.

Car rental

Car rental in the Ionian costs a minimum of £180/US$300 a week in high season for the smallest, Group A vehicle, including unlimited mileage and insurance; prices on the smaller islands are usually higher. Tour operators' brochures threaten alarming rates of £220/US$350 for the same period but, except in mid-August, no rental company in the islands expects to fetch that price for a car. Outside peak season, at the smaller local outfits in less touristed resorts, you can often get terms of about £22/US$35 per day, all inclusive, with better rates for a rental of three days or more. Shopping around agencies in the larger resorts – particularly on Corfu – can yield a variation in quotes of up to 15 or 20 percent for the same conditions over a four-to-seven-day period; a common hidden catch, however, is to charge extra for kilometres in excess of 100 per day. Open **jeeps**, an increasingly popular extravagance, begin at about £40/$US64 per day, rising to as much as £50/US$80 at busy times and places.

Many basic-rate rental prices in Greece don't include tax, collision damage waiver (CDW) and personal insurance, so check the fine print on your contract. Be careful of the hammering that cars get on minor roads; tyres, windscreen and the underside of the vehicle are almost always excluded from even supplementary insurance policies. All agencies will want either a credit card or a large cash deposit up front; minimum age requirements vary from 21 to 25. In theory an **International Driving Licence** is also needed, but in practice European, Australian, New Zealand and North American ones are honoured.

INTERNATIONAL CAR RENTAL AGENCIES

NORTH AMERICA

Avis ☎ 1-800/331-1084; *www.avis.com.*

Budget ☎ 1-800/527-0700; *www.budgetrentacar.com.*

Hertz US ☎ 1-800/654-3001; Canada

☎ 1-800/263-0600; *www.hertz.com.*

National ☎ 1-800/CAR-RENT; *www.nationalcar.com.*

Thrifty ☎ 1–800/367–2277; *www.thrifty.com.*

UK

Avis ☎ 0990/900 500.

Budget ☎ 0800/181 181.

Europcar-InterRent ☎ 0345/222525.

Hertz ☎ 0990/996 699.

Holiday Autos ☎ 0990/300 400; stations on Corfu, Kefalloniá, Zákynthos.

AUSTRALIA AND NEW ZEALAND

Avis Australia ☎ 1800/225 533; NZ ☎ 09/526 2847.

Budget Australia ☎ 1300/362 848; NZ ☎ 09/375 2222.

Hertz Australia ☎ 1800/550 067; NZ ☎ 09/367 6350.

In peak season only you may get a better price (and, more importantly, better vehicle condition) by booking through one of the **international companies**, rather than arranging the rental once you're in Greece; this may also be the only way to get hold of a car at such times. In the Ionian, Avis (Corfu, Kefaloniá, Zákynthos), Budget (Corfu, Lefkádha, Kefaloniá, Zákynthos), Europcar-InterRent/National (Corfu, Lefkádha, Kefaloniá) and Hertz (Corfu, Lefkádha, Kefaloniá, Zákynthos) all have outlets, mainly in island capitals, airports or major resorts.

In terms of **models**, the more competitive companies tend to offer the Subaru M80 or Subaru Vivio and the Suzuki Alto 800 as A Group cars, and Opel Corsa 1200 and Peugeot 106 in the B Group. The Suzuki Alto 600, Fiat Panda 750 and Seat Marbella should be avoided at all costs. More acceptable are the Fiat Cinquecento as an A Group choice or the Fiat Uno in the B Group. The standard four-wheel-drive options are Suzuki jeeps – great for bashing down rutted tracks to remote beaches.

Driving in Greece

Greece has the highest **accident rate** in Europe after Portugal, and many of the roads can be quite perilous: asphalt can turn into a one-lane surface or a dirt track without warning on secondary routes, and you're heavily dependent on magnifying mirrors at blind intersections in congested villages. Uphill drivers insist on their right of way, as do those first to approach a one-lane bridge – **flashed headlights** mean the opposite to what they do in the UK or North America, here signifying that the driver is coming through or overtaking.

Wearing a **seatbelt** is compulsory, and children under the age of 10 are not allowed to sit in the front seats. It's illegal to drive away from any kind of accident, and you can be held at a police station for up to 24 hours. If this happens, you have the right to ring your consulate immediately to summon a lawyer; don't make a statement to anyone who doesn't speak, and write, very good English.

Tourists with proof of membership of their home-motoring organization are given free **road assistance** from ELPA, the Greek equivalent, which runs breakdown services on the larger islands (not Paxí or Itháki); in an emergency ring their road assistance service on ☎104. Many car rental companies have an agreement with ELPA's equally widespread competitors Hellas Service and Express Service, but they're prohibitively expensive to summon on your own – over 40,000dr to enrol as an "instant member".

Buying fuel

Fuel currently costs around 215–230dr a litre for regular unleaded (*amólivdhi*), 230–245dr for super unleaded; as throughout the EU, leaded four-star became unavailable after January 1, 2000. Beware that many stations in island towns and rural areas close at 7pm sharp. Nearly as many are shut all weekend, and though there will always be at least one pump per district open, it's not always apparent which that is. Filling stations run by international companies (BP, Mobil and Shell) usually take **credit cards**; Greek chains like EKO, Mamidhakis and Elinoil don't.

Incidentally, the smallest grade of motor **scooters** (Vespa, Piaggio, Suzuki) consume "mix", a red- or green-tinted fuel dispensed from a transparent cylindrical device. This contains a minimum of three-percent two-stroke oil by volume; if this mix is unavailable, you brew it up yourself by adding to "super" grade fuel the necessary amount of separately bottled two-stroke oil (*ládhi dhío trohón*). It's wise to err on the side of excess (say five percent by volume); otherwise you risk the engine seizing up.

Motorbikes, mopeds – and safety

The cult of the **motorcycle** is highly developed in the Greek islands, presided over by a jealous deity apparently requiring regular human sacrifice. **Accidents** among both foreign and local motorbikers are common, and some package companies have taken to warning clients in print against renting motorbikes or mopeds. However, with a bit of caution and common sense – plus an eye to increasingly enforced traffic regulations – riding a bike on holiday should be a lot less hazardous than, say, dodging traffic in central London or New York.

Many tourists come to grief on rutted dirt tracks or astride mechanically dodgy machines. In many cases accidents are due to attempts to cut corners, in all senses, by riding two to an underpowered scooter. Don't be tempted by this apparent economy – and bear in mind, too, that you're likely to be charged an exorbitant sum for any repairs if you do have a wipeout.

One precaution is to wear a **crash helmet** (*krános*); many rental outfits will offer you one, and may make you sign a waiver of liability if you refuse it. Helmet-wearing is in fact required by law, and though very few comply at present, it's likely to be more strictly enforced in the future.

Above all, make sure your travel **insurance policy** covers motorcycle accidents. Reputable establishments require a full **motorcycle driving licence** for any machine over 75cc, and you will usually be required to leave a passport as security.

Mopeds and small motor scooters, known in Greek as *papákia* (little ducks) after their characteristic noise, are good transport for all but the hilliest islands. They're available for rent in most main towns or ports, and at the larger resorts, for 3000–4000dr (mopeds) or 3500–5000dr (scooters) a day. Rates can be bargained down out of season, or if you negotiate for a longer period of rental. Before riding off, make sure you check the bike's mechanical state, since many are only cosmetically maintained. Bad brakes and worn spark plugs are the most common defects; dealers often keep the front brake far too loose, with the commendable intention of preventing you going over the handlebars. If you break down it's your responsibility to return the machine, so it's worth taking down the phone number of the rental agency in case the bike gives out and you can't get it back, or if you lose the ignition key.

As far as **models** go, the three-speed Honda 50, Suzuki Townmate and Yamaha Birdie are workhorse favourites; gears are shifted with a left-foot pedal action, and (very important) they can be push-started if the battery fails. These carry two people easily enough, though if you have a choice the Cub series gives more power at nominal extra cost. A larger Vespa scooter is more comfortable, but less stable; the Suzuki Address is thirsty on fuel and cannot be push-started. Smaller but surprisingly powerful Piaggio Si or Monte Carlo models can take one person only along almost any road and are automatic. Bungy cords (*khtapódia* in slang) for tying down bundles are supplied on request.

Cycling

Cycling on the Ionian islands is not such hard going as you might imagine, unless you're planning to traverse island hill or mountain ranges, in which case a mountain bike and a mountain biker's stamina are essential. Away from the busier resorts and arterial roads, which are hellish for cyclists and pedestrians alike, cycling is an ideal form of transport. Virtually every resort will have bikes for hire, at around 1000–1500dr a day.

If you have your own mountain or touring bike, you might consider bringing it with you: bikes fly free on most airlines, if within your twenty-kilo luggage limit, and are free on most ferries. Any spare parts you might need, however, are best brought along, since there are no specialist bike shops in the islands beyond rental agencies, and parts are difficult to obtain.

Hitching

Hitching on the Ionian islands is a hit-and-miss affair, and carries the usual risks and dangers, particularly for solo women travellers. However, Greece is in general one of the safest places to hitch. These days, though, the key question is whether you'll find anyone prepared to stop. On the larger islands and in larger resorts, especially, it's almost taken for granted (not unreasonably) that foreigners should hire or pay for their own transport. In Greece's increasingly car-mad culture, the idea of not driving anywhere baffles most islanders under donkey-owning age. That noted, hitching is a great way to meet islanders and see the landscape, particularly in outlying areas, where it's not uncommon for villagers to stop and offer lifts unasked. Just don't expect to get very far very fast.

Taxis

Greek **taxis** and tariffs are a law unto themselves. Most vehicles in the Ionians are fitted with meters, and there are various regulations on metering, but for most visitors the back of a cab is hardly the place to start arguing the toss about Greek transport law. Always request and negotiate a price beforehand, ideally in Greek, however basic your Greek is. Expect to be overcharged on journeys from airports to capitals (around 2000dr at Corfu, 3500dr at Kefalloniá). Away from airport rides, taxis are still roughly half the price paid to cover a similar distance in Britain. In rural areas, taxis respond to hailing, and will even return to collect you if full. Taxi-sharing is common, though if you board a taxi that already has a passenger (whom you don't know) inside, you are each expected to pay your full share.

Accommodation

Even though 1999's statistics showed that tourist numbers were on the increase again after an early nineties slump, there are still a great number of beds available for tourists in the Ionian islands. At most times of the year you can rely on turning up anywhere and finding a room – if not in a hotel, then in a private house or block of rooms (the standard island accommodation). All the larger islands have at least one basic but inexpensive campsite, too.

However, from late July to early September, when large numbers of Greeks and Italian visitors (though the latter were in shorter supply during the last summer of the millennium) arrive in the islands, you may well experience problems if you haven't booked accommodation in advance. The first three weeks of August constitute the peak of high season, when rooms are like gold dust almost everywhere. Some resorts can literally fill up, and in busy periods room owners, and even hoteliers, are less inclined to rent for one or just a few nights; some won't even contemplate stays of less than a week. At these times, it's worth looking away from the obvious tourist areas, turning up at each new place early in the day, and taking whatever is available in the hope of exchanging it for something better later on.

Out of season, there's a different problem: rooms close from November to March (campsites even earlier), leaving hotels your only option, probably in the island's main town or port; there'll be very little life outside these places, anyway, with all the seasonal bars and restaurants closed. Just one hotel, the *Mentor*, stays open on Itháki; there are none on Paxí. If you're set on travelling out of season, local travel companies can sometimes help to find suitable accommodation, often at bargain prices.

Private rooms

The most common form of island acommodation is **privately let rooms** – *dhomátia*. These are regulated and officially classified by the local tourist police, who divide them into three classes (A down to C), according to their facilities. These days the bulk of them are in new, purpose-built low-rise buildings, but a few are still in people's homes, where you'll occasionally be treated to disarming hospitality. The purpose-built apartments are more commonly known as *dhiamerísmata* in Greek.

Rooms are almost always scrupulously clean, whatever their other qualities. At their simplest, you'll get a bare, concrete or wood room, with basic furnishing and shared toilet facilities (cold water only). At the fancier end of the scale, you'll find modern, purpose-built and fully furnished rooms with a smart modern bathroom attached. Sometimes there's a choice of rooms at various prices – owners will usually show you the most expensive first. Room prices and standards are not necessarily directly linked, so always ask to see the room before agreeing to take it and settling on the price.

Areas to look for rooms, along with recommendations of the best places, are included in the Guide. But as often as not, the rooms find you: owners descend on ferry or bus arrivals to fill any space they have, sometimes waving photos of the premises. In smaller places you'll often see rooms advertised, usually in English but sometimes in German (*Zimmer*) or Italian (*camare*). The Greek signs to look out for are "*Enoikiázontai dhomátia/dhiamerísmata*" or "*Enoikiazómena dhomátia/dhiamerísmata*" – "Rooms/apartments to let". If you can't find rooms or, as is sometimes the case, there are no signs for them, ask in a shop, *kafenío* or taverna: if they don't have rooms themselves, they'll often know someone who does. Even in small villages, there is often someone prepared to earn some money by putting you up.

It's quite usual for room owners to ask to keep your passport – ostensibly "for the tourist police", but in reality to prevent you departing without paying.

Some owners will be satisfied with taking your passport details, or simply ask you to pay in advance. They'll usually return the documents once they've got to know you, or if you need them for another purpose (to change money, for example).

Hotels

There are **hotels**, from basic to luxury, in most island towns, ports and resorts in the Ionian. In the larger resorts, however, many are block-booked by package holiday companies.

Like private rooms, hotels are **categorized** by the tourist police. They range from Luxury down to E-class, and all except the top category have to keep within set price limits. Letter ratings are supposed to correspond to facilities available, though in practice categorization often depends on location and other, less obvious criteria (some decent hotels in quieter areas, because they are away from the main resorts, receive a relatively low categorization, and are therefore surprisingly good value). D-class usually have attached baths, while in C-class this is mandatory, along with a bar or breakfast area. The additional presence of a pool and/or tennis court will attract a B-class rating,

while A-category hotels must have a restaurant, bar and extensive common areas. Luxury hotels are in effect self-contained holiday villages; both they and A-class outfits usually back a private beach. **Prices** have to be displayed in the room, although outside the high season you will normally find yourself paying less than the advertised price. As a rough guide, D- and E-class hotels usually cost around £20–25/US$32–40 for a double room, only slightly less for single occupancy.

In terms of **food**, C-class hotels are required only to provide the most rudimentary of continental breakfasts – in practice, most now let you choose whether to take a room with or without breakfast – while B-class and above will usually offer some sort of buffet breakfast including cheese, cold cuts, sausages, eggs, etc. With some outstanding exceptions, noted in the Guide, lunch or supper at hotel-affiliated restaurants is bland and poor value.

Villas and long-term rentals

The easiest – and usually most reliable – way to arrange a **villa rental** is through one of the package holiday companies detailed in the "Getting there" sections above. They can offer some

---

Accommodation price codes

Rooms and hotels listed in this book have been price-coded according to the scale outlined below. The rates quoted represent the cheapest available double room in high season. Out of season, rates can drop by as much as fifty percent or more, especially if you negotiate for a stay of three or more nights. Single rooms, where available, cost around seventy percent of the price of a double.

① up to 6000dr	⑤ 16,000–20,000dr
② 6000–9000dr	⑥ 20,000–30,000dr
③ 9000–12,000dr	⑦ 30,000dr upwards
④ 12,000–16,000dr	

Very little accommodation beyond campsite bungalows and drastically simple, cold-water rooms falls into the ① category. Most private rooms tend to fall into the ② or ③ categories, some (falling mostly in the latter category) with en-suite toilet and shower facilities. The more modern apartments, which always have their own bathrooms and usually at least a rudimentary kitchen, are mostly in the ④ category, though they can easily fall into the categories either side. These overlap in price terms with C-category hotels, the smarter or more recently built of which edge into the ⑤ bracket. Most ⑤ and some ⑥ hotels are B-class, with en-suite facilities, air conditioning, phone and TV. The remainder of ⑥ and all ⑦ category are A or Luxury, top-of-the-range hotels, which can charge in excess of £150/US$240 a night.

Prices in any establishment should by law be displayed on the back of the door of your room. If you feel you're being overcharged at a place that is officially registered, threaten to report it to the tourist police, who will generally adopt your side in such cases. Small increases over the listed prices may be legitimately explained by local tax or outdated lists. Out of high season, you may well find yourself paying much less than the listed amount.

---

superb places, from simple to luxury, and costs can be very reasonable, especially if shared between four or more people. Several of the companies we list will arrange "multi-centre" stays on two or more islands.

On the islands, a few local travel agents arrange villa rentals, mostly places not booked or listed by the overseas companies, and sometimes representing excellent value. **Out of season**, you can sometimes get a good deal on villa or apartment rental for a month or more by asking around locally, though in these days of EU convergence and the increasing desirability of the islands as year-round residences, "good deal" means anything under 50,000dr per month for a large studio (*garsoniéra*) or small one-bedroom flat.

Camping

Officially recognized **campsites** in the Ionian are restricted to Corfu (nine), Paxí (one, currently closed), Lefkádha (seven), Kefalloniá (two) and Zákynthos (six); see the Guide for full descriptions. Most places cost from 900dr a night per person, roughly the same fee per tent, and 1500dr per camper van, but at the fanciest sites,

rates for two people plus a tent can almost add up to the price of a basic room. Generally, you don't have to worry about leaving tents or baggage unattended at campsites; the Greeks are one of the most honest nationalities in Europe. The main risk comes from other campers.

Freelance camping – outside authorized campsites – is such an established element of Greek travel that few people realize that it's officially illegal. Since 1977 it has actually been forbidden by a law originally enacted to harass gypsies, and regulations are increasingly enforced. If you do camp rough, it's vital to exercise sensitivity and discretion. Police will crack down on people camping (and especially littering) around popular tourist beaches, particularly when a large community of campers develops. Off the beaten track, however, nobody is very bothered, though it is always best to ask permission locally in the village taverna or café. During high season, when everything may be full, attitudes towards freelance camping are more relaxed. At such times the best strategy is to find a sympathetic taverna, which in exchange for regular patronage will probably be willing to guard small valuables and let you use their facilities.

Eating and drinking

Greeks tend to socialize mostly outside their homes, and sharing a meal is one of the chief ways of doing it. The atmosphere is always relaxed and informal, with an accent on celebration, usually with children, grandparents, other relatives and friends in tow. Greeks are not big drinkers – what drinking they do is mainly to accompany food, as an appetizer or *digestif* – though in the resorts a whole range of bars, pubs and cocktail joints have sprung up principally to cater for tourists.

Breakfast, picnic fare and snacks

Greeks don't generally eat **breakfast**, so the only egg-and-bacon kind of places are in resorts where the British congregate; this can vary drastically in value (1200–2500dr for the works), depending on the competition. More indigenous alternatives are sweet or savoury pies and pretzel rings from a street stall (see "Snacks", opposite), or the fare on offer at *galaktopolía* or *zaharoplastía* (see "Sweets and desserts", p.44).

Picnic fare is good, cheap and easily available at bakeries and *manávika* (fruit-and-veg stalls). **Bread** is often of minimal nutritional value and inedible within a day of purchase. It's worth paying extra at the bakery (*foúrnos*) for *olikís* (wholemeal), *sikalísio* (rye bread), *oktásporo* (eight-grain), or even *enneásporo* (nine-grain) which are particular specialities of wheat-growing Lefkádha. Although the Ionian archipelago is an olive-producing region, local **olives** are hard to find; they take forty days of daily rinsing with salted water before they leach natural poisons and become edible, so don't try tasting one off a tree. Local **olive oil** is, however, available – and delicious – usually from oil-pressing factories or the older shops. However, it rarely makes it into tavernas or restaurants. **Féta cheese** is ubiquitous – often, these days, imported from Holland or Denmark, though local brands are usually better and not much more expensive. The goat's milk variety can be very dry and salty, so ask for a taste before buying; if you have a fridge, leaving the cheese in water overnight will solve both problems. This sampling advice goes for other indigenous cheeses as well, the most palatable of which are the expensive Gruyère-type *graviéra*. Despite the presence of farmland and the rainy winters, **fruit and vegetables** are fairly basic in the islands: roots such as potatoes, carrots and onions, and legumes such as courgettes and aubergine form the staple in shops on small islands such as Paxí, with little variation on the larger islands. Salad vegetables are more widely available, although lettuces are as rare as hen's teeth on some islands, hence the ubiquity of *horiátiki* (peasant) salad: cucumber, onion, tomato, olives and féta cheese. Apples, pears, peaches, bananas, grapes and mountains of various melons are also plentiful and usually cheap. Useful **phrases** for shopping are *éna tétarto* (250g) and *misó kiló* (500g). If you're self-catering and know your herbs by sight or smell, they're often available for free in the open countryside, in particular thyme, rosemary and oregano. Cheap local red wines are unbeatable with oil in salad dressings.

Snacks

Traditional **snacks** can be one of the distinctive pleasures of Greek eating, though they are being increasingly edged out by an obsession with *tóst* (toasted sandwiches) and pizzas. However, small kebabs (*souvlákia*) are widely available, and in most larger resorts and towns you'll find *yíros* – doner kebab with garnish in thick, doughy *píta* bread that's closer to Indian nan bread, often with *patátes* (the Greek equivalent of chips) and *tzatzíki* or a spicy sauce.

FOOD AND DRINK GLOSSARY

BASICS

Aláti	Salt	*Méli*	Honey
Avgá	Eggs	*Neró*	Water
(Horís) ládhi	(Without) oil	*Psári(a)*	Fish
Hortofágos	Vegetarian	*Psomí (olikís)*	Bread (wholemeal)
Katálogos	Menu	*Thallassiná*	Seafood (non-fish)
Kréas	Meat	*Tyrí*	Cheese
Lahaniká	Vegetables	*Yiaoúrti*	Yoghurt
O logariasmós	The bill	*Záhari*	Sugar

COOKING TERMS

Akhnistó	Steamed	*Stó foúrno*	Baked
Psitó	Roasted	*Tiganitó*	Pan-fried
Saganáki	Fried in a small pan (usually cheese)	*Tís óras*	Grilled/fried to order
		Yahní	Stewed in oil and tomato sauce
Skáras	Grilled		
Stí soúvla	Spit-roasted	*Yemistá*	Stuffed (squid, vegetables, etc)

SOUPS AND STARTERS

Avgolémono	Egg and lemon soup (rare in the Ionian)	*Skordhaliá*	Garlic dip for certain fish
Dolmádhes	Stuffed vine leaves	*Soúpa*	Soup
Fasoládha	Bean soup	*Taramosaláta*	Cod roe paté
Kopanistí	Spicy cheese dip	*Tzatzíki*	Yoghurt, garlic and cucumber dip
Melitzanosaláta	Aubergine/ eggplant dip		

VEGETABLES

Angoúri	Cucumber	*Hórta*	Greens (usually wild)
Bámies	Okra/ladies' fingers	*Kolokythákia*	Courgettes/zucchini
Bouréki	Courgette/ zucchini, potato and cheese pie	*Maroúli*	Lettuce
		Melitzána	Aubergine/eggplant
Briám	Ratatouille	*Papoutsákia*	Stuffed aubergine/eggplant
Domátes	Tomatoes	*Patátes*	Potatoes
Fakés	Lentils	*Rízi/piláfi*	Rice (usually with *sáltsa* – sauce)
Fasolákia	French (green) beans		
Frésko kremýdhi	Spring onions	*Saláta*	Salad
Horiátiki (saláta)	Greek (literally "peasant") salad (usually cucumber, onion, tomato, olives and féta cheese)	*Spanáki*	Spinach
		Yígandes	White haricot beans (usually in tomato sauce)

MEAT AND MEAT-BASED DISHES

Arní	Lamb	*Païdhákia*	Lamb chops
Biftéki	Hamburger	*Pastítsio*	Macaroni baked with meat
Brizóla	Pork or beef chop	*Soutzoukákia*	Mincemeat rissoles/beef
Hirinó	Pork		patties in seasoned
Keftédhes	Meatballs		tomato sauce
Kokorétsi	Liver/offal kebab	*Stifádho*	Meat stew with
Kotópoulo	Chicken		tomato sauce
Loukánika	Spicy homemade sausages	*Sykóti*	Liver
Moskhári	Veal	*Youvétsi*	Baked clay casserole
Moussakás	Aubergine/eggplant, potato		of meat and pasta
	and meat pie with		
	béchamel sauce topping		

SWEETS AND DESSERTS

Baklavás	Honey and nut pastry	*Karidhópita*	Walnut cake
Bougátsa	Creamy cheese pie served	*Kréma*	Custard pudding
	warm with sugar and	*Pagotó*	Ice cream
	cinnamon	*Pastélli*	Sesame and honey bar
Galaktoboúreko	Custard pie	*Rizógalo*	Rice pudding
Halvás	Sesame or semolina		
	sweetmeat		

FRUIT AND NUTS

Fistíkia	Pistachio nuts	*Míla*	Apples
Fráoules	Strawberries	*Pepóni*	Melon
Karpoúzi	Watermelon	*Portokália*	Oranges
Kerásia	Cherries	*Rodhákino*	Peach
Krystália	Green miniature pears	*Sýka*	(Dried) figs
Lemóni	Lemon	*Stafýlia*	Grapes

CHEESE

Féta	Salty, white cheese	*Katsikísio*	Goat's cheese
Graviéra	Gruyère-type hard cheese	*Myzíthra*	Sweet cream cheese
Kasséri	Medium cheese	*Próvio*	Sheep's cheese

DRINKS

Bíra	Beer	*Rozé/kokkinéli*	Rosé
Boukáli	Bottle	*Lemonádha*	Lemonade
Gála	Milk	*Metalikó neró*	Mineral water
Gazóza	Generic fizzy drink	*Portokaládha*	Orangeade
Kafés	Coffee	*Potíri*	Glass
Krasí	Wine	*Stinyássas!*	Cheers!
Áspro/lefkó	White	*Tsáï*	Tea
Kókkino	Red		

Other common snacks include *tyrópites* (cheese pies) and *spanakópites* (spinach pies), which can usually be found at the baker's, as can *kouloúria* (crispy pretzel rings sprinkled with sesame seeds) and *voutímata* (heavy biscuits rich in honey or cinnamon). Snack bars in towns and resorts usually also sell savoury pies with sausages (*loukánika*), and sweet ones with cream (*kréma*), fruit (*froúta*) or chocolate (*sokoláta*), and are an excellent source of cheap fuel food at any mealtime.

Restaurants

Greek cuisine and **restaurants** are simple and straightforward. There's no snobbery about eating out; everyone does it some of the time, and it's still reasonable – around 3000–4000dr per person for a substantial meal with a fair measure of house wine.

In choosing a restaurant, the best strategy is to go where the Greeks go. They eat late: 2pm to 3pm for **lunch**, 9pm to 11pm or even later for **dinner**. You can eat earlier, but you're likely to get indifferent service and cuisine if you frequent establishments catering to tourist timetables. Chic appearance is not a good guide to quality; often the more ramshackle, traditional outfits represent the best value – one good omen is the waiter bringing a carafe of refrigerated water, unbidden, rather than pushing you to order bottled stuff.

In resort areas, it's wise to keep a wary eye on the **waiters**, who are inclined to urge you to order more than you want, then bring things you haven't ordered. They still sometimes don't actually write anything down and may work out the **bill** by examining your empty plates. Although cash-register receipts are now officially required in all establishments, these are often only for the grand total, and even if the accompanying handwritten bill is itemized, it will probably be illegible. Where prices are printed on menus, you'll be paying the right-hand (higher) set in the case of those with a double column; the figure is inclusive of all taxes and **service charge**, although a small tip (150–200dr) is standard practice for the lad who lays the table, brings the bread and water, and so on.

Bread costs extra but consumption is not obligatory unless it is part of the **cover charge** (150–200dr), as it often is; you'll be considered deviant for refusing it (just say you're on a diet or

diabetic), but be warned that outside the very smartest places and those with a predominantly Greek clientele, much restaurant bread might be better taken home to build a sauna. If you do like the bread, you will not be charged for ordering more. **Children** are normally very welcome at restaurants and tavernas, day or night, and owners have a high tolerance of children playing around tables, although this may not be the case with neighbouring tables. Feeding the inevitable crowd of mendicant cats is frowned on, and unhygienic anyway.

Estiatória

There are two basic types of restaurant: the **estiatório** and the taverna. Distinctions between the two are minimal, though the former is more commonly found in town centres and tends to have the slightly more complicated dishes termed **mayireftá** (literally, "cooked"). An *estiatório* will generally feature a variety of oven-baked casserole dishes: *moussakás*, *pastítsio*, stews like *stifádho*, *yemistá* (stuffed tomatoes or peppers), the oily vegetable casseroles called *ladherá* and oven-baked meat or fish. Choosing these dishes is commonly done by going back to the kitchen and pointing at the desired trays.

Batches are cooked in the morning and then left to stand, which is why the food is often lukewarm or even cold. Greeks don't mind this (most believe that hot food is bad for you). If you do mind, ask for it *zestó* (hot). Some meals actually benefit from being allowed to marinate in their own juices before warming again. Similarly, you have to specify if you want your food with little or no oil (*horís ládhi*), but once again you will be considered a little strange, since Greeks regard good olive oil as essential to digestion. A sure sign of a primarily touristic restaurant is if the salad automatically comes without a lashing of oil on it.

Desserts (*epidhórpia* in formal Greek) of the pudding-and-pie variety don't exist at *estiatória*, and yoghurts only occasionally. Fruit is always available in season – watermelons and melons are the summer standards, grapes come in towards the end of summer, while apples and oranges fulfil the role during winter. Autumn treats worth asking after include *kydhóni* or *akhládhi stó foúrno*, baked quince or pear with some sort of syrup or nut topping.

Tavernas

Tavernas range from the smart and fashionable to rough-and-ready huts set up behind a beach, under a reed awning. Basic tavernas have a very limited menu, but the more established will offer some of the main *estiatório* dishes mentioned opposite, as well as the standard taverna fare. This essentially means *mezédhes* (hors d'oeuvres) and *tís óras* (meat and fish, fried or grilled to order). Increasingly, under the influence of tourism, tavernas serve up more adventurous international cuisine

Since the idea of courses is foreign to Greek cuisine, starters, main dishes and salads often arrive together unless you request otherwise. The best thing is to order a selection of *mezédhes* and salads to share, in true Greek fashion. Waiters encourage you to take the *horiátiki* **salad** – the so-called "Greek salad" with *féta* cheese – because it is the most expensive. If you only want tomato, or tomato and cucumber, ask for *domatosaláta* or *angourodomáta*. *Láhano* (cabbage) and *maroúli* (lettuce) are the typical winter and spring salads.

The most interesting **mezédhes** are *tzatzíki* (yoghurt, garlic and cucumber dip), *melitzanosaláta* (aubergine/eggplant dip), *kopanistí* (spicy cheese dip), *kolokythákia tiganitá* (courgette/zucchini slices fried in batter) or *melitzánes tiganités* (aubergine/eggplant slices fried in batter), *yígandes* (white haricot beans in vinaigrette or hot tomato sauce), *tyropitákia* or *spanakópites* (small cheese and/or spinach pies) and *okhtapódhi* (octopus).

Among **meats**, *souvláki* (shish kebab) and *brizóles* (chops) are reliable choices. In both cases, especially the latter, pork (*hiriní*) is usually better and cheaper than veal (*moskharísia*). The best *souvláki*, though not often available, is lamb (*arnísio*). The small lamb cutlets called *païdhákia* are very tasty, as is roast lamb (*arní psitó*) and roast kid (*katsíki stó fournó*) when obtainable. *Keftédhes* (meatballs), *biftékia* (a sort of hamburger) and the homemade sausages called *loukánika* are cheap and good. *Kotópoulo* (chicken) is also usually a safe bet.

Seafood dishes such as *kalamarákia* (fried baby squid) and *okhtapódhi* (octopus) are a summer staple of most seaside tavernas, and in some places *mýdhia* (mussels) and *garídhes* (small prawns) will be on offer at reasonable prices; *mýdhia saganáki* (mussels fried in a cheese and tomato sauce) is a particular treat.

Keep an eye out, however, for freshness and season – mussels in particular are a common cause of stomach upsets in mid-summer. Seaside tavernas also offer **fish**, though the choicer varieties, such as *barboúni* (red mullet), *tsipoúra* (gilt-head bream), or *fangrí* (common bream), are expensive. The price is usually quoted by the kilo, which should be not much more than double the street market rate – eg if squid is 2000dr a kilo at the fishmongers, that sum should fetch you two 250-gramme portions. It is procedure to go over to the cooler and pick your own, but if this isn't an option you should always specify how little or much you want.

As in *estiatória*, traditional tavernas offer fruit rather than **desserts**, though nowadays these are often available, along with coffee, in tavernas frequented by foreigners.

Specialist tavernas – and vegetarians

Some tavernas specialize. **Psarotavérnes**, for example, feature fish, while **psistariés** serve spit-roasted lamb, pork or goat (generically termed *kondosoúvli*), grilled chicken (*kotópoulo skáras*) or *kokorétsi* (grilled offal).

If you are **vegetarian**, you may be in for a hard time, and will often have to assemble a meal from various *mezédhes*. Even the excellent standbys of yoghurt and honey, *tzatzíki* and Greek salad begin to pall after a while, and many of the supposed "vegetable" dishes on the menu are cooked in stock or have pieces of meat added to liven them up. Restaurants wholly or largely vegetarian are slowly on the increase in touristed areas; this guide highlights them where appropriate, as well as those with a decent range of vegetable alternatives.

Wines

Both *estiatória* and tavernas will usually offer you a choice of bottled **wines**, and many have their own house variety kept in barrels, sold in bulk by the quarter-, half- or full litre and served either in glass flagons or brightly coloured tin "monkey-cups". Not as many tavernas stock their own wine as once did, but always ask whether they have wine *varelísio* or *hýma* – respectively meaning **"from the barrel"** and **"bulk"**. Non-resinated bulk wine is almost always more than decent. **Retsina** – pine-resinated wine, a slightly acquired taste – is also usually better, and startlingly cheap, straight from the barrel. Some of the older village shops stock it as well as tavernas. Kourtaki retsina in the small tin-top bottles is the most basic, and best served extra-chilled. The cork-bottle, 75cl version, is slightly more palatable.

Among the more common bottled wines, Calliga, Boutari and Lac de Roches are good, inexpensive whites, while Boutari Nemea is perhaps the best mid-range red. If you want something better but still moderately priced, Tsantali Agioritiko is an excellent white or red, and Boutari has a fine "Special Reserve" red. Local bottled wines of note, such as Kefalloniá's fine Rombola, are mentioned in the relevant chapters.

The kafenío

The **kafenío** is the traditional Greek coffee shop or café, found in every town, village and hamlet in the country. Although its main business is Greek coffee – prepared *skéto* or *pikró* (unsweetened), *métrio* (medium) or *glykó* (sweet) – it also serves spirits such as *oúzo* (see below), brandy (Metaxa or Botrys brand, in three grades), beer and soft drinks. Another refreshing drink sold in cafés is *kafés frappé*, a sort of iced instant coffee with or without milk and sugar – uniquely Greek despite its French-sounding name. Like Greek coffee, it is always accompanied by a welcome glass of cold water. Standard fizzy soft drinks are also sold in all *kafenía*.

Usually the only **snacks** available are variants on those in the street snack bars, or biscuits, cakes and sweets – increasingly pre-packaged, as a new generation of Greeks discover their sweet teeth and a taste for junk food.

Like tavernas, *kafenía* range from the plastic and sophisticated to the old-fashioned, spit-on-the-floor variety, with marble or brightly painted metal tables and straw-bottomed chairs. An important institution anywhere in Greece, they are the focus of life in more remote villages. You get the impression that many men spend most of their waking hours there. Greek women are rarely to be seen in the more traditional places – and foreign women may sometimes feel uneasy or unwelcome in these establishments. Even in holiday resorts, you will usually find there is at least one coffee house that the local men have kept intact for themselves.

Some *kafenía* close at siesta time, but many remain open from early in the morning until late at night. The chief socializing time is 6–8pm, immediately after the siesta. This is the time to take your pre-dinner *oúzo*, as the sun begins to sink and the air cools down. The more westernized, posh places with padded seats, popular with trendy Greeks, do not really classify as *kafenía* and are referred to as cafeterias.

Oúzo and mezédhes

Oúzo is a simple spirit of up to 48 percent alcohol, distilled from the grape-mash residue left over from wine-making, and then flavoured with herbs such as anise or fennel. It's comparable to a very rough schnapps, aqua vit or genever. When you order, you will be served two glasses: one with the *oúzo*, and one full of water that you tip into the former until it turns a milky white. You can drink it straight, but the strong, burning taste is hardly refreshing. It is increasingly common to add ice cubes.

Until not long ago, every *oúzo* you ordered was automatically accompanied by a small plate of **mezédhes**, on the house: bits of cheese, cucumber, tomato, a few olives, sometimes octopus or even a couple of small fish. Unfortunately these days you usually have to ask, and pay, for them, although bars on some of the islands – notably Lefkádha and Kefalloniá – have preserved the tradition. As these tend to be some of the best such establishments, we list them where we find them.

Sweets and desserts

Similar to the *kafenío* is the **zaharoplastío**, a cross between café and patisserie, which serves coffee, alcohol, yoghurt with honey, and sticky cakes.

The better establishments offer an amazing variety of pastries, cream and chocolate confections, honey-soaked Greco-Turkish sweets like *baklavás*, *kataïfi* (honey-drenched "shredded wheat"), *galaktoboúreko* (custard pie), and so on. The latter is something of a rarity nowadays, and when encountered should be tried.

If you want a stronger slant towards the dairy products and away from the pure sugar, seek out a **galaktopolío**, where you'll often find *rizógalo* (rice pudding – rather better than the English school-dinner variety), *kréma* (custard) and home-made or at least locally made *yiaoúrti* (yoghurt), best if it's *próvio* (from sheep's milk). These establishments, however, are definitely on the decline

Ice cream, sold principally at the gelaterias which have carpeted Greece of late, can be very good and almost indistinguishable from their

Italian prototypes. A scoop (*baláki*) costs 250–400dr; you'll be asked if you want it in a cup (*kýpello*) or a cone (*konáki*), or with *sandiyí* (whipped cream) on top. By contrast, mass-produced stuff like Delta or Evga brand is pretty trashy, with the honourable exception of Mars and Opal Fruit ices and Dove Bars.

Both *zaharoplastía* and *galaktopolía* are more family-oriented places than the *kafenío*, and many also serve a basic continental-type **breakfast** of *méli me voútiro* (honey poured over a pat of butter) or jam (all kinds are called *marmeládha* in Greek; ask for *portokáli* – orange – if you want proper marmalade) with fresh bread or *friganiés* (melba-toast-type slivers). You are also more likely to find proper (*evropaïkó*) tea and non-Greek coffee. *Nescafé* has become the generic term for all instant coffee, regardless of brand; it's generally pretty vile, and in resort areas smart proprietors have taken to offering genuine filter coffee, dubbed "*gallikós*" (French).

Bars – and beer

Bars (*barákia*), once confined to towns, cities and holiday resorts, are now found all over Greece. They range from clones of Parisian cafés to seaside cocktail bars, by way of imitation English pubs, with satellite channels offering Premier League football or MTV-type videos running all day. Once twenty-hour-a-day operations, most bars now close at about 2am or 3am, depending on the municipality; during 1994 they were required by the Ministry of Public Order to make an admission/cover charge which included the first drink. This decree, met with a storm of street protests and other mass civil disobedience, is presently in abeyance but could be revived at any time.

For that and other reasons, drinks are invariably more expensive than in a café. Bars are, however, most likely to stock a range of **beers**, all foreign labels made locally under licence or imported, with the exception of the new Greek brew Mythos. Kronenbourg and Kaiser are also commonly found, with the former available in both light and dark; since 1993 a tidal wave of even pricier, imported German beers, such as Bitburger and Warstein, has washed over the fancier resorts. Amstel and Henninger are the two ubiquitous cheapies, rather bland but inoffensive; the Dutch themselves claim that the former is better than the Amstel available in Holland. A possible compromise in both taste and expense is the sharper-tasting Heineken, universally referred to as a "*prássini*" by bar and taverna staff after its green bottle. Incidentally, try not to get stuck with the 330ml cans, vastly more expensive (and more of a rubbish problem) than the returnable 500ml bottles.

Communications: mail, phones and the media

Postal services

Most **post offices** are open Monday to Friday from about 7.30am to 2pm, though in certain large towns – for example Corfu, Lefkádha and Argostóli – they also have evening and weekend hours.

Airmail **letters** from the islands take three to seven days to reach the rest of Europe, five to twelve days to North America and a little longer to Australia and New Zealand. Generally, the larger the island (and the planes serving its airport, if it has one), the quicker the service. Aerograms are slightly faster, and for a modest fee (about 500dr), you can further cut delivery time to any destination by using the express (*katepígonda*) service. Registered (*sistiméno*) delivery is also available, but it is quite slow unless coupled with express service. If you are sending large purchases home, note that **parcels** should, and often can only, be handled in the main island capitals.

For a simple letter or card, **stamps** (*grammatósima*) can also be purchased at a *periptero* (kiosk). However, the proprietors charge ten percent commission on the cost of the stamp, and never seem to know the current international rates. At the time of writing these had just increased to 180dr within Europe and 220dr to all destinations outside Europe for postcards and

letters under 20gm. Ordinary **postboxes** are bright yellow, with the hunting horn logo, and express boxes dark red; if you are confronted by two slots, "*esoterikó*" is for domestic mail, "*exoterikó*" for overseas.

Receiving mail

The **poste restante** system is reasonably efficient, especially at the post offices of larger towns. Mail should be clearly addressed and marked "poste restante", with your surname underlined, to the main post office of whichever town you choose. It will be held for a month, and you'll need your passport to collect it.

Telephones

Telephone calls are relatively straightforward. Street-corner call boxes work only with **phone cards**; these come in three denominations – 100, 500 and 1000 units – and are available from *periptera* (kiosks), OTE offices (*Organismós Tilepikinoníon tis Elládhos*) and newsagents. You will probably have to go to OTE for the higher denominations, which, unsurprisingly, are the best value. *Periptera* usually only carry the basic 100 unit (1000dr) cards.

It's easy enough to use up any remaining phone card units with a quick call home, but you can also make **local calls** from a *periptero*, or **street kiosk**. Here the phone is connected to a meter, and you pay after you have made the call. Very occasionally you come across a chunky coin-operated phone at a *periptero*. While local calls are reasonable (30dr for the first six minutes), long-distance ones have some of the most expensive rates in the EU – and definitely the worst connections, although the situation is gradually improving as exchanges are digitalized. Other options for local calls are from a *kafenío* or **bar** (same 30dr charge as at kiosks), but you won't be allowed to use these for trunk or overseas calls unless the phone is metered: look for a sign saying "*tiléfono me metrití*".

PHONING GREECE FROM ABROAD

Dial the international access code (given below) + 30 (country code) + area code (minus initial 0) + number

Australia ☎ 0011	New Zealand ☎ 00
Canada ☎ 011	UK ☎ 00
Ireland ☎ 010	US ☎ 011

PHONING ABROAD FROM GREECE

Dial the country code (given below) + area code (minus any initial 0) + number

Australia ☎ 0061	New Zealand ☎ 0064
Canada ☎ 001	UK ☎ 0044
Ireland ☎ 00353	US ☎ 001

USEFUL GREEK TELEPHONE NUMBERS

ELPA Road Service ☎ 104	Operator (international) ☎ 161
Fire brigade ☎ 199	Police/Emergency ☎ 100
Medical emergencies ☎ 166	Speaking clock ☎ 141
Operator (domestic) ☎ 132	Tourist police ☎ 171

PHONE CREDIT CARD OPERATOR ACCESS NUMBERS FROM GREECE

AT&T USA Direct ☎ 00 800 1311	British Telecom ☎ 00 800 4411
Australia ☎ 00 800 61 11; (Ortus) ☎ 00 800 6121	Cable & Wireless ☎ 00 800 4422
	Canada ☎ 00 800 1611
Bell Atlantic ☎ 00 800 1821	MCI ☎ 00 800 1211
Bell South ☎ 00 800 1721	Sprint ☎ 00 800 1411

For inter-island or **international** (*exoterikó*) **calls**, it's better to use either card phones or the very few remaining inside the premises of the nearest OTE office. As of writing, many OTE branches have withdrawn from the business of providing call facilities, with opening hours drastically shortened, and now generally resemble a UK high-street BT Phone Store with their array of phones and fax machines for sale. **Faxes** are best sent from post offices and some travel agencies – at a price; receiving a fax may also incur a small charge. **Avoid** making long-distance calls from a hotel, as they slap a fifty-percent surcharge onto the already outrageous rates.

Calls a 1000dr card get you about five minutes to all EU countries and much of the rest of Europe, and around three to North America, Australia or New Zealand. **Cheap rates**, a reduction of ten to fifty percent depending on call distance, apply from 10pm to 8am daily, plus all day Sunday, for calls **within Greece**; calling **internationally**, cheap rates take effect from 10pm to

6am for Europe, 11pm to 8am for North America, and 8pm to 6am for Australia. Discounts for other destinations are minimal. With access to a subscriber line, night rates to any EU country are about 21p per minute equivalent.

Mobile phones are an essential fashion accessory in Greece, with the highest per-capita use in Europe outside of Italy. There are three networks at present: Panafon, Telestet and Kosm OTE. Ringing any of them from Britain, you will find that costs are exactly the same as calling a fixed phone, though of course such numbers are pricey when rung locally. UK users should note that only GSM phones will work in Greece. Coverage country-wide is fairly good, though there are a number of "dead" zones in the shadows of mountains and on really remote islets. Pay-as-you-go, contract-free plans are being heavily promoted in Greece (such as Telestet B-Free and Panafon À La Carte), and if you're going to be around for a while – for example, working a season in the tourist industry – an outlay of

£80 or less will see you to a decent apparatus and your first calling card, which lasts six months rather than the sixty-day norm in Britain.

British Telecom, as well as North American long-distance companies like AT&T, MCI and Sprint, provide **credit card call** services from Greece, but only back to the home country. There are now local-dial numbers with some cards, such as BT, which enable you to connect to the international system for the price of a one-unit local call, then charge the international call to your home phone – cheaper than the alternatives.

Email

Email and **Internet** use is catching on slowly but surely in Greece; electronic addresses or Web sites are given for the few travel companies and hotels that have them. Greeks connected privately at their homes, often as an indulgence to the kids, far outnumber the businesses that have got clued in. For your own email needs, you're best off using the various Internet cafés which have sprung up in the larger towns – street addresses are given where appropriate.

The media

British **newspapers** are fairly widely available in Greece at a cost of 500–700dr for dailies, or 900–1000dr for Sunday editions. You'll find day-old copies of *The Independent* and *The Guardian*'s European edition, plus a few of the tabloids, in all the resorts as well as in major towns. American and international alternatives include the turgid *USA Today* and the more readable *International Herald Tribune*, the latter including as a major bonus a free, complete English translation of the respected Greek daily *Kathemerini* (see below). *Time* and *Newsweek* are also widely available, as are popular publications in other European languages.

Greek publications

Although you will probably be excluded from the **Greek print media** by the double incomprehensibilities of alphabet and language, you can learn a fair bit about your Greek fellow-travellers by their choice of broadsheet, so a quick survey of Greek magazines and newspapers won't go amiss.

Many papers are funded by **political groups**, which tends to decrease the already low quality of Greek dailies. Among these, only the centrist

Kathemerini – whose former proprietor Helen Vlahos attained heroic status for her defiance of the junta – and the now daily *Vima* approach the standards of a major European newspaper. *Eleftherotypia*, once a PASOK mouthpiece, now aspires to more independence, and has editorial links with Britain's *Guardian*; *Avriani* has now taken its place as the PASOK cheerleading section; *Ta Nea* is mostly noted for its extensive small ads. On the **left**, *Avyi* is the Eurocommunist forum with literary leanings, while *Rizospastis* acts as the organ of the KKE (unreconstructed Communists). *Ethnos* was also shown some years back to have received covert funding from the KGB to act as a disinformation bulletin. At the other end of the political spectrum, *Apoyevmatini* and *Eleftheros Typos* generally support the **centre-right** Néa Dhimokratía party, while *Estia*'s no-photo format and reactionary politics are both stuck somewhere at the turn of the century. The **nationalist**, lunatic fringe is staked out by paranoid *Stohos* ("Our Goal: Greater Greece; Our Capital: Constantinople"), while *Eleftheri Ora* still harps on about the unjust treatment received by the surviving colonels of the junta. Given the generally low level of journalism, there is little need for a soft-porn or gutter press, unlike in Germany or the UK.

Among **magazines** that are not merely translations of overseas titles, *Tahydhromos* is the respectable news-and-features weekly; *Ena* is more sensationalist, *Klik* a crass rip-off of *The Face* and *To Pondiki* (The Mouse) a satirical weekly revue in the same vein as Britain's *Private Eye* or *Spy*; its famous covers are spot-on, and accessible to anyone with minimal Greek. More specialized niches are occupied by low-circulation titles such as *Adhesmatos Typos* (a muckraking journal) and *Andi*, an intelligent biweekly somewhat in the mould of Britain's *New Statesman*.

Radio

If you have a **radio**, playing dial roulette can be rewarding. As the government's former monopoly of wavelengths has ended, regional stations have mushroomed and the airwaves are now positively cluttered. On Corfu, frequencies around 100 FM play host to a variety of fairly forgettable local radio stations. The **BBC World Service** broadcasts on short-wave throughout Greece; 9.41, 15.07 and 12.09 MHz are the most common frequencies.

TV

Greece's three government-owned **TV stations**, ET1, NET and (from Thessaloníki) ET3 nowadays lag behind private, mostly right-wing channels – Mega-Channel, New Channel, Antenna, Star and Seven-X – in the ratings, although their quality is far superior. They are the only ones to provide a decent range of educational programmes such as documentaries, along with current affairs, sport and quality cinema, including works from around Europe and further afield, not just America. On NET, news summaries in English are broadcast daily at 6pm. Programming on the private channels tends to be a mix of soaps (especially American, Italian, Spanish and Latin American), game shows, Hollywood movies of varying quality and more sports.

Local stations in the Ionian, as elsewhere in Greece, offer little more than regional news and sporting events, plus second-rate serials and foreign movies, unless they spring into life with a belting display of folk music from a recent festival. It should also be noted that Greek censors have a high tolerance level when it comes to sex, and the private channels can get pretty raunchy late at night; if your hotel subscribes to Filmnet, then you are in for an eyeful of hardcore porn if you go channel-hopping after midnight. Whatever the channel, all foreign films and serials are broadcast in their original language, with Greek subtitles. Except for the 24hr channels, Skai, Mega and Antenna, most broadcast from breakfast time, or just after, until the small hours. Numerous **cable and satellite** channels are received, including Sky, BBC World, CNN, MTV, Super Channel, French Canal Cinque, German Sat and Italian Rai Uno or Due. The range available depends on the area (and hotel) you're in.

Opening hours and public holidays

The one constant about Greek opening hours is change. Hours may alter for reasons that elude those who happily alter them. The traditional timetable starts at a relatively civilized hour, with shops opening between 8.30 and 9.30am, then runs through until lunchtime, when there is a long break for the hottest part of the day. Things (but not banks) may then reopen in the mid- to late afternoon.

Tourist areas tend to adopt a slightly more northern timetable, with shops and offices, as well as the most important archeological sites and museums, usually open throughout the day.

Business and shopping hours

Most **government agencies** are open to the public on weekdays from 8am to 2pm. In general, however, you'd be optimistic to show up after 1pm expecting to be served the same day. Private businesses, or anyone providing a service, frequently operate a 9am–6pm schedule. If someone is actually selling something, then they are more likely to follow a split shift as detailed below.

Shopping hours during the hottest months are theoretically from approximately 9am to 2.30pm, and from 6 to 9pm. During the cooler months the morning schedule may start and finish slightly later, the evening trade a half-hour or even a full hour earlier. There are so many exceptions to these rules, though, that you can't count on getting anything done except from Monday to Friday, between 9.30am and 1pm. It's worth noting that delis and **butchers** are not allowed to sell fresh meat during summer afternoons (though some flout this rule); similarly, **fishmongers** are only open in the morning, as are **pharmacies**, which additionally are shut on Saturday, except for the duty rota. Tourist shops and minimarkets, especially in the busier resorts, tend to be open all day until quite late in the evening as long as there are people around

PUBLIC HOLIDAYS

January 1	May 1
January 6	Whit Monday/Pentecost (50 days after Easter,
March 25	usually in June)
First Monday of Lent (Feb/March; see below)	August 15
Easter weekend (according to the Orthodox	October 28
festival calendar; see below)	December 25 & 26

There are also a large number of local holidays, which result in the closure of shops and businesses, though not government agencies.

VARIABLE RELIGIOUS FEASTS

	Lent Monday	Easter Sunday	Whit Monday
2000	March 13	April 30	June 19
2001	February 26	April 15	June 4
2002	March 18	May 5	June 24

All of the above opening hours will be regularly thrown out of sync by the numerous **public holidays and festivals**. The most important, when almost everything will be closed, are listed in the box above.

Ancient sites and monasteries

Opening hours of **ancient sites** vary considerably. As far as possible, individual times are quoted in the text, but bear in mind that these change with exasperating frequency and at smaller sites may be subject to the whim of a local keeper. The times quoted are generally summer hours, which operate from around late April to the end of September. Reckon on similar days but later opening and earlier closing in winter. Reductions on entry fees of approximately 25 percent often apply to senior citizens, 50 percent to students with proper identification. In addition, entrance to all state-run sites and museums is **free** to all EC nationals on Sundays and public holidays outside of peak season – non-EU nationals are unlikely to be detected as such unless they go out of the way to advertise the fact.

Smaller sites tend to close for a long lunch and siesta (even where they're not supposed to), as do **monasteries**. The latter are generally open from about 9am to 1pm and 5 to 8pm (3.30–6.30pm in winter) for limited visits. Most operate a fairly strict **dress code** for visitors; shorts on either sex are unacceptable, and women are often expected to cover their arms and wear skirts – wraps are sometimes provided on the spot. It's free to take **photos** of open-air sites, though museum photography and the use of videos or tripods anywhere requires an extra fee and written permit. This usually has to be arranged in writing from the nearest Department of Antiquities (*Eforía Arheotíton*). It's also worth knowing that Classical studies students can get a free annual pass to all Greek museums and sites by presenting themselves at the office on the rear corner (Tossítsa/Bouboulínas) of the National Archeological Museum in Athens – take documentation, two passport-sized photographs and be prepared to say you're a teacher (anyone with a university degree in Greece is automatically regarded as a teacher of that subject).

Festivals

Many of the big Greek festivals (see the box overleaf) have a religious basis, and are observed in accordance with the Orthodox calendar. Give or take a few saints, this is similar to the regular Catholic liturgical year, except for Easter, which can fall as much as three weeks on either side of the Western festival.

Easter

Easter is by far the most important festival of the Greek year – infinitely more so than Christmas – and taken much more seriously than in western Europe. The festival is an excellent time to be in Greece, both for its beautiful religious ceremonies and for the days of feasting and celebration that follow. Corfu, in particular, is a good place to be, but each village celebrates the event, and in the smaller villages you're more likely to find yourself invited to join in. Similarly, each island and village has its own variations on the main ceremonies. Corfu continues its tradition of pottery-smashing from windows around the old town on Easter Saturday morning (Lefkádha and Zákynthos have a similar tradition), and the spectacular firework display at midnight over the Spianádha. Each town and village parades its saints' icons in great panoply and, on Paxí, islanders strew the country lanes with flowers from their gardens. Zákynthos has a tradition dating from the Middle Ages of practical jokes played on shop-owners through the Easter period.

The first great public ceremony takes place on **Good Friday** evening as the Descent from the Cross is lamented in church. At dusk the *Epitáfios*, Christ's funeral bier, lavishly decorated with flowers by the women of the parish, leaves the sanctuary and is paraded solemnly through the streets.

Late Saturday evening sees the climax in a majestic *Anástasis* Mass to celebrate Christ's triumphant return. At the stroke of midnight all lights in each crowded church are extinguished, plunging the congregation into the darkness that envelops Christ as he passes through the underworld. Then there's a faint glimmer of light behind the altar screen before the priest appears, holding aloft a lighted taper and chanting *"Avtó to Fos"* (This is the Light of the World). Stepping down to the level of the parishioners, he touches his flame to the unlit candle of the nearest worshipper, intoning *"Dhévte, lávete Fos"* (Come, take the Light). Those at the front of the congregation and on the aisles do the same for their neighbours until the entire church is ablaze with burning candles and the miracle reaffirmed.

Even the most committed agnostic is likely to find this moving. The traditional greeting, as an arsenal's worth of fireworks explode around you in the street, is *"Khristós anésti"* (Christ is risen), to which the response is *"Alithós anésti"* (Truly He is risen). In the week up to Easter Sunday you should wish people a Happy Easter: *"Kaló Páskha"*; after the day, you say *"Khrónia pollá"* (Many Happy Returns, literally Many Years).

Worshippers then take the burning **candles** home, and it brings good fortune on the house if they arrive still lit. On reaching the front door it is common practice to make the sign of the cross on the lintel with the flame, leaving a black smudge visible for the rest of the year. The **Lenten fast** is traditionally broken early on **Sunday** morning (usually just after midnight) with a meal of *mayirítsa*, a soup made from lamb tripe, rice and lemon. The rest of the lamb will be roasted on spits for Sunday lunch, and festivities often take place through the rest of the day.

The Greek equivalent of **Easter eggs** are hard-boiled eggs (painted red on Holy Thursday), which are baked into twisted, sweet bread-loaves (*tsourékia*) or distributed on Easter

FESTIVALS

January 1
New Year's Day (*Protokhroniá*) in Greece is the feast day of Áyios Vassílios (St Basil), and is celebrated with church services and the making of a special loaf, *vassilópitta*, in which a coin is baked which brings its finder good luck throughout the year. The traditional New Year greeting is *"Kalí Khroniá"*.

January 6
Epiphany (*Áyia Theofánia*, or *Ta Fóta* for short), when the *kalikántzari* (hobgoblins) who run riot on earth during the twelve days of Christmas are banished back to the nether world by various rites of the Church. The most important of these is the blessing of baptismal fonts and all outdoor bodies of water.

Pre-Lenten carnivals
This period, known as *Apókries* throughout Greece, spans three weeks, climaxing during the seventh weekend before Easter and finishing on *Katharí Dheftéra* (Clean Monday), the start of Lent. All the islands in this guide have the most elaborate festivities, parties and parades, usually based around the capital towns; in the Ionian, the tradition harks back to the Venetian era, and is dubbed *Karnaváli* (Carnival).

March 25
Independence Day and the Feast of the Annunciation (*Evangelismós*) is both a religious and a national holiday, with, on the one hand, military parades and dancing to celebrate the beginning of the revolt against Turkish rule in 1821 and, on the other, church services to honour the news being given to Mary that she was to become the Mother of Christ. There are major festivities at any place with a monastery or church named *Evangelístria* or *Evangelismós*.

April 23
The feast of **St George** (*Áyios Yeóryios*), the patron of shepherds, is a big rural celebration, with much dancing and feasting at associated shrines and towns. If April 23 falls before Easter, ie during Lent, the festivities are postponed until the Monday after Easter.

May 1
May Day is the great urban holiday when townspeople traditionally make for the countryside for picnics and return with bunches of wild flowers. Wreaths are hung on their doorways or balconies until they are burnt on Midsummer's eve. There are also large demonstrations by the Left, claiming the *Ergatikí Protomayiá* (Working Class First of May) as their own.

May 21
Ionian Day is the anniversary of the islands' union with Greece in 1864, celebrated on Corfu with marches, wreath-laying, flybys and much military pageant. Also the saints' days of **Áyios Konstandínos** and **Ayía Eléni**, therefore the most celebrated name day in Greece.

Late June to early September
Lefkádha Festival of Language and Arts. Launched in a postwar atmosphere of internationalism, this aims to bring together disparate cultures to enhance understanding. Spread out over a three-week period, the festival mixes music and dance from South America, Europe and the Mediterranean countries.

June 29
The **Holy Apostles** (*Áyii Apóstoli*), Petros and Pavlos (Peter and Paul). Two of the more widely celebrated name days.

Sunday. People rap their eggs against their friends', and the owner of the last uncracked one is considered lucky.

The festival calendar

Most of the other Greek festivals are in honour of one or another of a multitude of **saints**. The most important are detailed in the box above: a village or church bearing one of the saint's names mentioned here is a sure sign of celebrations – sometimes right across the town or island, sometimes quiet, local and consisting of little more than a special liturgy and banners adorning the chapel in question. Saints' days are also celebrated as **name days**; if it's a friend's name day, you wish them *"Khrónia pollá"* (Many Happy Returns). Also detailed are a few more **secular holidays**, most enjoyable of which are the pre-Lenten carnivals.

July 26

Ayía Paraskeví is celebrated in the many parishes and villages bearing that name.

August 11

Áyios Spyrídhon. The one fixed date of the Corfiot patron saint's four festival days, each remembering the saint's intervention when disaster threatened the island. The gold casket containing the saint's remains is paraded around the centre of the town. (The other days, floating in the calendar, are Palm Sunday, Easter Saturday and the first Sunday in November.) The saint's day is also a major celebration in Karyá on Lefkádha.

August 15

Apokímisis tis Panayías (Assumption or Dormition of the Blessed Virgin Mary). This is the day when people traditionally return to their home village, and in many places there will be no accommodation available on any terms. Even some Greeks will resort to sleeping in the streets. There are major festivities throughout the islands – strangest of all is the ritual **snake-handling** at the village of Markópoulo on Kefalloniá.

August 24

Áyios Dhionýsios. One of two days (the other is the visitor-unfriendly December 24) for the saint, with major celebrations held around Áyios Dhionýsios churches, notably at Zákynthos Town.

September 8

Yénisis tis Panayías (Birth of the Virgin Mary) sees special services in churches dedicated to the event.

September 14

A last major summer festival, the **Ípsosis tou Stavroú** (Exaltation of the Cross).

October 26

The feast of **Áyios Dhimítrios**, another popular name day. New wine is traditionally tapped on this day, a good excuse for general inebriation.

October 28

Óhi Day, the year's major patriotic shindig – a national holiday with parades, folk-dancing and speechifying to commemorate Metaxas's apocryphal one-word reply to Mussolini's 1940 ultimatum: "*Óhi!*" (No!).

November 8

Another popular name day, the feast of the **Archangels Michael and Gabriel** (Mihaíl and Gavriíl, or the Taxiarhón), marked by rites at the numerous churches named after them, particularly at the rural monastery of Taxiárhis on Itháki.

December 6

The feast of **Áyios Nikólaos**, the patron of seafarers, consequently a big favourite on all islands, with many chapels dedicated to him.

December 25

A much less festive occasion than Greek Easter, **Christmas** (*Khristoúyenna*) is still an important religious feast. In recent years it has acquired all of the commercial trappings of the Western Christmas, with decorations, trees and gifts. December 26 is not Boxing Day as in England, but the **Sýnaxis tis Panayías** (Meeting of the Virgin's Entourage), a legal holiday.

December 31

New Year's Eve (*Paramoní Protokhroniás*), when, as on the other twelve days of Christmas, children go door to door singing the traditional *kálanda* (carols), receiving money in return. Adults tend to play cards, often for money. The *vassilópitta* is cut at midnight (see January 1).

In addition to the specific dates mentioned, there are literally scores of **local festivals** (*paniyíria*) celebrating the patron saint of the village church. With hundreds of possible name-saints' days (liturgical calendars list two or three, however arcane, for each day) you're unlikely to travel around Greece for long without stumbling on something. Those that fall in the warmer months are usually lively outdoor events lasting most of the night. Apart from the general list above, the location and date of many specific ones are mentioned in the course of the Guide.

It is important to remember the concept of the **paramoní**, or eve of the festival. Most of the events listed above are celebrated on the night before, so if you show up on the morning of the date given you will very probably have missed any music, dancing or drinking.

Watersports

The Ionian islands can claim some of the finest watersports facilities in the Mediterranean. Watersport equipment – from the humble pedalo to top-of-the-range competitive windsurf boards and sails – can be rented out in most resorts, and larger resorts have waterskiing and parasailing facilities.

The last few years have seen a massive growth in the popularity of **windsurfing** in Greece. The country's bays and coves are ideal for beginners, and boards can be rented in literally hundreds of resorts. Because of the shared geography and prevailing winds of the Ionian islands, it is typically the sandy or pebbly parts of the west coasts, often inaccessible except by boat, that provide the best conditions. Only Paxí and Zákynthos are exceptions to this rule, with west coasts dominated by high, hostile cliffs. Morning winds are gentle, ideal for novices, and the afternoon winds will test even the most experienced. Rentals start from around £6/US$10 an hour. Fully inclusive windsurf holidays on islands such as Lefkádha start at around £350/US$560 a week.

Waterskiing is available at a number of the larger resorts, and even on the smaller islands. By the rental standards of the ritzier parts of the Mediterranean, it is a bargain, with twenty minutes' instruction often available for around £8–10/US$13–16. At many resorts, **parasailing** (*parapént*) is also possible; rates start at £10/US$16 a go.

A combination of steady winds, appealing seascapes and numerous natural harbours has long made the Greek islands a tremendous place for **sailing**. Holiday companies offer all sorts of packaged and tailor-made cruises (see the "Getting there" sections above). Locally, small boats and dinghies are rented out by the day at many resorts. Larger craft can be chartered by the week or longer, either bareboat or with skipper, from marinas on Corfu and bases in most of the islands. Where the Aegean has its notorious

meltémi, the Ionian has its equivalent **maéstro**, which can blow for up to three days and make for pretty nauseating sailing, most often at either end of the season, but sometimes at points during it. More and more companies are offering sailing as options, and there are numerous agencies who will organize skippered or bareboat charters. For more details, contact the Hellenic Yachting Federation, Aktí Navárhou Koundourióti 7, 185 34 Pireás ☎01/41 37 351; fax 41 31 119.

Scuba-diving is still a minority sport in the Ionian, but growing fast because of its popularity among north European visitors. Many schools are in fact run by visitors from Germany and the Nordic countries, with some Brits now muscling in on the act and an increasing number of Greeks catching on. We list diving schools in the Guide and more extensive information can be obtained in Britain from the British Sub-Aqua Club (Seymour Leisure Centre, Seymour Place, London SW1 ☎020/7723 8336) or from GNTO offices in other countries. In Greece you can contact the Union of Greek Diving Centres (☎01/92 29 532 or 41 18 909).

Public beaches, sunbeds and umbrellas

Not many people realize that all **beaches** in Greece are public land; that's understandable, given the extent to which luxury hotels encroach on them, and the sunbeds and umbrellas that carpet entire strands. Greek **law**, however, is very clear that the shore from the winter high-tide mark down to the water must be freely accessible, with a right of way provided around hotels or resorts, and that no permanent structures be built in that zone. Accordingly, you should resist pressure to pay rental for unwanted **sunbeds** or **umbrellas**, particularly the latter, which are often anchored with permanent, illegal concrete lugs buried in the sand.

Police and trouble

Greece is one of Europe's safest countries, with a low crime rate and an almost unrivalled reputation for honesty. If you leave a bag or wallet at a café, you'll most likely find it scrupulously looked after, pending your return. Similarly, Greeks are relaxed about leaving possessions unlocked or unattended on the beach, in rooms or on campsites. However, in recent years there has been a large increase in theft and crimes, perpetrated mainly by fellow tourists, particularly in the cities and resorts, so it's wise to lock things up and treat Greece like any other European destination. Below are a few pointers on offences that might get you into trouble locally, and some advice on sexual harassment – all too much a fact of life given the classically Mediterranean machismo of Greek culture.

Offences

The most common causes of a brush with authority are nude bathing or sunbathing, and camping outside an authorized site.

Nude bathing is legal on only a very few beaches, and is deeply offensive to the more traditional Greeks. You should exercise considerable sensitivity to local feeling: it is, for example, very bad etiquette to swim or sunbathe nude within sight of a church. Generally, though, if a beach has become fairly established as naturist, or is well secluded, it's highly unlikely that the police are going to come charging in. Where they do get

bothered is if they feel a place is turning into a "hippie beach" or nudity is getting too overt on mainstream tourist stretches. Most of the time, the only action will be a warning, but you can officially be arrested straight off – facing up to three days in jail and a stiff fine.

Topless (sun)bathing for women is technically legal nationwide, but specific locales sometimes opt out of this by posting signs, which should be heeded, although they are extremely rare in the Ionian.

Very similar guidelines apply to **freelance camping** – though for this you're still unlikely to incur anything more than a warning to move on. The only real risk of arrest is if you are told to move on and fail to do so. In either of the above cases, even if the police do take any action against you, it's more likely to be a brief spell in their cells than any official prosecution.

Incidentally, any sort of **disrespect** towards the Greek State or Orthodox Church in general, or Greek civil servants in particular, may be construed as offences in the most literal sense, so it's best to keep your comments on how things are working (or not) to yourself. This is a society where words count, with a consistent backlog of court cases dealing with the alleged public utterance of *malákas* (wanker). While you'll hear it bandied about endlessly, don't be tempted to use it yourself unless your Greek is good enough to appreciate the register of the conversation: you may well land yourself in hot water.

Drug offences are treated as major crimes, particularly since there's a growing local use and addiction problem, even on the smaller islands. The maximum penalty for "causing the use of drugs by someone under 18", for example, is life imprisonment and at least a ten-million-drachma fine. Theory is by no means practice, but foreigners caught in possession of even small amounts of grass do get long jail sentences if there's evidence that they've been supplying the drug to others.

If you get arrested for any offence, you have a right to contact your **consulate**, which will arrange a lawyer for your defence. Beyond this, there is little they can or (in most cases) will do.

In an **emergency**, dial ☎100 for the police; ☎171 for the tourist police; ☎166 for an ambulance; ☎199 for the fire brigade.

Sexual harassment

Thousands of women travel independently about the Ionian without being **harassed** or feeling intimidated. Greek machismo, however, is strong, if less upfront than that of southern Italy, for example. Most of the hassle you are likely to get is from a small minority of Greek males, known as *kamákia* (fish harpoons), who migrate in summer to the beach bars and discos of the main resorts and towns, specifically in pursuit of "liberated, fun-loving" tourists. Indigenous Greeks, who are increasingly protective of you as you become more of a fixture in any one place, treat these outsiders with

contempt. Words worth remembering as unambiguous responses include *pápste* (stop it), *afísteme* (leave me alone) and *fiyete* (go away), the latter intensified if followed by *dhrómo!* (road, as in "hit the road"). **Hitching** is not advisable for lone women travellers, but **camping** is generally not a problem, though away from recognized sites it is often wise to attach yourself to a local family by making arrangements to use nearby private land. On the more remote islands you may feel more uncomfortable travelling alone. The intensely traditional Greeks may have trouble understanding why you are unaccompanied, and might not welcome your presence in their sometimes exclusively male *kafenía* – often the only place where you can get a drink. Travelling with a man, you're more likely to be treated as a *xéni*, a word meaning both (female) stranger and guest.

Work

Since Greece's full accession to the European Union in early 1993, a citizen of any EU state has (in theory) the right to work in Greece. In practice, however, there can be a number of bureaucratic hurdles to overcome. In the Ionian islands the number of teaching posts in the private language schools (*frondistíria*) was always limited in comparison to the mainland, and

lately restrictions on the availability of such positions for non-Greeks have made matters more difficult, so you may stand more chance in a commercial or leisure-orientated trade, most likely tourism-related.

If you plan to work for someone else you may find yourself involved in a bureaucratic process despite the theoretical freedom of employment. You first visit the nearest Department of Employment and collect two forms: one an **employment application** which you fill in, the other for the formal offer of work by your prospective employer. Once these are vetted, and revenue stamps (*hartósima*, purchased at kiosks) applied, you take them to the Aliens' Bureau (*Ipiresía Allodhapón*) or, in its absence, the central police station, to support your application for a **residence permit** (*ádhia paramonís*). For this, you will also need to bring your passport, two photographs, more *hartósima* and a stable address (not a hotel). Permits are given for terms of three or six months (white cards), one year (green triptych booklets), or even five years (blue booklets) if they've become well acquainted with you. For one- or five-year permits, a **health examination** at the nearest public hospital is required, to screen for TB, syphilis and HIV. The situation is constantly evolving, so check with your employer if all this is necessary; just don't presume that he or she will know the current official policy.

The reality is that an EU passport and the unwillingness of the Greek government to be taken to the European Court of Justice make you pretty safe from prosecution for ignoring any regulations, and it is easy to pick up **casual work**. As fruit-picking and manual labour is now the exclusive domain of illegal and underpaid Albanian refugees, your best chance is in tourism-related jobs. Most women and some men working casually in Greece find jobs in **bars** or **restaurants** around the main resorts. Men, unless they are "trained" chefs, will be edged out by Albanians even when it comes to washing up.

If you're waiting or serving, most of your wages will probably have to come from tips, but you may well be able to get a deal that includes free food and lodging; evening-only hours can be a good shift, leaving you a lot of free time. The main drawback may be the machismo and/or chauvinist attitudes of your employer. Ads in the local press for "girl bar staff" are certainly best ignored; see "Sexual Harassment" opposite. The large resorts of Corfu and Zákynthos are the easiest places in the Ionian to find bar work.

On a similar, unofficial level you might be able to get a sales job in **tourist shops** anywhere with a high concentration of foreigners or (if you've the expertise) helping out at one of the many **windsurfing** or less numerous **scuba-diving** schools that have sprung up all around the coasts. **Yacht marinas** can also prove good hunting-grounds, though less for the romantic business of crewing, than scrubbing down and repainting. The best possibilities are likely to be on Corfu or Lefkádha.

Perhaps the best type of tourism-related work, though, is that of courier/greeter/group co-ordinator for a **package holiday company**. With such a British tour operator presence as there is in the Ionians, there are plenty of opportunities and, although some knowledge of Greek is an advantage for dealing with local room owners and the like, it is not a requirement as your main mandate is to keep the punters happy. Many

such staff are recruited through ads in newspapers issued outside Greece, but it's by no means unheard of to be hired on the spot in April or May. A big plus, however you're taken on, is that you're usually guaranteed about six months of steady work, and that if things work out you may be re-employed the following season with contract and foreign-currency wages from the home company, not from the local affiliate.

You may do even better by working for yourself. Travellers report rich pickings during the tourist season from **selling jewellery** on island beaches, or on boats – trinkets from Asia are especially popular with Greeks. Once you've managed to get the stuff past the customs officials (who will be sceptical, for instance, that all those trinkets are presents for friends), there rarely seem to be problems with the local police, though it probably pays to be discreet. **Busking** can also be quite lucrative; playing on a shady street corner, it's common to make around 2000dr per hour, more if you're lucky.

At the present time, all **non-EU nationals** who wish to work in Greece do so surreptitiously, unless employed by their government or a multinational company, with the ever-present risk of denunciation to the police and instant deportation. Having been forced to accept large numbers of EU citizens looking for jobs in a climate of rising unemployment, Greek immigration authorities are cracking down hard on any suitable targets, be they Albanian, African, Swiss or North American. That old foreigners' stand-by, teaching English, is now officially available only to TEFL certificate-holders, preferably Greek, non-EU nationals of Greek descent, or EU nationals in that order. Many *frondistíria*, however, still employ teachers without worrying about the paperwork. If you are a non-EU foreign national of Greek descent, you are termed *"omólogos"* (returned Greek diaspora member) and in fact have tremendous employment and residence rights – you can, for example, open your very own *frondistírio* with minimum qualifications (something painfully evident in the often appalling quality of English instruction in Greece). The downside, if you are male and under 40, is that you may find yourself being drafted into military service.

Directory

BARGAINING This isn't a regular feature of life, though you'll find it possible with private rooms and some hotels out of season. Similarly, you may be able to negotiate discounted rates for vehicle rental, especially for longer periods. Services such as shoe, watch and camera repair don't have iron-clad rates, so use common sense when assessing charges (advance estimates are not routine).

CHILDREN Kids are worshipped and indulged in Greece, and present few problems when travelling. Baby foods and nappies (diapers) are ubiquitous and reasonably priced, plus concessions are offered on most forms of transport. Private rooms and luxury hotels are more likely to offer some kind of babysitting service than the mid-range hotels.

CINEMA Greek cinemas show a large number of American and British movies, always in the original language, with Greek subtitles. They are highly affordable, currently 1600–2500dr depending on location and plushness of facilities. In the Ionians, however, there are only indoor cinemas on Corfu and Lefkádha, with occasional showings in town halls on Zákynthos and elsewhere. An outdoor movie in summer at the more numerous garden cinemas is worth catching at least once for the experience alone, though it's best to opt for the earlier screening (approximately 9pm) since the soundtrack on the later show tends to be turned down or even off to avoid complaints from adjacent residences.

DEPARTURE TAX This is levied on all international ferries – currently 1500dr per person *and* the same again for any car or motorbike within the EU. There's also an airport departure tax, currently 3700dr for destinations under 1200km away, 7200dr for remoter ones, but it's always included in the price of the ticket – there's no collection at the airport itself.

ELECTRICITY 220 volt AC throughout the country. Wall outlets take double round-pin plugs as in the rest of continental Europe. Three-to-two-pin adaptors should be purchased beforehand in the UK, as they can be difficult to find in Greece; the standard five-amp design will allow use of a hair-dryer. North American appliances will require both a step-down transformer and a plug adapter.

FILM Fuji, Kodak and Agfa print films are reasonably priced and easy to have processed – you practically trip over "One Hour Foto" shops in some resorts. Fuji and Kodak slide film can be purchased, at a slight mark-up, on the larger islands, but it cannot be processed there – whatever you may be told, it will be sent to Athens, so it's best to wait until you return home.

FOOTBALL Soccer is by far the most popular sport in Greece. The most important (and most heavily sponsored) teams are Panathanaïkós and AEK of Athens, Olympiakós of Pireás, and PAOK of Thessaloníki. Most Ionian residents support these clubs, especially as none of the islands has a team higher than the fourth division.

GAY LIFE Male homosexuality is legal over the age of 17 in Greece, but still very covert. Male bisexuality is common but rarely admitted. Out gay Greeks are rare, and out lesbians rarer still: they suffer harassment and even violence from peers, although thanks to the culture of *filoxénia* (hospitality) gay visitors will encounter few, if any, problems. Most Greeks regard same-sex couples with bemusement, although younger males have adopted the homophobia of some British visitors. Gay and lesbian tourists are discreetly visible on virtually all the Ionian islands. There are gay-owned/run bars and businesses in the islands, but they rarely advertise the fact. Greek men are terrible flirts – cruising them is a semiotic mine-field and definitely at your own risk (references in gay guides to male cruising grounds should be regarded with great caution). Native lesbians are virtually invisible in Greece, and are unusually absent from Lefkádha, despite its claim to a major role in queer history – proto-dyke Sappho is said to have committed suicide by throwing herself from the cliffs of Cape Lefkáta.

HIKING Greeks are just becoming used to the notion that anyone should want to walk for plea-sure, yet if you have the time and stamina it is probably the best way to see many of the islands. This guide includes tips on good bases and routes; for advice on maps see pp.29–31.

LAUNDRETTES (*plindíria*) are rare in the Ionian, except in main towns, but they are beginning to crop up in some of the main resort towns; some-times an attended service wash is available for little or no extra charge over the basic cost of 1500–1800dr per wash and dry. Dry cleaning can run to 300dr an item. Otherwise, ask room own-ers for a *skáfi* (laundry trough), a bucket (*kouvás*) or the special laundry area; they freak out if you use bathroom washbasins, Greek plumbing and wall mounting being what they are.

PERÍPTERA These are street-corner kiosks, or sometimes a hole-in-the-wall shop front. They sell everything from pens to disposable razors, stationery to soap, sweets to condoms, cigarettes to plastic crucifixes – and are often open when nothing else is.

TIME Greek summertime now falls in line with the rest of the EU, beginning at 4am on the last Sunday in March, when the clocks go forward one hour, and ending at 4am the last Sunday in October, when they go back. Be alert to this, as the change is not well publicized, leading scores of visitors to miss planes and ferries every year. Greek time is two hours ahead of Britain. For North America, the difference is seven hours for Eastern Standard Time, ten hours for Pacific Standard Time, with again an extra hour plus or minus for those weeks in April and October if one place is on daylight savings and the other isn't. A recorded time message (in Greek) is available by dialling ☎141.

TOILETS Public ones in towns are usually in parks or squares (such as Corfu Town and Argostóli), often subterranean; otherwise try a bus station. Public toilets tend to be pretty filthy – it's best to use those in restaurants and bars. Note that throughout Greece you drop toilet paper in the adjacent waste bins, not in the bowl.

USEFUL THINGS A small alarm clock for early buses and ferries; a flashlight if you're camping out; sunscreen of high SPF (15 and above; some-times unavailable in Greece); a pocket knife (Swiss army type or similar); a universal sink plug; and earplugs for noisy ferries or hotels.

The Guide

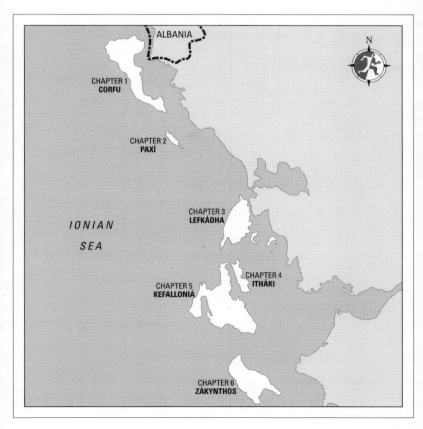

Chapter 1

Corfu (Kérkyra)

Dangling between the southern tip of Italy and the west coast of mainland Greece, at the point where the Adriatic meets the Ionian Sea, the lush green sickle of **Corfu (Kérkyra)** was one of the first Greek islands to attract mass tourism in the 1960s. Since then it has acquired the sleaziest reputation among the islands, although much of this is exaggerated and due more to snobbery than actual fact. It's true that indiscriminate exploitation by package tour operators and their willing Corfiot partners turned parts of Corfu into eyesores, but many of the island's resorts have developed a more moderate form of tourism and even in the most overrun resorts unspoilt parts of the coast and interior are often only a few minutes away on foot. The island has some of the best beaches in the whole archipelago – no fewer than 24 of them were awarded blue flags in 1999 – and idyllic bays that still resemble the "delectable landscape" Lawrence Durrell described in *Prospero's Cell*. The main settlement, **Corfu (Kérkyra) Town**, for many years a mess of collapsing tenements and traffic congestion, was renovated for the 1994 EC summit and is now one of the most elegant island capitals in the whole of Greece, with indubitable charm and a number of cultural attractions.

Tourism has tended to stick to the coasts, in clusters that are handy either to base yourself in or to avoid. There are no high-rise hotels

---

Accommodation price codes

Rooms and hotels listed in this book have been price-coded according to the scale outlined below. The rates quoted represent the cheapest available double room in high season. Out of season, rates can drop by as much as fifty percent or more, especially if you negotiate for a stay of three or more nights. Single rooms, where available, cost around seventy percent of the price of a double. For further information, see p.36.

① up to 6000dr	⑤ 16,000–20,000dr
② 6000–9000dr	⑥ 20,000–30,000dr
③ 9000–12,000dr	⑦ 30,000dr upwards
④ 12,000–16,000dr	

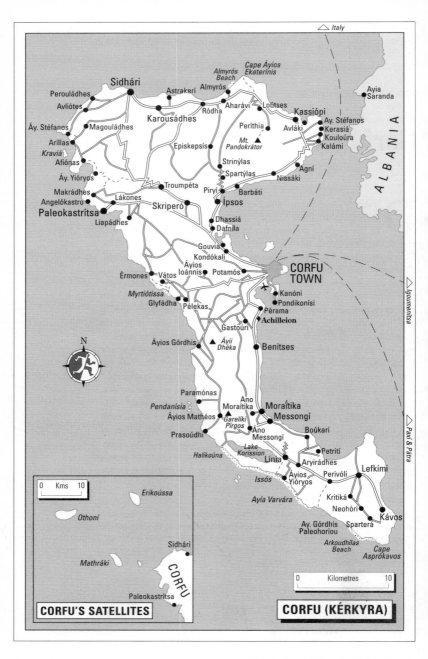

here in the Spanish mould: **accommodation** tends to be in apartments, rooms, villas and small hotels, while the larger resort hotels are horizontal rather than vertical, never more than five storeys high. Transport on the island's **bus** system is cheap, reliable and will get you to almost every village or resort. The island-wide green buses stop at between 6 and 8pm, and restricted services run on Sundays, while the blue suburban buses that run within a 10km radius of Corfu Town operate till around 10pm. Both systems radiate out from Corfu Town, and less than a thousand drachmas will get you to the furthermost points at the north or south of the island in an hour and a half.

The island's finest scenery is along the northeast coast, served by a single mountain road with turnings leading down to small pebbly bays and clear blue water, and in the northwest, with its towering cliffs and wide sandy bays. The north is dominated by the bulk of **Mount Pandokrátor** and neighbouring peaks, whose foothills and summits offer great walks and even better views – though the mountain attracts more than its fair share of bad weather, particularly in low and shoulder seasons. The centre and south is less hilly and more verdant: the lush farmland of the **Ropa plain,** which extends south from just below the resort of Paleokastrítsa, is the island's fruit (and veg) basket. The south has two distinct sides: narrow stony beaches and a few hidden beauty spots face the mainland, while the southwest-facing coast is backed by verdant countryside and features some of the best sandy beaches on the island.

If you want to see the whole island, it's probably best to get the south out of the way first; apart from a handful of beauty spots detailed below, it doesn't have the scenery and variety found elsewhere, and although the north has more overall development these days, the southern resorts have fewer redeeming factors, and there is little of interest away from them. Hardened **beach** nuts go west, to Myrtiótissa and other strands to the south. If you want scenery and unspoilt bays, head for the northeast coast between Nissáki and Kassiópi. Resorts for **nightlife** include Kassiópi, Sidhári, Ípsos and, notoriously, **Kávos**, still a favourite with teenage ravers. If you're on a tight schedule, spend a day in Corfu Town, move north to Kalámi, Kouloúra and Áyios Stéfanos, and then head for the west coast.

Despite the complaints of overdevelopment, many northern Europeans have been returning to the island for twenty or thirty years. The Corfiots' friendliness and kindness to strangers, the quality of *filoxenía* that has been eroded in some larger resorts, can still astonish with its generosity and grace. In particular, the Corfiots retain a great affection for the British – something the island's former rulers didn't actually earn or deserve – and the decline in visitors from the UK during the tourism slump of the early to mid-1990s, when islanders accused British travel operators of virtually blockading the island by cutting flights and reducing the length of the season, left many Corfiots perplexed.

Igoumenítsa

IGOUMENÍTSA, the third busiest passenger port in Greece, is Corfu's major link with the mainland, and a key stop on **ferry routes** between Italy, Corfu Town and Pátra; boats also ply daily to Paxí. The town is an important crossroads for mainland **bus services**, with connections to Athens and Thessaloníki, inland to Ioánnina and south to Párga and Préveza; the **bus station** is at Kýprou 47, the main shopping street, a few blocks away from the southeast corner of the town's main square, Platía Dimarhíou, which stands two blocks back and a few blocks east of the port. There's little in this busy industrial port to detain travellers, and most people travelling in either direction will find connections onwards: ferries to Corfu Town's New Port run from 4.30am to 10pm daily, although buses to Athens stop at 6pm, to Ioánnina at 8pm. At the time of writing, the one Thessaloníki bus leaves at 11.45am (Mon–Sat).

It's possible, however, that bad connections, or a tiring journey, may force you to **stay** in Igoumenítsa. The town is not large but hotels are plentiful, if somewhat miserable; most are to be found either along or just back from the seafront. The nearest budget hotel to the port is the *Acropolis* at Ethnikís Andístasis 58A (☎0665/22 342; ②), although the *Stavrodhrómi* (☎0665/22 343; ②) at Soulíou 14, the street leading diagonally uphill and northeast from the square, is better value; neither has en-suite rooms. A smarter option with a striking modern design on the Ethnikís Andístasis seafront is *Hotel El Greco* (☎0665/22 245, fax 25 073; ⑤), while a cheaper but comfortable choice with en-suite rooms is the *Egnatia* (☎0665/23 648; ③), at the southeast corner of the main platia. The closest **campsite** is the *Kalami Beach* (☎0665/71 211), just before Platariá, a 9km bus ride away.

A walk away from the Corfu dock west along the seafront will bring you to a marina used by visiting yachts, where the concrete quay has recently been transformed into an elegant, illuminated promenade. Here on Antístasis, you'll find some stylish **bars**, catering to high-spending Greeks who hang out at *Art*, *Memphis*, *Metropole* and *Opera*, and some of the better **restaurants**, such as the *Petros* and *Emilios psistariés*. Next to the large, open-air *Traffic Bar*, there's a **cinema**, *Pame*, which sometimes screens English-language films. Another direction to head in search of food is to the north end of the front, where several fish tavernas and ouzeris come to life in the evening.

There are **banks** and 24-hour cash dispensers opposite the ferry docks on Apostólon, as well as **international ferry offices**, and a **post office** on Evangelístrias, just behind the north end of the seafront. **Corfu ferries** dock at the open quay beyond the secured international terminal; different boats operate their own ticketing systems, with the name of the ferry posted on one of two ticket kiosks opposite the loading ramps. If you miss or skip a sailing, your ticket may not be valid for a later one, though usually you can change it. Crossing times depend on the boat: the regular open-topped ferries take just under two hours; the larger *Áyios Spirídion* is slightly more expensive but cuts the journey time in half.

Numbers have picked up again in recent years, and there is now a better balance between mass and individual tourism than on some of the smaller islands. This benefits both the independent traveller, by offering more availability at lower prices, and the small-time local operator, by allowing more chance to compete with the big boys. The island authorities have also taken steps – a little late in the day, some would say – to reverse its fortunes. The successful renewal of Corfu Town has prompted similar programmes in other parts of the island. The authorities have made determined attempts to attract a more moneyed type of tourist, but it is still too early to say if there has been any real shift in the demographic profile of the average visitor. Many of the British family holidaymakers who helped build Corfu's tourism economy have been lured away to cheaper deals in Turkey and Florida. It may be, however, that the island really is undergoing a sea change because of the recent downturn. **Benítses**, for example, once reviled as the home-from-home of lager-loutism, has, under a new mayor, begun to revert to a whitewashed island village splashed with purple bougainvillea.

Some history
Although important defensive structures were built at outposts such as Kassiópi and Paleokastrítsa during the Middle Ages, the island's history is essentially that of its main town. Indeed, the name "Corfu" is an Italian corruption of the ancient Greek word *koryphai*, the "hills" on which the town's two forts were built.

Archeological finds carbon-dated to the middle Paleolithic – when the island was still part of the mainland, and much of the Adriatic was dry land covered by vast forests – indicate that there's been a settlement of sorts on the site of the town for over fifty thousand years. Much of prehistoric Corfu has been discovered around the sites of two ancient natural harbours: one at the opposite end of Garítsa Bay to the town centre, near Mon Repos; and the other in the Hyllaic Harbour, now the Halikópoulou lagoon, bisected by the airport runway. The latter is also thought to have been the site of settlements of **Eretrians**, mainland Greeks who overran tribes of Liburnians, in what is now Albania, in 750 BC. They were soon followed, and displaced, by invaders from **Corinth**, who made Corfu Town (which they called Corcyra, from which modern Greek Kérkyra is derived) one of the most powerful forces in ancient Greece, turning it into a mighty walled city and a major sea power in the region. During the Persian Wars of the fifth century BC, Corfu provided the second largest naval force after Athens. Along with other Ionian islands, it fought alongside Athens against the Spartans in the Peloponnesian War, which was in part caused by political tensions beween Corfu and Corinth to the south.

Much to the relief of the inhabitants, who had been overrun by Illyrian pirates, the city was taken over by the **Romans** in 229 BC. It remained under Rome's rule, supplying men and ships in its wars, and after the division of the empire in 395 AD both city and island came under the control of the eastern or **Byzantine empire**. Corfu was nominally Byzantine for over eight centuries, but as one of the most distant outposts of the empire, it was prone to raids by Vandals, Goths, Saracens, Normans and others. It was seized, briefly, by the Venetians in 1205, who were followed by the Despots of Epirus and the Angevins. After further suffering at the hands of pirates, the islanders asked for help from **Venice** in 1386, under whose rule they remained until 1797. The Venetians imposed their own laws, language, art and architecture, and began the construction of the town as it is seen now, including structures on both the Paleó and Néo Froúrio hills.

Following Napoleon Bonaparte's defeat of the Republic of Venice in 1797, Corfu and the other Ionian islands were acquired by **France**. The French began what was proposed as an extensive plan of development, which resulted in the construction of the famous Listón, modelled on the rue de Rivoli in Paris. Bonaparte's true legacy to the islanders, however, was a taste for independence and republicanism, which was vigorously and even violently discouraged when the city and island were taken by the **British** in 1814. The British began the last notable stage of civic construction, building the Palace of SS George and Michael, as well as various public amenities, under lords Guildford and Maitland. Despite these efforts, the British rulers were not liked by the general populace; Maitland, in particular, was despised for his arrogant attitude towards the islanders, who nicknamed him "The Abortion". The Ionian islands were finally offered to Greece by Queen Victoria – whose great-great-great-nephew Prince Philip was born in the Mon Repos estate in Garítsa Bay – in her speech at the opening of Parliament in 1864.

During **World War II**, Corfu was occupied by the Italians and Germans between 1941 and 1944, and was heavily bombarded by Nazi planes. Over a quarter of Corfu Town was destroyed, including the library, parliament and numerous churches. Most, if not all, of the town's Jewish population, who had found refuge here over the centuries after pogroms elsewhere in Europe, were arrested and shipped off to the Nazi death camps. The elegant Listón makes a haunting appearance in Claud Lanzman's epic Holocaust documentary, *Shoah*, as the place where Corfu's Jews were rounded up.

Corfu Town

CORFU TOWN (Kérkyra in Greek) is the place where the island's heritage and commerce collide with an almighty bang. In high summer it can seem hellish, with a seemingly endless stream of tour coaches dumping even more tourists on a town that's already overflowing with its own hotel guests and a native population heading for 40,000. It's not a place to come for peace and quiet, and certainly not a place to arrive without checking on accommodation beforehand; even in deep winter some hotels are fully booked. Yet if you intend to see much of the island by bus, it's the only place to base

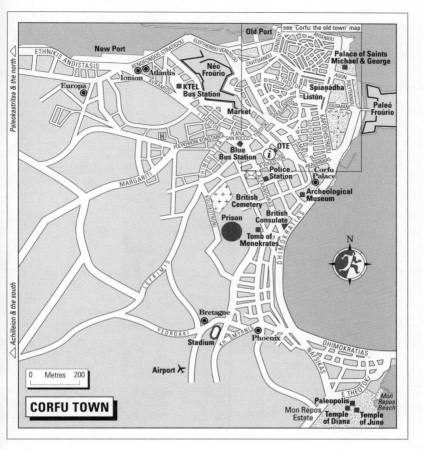

CORFU TOWN

0 Metres 200

yourself, and the recent renovations to its older buildings, and the appearance of new restaurants, galleries and other attractions, have made Corfu Town more attractive than it has been for decades.

Beneath all the bustle there remains a beautiful city in miniature, fortified since Byzantine times, developed by the Venetians, added to by the French – and, some would say, desecrated by the British. It's one of the most attractive towns in the Greek islands, and certainly the most stunning in the Ionian. When the crowds subside, at siesta time and in low season, it's well worth ambling around its elegant arcades, boulevards and squares. If you're just visiting on a day-trip, you shouldn't miss, first of all, the two forts, both now open daily, the palace, the warren of alleys in the Campiello and the old streets behind the Listón, including exquisite Áyios Spyrídhon

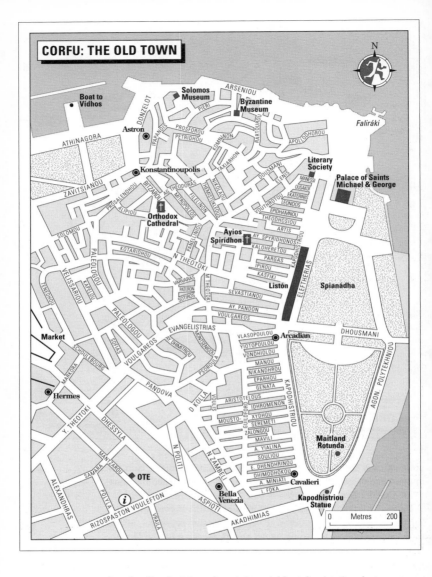

CORFU: THE OLD TOWN

N

Boat to Vídhos

Solomos Museum

Byzantine Museum

ARSENIOU

DONZELOT

PIERI

Faliráki

Astron

PROSFOROU

PETRIDHOU

ATHINAGORA

IRAPANDIS

KOMNINON

APOLLODHOROU

Konstantinoupolis

ZAVITSIANOU

PROSALENDHOU

BIZAROU

THEODORAS

MITROPOLEOS

TILELLINON

THEOTOKI

TAXIARHON

NIKOFOROU

THEOTOKOU

DOUSMANI

ELENIS

Literary Society

Palace of Saints Michael & George

ALTIPIOU

Orthodox Cathedral

MANESSI

OUSAKOF

LEONDOS

YOUHROTOU

EKATERINIS

EPIDHAMNOU

THEODHOSIOU

ARTIS

SOLOMOU

KOTARIDHOU

N THEOTOKI

PANELI

Áyios Spirídhon

AY. SPYRIDHONOS

PALEOLOGOU

VELISSARIOU

KAPETOU

VARVARAS

PATERON

SOTIROS

M THEOTOK

KALOHÉRETOU

PARGAS

IPIROU

KASFIKI

Listón

KAPODHISTRIOU

ELEFTHERIAS

Spianádha

ENEDIOU

KOTARIDHOU

SEVASTIANOU

AY. PANDON

VOULGAREOS

Market

PALEOLOGOU

SOTIRA

VOULGAREOS

EVANGELISTRIAS

AY. DHIMITRIOU

MANISMENGOLA

VLASOPOULOU

YIOTOPOULOU

VONDHIOLOU

Arcadian

DHOUSMANI

PSOROULA

MANOU

NIKANDHROU

EPARHOU

GENATA

Hermes

PANDOVA

ARISTOTELOUS

D KOLLA

VOULIS

IDHROMENON

XYDHOU

SEREMETI

KAPODHISTRIOU

AGON POLYTEKHNIOU

Y. THEOTOKI

DHESSYLA

MOUSTO

GUILFORD

ZALONGOU

MAVILI

A. YIALINA

SOULIOU

Maitland Rotunda

MANTZAROU

N POLITI

N ZAMBELI

E. DHENDHRINOU

DHIMODHOKOU

A. MINIATI

Cavalieri

ALEXANDRAS

SAMARA

POLITA

OTE

ASPIOTI

I. FOKA

RIZOSPASTON VOULEFTON

VOULEFTON

Bella Venezia

Kapodhistriou Statue

VRAILA

AKADHIMIAS

0   Metres   200

church. Coach trips almost invariably take in tiny but overrun Mouse Island, but independent travellers would be better advised to track down the newly excavated Doric temples in the recently opened Mon Repos estate, seek out the British cemetery or hop on a boat to Vídhos islet.

Surviving Corfu airport

Described by one respectable British newspaper as "European air travel's answer to the Black Hole of Calcutta", **Corfu airport** has come to present a special challenge to seasoned aeronauts. The airport doubled in size when an extension was built for the 1994 EC summit, but that was only opened to the general public late in 1996, with little to offer the traveller beyond more floor space. Passage through what is basically one big glass box is invariably traumatic, with occasional air-traffic delays of up to twelve hours or more (though these are mercifully less frequent now) exacerbating the problem. A few tips can ease your passage through the "Black Hole".

On **arrival** from international flights, unless you're racing to catch a ferry, don't rush to get off the plane. Even if you were lucky enough to get one of the few seats in Arrivals, you'd only be doing what you can do in the cool of the plane. Baggage takes ages, and Arrivals is an airless glass-house, even in winter. Domestic Arrivals is more organized, so you should be able to pick up bags and make a break for it fairly quickly.

When **departing** internationally, do not go through passport control unless you know your plane home has landed. Once through, you won't get back out, and if delayed you'll be stuck with a choice of naff snacks and expensive drinks from a tiny bar with long queues, and no shop or exchange facilities – no fun if you end up with a major delay. Things worsen as people departing on other flights come in behind you (the so-called Black Hole effect), until the departure lounge and tiny balconies begin to resemble the rock festival of your nightmares, only without the music. It's far better to wait in the areas outside passport control or in the cafeteria upstairs. Keep an eye on the passport gate, though: it opens and closes at whim, so leave time to get through (at least thirty minutes before takeoff). If you are facing a long delay, you can escape the building and go back into town, or to the shops and bars of Garítsa ten minutes' walk back from the airport; however, you should only leave the airport if you can confirm a departure time or length of delay with an airline representative.

Arrival and information

Most visitors arrive at Corfu's notorious **airport** (see box above), 2km south of the centre of the town. There are no airport buses, and taxis have a tradition of overcharging (expect to pay around 2000dr) but with a pack or other manageable bag it's an easy walk into town; car rental agencies at the airport are listed on p.84.

Corfu has two distinct ports, though they're near to each other on the same straight seafront. The **new port (Néo Limáni)**, just beyond Platía Athinágora in the old town, serves most of the passenger vessels; the major ferry links with Brindisi, Bari and Ancona in Italy, with Paxí and with Igoumenítsa and Pátra on the Greek mainland, all moor here. Only excursion boats, the shuttle across to Vídhos and private craft use the **old port (Paleó Limáni)**, right by the *platía*. Neither port is much more than ten minutes' walk from the heart of the town, and the island-wide bus station is a short walk from either. Taxis meet ferries day and night, as do room owners.

For details of the frequencies and journey times of buses, ferries and domestic flights from Corfu Town, see p.117. For information on buying tickets, see "Listings" on p.84.

Corfu Town

Buses from Athens and the island's outlying towns and communities arrive at the main bus station on Avramíou, behind the agricultural co-operative building; the suburban bus station is in Platía Y. Theotóki (aka Platía Saróko, anglicized to San Rocco). For those visiting in a rented vehicle, a new one-way system has further complicated the town's traffic system, with an anticlockwise flow around the arterial road that runs along the seafront. Much of the centre is inaccessible by car, and poor for **parking** – it's best to park away from the centre, or choose the quieter side-streets in the Garítsa district.

The **tourist office** (Mon–Fri 8am–2pm; ☎0661/37 520 or 37 638, fax 30 298) is on Rizospáston Vouleftón, a short way up from Leofóros Alexándhras. The office is very friendly, and keeps accommodation details as well as the usual glossy brochures. Several **publications** provide useful information: the free monthly *Liston* magazine (bilingual Greek/English) includes a detailed calendar and entertainment suggestions; the monthly English language *Corfiot* newspaper (500dr) has interesting articles as well as info on events, eating out, timetables etc.; and the monthly *Exit stin Kérkyra* magazine (500dr) has cultural features, a great music section and nightlife tips, if your Greek is up to it.

Accommodation

Accommodation in Corfu Town is notoriously hard to come by and, when found, notoriously expensive and cramped – it's cold comfort to know that, because of the town's topography, even middle-class apartments in the old town tend to be tiny. The surrounding bluffs hinder further construction, and the airport and adjacent farmland prevent much more expansion, so new accommodation developments have been squeezed north to Kondókali and beyond, and south to Pérama and further. And even in midwinter the hotels can fill up with mysterious crowds of businesspeople and visitors who don't seem visible on the streets. At any time of year, it's best to call ahead.

Both the tourist office (see above) and the tourist police (see p.85) keep lists of private rooms.

Private rooms tend to be in the old town and Mandoúki area by the two ports; a small crowd of room owners meets each ferry arrival in the New Port. If you want to phone ahead, try George Skordhilis (☎0661/24 252 or 43 421; ③) or K. Nikis (☎0661/35 827 or 26 956; ③). A number of agencies near the Néo Froúrio offer rooms in the Mandoúki area, including the seafront Katsaros Travel, Andhréa Kálvou 6 (☎0661/27 002, fax 42 413). Budget travellers might be advised to head straight for a **campsite**, although the nearest one, since the closure of the site in the suburb of Kondókali, is 7km away at Dhassiá (see p.87).

Inexpensive to moderate hotels

Arcadian, Kapodhistríou 44 (☎0661/37 670, fax 45 087). Mid-range hotel in a central setting, with en-suite rooms with balconies and views over the Listón and Spianádha. Street noise can be a problem, especially at weekends. ④.

Europa, Yitsiáli 10 (☎0661/39 304). Small family hotel one block back from Néo Froúrio quay; ideal if arriving by ferry. Cosy en-suite rooms. ③.

Hermes, Markorá 14 (☎0661/39 268 or 39 321, fax 31 747). Not quite the budget place it was, with average rooms and friendly staff who do not always speak English. Its main drawback is that it overlooks the lively market behind San Rocco. Open year round. ④.

Ionion, Xenofóndos Stratigoú 46 (☎0661/39 915, fax 44 690). Large functional hotel on the seafront in the New Port. Quite friendly and better value than the expensive *Atlantis* next door. ③.

Phoenix, Khris. Smýrnis 2, Garítsa (☎0661/42 290, fax 42 990). Small, stylish hotel between the airport and the seafront. Handy for flights at awkward hours. ④.

Upmarket hotels

Astron, Dónzelot 15 (☎0661/39 505 or 39 983, fax 33 708). This long-standing travellers' favourite has now been completely renovated and gone decidedly upmarket. One of the smartest in the New Port, with all mod cons. Open year round. ⑥.

Atlantis, Xenofóndos Stratigoú 48 (☎0661/35 560–2, fax 46 480). Large and spacious air-conditioned hotel, with a bar and taverna attached. Open year round. Most credit cards accepted. ⑥.

Bella Venezia, Zambéli 4 (☎0661/46 500 or 44 290, fax 20 708). Best of the posher hotels: lovely, colourful Neoclassical building just behind the *Cavalieri*, with all the *Cavalieri*'s comforts but far cheaper. Most credit cards accepted. ⑤.

Bretagne, K. Yeorgáki 27 (☎0661/30 724, 31 129 or 35 690, fax 28 027). Not the place for a quiet night, barely 100m from the airport runway, but useful if arriving late or leaving early. A comfortable modern hotel with en-suite rooms with balconies, a restaurant and bar; also recommended to those escaping the airport or sitting out a flight delay. ⑤.

Cavalieri, Kapodhistríou 4 (☎0661/39 041 or 39 336, fax 39 283). Smart and friendly, with great views and a roof bar open to the public. Smart plush rooms and full service. ⑦.

Corfu Palace Hotel, Leofóros Dhimokratías 2 (☎0661/39 485–7, fax 31 749). Luxury hotel with pools, landscaped gardens and magnificent rooms, but beware: the bed linen is sadistically rubberized and the restaurant operates a dress code. ⑦.

Konstantinoupolis, K. Zavitsiánou 1 (☎0661/48 716–7, fax 48 718). Classy hotel in the Old Port with tasteful decoration and comfortable rooms. ⑤.

The Town

Though compact, in parts claustrophobically so, Corfu Town is actually a collection of quite different areas, each with a distinct character. The **Campiello**, the oldest district, sits on the hill above the old port (roughly between the Palace of SS Michael and George, the Listón and the cathedral), while the streets running between the Campiello and Velisáriou, to the west, are what remains of the town's **Jewish Quarter**. These districts form the core of the old

Corfu Town

Corfu Town is best explored on foot, but if you're flagging, you might consider catching the bizarre, theme park-style miniature train that runs from the far end of the Listón, circling the old town and the Néo Froúrio (1000dr, or 1500dr including admission to the Néo Froúrio).

The Paleó Froúrio (1000dr) and the Néo Froúrio (500dr) are open daily 9am–9pm.

town, and their tall, narrow alleys conceal some of Corfu's most beautiful Venetian architecture. **Mandoúki**, beyond the old port, is a commercial and dormitory area for the port, and well worth exploring, not least for its small bars and restaurants.

The town's main **commercial area** lies inland from the **Spianádha** (Esplanade), roughly between Y. (Yioryíou) Theotóki, Alexándhras and Kapodhistríou streets, with most shops and boutiques around the meeting of Voulgaréous and Y. Theotóki and the streets radiating off Platía Theotóki. The alleys between Theotóki and Platía Athinágora, in particular, cater to Corfu's most feared latter-day invaders, shoppers with attitude: windows sparkle with gold, silver and jewellery, and craft stores recycle the island's surplus olive wood into as many shapes as tourists can be persuaded to buy. Tucked behind the corner of Platía Saróko and Odhós Theotóki is the old **morning market**, specializing in farm produce, fish and other comestibles. This is a lively place, full of exciting smells, and is great if you're self-catering. The smarter areas of **San Rocco** and **Garítsa**, to the west and south, give a good idea of the town's nineteenth-century heyday, especially in the mansions of Odhós Alexándhras and the Garítsa seafront.

The Paleó Froúrio and the Néo Froúrio

Jutting up above its rooftops like two miniature volcanoes, Corfu Town's most obvious sights are the forts, the **Paleó Froúrio** and the **Néo Froúrio**. Their designations (*paleó* – "old", *néo* – "new") are a little misleading, since most of the visible exterior of both forts is the work of the Venetians over a period of less than two hundred years, and both were modified in tandem by subsequent occupiers. The Paleó Froúrio, however, had its origins in the sixth century after the ancient city was destroyed by the Goths, and was gradually fortified by the Byzantines, particularly in the eleventh century. Up to the thirteenth century it contained the town within its walls and was topped by two castellated towers until the Venetians replaced the old fortifications early in the fifteenth century. The Néo Froúrio was constructed by the Venetians on the hill of St Mark between 1572 and 1645, although the buildings within all date from the British occupation. They have both been damaged down the years by various besiegers and careless overlords.

The Paleó Froúrio is regarded as a masterpiece of military engineering, especially for the casemates inside the main western **bastions**, the largest in the Ionian, which face the municipal gardens across the moat. The small Venetian harbour, the artificial canal joining the northern harbour to the bay of Garítsa, the iron bridge across it, replacing two earlier ones, and the inner dry moat are all still there. The most noteworthy building is the Neoclassical **shrine of St George**, built by the British in the 1840s and consecrated as Orthodox after their departure; the six unfluted Doric columns reflect the prevailing taste for classicism. The British barracks also survive. The latest contribution was an extensive but rather sterile renovation at the time of the 1994 EC Summit in the town.

Looming above the old port, the Néo Froúrio, which has only been opened to the public this decade, is by far the more interesting of the two forts for the lay visitor to amble around. The entrance, tucked away at the back of the fort up steps beyond the *Tenedos Taverna* on Odhós Solomoú, gives onto a complex of cellars, dungeons, tunnels and battlements, with excellent **views** over the old town and bay, and a small gallery and café at the summit. Among the British additions are the stone defensive building that crowns the fort and the brick one, overlooking the harbour and now used by the Corfu Naval Station. The **dry moat** that runs along the western side of the fort, starting by the market, is still in excellent condition and a fine example of its kind. Look out for the two lions of St Mark and Venetian inscriptions on the bastion walls above.

The Listón and the Spianádha

The **Listón**, an arcaded street designed during the French occupation, and the green **Spianádha** (Esplanade) it overlooks, are the focus of town life, even if the *kafenía* here charge exorbitant prices. People still play cricket on the Spianádha some afternoons, a tradition (like the local *tsitsibíra*, ginger beer) left over from the British administration, and it's possible to linger for hours over one drink. This is the venue for Corfu Town's evening *vólta*, a relaxed parade of strolling friends, couples and overdressed teenage posers. At the south end of the Spianádha, the **Maitland Rotunda**, now covered in graffiti, was constructed in 1821 to honour the first British High Commissioner of Corfu and the Ionian islands. Built in the form of a circular Ionic temple, it covers an earlier underground cistern. The neighbouring **statue of Ioannis Kapodhistrias** celebrates the local hero and consummate statesman (1776–1831), who led the diplomatic efforts for Greek independence and was made its first president in 1827.

The Palace of SS Michael and George

Renovated for the 1994 summit – hence the incongruously space-aged glass structure to the rear – the interior of **Palace of SS Michael and George** is currently barred to the public, except for the Asiatic Museum and the new Municipal Art Gallery. It is, however, the grandest edifice left by the British, and the grounds are open, allowing you to admire its main facade, with a portico supported by twenty Doric columns running its whole length and bending round to the side-wings. You can pass through the two elaborate gates, one for each saint, and gain limited access to the magnificent gardens. The palace

Corfu Town was built between 1819 and 1823 to honour British civil servants in the Ionian and on Malta; the imposing statue on a moated pedestal in the gardens is of the British High Commissioner of the time, Sir Frederic Adam.

The Asiatic Museum, when fully operational, is usually open Tues–Sun 8am–3pm; 500dr.

Said to be the only one of its kind in Greece, the **Asiatic Museum** is a must for aficionados of Oriental culture, and has more than enough to detain the casual visitor. Amassed by Corfiot diplomat Grigorios Manos (1850–1929), the collection of over 10,000 pieces was given to the Greek government in 1926, and is displayed in elegant staterooms on the first floor of the palace. It includes Noh theatre masks, exquisite woodcuts, erotic wood and brass statuettes, samurai weapons and decorated screens and fans, as well as art works from Thailand, Korea and Tibet. At the time of writing only parts of the collection were open; protracted negotiations were in progress to extend the museum to display the remainder, also more Eastern artefacts privately amassed by other connoisseurs.

The Municipal Art Gallery is open daily 9am–9pm; 500dr.

Opened in 1996, the **Municipal Art Gallery** holds a small but growing collection of contemporary art, much of it local. It's well worth a visit to see what Greek artists are currently producing, and to take in the gardens and pleasant café-bar, a quiet haven away from the busy tourist routes through the old town.

Opposite the west front of the palace, another elegant nineteenth-century building houses the **Reading Society of Corfu**, which is the oldest cultural institution in modern Greece and contains a vast collection of works on Corfu and the other Ionian islands in Greek, English, French and other languages. There is also a growing collection of maps, engravings, photographs, periodicals and newspapers. The library is open to the public but times vary.

The Solomós and Byzantine museums

The Solomós Museum is open Mon–Fri 5–8pm; 300dr. The Byzantine Museum is open Tues–Sun 9am–3pm; 500dr.

In a nearby backstreet off Arseníou, five minutes' walk from the palace, a former private house, restored in 1979, houses a museum dedicated to modern Greece's most famous poet, **Dhionysios Solomos**. Born on Zákynthos, Solomos was author of the poem *Ýmnos is tin Eleftherían* (Hymn to Liberty), which was to become the Greek national anthem. He studied at Corfu's Ionian Academy, and lived in a house on this site for much of his life (it was destroyed in the war and rebuilt). The museum contains a small collection of Solomos manuscripts and effects but, frustratingly, is labelled solely in Greek. If you're also travelling to Zákynthos, visit the far more enlightening museum dedicated to the native poet there (see p.232).

Up a short flight of steps on Arseníou, the **Byzantine Museum** is housed in the restored church of the Panayía Andivouniótissa (it is also known by this name), which dates from the mid-sixteenth century. Despite its name, it houses Christian and pre-Christian artefacts,

The Ionian School of painting

The Ionian islands have a strong tradition of excellence in the fine arts, particularly iconography. They were in a unique position to bring Greece more in touch with mainstream developments in Western European ideas and art, having spent centuries occupied by the Venetians and later the British, rather than under the Turkish yoke.

The founder of the **Ionian School of painting** is considered to be **Panayiotis Dhoxaras**, who was born in the Peloponnese in 1662 but, after studying in Venice and Rome, moved to Zákynthos and later lived and worked in Lefkádha and Corfu until his death in 1729. Until the late seventeenth century, religious art in the Ionians, as elsewhere, was dominated by the Cretan School; Crete was another Venetian possession, and there was a great deal of contact between the two islands. Exponents of this school were intent on maintaining the stylistic purity and dignified austerity of the Byzantine tradition. Dhoxaras, however, having absorbed the spirit of Italian Renaissance art, brought a greater degree of naturalism into iconography by showing his subjects, usually saints, in more human poses amid everyday surroundings. He is also credited with introducing the technique of oil painting into Greece in place of the older method of mixing pigments with egg yolk. He translated da Vinci's *Treatise on Painting* into Greek and published his own *Manual of Painting*. His most lauded work was the ceiling of Áyios Spyrídhon church in Corfu Town, which succumbed to damp in the mid-nineteenth century and had to be redone by Nikolaos Aspiotis. Originals of his do survive in the Panayía church of Áno Garoúna in Corfu and Áyios Dhimítrios in Lefkádha Town, among other places.

Dhoxaras' work was carried on by his son, Nikolaos, whose best work is the ceiling of Áyios Minás in Lefkádha Town, and over the next two centuries the tradition has flourished through the skilled brushwork of a host of talented artists. Among these, **Yioryios Khrysoloras**, another eighteenth-century Corfiot, painted a number of the works on display at Corfu's Byzantine Museum; the Zakynthian **Nikolaos Kandounis** (1767–1878), creator of *The Last Supper* and *Washing of the Feet* at the Panayía Platytéra, was another prolific exponent; and three generations of the Proselandis family, starting with **Pavlos Proselandis** (1784–1837), have left work in various locations. Other artists of the school are mentioned in appropriate sections of the text.

religious and secular, including sculptures and sections of mosaic floors from Paleópolis, sections of Byzantine church **frescoes**, a collection of ninety **icons** dating from the fifteenth to nineteenth centuries, and other religious paraphernalia from around the island. The collection of Byzantine art is one of the finest in the country, rivalling that of the Byzantine Museum in Athens. Some of the more striking images are the dark, gruesome depictions of a beheaded John the Baptist, triumphant scenes of St George slaying the dragon and a moving portrayal of Christ trampling down the gates of Hell to rescue the holy dead. The anti-clockwise direction from the entrance follows a generally chronological order, and culminates in the centre with the atmospherically recreated inner shrine.

Corfu Town

Áyios Spyrídhon is open daily, but should be avoided during services, unless you are entering in a spirit of worship.

Áyios Spyrídhon Church

A block behind the Listón, down Odhós Spyrídhonos, is the most famous structure on the whole island: the **church of Áyios Spyrídhon**, whose maroon-domed campanile, the highest on the island, dominates the town and serves as a handy navigation mark. The church is dedicated to **St Spyridhon**, a bishop of Cyprus and prominent father of Orthodoxy, who was born in the late third century and whose relics were kept in Constantinople until the fall of the Byzantine empire, when refugees managed to salvage them. Having finally arrived on Corfu in 1489, the relics were credited with saving the islanders from a famine in 1553: a sea captain carrying grain claimed that the saint appeared to him in a dream and told him to take it to Corfu. Since then Spyridhon has been credited with saving the island from various plagues, invasions and other disasters. His position as **patron saint** is reflected in the popularity of the name Spyros; it can seem that just about every other male here answers to it.

The saint's mysteriously preserved body is kept in a silver and ebony **sarcophagus** near the altar, and on Palm Sunday, Easter Saturday, August 11 and the first Sunday in November, he is paraded through the city. For days leading up to these festivals the casket is opened for the faithful, who queue up to view the body. Corfiots visiting the shrine on his name day (December 12) kiss his robe to petition for good luck. St Spyridhon is believed by some to be a peripatetic saint, given to the odd *vólta* around town by himself, and each year he's given a new pair of slippers; apocryphal lore holds that the old slippers have been found scuffed from use.

This "new" church was built in 1590 after the original, founded in the fifteenth century in the suburb of San Rocco, had to be destroyed because of structural faults. The **ceiling** features ornate gilt-framed scenes from the saint's life, nineteenth-century copies of earlier originals by the painter Panayiotis Dhoxaras, leader and instigator of the Ionian School (see box on p.77, which were destroyed by damp. One of the most interesting depicts St Spyridhon breaking a tile into its constituent elements of earth, water and fire, thus demonstrating the tripartite nature of God to support the doctrine of the Trinity. The exquisite iconostasis of white Parian marble has a finely balanced picture of the Last Supper in its central upper panel. On the wall to its right is a splendid icon of the saint, dressed in a brown robe patterned with repeated crosses, by eighteenth-century local artist Konstandinos Kondarinis; it is considered to be the finest on the island. The rest of the church is a riot of icons, frescoes and gilt ornaments.

The Mitrópolis

The other unmissable church in Corfu Town is the **Mitrópolis** (Orthodox Cathedral), which stands above its eponymous square near the Old Port. Originally built in 1577 as Panayía Spiliótissa (The Virgin of the Grotto) because of a nearby cave, it is still sometimes referred to by that name. The exterior is typically plain, although the front was modernized in Baroque style in the earlier twentieth century. Within, the Mitrópolis boasts a wealth of Orthodox art. Apart from another splendid iconostasis, some fragments of seventeenth-century frescoes and the expected array of beautiful icons from different epochs, there are three remarkable paintings of scenes from the Old Testament on the side walls; the unknown artists were clearly influenced by Italian Mannerism. There is also some excellent wrought-ironwork on the grilles to either side of the main door and on the railing that separates the raised area before the iconostasis from the rest of the nave.

The Mitrópolis has its resident saint too: in a casket beside the altar lies the body of **St Theodhora**, which was rescued from Constantinople at the same time as that of St Spyridhon. Theodhora was born in Asia Minor in 815 and later married to Emperor Theophilos, taking over the reins of empire on his death until her son attained majority. She was renowned for her beauty and accomplishments, but her greatest achievement was to re-establish the cult of icons at a brilliant ceremony in Ayía Sofía, Constantinople, on March 11, 843, thus ending the bitter controversy over their veneration that had riven the Orthodox world for a century. She was canonized for this act, which is still celebrated on the first Sunday of Lent; since 1985, her body has been solemnly paraded around the streets on that day.

The Archeological Museum

Corfu Town's **Archeological Museum**, a few blocks south from the Maitland Rotunda, just off the seafront, is the biggest and best in the archipelago, and the ideal place to catch a glimpse of ancient Corfu, at least in the form of architectural details and artefacts from the era. It contains fragments of Neolithic weapons and cookware, coins, pots and sculpture from the Corinthian era, and Roman architectural features. Its most impressive exhibit is the massive west pediment excavated from the Archaic temple of Artemis at Paleópolis, just south of Corfu Town: at around 17m long, this dominates an entire room on the first floor, its mesmerizing central Gorgon figure flanked by panthers and battle scenes between the gods. The North Room also contains a huge pediment, from an unidentified classical building discovered near Kanóni in 1973, and a fine sixth-century BC *kouros* head. Another extremely rare example of early sculpture is the magnificent crouching lion (probably placed on a tomb as a guardian of the dead), believed to be the work of a seventh-century BC Corinthian craftsman, in the South Room.

The British Cemetery

South of Platía Saróko and signposted on the corner of Methodhíou and Kolokotróni, just beyond the psychiatric hospital, the **British Cemetery** – which is still used for civilian burials – features some

The Archeological Museum is open Tues–Sun 8.30am–3pm; 1000dr, free on Sun. Full wheelchair access.

elaborate civic and military memorials. Most notable is a memorial to the 44 seamen killed in a naval incident in 1946, when an Albanian vessel sank two British warships, leading to the severing of diplomatic ties between the countries. Despite its grim history, the cemetery is a quiet green space away from the madness of San Rocco at any time of the year, and in spring and early summer it's alive with dozens of species of orchids and other exotic blooms.

Around Corfu Town

Each of the following sights on the outskirts of the city is easily seen in a morning or afternoon, and best visited from the town rather than from the outlying resorts.

Mon Repos

Mon Repos is open daily 8am–8pm; 200dr.

Around the bay from the Rotunda and Archeological Museum, and tucked behind popular Mon Repos beach, the estate around **Mon Repos** villa contains the most accessible archeological remains on the island. The villa itself, a Neoclassical structure built by British High Commissioner Frederic Adam in 1824, became the property of the Greek royal family when Britain ceded the island to Greece in 1864. The Corfu authorities stirred up a minor international spat in 1996 – at least in right-wing British tabloids – when they unilaterally took over the property – where Prince Philip was born – and began to redevelop it for public visits. The grounds are already open to the public, accessible via the gate just beyond Mon Repos beach, but the building itself has been undergoing lengthy restoration and is not due to open until early in the new millennium.

The estate makes a pleasant shady walk, its thick woodlands concealing the remains of two **Doric temples**, dedicated to Hera and Artemis. The first has some recognizable features such as an altar and fragments of columns. The second, near the low cliffs overlooking the coast, is better preserved, with walls, foundations, columns and other details partly excavated in a pit.

Vlahérna and Pondikoníssi

The most famous excursion from Corfu Town is to the islets of **Vlahérna and Pondikoníssi**, 2km south of town – you can either walk there, along the road past Mon Repos beach or over the causeway that crosses the lagoon from Pérama, or take a suburban bus from Platía Saróko to the suburb of Kanóni (20min). Joined to the mainland by a short causeway, the tiny white convent of Vlahérna is surrounded by tall cypresses, and must be one of the most photographed images in Greece. The crowds, however, as well as the roar from planes at the nearby airport, significantly detract from what can look like an idyllic setting through a camera lens. Nearby, the small wooded island of Pondikoníssi (aka Mouse Island) can be reached by a short boat trip from the dock (500dr). It's reckoned to be the petrified remains of one of Odysseus's ships, an act of revenge by Poseidon after the blinding of Polyphemus in the cave – although it's only one of a number of rocks in the region that are said to be this vessel. Barely a hundred metres across, Pondikoníssi also suffers from brief but intense over-population by day-trippers.

Vídhos

A far quieter destination than Vlahérna and Pondikoníssi is **Vídhos**, the larger wooded island visible from the port in Corfu Town. Vídhos has been a strategic point in defending, and attacking, Corfu over the centuries, and over the years has been the site of a prison, a cemetery and an execution ground. Regardless of its history, it's a pleasant place for a picnic and is uninhabited apart from a seasonal scout camp. A free shuttle *kaïki* runs back and forth between the Old Port and Vídhos hourly, the last one returning at 1.30am to encourage people to dine at the excellent municipally owned restaurant and bar. With a fine range of dishes at reasonable prices, subtle live music from an accomplished local duet and unparalleled views of the illuminated forts and old town, this makes for an unforgettable evening out. Hard by the Vídhos *kaïki* moors the *Calypso Star*, a large, glass-bottomed semi-submersible boat, which, for 4000dr a head (children half-price), takes parties out to explore the waters around Vídhos and to see divers at work.

Achilleion Palace

Built in 1890–91 for Empress Elizabeth of Austria, this Neoclassical folly of a summer residence attracts a huge number of coach tours, despite an alarming mishmash of styles that led Henry Miller to describe it (in *The Colossus of Maroussi*) as a "madhouse" and "the worst piece of gimcrackery I have ever laid eyes on". It's certainly a curiosity in its setting, but no more interesting than an average minor country house in England – those on a tight schedule could avoid it with few qualms. If you're tempted, it's located 4km through the bad-lands of suburban Corfu, and therefore best reached on the dedicated bus from Platía Saróko.

The Achilleion Palace is open daily 9am–3pm; 1000dr.

The **house** itself is not particularly large, and only half a dozen ground-floor rooms are open. Pause to take in the colourful, if rather overdone, ceiling painting in the entrance hall. On display inside you'll find furniture, portraits, statuary, jewellery and bas-reliefs, as well as personal effects of the empress and of Kaiser Wilhelm II, who bought the Achilleion after her assassination by an Italian anarchist in 1898. It's difficult to really appreciate the displays as, like much of the building, they're roped off and festooned with "Do not touch" signs.

The terraced **gardens**, planted mainly with indigenous flora, are more worthwhile than the interior. The different tiers afford a range of vantage points with fine views over town and coast. The surrounding flowerbeds are magnificent, and a beautiful double pergola leads to Herter's monumental statue of **The Dying**

Achilles, from whom the building takes its name ("I want a palace...worthy of Achilles," the empress is reported to have said). A closed path leads down to the remains of **Kaiser's Bridge**, destroyed by the Nazis, ironically, so they could roll their panzers underneath it. The structure used to span the coast road and led to an elegant Neoclassical stone jetty, which still survives.

You may well find yourself being invited into the tasting room of *Vassilakis* distillery, right opposite the Achilleion entrance, for a nip of liqueurs made with kumquats and other fruit. This is a harmless diversion, especially if you haven't tried the sticky concoction, and there is no compulsion to buy a bottle. Indeed, some locals claim that you are far better off getting to the kumquat-producing villages of the northeast in order to procure the best quality.

Aqualand

Basic entry to Aqualand is reasonable at 1000dr per person, but the extra cost of special attractions and refreshments can easily make an expensive day of it.

If you are on holiday with children or are a child at heart, then you will probably want or be coerced to visit **Aqualand**, Corfu's well-advertised "water paradise" at Áyios Ioánnis, 5km west of Corfu Town. Reckoned to be one of the biggest water parks in Europe, it features multiple opportunities to get wet on attractions with names like Black Hole, Kamikaze, Hydro-tube and Twister, as well as the usual assortment of pools with slides and diving boards. Plenty of overpriced junk food and drinks are available in time-honoured theme-park tradition. The dedicated blue bus #8 leaves regularly from San Rocco square.

Eating and drinking

It is a pity that so many visitors return to the resort they're based in for their evening meal, as the island's capital offers the variety of eating possibilities that you would expect of a cultured town. Most **restaurants** are in or around the old town, with some hard-to-find places favoured by locals concealed in the maze of the Campiello. Restaurants on the main thoroughfares – the Listón, Arseníou, around Theotóki/San Rocco square – tend to be fast, snacky and indifferent. The Garítsa seafront has a number of excellent fish restaurants with outdoor seating and views of the bay, although you need to be careful what you order to avoid an exorbitant bill.

Aleko's Beach, Faliráki jetty. Sharing the tiny harbour below the palace with the *Faliraki*, this place offers simpler meat and fish dishes at good prices.

Averof, in the alley leaving the cathedral steps behind Zavitsiánou. Long-running Corfu institution, offering above-par if fairly unimaginative *estiatório* cuisine.

Faliraki, below the Palace of SS Michael and George, down a sunken slope that passes through an arch onto the Faliráki jetty. Crumbling medieval buildings renovated as a restaurant, reasonably priced for its setting and with an imaginative menu: marinated salmon, cod croquettes, steamed mussels, designer pasta, prosciutto and other dishes not normally spotted in Corfu. The restaurant's large patio overlooks the bay, and when not busy is a good place for just a drink and a rest.

The Listón, Corfu Town

Vlahérna convent, Corfu

Achilleion Palace, Corfu

Kassiópi, Corfu

Mon Repos, Corfu

Palm procession during Easter celebrations, Corfu

Kalamítsi beach, Lefkádha

Gáïos, Paxí

Longós, Paxí

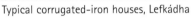
Typical corrugated-iron houses, Lefkádha

Pandokrátor Church, Lefkádha

Egremní beach, Lefkádha

Mourayia, Arseníou 15–17. Unassuming and good-value *ouzerí* near the Byzantine Museum. A range of tasty *mezédhes*, including sausage and seafood such as mussels and shrimp. One of the best seafront establishments.

Orestes, Xenophóndos Stratigoú, in Mandoúki. Probably the best fish and seafood restaurant in town, and better priced than the central restaurants.

Quattro Stagione, in an alley on the north side of N. Theotóki. A mix of Italian and Greek but, as the name implies, it concentrates on pizzas and pastas.

Rex, Zavitsiánou behind the Listón. Pricey, but some of the best food in the centre, mixing Greek with north European.

Sze Chuan, Ethnikís Andístasis 61. If you need a break from Greek food, this Chinese restaurant in the New Port provides all the old favourites, but at a price. Closed Mon.

Tenedos, 1st Párodhos Solomoú 1, Spiliá. At the foot of the steps to the Néo Froúrio, this place offers an excellent range of *mezédhes* like courgette fritters and *yígandes* plus succulent meat dishes to the accompaniment of live guitar music.

Venetian Well Bistro, Platía Kremastí. One of the best-kept secrets in Corfu, mainly because it's so difficult to find, tucked away in a tiny square a few alleys to the south of the cathedral. This is the nearest you're likely to get to Greek *nouvelle cuisine*, but with large portions, and exotica such as Iraqi lamb and Albanian calves' livers done in ouzo. One warning: beyond the barrelled variety, the wine-list prices climb alarmingly. Sometimes closes Mon.

Nightlife

Corfu's self-proclaimed **Disco Strip** lies a few kilometres north of town, en route to Kondókali, a trip best made by bus or taxi – on foot along the road, it's a game of chicken with the local daredevils. Here, at such places as the (unofficial) *Hard Rock Café*, the *Hippodrome* disco complex (the town's biggest, with its own pool), the bizarrely decorated *Apokalypsis* and *Coca*, party animals dress up for wild and fairly expensive nights out with gaggles of friends. Some smaller joints such as *Rondo*, for soul and rock, or *Confusio* operate within the Emborikó Kéndro (Trade Centre) besides *Coca*.

If that's not your bag, Corfu Town has plenty to offer in the way of **bars**, outdoor restaurants and streetlife at night. The Listón stays open until late, and has its own special atmosphere at night, with prices to match: if you're drinking here, avoid the eyebrow-raising mark-ups at the *Magnet*, and follow the locals to *Koklia*, *Aegli* or *Olympia*. The San Rocco square bars are bedevilled by traffic noise and fumes, but you will find some quieter open-air spots around Zavitsiánou. Another alternative is to drink in one of the smarter hotels, which all open their bars to outsiders: the *Cavalieri* rooftop in particular can be a dream at night.

If you're looking for a little local atmosphere, try the cheap and cheerful *Dirty Dick's*, on the corner of Arseníou and Zavitsiánou, or the more sophisticated *Art Café* behind the palace gardens. If you prefer world music, head for *Ethnik* at Ethnikís Andístasis 12.

The Pallas cinema, on Y. Theotóki, and the Orfeus, on the corner of Akadhimías and Aspióti, regularly show English-language films.

Listings

Albania Tours Day-trips to nearby Albania were suspended again in 1999 because of the Kosovo crisis. If the situation is calm, they will probably be resumed in 2000, and are widely advertised at agencies around the island. The tours cross from the Old Port to Ayía Saránda, where a coach transfer takes you to some extensive Roman ruins before returning for a meal and shopping. Expect to pay 9–10,000dr and as much again for the visa.

American Express Kapodhistríou 20a (Mon–Fri 8am–2pm; ☎0661/30 883).

Banks and exchange The town's banks are almost all based on Y. Theotóki, and around Platía San Rocco; most have cash machines that accept international credit and debit cards. There are two 24hr automatic currency exchange machines on Alexándhras, on the left leaving San Rocco.

Beaches and lidos There are no beaches in town, but two lidos offer deep-water swimming off jetties and platforms. The main lido is at Faliráki, below the palace, reached by the sunken road leading down from the corner of Arseníou and Kapodhistríou. It has loungers, changing facilities and a café, and charges 200dr entry. The second is the public swimming area below the Old Fort near the *Corfu Palace Hotel*. Mon Repos Beach, a small private beach of imported sand at Garítsa, a 15min walk south of the Spianádha (daily 9am–6pm; 200dr), is very popular with townspeople, despite what looks like a sewage outfall just metres outside its northern boundary. There's a bar and taverna, changing rooms, showers, toilets, sunbeds and a diving jetty plus the ancient ruins behind.

Bookshops Surprisingly for a town with such British connections, there is no real specialist English bookshop. Lykoudis, next to the National Bank, Voulgaréos and Xenoglossa, Y. Markorá 45, have a limited selection of fact and fiction; the pulp variety is available at kiosks and tourist shops all over the island.

Bus departures Corfu Town's suburbs, and outlying resorts as far south as Benítses and north to Dhássia, are served by the blue bus system, which is based in San Rocco square (Platía Y. Theotóki). Some services, notably to Benítses, leave from a stop 100m down Methodhíou, the road leaving the square by the bus stand. For these conductorless buses you'll have to buy tickets either at the San Rocco bus stand or the *kafenío* by the Methodhíou bus stop. Island-wide and mainland services leave the KTEL green bus station on Avramíou near the new port. Here, tickets are bought on board, apart from Athens and Thessaloníki departures.

Car rental Avis, Ethnikís Andístasis 42 ☎0661/24 404, plus an office at the airport; Budget, Venizélou 22 ☎0661/49 100, and at the airport ☎0661/44 017; Hertz, at the airport ☎0661/33 547. Among local companies, try Sunrise, Ethnikís Andístasis 14, in the new port ☎0661/44 325.

Consulates Belgium, Alexándhras 44 ☎0661/33 788; Denmark, Ethnikís Andístasis 4 ☎0661/35 698; Eire, Kapodhistríou 20A ☎0661/32 469; France, I. Pólyla 22 ☎0661/26 312; Germany, 57 Guildford St. ☎0661/31 453; Italy, Alexándhras 10 ☎0661/37 351; Netherlands, Idroménou 2 ☎0661/39 900; Norway, Donzelot 9 ☎0661/39 667; Spain, Sweden, Platía Skaramangá 7 ☎0661/36 241; Switzerland, Corfu Palace Hotel 0661/39 485; UK, Menekrátous 1 ☎0661/30 055.

Doctor The British general practitioner, Dr Yiannopapas, with training and experience in England, serves the expat community and has been recommended by some travellers; surgery at Mantzárou 1, near OTE (☎0661/49 530), or in emergency call home (☎0661/49 530).

Email Full Internet facilities are available at Netoikos Internet Café, Kaloherétou 14, near Áyios Spyrídhon church; Mon–Sat 9am–midnight, Sun 5pm–midnight (☎0661/47 481).

Ferry offices There are ticket agencies inside the new port buildings, and franchises of the major ferry companies on Ethnikís Andístasis opposite: Minoan (☎0661/25 000); Strintzis (☎0661/25 332); Anek (☎0661/24 504); Adriatica (☎0661/38 089); HML (☎0661/39 747); and Ventouris (☎0661/32 664). High-season ferries to Italy fill quickly, especially car spaces, so phoning ahead is advised. Tickets for other ferries are usually available prior to departure at booths or agencies near the quay.

Hospital On the corner of I. Andhreádhi and Polykhroníou Konstánda, off Platía San Rocco (☎0661/45 811–7 or 25 400). ☎166 gets an ambulance.

Laundry There are at least three ancient *plyndíria* hidden in the alleys of Corfu Town. Most central is the Kyknos on Néa Paleológou, behind the Pisteos Bank on Voulgaréos. Also handy is the Perioteri, in the first block of I. Theotóki off San Rocco. And tucked in an alleyway to the left of the Orthodox cathedral's front entrance stands the Christos *plyndírio*. None of their staff speaks English.

Motorbike rental Most bike rental firms are based in or around the new port: Easy Rider, I. Theotóki 128 (☎0661/43 026), is a good place to start, but if you have time shop around.

Olympic Airways Polylá 11 ☎0661/38 694; airport ☎0661/30 180 or 37 398.

OTE Mantzárou 3 (daily 8am–2.30pm).

Police Alexándhras 19 ☎0661/38 661 or 39 509.

Port Authority in the New Port for up-to-date sailings: domestic ☎0661/32 655, international ☎0661/30 481.

Post office Corner of Alexándhras and Zafirópoulou (Mon–Fri 7.30am–8pm).

Taxis There are taxi ranks at the airport; by the new and old ports ☎0661/37 993; at the Spianádha end of the Listón ☎0661/39 926; on Platía Saróko ☎0661/30 383; and on Theotóki ☎0661/39 911. Alternatively, call Radio Taxi ☎0661/33 811–2.

Tourist police Samartzí 4, Platía Saróko ☎0661/30 265.

Travel Agents Corfu Town is crawling with travel agents, especially around the New Port and Platía Saróko. Two which are recommended for a variety of services, including cheap flights to Britain and northern Europe are: Corfu Infotravel, Ethnikís Andístasis 14, New Port (☎0661/41 550 or 25 933, fax 23 829) and Eurocorfu Travel, Alexándhras 40, San Rocco (☎0661/46 886 or 21 886, fax 46 887).

The northeast and the north coast

The northeast is the most stereotypically Greek part of Corfu: mountainous, with a rocky coastline chopped into pebbly bays and coves, above a sea that's often as clear as a swimming pool. A green **bus** route between Corfu Town and Kassiópi serves the resorts along the single coastal road, along with some blue suburban bus services as far as Dhassiá. A bus from the island capital connects Kassiópi to the family-oriented resort of Aharávi, but otherwise the north coast resorts – as far west as brash Sidhári and the nearby hill town of Avliótes – are served by direct buses from Corfu Town that travel via often spectacular inland routes.

Kondókali and Gouviá

The landscape immediately to the north of Corfu Town as far as Kondókali is little more than motorway and industrial sites, and has about as much rural charm as Brooklyn or Lewisham. Things don't improve much at **KONDÓKALI** itself, a small village overrun by holiday developments, which serves the nearby marina at Gouviá. The old town consists of a short street with a number of bars and traditional *psistariés* – notably, *Gerekos* and *Takis* – and a couple of smarter restaurants; *Flags*, with an imaginative menu (fish and steaks in exotic sauces) aimed at the yachting fraternity, who comprise much of Kondókali's passing trade, and *Lithari*, a pricey music taverna popular with well-heeled Greeks. There's very little independent accommodation here: many holiday lets reverted to domestic tenancies during the tourism slump earlier in the decade and, wisely, no one has tried to tempt people back into using it as a base, other than those who buy a pig-in-a-poke package.

Kondókali's neighbouring resort, **GOUVIÁ**, is the site of Corfu's largest yachting marina, and the launching point of most flotilla and bareboat holidays. As the first half-decent resort north of Corfu Town, it also tends to fill up with tourists off the ferries, particularly in high summer. Besides the marina facilities and several unappealing luxury hotels on the main highway, the village boasts a couple of small **hotels**, notably the *Hotel Aspa* (☎0661/91 165 or 91 292; ④), and some **rooms** – try Maria Lignou (☎0661/91 348; ③) or Yiorgos Mavronas (☎0661/91 297 or 90 297; ③). Catering largely to the flotilla culture are a number of decent **restaurants**, including *The Captain's Table* and *Aries Taverna*, the highly rated *Gorgona* fish taverna and a couple of pizzerias, *Bonito* and *Palladium*. For a drink and bop there are the curious Spanish-themed *Borracho* bar and the *Adonis* disco. The very narrow shingle **beach**, barely 5m wide in parts, shelves into sand, but given the amount of yacht traffic in the area, water quality must be at best uncertain. Behind the fenced-in marina are the skeletal remains of a **Venetian armoury**, an almost surreal collection of stone buttresses standing in a meadow.

Gouviá's marina has become safe again after a scare in the mid-1990s, when it became the target of armed Albanian criminals, who stole yachts either to sell on or to strip for equipment. The problem was blown out of proportion in the British media, but early in 1996 the Foreign Office did issue a safety warning and later in the year a British yachtsman was shot dead by one such gang aboard a yacht off Cape Komméno to the north of Gouviá. Since then concerted naval patrolling and an amelioration of the Albanian situation have dispelled the threat, which at no time affected land-based tourists.

Dhassiá and Dhafníla

Two kilometres beyond Gouviá are **DHASSIÁ** and **DHAFNÍLA**, set in two small wooded bays where developments have largely merged into one. The beaches here are pebble, with two outfits, Corfu Ski Club and Club 2001, offering paragliding and other **watersports** at either end of the Dhassiá beach. Two large A-class **hotels**, the *Dasia Chandris* and *Corfu Chandris* (both ☎0661/97 100–3, fax 93 458, email *chandris@ker.forthnet.gr*; ⑦) dominate Dhassiá. The hotels are next to each other but set in their own extensive grounds, with pools and sports facilities, shops, restaurants, bars and beach frontages. Both take block bookings from north European package companies, but have rooms available for most of the season.

A notch or two below these, the *Livadi Nafsika* (☎0661/93 276 or 93 174, fax 93 494; ⑥) is another huge hotel with all amenities and ample grounds, while, more reasonably, the *Hotel Amalia* (☎0661/93 523; ④) has pleasant en-suite rooms and its own pool and garden, set back from the main road opposite the *Chandris* hotels. Another medium-size, comfortable hotel on the main road is *Penelope* (☎0661/93 638; ④). There are numerous other hotels near the main road or down by the beach; two of these are the large *Dassia Beach* (☎0661/93 224 or 93 268; ⑤) and more modest *Spiros Beach* (☎0661/93 666; ④). Private **rooms** are scarce in the resort, although Spyros Rengis, who runs the local minimarket, has a few (☎0661/90 282; ③), and *Hermes Apartments* (☎0661/93 314, fax 93 373; ④) can offer studios and apartments.

Dhassiá does, however, have the best **campsite** on the island and closest to Corfu Town, *Dionysus Camping Village* (☎0661/91 417 or 93 785, fax 91 760) on the Dhafníla side. While it doesn't have direct access to the sea, it's only a few hundred democratic metres from the beach the two *Chandris* joints use. As well as camping space under terraced olive trees, *Dionysus* has simple bungalow huts (①), a pool, shop, bar and restaurant. The camp attracts an international crowd, some of whom appear still to be on their way home from the Isle of Wight pop festival, and the friendly, multilingual owners will offer a ten percent discount if you wave this book at them (nicely). Another more family-oriented campsite, *Karda Beach Camping* (☎ & fax 0661/93 595), is situated off the main road on the north side of Dhassiá.

Eating in the Dhassiá area is mostly a functional affair. Many of the seaside hotels have adequate restaurants with staple diets on offer and competition keeps prices reasonable. The *Karydia* in Dhassiá is a cut above most, with a wide menu of meat and fish in some delightful sauces, and a popular weekend escape for townsfolk. On the main road through Dhafníla, the *Greco* taverna is famed for excellent home-cooking, such as freshly baked Ioánnina-style pies with a variety of fillings, and good Macedonian barrelled wine.

If you fancy trying some watersports, the following prices from Club 2001 are indicative: banana ride 2500dr; towed dinghy 4000dr; water-ski 6000dr; and paragliding 9000dr (14,000dr for two goes).

Ípsos

ÍPSOS, 2km and one bay north of Dhassiá, can't really be recommended to anyone but hardened bar-hoppers. There isn't room to
swing a cat on the long, thin pebble beach, which lies right beside
the busy coast road, and the atmosphere suggests the resort has
been twinned with Southend or Coney Island. The seafront comprises a kilometre-long row of snack joints, vehicle rental firms,
one laundromat (the subversively named *My Beautiful
Laundrette*) and cocktail bars with names like *Alcoholics
Anonymous*, *The Shamrock* and *The Victoria Pub*, which draw a
young, boozy crowd with adverts for "Sex on the Beach" cocktails
– and, on the irregular visits by the US Navy on R&R shore trips,
bar notices asking "Fancy a date with four thousand sailors?"

Most **accommodation** has been taken over by British package companies, although Ipsos Travel (☎0661/93 661 or 93 920–1) can offer
rooms, as well as car rental and other facilities, and the *Hotel Mega*
(☎066193 208 or 93 216, fax 93 566; ⑤), complete with pool, bars
and restaurants, often has vacant rooms. *Corfu Camping Ipsos*
(☎0661/93 579 or 93 246), in the centre of the strip, has a motel-style
reception with bar and restaurant and offers standing tents to those
without their own equipment. Ípsos is also the base for a major **diving
centre**, Waterhoppers (☎0661/93 876), which is registered with the
British Sub-Aqua Club and run on their guidelines. Claiming to be the
only dive outfit in Greece with a 54-inch decompression chamber, the
club caters for beginners and advanced divers, as well as offering a
number of BSAC and CMAS courses. The daily trips on its own *kaïki*
also welcome snorkellers and those who prefer to remain dry.

Eating on Ípsos' main drag is a hit-and-miss affair, although it
does have a large and stylish Chinese, the *Peking House*, looming
over it. A more traditional meal and a quieter setting can be found in
the *Akrogiali Psistaria* and *Asteria Taverna*, by the small marina
at the southern end of the strip. **Drinking** in Ípsos is mandatory, but
if you want to avoid droves of bevvied-up lads in full flight, head for
one of the quieter bars at the southern end of the seafront.

Mount Pandokrátor

Ípsos has now all but engulfed the neighbouring hamlet of Pyryí, at
the end of the strip, but it is still much quieter here, and all right if
you want a seaside walking base on this stretch of coast; try the
pleasant *Hotel Pirgi* (☎0661 93 266 or 97 867, fax 97 867; ④).
Pyryí is the main point of access for the hill villages and routes leading up to the island's largest mountain, **Mount Pandokrátor**. The
access road, initially signposted "Spartílas", is 200km beyond the
main junction in Pyryí. A popular base for walkers is the village of
STRINÝLAS, 16km up the road from Pyryí. Accommodation is basic
but easy to come by: most of it is in private houses, but the *Elm Tree*

Taverna in Strinýlas, a long-time favourite with walkers, can point you in the direction of rooms.

The presence of an unattractive communications station on the top of Mount Pandokrátor, complete with two large radio masts, has meant that the path leading up to the neighbouring Pandokrátoras monastery has now become a road. Cars and tour coaches can almost reach the summit, stopping at the hamlets of Petália, if coming from the south, or Períthia from the north. In Períthia there is a good place to assuage your hunger, if you've done it the hard way, in the shape of the *Old Peritheia* taverna. In summer the main routes become quite busy, but there are quieter walks to be had by taking in the handsome Venetian village of **Epískepsi**, 5km northwest of Strinýlas; quietest of all is the trail from Agnitsíni (on the main northeast coast road by the turn-off for Áyios Stéfanos), which leads to the tiny hamlet of Tritsí and on to the near-deserted Venetian village of **Áno Períthia**, from where a path leads up to the summit.

In spring and early summer, the route up to the summit blossoms with dwarf cyclamen, irises and orchids, and birds of prey – including the rarely seen golden eagle – patrol thermals above the slopes. Rules about hill walking – taking liquids, cover, sensible clothing, leaving note of your destination – should be followed. Pandokrátor is a magnet for bad weather, so take local advice if it looks at all changeable. Storms and low cloud are not uncommon in all but the driest of high seasons.

Barbáti, Nissáki and Agní

The coast road beyond Ípsos mounts the lower slopes of Pandokrátor towards **BARBÁTI**, some 4km on. Here you'll find the best beach on this stretch of coast: long and wide, away from traffic, with a gently shelving shore of pebbles and sand, and ample facilities. It's a favourite with families, and much of the **accommodation** here is booked throughout the summer by north European travel companies. However, there are some rooms – *Paradise* (☎0663/91 320;③) and *Roula Yeranou* (☎0663/92 397;③) – and a friendly travel agency on the main road, named Helga after its owner, has a range of accommodation (☎0663/91 547; ②–③). Apart from these places and a number of **tavernas** – including the *Lord Byron*, and the more traditional *Alexiou* and *Chryso Varelli* – there's not much else. Barbáti gets the morning sun, but the steep mountain bluffs behind it lose light early, and when bad weather is snagged by Mount Pandokrátor, the coast here tends to get dumped on.

The mountainside becomes steeper and the road higher above the sea beyond Barbáti, as the population of the coastline thins drastically. **NISSÁKI** is more a vague area than a place: three excellent pebble beaches, one dominated by the gigantic and rather soulless *Nissaki Beach Hotel* (☎0663/91 232–3; ⑦), a couple of shops and a bakery, and a few travel and **accommodation agencies**. The

Anyone interested in walking the Pandokrátor paths is advised to get the map of the mountain by island-based cartographer Stephan Jaskulowski and the useful "Second Book of Corfu Walks" by Hilary Whitton Paipeti (see p.280).

At Nissáki and beyond, watch out for blue signs saying "to paralía" (the beach), which point out short-cut paths to the beaches below.

British-owned Falcon Travel (☎0663/91 318, fax 91 070, email *falcon@ker.forthnet.gr*) rents out apartments above the first beach, a tiny, white-pebble affair with deep-blue water that's home to a trio of fine tavernas. Also worth contacting for apartments and villas are the Nissaki Holiday Center (☎0663/91 116 or 91 448, fax 91 206) and Vally's Tours (☎0663/91 294, fax 91 071), or for rooms, *Studios Aliki* (☎0663/91 041; ④) by the bus stop. One **restaurant** on the main road deserves a mention: *Taverna Giorgos*, opposite Club Med's quasi-military security gates, which specializes in Italian and German dishes.

A real gourmet's treat, however, is the tiny bay of **AGNÍ** a little further along. The only buildings backing onto the white pebble beach are a trio of fine tavernas; *Nikolas* does specialities like lamb in lemon sauce and liver in wine, *Agni* is good for seafood and veggies, as well as unusual items such as Spanish-style chicken, while *Toula's* is also very strong on seafood, with delights such as *mýdhia saganáki* (mussels fried in cheese sauce) and prawns pilaff.

Kalámi and Kouloúra

The two places no one visiting the northeast coast should miss are neighbouring Kalámi and Kouloúra: the first for its Durrell connection, the latter for its exquisite bay and sole taverna (though it has to be said that neither has a beach worth mentioning). Sadly, **KALÁMI** is on the way to being spoiled – already, the hillside above the bay is scarred by ugly purple apartment blocks that must have been designed with the help of hallucinogenic drugs – but the village itself is still small and, if you squint, you can imagine how it would have been in the year Lawrence Durrell spent there on the eve of World War II, when, according to Henry Miller, "days in Kalámi passed like a song". The beach is stony, and pebbly in the water, but many who holiday here hire boats to explore nearby coves. The **White House**, where Durrell wrote *Prospero's Cell*, is now split in two: the ground floor is an excellent taverna; the upper floor is let by the week through CV Travel (see p.6), although it tends to be prebooked months in advance.

Most of the **accommodation** in Kalámi – like much of the arc between Nissáki and Kassiópi – has been sewn up by blue-chip villa companies such as CV, Simply Ionian and Corfu à la Carte; anything left over for independent travellers probably needs to be booked in advance. *Vila Rita* (☎0663/91 030; ④) is a small block of well-appointed rooms; Tassos Athineos (☎0663/91 251) has rooms, and Yiannis Vlahos (☎0663/91 077–8 or 91 094, fax 91 077) has rooms, apartments and studios in the bay; Sunshine Travel (☎0663/91 170 or 91 572–3) and Kalami Tourist Services (☎0663/91 062, fax 91 369) also offer car, bike and boat rental, and exchange facilities. *Matella's* restaurant at the back of the village can also find you a room.

The **restaurant** at the White House is recommended, as is *Matella's* for its range of vegetarian and north European dishes,

The Durrells and Corfu

Between them, brothers **Gerald** and **Lawrence Durrell** unwittingly persuaded untold hundreds of thousands of Britons to visit Corfu – a fact the former would live to rue. Gerald (1925–95) described the family's arrival on the island in the early 1930s in *My Family and Other Animals;* the "strawberry-pink" villa the family moved into was in Pérama, although later they would move to another house in the hills above Kalámi. Lawrence (1912–90) was in his twenties and had already published a first novel (*Panic Spring*) pseudonymously when he arrived in 1937 to spend a year and a half living in "an old fisherman's house in the extreme north of the island – Kalamai". The book he produced describing this idyll, *Prospero's Cell* – the title taken from the theory that Corfu was the setting for Prospero's and Miranda's exile in Shakespeare's *The Tempest* – remains in print half a century on and portrays an island that can still be glimpsed in the more remote corners of the northeast coast.

Lawrence left the island at the outbreak of World War II – Henry Miller's *Colossus of Maroussi* describes a holiday with Durrell on the eve of war – but returned later, and shorter pieces on the island can be found in his collected prose works, *Spirit of Place*. *Prospero's Cell* was to form part of an island trilogy – joined later by *Reflections on a Marine Venus*, based on his postwar visit to Rhodes, and *Bitter Lemons*, on a later visit to Cyprus.

While Lawrence travelled widely, eventually settling in France, Gerald retained his contact with Corfu up until his death. The environmentalist and author was particularly outspoken about the dangers of chemical pesticide sprays on the olive trees, particularly when an alfresco lunch party of his was "accidentally" sprayed with noxious chemicals. His green successors have managed to get chemical spraying banned in inhabited areas and are fighting for total prohibition. For an interesting and detailed account of the Durrell brothers in Corfu, look for Hilary Whitton Paipeti's little book *In the Footsteps of Lawrence Durrell and Gerald Durrell in Corfu (1935–39)*.

even though it's away from the view. The *Kalami Beach Taverna* also has a lengthy list of vegetarian alternatives to Greek staples. *Pepe's* on the beach offers a mix of pizzas and local dishes, and holds traditional Greek music nights.

The tiny harbour of **KOULOÚRA** has managed to retain its charm, set at the edge of a (so far) totally undeveloped bay with nothing in it but pine trees, *kaïkia* and a single **taverna**. This fine, authentic restaurant has to be the most idyllic setting for a meal in the whole of Corfu, which accounts for its great popularity, particularly with drivers: if you're coming for lunch, arrive early, as it fills up quickly even in low season.

Kerasiá, Áyios Stéfanos and Avláki

Two pleasant kilometres by lane beyond Kouloúra, the large, shady cove of **KERASIÁ** shelters the friendly, family-run *Kerasia Beach Taverna* and a strip of villas along the shore, handled by CV Travel and others. The beach has a jetty, and with reason: it tends to attract day-trip boats most summer afternoons, when those staying here leave as fast as their outboards will take them.

Áyios Stéfanos
is connected to
Kerasiá by a
two-kilometre
lane passing
through olive
groves and an
estate owned
by the
Rothschild
clan.

Without doubt the most attractive resort on this stretch of coast, some 3km down a winding lane from the village of Agnitsíni on the main coast road, is **ÁYIOS STÉFANOS**, not to be confused with the resort of the same name on the west coast above Paleokastrítsa. Buses marked "Áyios Stéfanos" from Corfu Town go to the latter; this Áyios Stéfanos is only ever served by the Kassiópi bus, which will drop you at Agnitsíni. From there, it's a beautiful walk down to the resort, through olive groves and then open country with views across to nearby Albania – though quite a slog on the way back up.

Áyios Stéfanos is probably the most remote resort on Corfu, and the bare countryside around it and across in Albania increases this pleasant – and, for Corfu, rare – sense of isolation. Most **accommodation** here consists of upmarket villas and apartments run by British travel companies, and the village has yet to succumb to any serious development, which means that available space is thin on the ground; so far, only the *Kohyli* pizzeria and snack bar has rooms and apartments for independent travellers (☎0663/81 522; ③). The handful of **tavernas** reflects this upmarket exclusivity in their pricing and the fact that they almost all take credit cards. Recommended are the *Garini* and *Kaporelli* tavernas on the seafront, which mix high-class Italian and Greek, and the *Eucalyptus* over by the village's small and rather gravelly beach.

Half an hour's walk from the coastguard station above Áyios Stéfanos, along a newly paved road, is the beach of **Avláki**. In season, it's favoured by those fleeing the crowds on the more accessible beaches to the south and at Kassiópi. The pebble bay faces north-northwest, and its cliffs scoop up the prevailing winds, providing lively conditions for the **windsurfers** who visit the beach's small windsurf club (board hire starts at around 3000dr). There are two **tavernas**, the *Barbaro* and *Avlaki*, and some **rooms** a few hundred metres back from the beach – *Mortzoukos* (☎0663/81 196; ③) and *Tsirimiagos* (☎0663/81 522; ④) – but nothing else.

Kassiópi and around

About 2km around the coast from Avláki is **KASSIÓPI**, a small fishing village with a long history that's been transformed into a major party resort. Emperor Tiberius had a villa here, and the village's sixteenth-century church, locked and a little careworn these days, stands on what is believed to have been the site of a temple of Zeus once visited by Nero. Very little evidence of Kassiópi's longevity survives, however, apart from a sadly derelict thirteenth-century Angevin *kástro* on its headland. This is where the Angevins made their last stand against the Venetian invaders, who dismantled it, once taken, so that it would not fall into the hands of the Genoese. These days the only invaders are northern Europeans with their sights fixed on the nightlife – clubs, video bars, restaurants – and some small pebbly beaches around the headland. Package tourism dominates, and the Greek language is on its way out, but the original architecture of some of the streets around the harbour is still attractive.

Kassiópi's **beaches** are hidden below its ruined castle and reached by paths leaving the harbour and the village church. They are small but well protected and, because of their geographical distribution, at least two of them should be sheltered, regardless of which way the wind is blowing. Only a few minutes' walk from the town centre, Kalamíonas is the largest, Pipítos the smallest and Kanóni and Bataría the quietest, although even these two fill up very easily.

Inland from Kassiópi, the tiny village of Loútses has no shops, tavernas or other facilities (though buses run there from Corfu Town), but the open countryside around is excellent walking terrain, mainly grazing land or wild maquis, free of trees and with fine views over Albania. The walk from Kassiópi, a simple stroll along the coast road to the signed turning for Loútses, can be done in under an hour. For more serious walkers, the Loútses route continues to Períthia, where a path leads onto the summit of Mount Pandokrátor (see p.89).

Practicalities

Most **accommodation** in Kassiópi is through village agencies who, because they're in the marketplace with cut-price package operators, tend to be cheaper than in the tonier resorts to the south. The largest, Travel Corner (☎0663/81 220 or 81 213, fax 81 108; ② and up), is a good place to start if you're planning to stay a while in Kassiópi and want a choice of accommodation. Beri's Travel (☎0663/81 682 or 81 681), Salco Holidays (☎0663/81 040) and Cosmic Tourist Centre (☎0663/81 624 or 81 686) also have a range of rooms, apartments and villas. An independent alternative, the rather smart *Kastro* café-pension, is set away from the hubbub of town, overlooking the beach behind the castle (☎0663/81 045; ⑤). And if they aren't overrun by package bookings, *Theofilos* (☎0663/81 261; ②) offers good rooms on Kalamíonas beach at a bargain price and *Edem* (☎0663/81 431; ③) has decent basic rooms back in the village.

Anglicized cuisine and fast food dominate **eating** in Kassiópi. For something more traditional, head for the *Three Brothers* taverna on the harbourfront, which has a vast menu, and the neighbouring *Porto* fish restaurant. At night, Kassiópi rocks to the cacophony of its music and video **bars**. Flashest has to be the gleaming, hi-tech *Eclipse*, closely followed by the *Baron*, *Angelos* and *Jasmine*, all within falling-over distance of the small town square. The *Axis Club* (daily 11pm–late; entrance free) specializes in house, techno and other dance strains mixed by imported British DJs; frolics sometimes extend onto the beach until dawn.

Kassiópi is home to one of Corfu's best scuba diving operations, the partly British-run Corfu Divers (☎0663/81 218), with reliable equipment and experienced instructors.

Almyrós and Aharávi

The coastline on from Kassiópi becomes slightly overgrown and marshy, until reaching the little-used **Almyrós beach**. Almyrós is in fact an extension of the same beach as at Aharávi and Ródha, and as such is one of the longest on the island. So far, it is also the most undeveloped, with only a few apartment buildings, some package-tour rooms and a handful of shops, cafés and restaurants at the hamlet of **ALMYRÓS**. The beach is wild and near deserted, although it gets busier as it approaches Aharávi with sporadic accommodation; a pleasant place to stay along this stretch is *Anastassia Beach Apartments* (☎0663/63 360; ④). The far eastern end, towards Cape Ayías Ekaterínis, is backed by the **Andinióti lagoon**, smaller than Korissíon in the south of the island, but still a haven for waterfowl, waders, marsh species and any number of other birds lured by the fish farms in the lagoon.

With its wide main road, **AHARÁVI** at first sight resembles a rather unappealing American Midwest truck stop, but the village proper is in fact tucked away behind this new highway, in a small, quiet crescent of old tavernas, bars and shops. The sand and pebble beach is very popular with family holidaymakers, who arrive in their coachloads with the British travel majors, but also attracts German and north European tourists to a number of seriously expensive resort hotels.

On the whole, Aharávi makes a decent, quieter alternative to the beaches in the southwest, and should also be considered by those looking for alternative routes up onto **Mount Pandokrátor** (see p.88). Signposted roads leaving the Aharávi main road for small mountain hamlets such as Áyios Martínos and Láfki connect with well-signed routes up onto the mountain, and even a walk up from the backstreets of Aharávi will find you on the mountain's upper slopes in under an hour. The dip slopes around Aharávi also have some excellent walks through them, although, given the maze of paths through the olive groves and lack of identifying topography, these are almost impossible to identify. As elsewhere in the region, though, the olive grove paths are there for a specific purpose, and will invariably bring you out to another road or village, although not always the one you might expect. The views from the open roads around Láfki, down over Aharávi and Cape Ayías Ekaterínis, are stunning, sometimes vertiginous.

Aharávi practicalities

Independent **accommodation** isn't too easy to find in Aharávi, but a good place to start is Castaway Travel (☎0663/63 541 or 63 843, fax 63 376). Run by a long-term English resident of the village, Sue Tsirigoti, and her husband Theo, the company handles a wide range of rooms and apartments, and offers other services such as vehicle rental, currency exchange and excursions. HN Travel (☎0663/63 458, fax 63 454) is also friendly and offers a range of accommodation and other

Day-trips to Erikoússa (see p.116), run weekly by Castaway Travel, cost around 5000dr per person.

services. Another of the village's travel companies, Oracle (☎0663/63 265 or 63 262, fax 63 441), has a smaller range of mainly upmarket accommodation, much of it committed to German holidaymakers, and offers car rental. One large but reasonable hotel down by the beach that may have space left over from its tour-group commitments is *Seven Islands* (☎0663/63 129; ④).

There are a number of good **restaurants** on Aharávi's main drag, among them the *Pump House* steak and pasta joint, which also offers a wide range of Italian, German and Greek dishes. There's a similarly catholic choice at *Gloo Gloo* (only ask them the meaning of the name if you've got time on your hands), and the traditional *psistariés Chris's* and *George's* are also recommended. A few hundred metres out of town towards Ródha, the smaller *Young Tree* specializes in Corfiot dishes such as *sofríto* and *pastitsáda*. A couple of quieter and more traditional places to eat can be found in the old village. The bar-restaurants on the main drag tend to get quite rowdy at night, although the light and airy *Captain's Bar*, where the counter is actually the owner's old *kaïki*, is a pleasant place to drink. For a quieter drink still, head for the leafy awning of the friendly *Vevaiotis kafenío* in the old village.

Ródha

Where Aharávi pulls up short of overdevelopment, **RÓDHA** has tipped over into it, and can't really be recommended to the independent traveller. Its central crossroads has all the charm of a motorway service station, and the beach, though an extension of Aharávi's, is rocky in parts and swampy to the west. "Old Ródha", as the signposts call it, is a small triangular warren of alleys between the main road and the seafront, where you'll find the best **restaurants and bars**: the *Taverna Agra*, oldest in Ródha, overlooking the beach, is the best for fish, and both the *Rodha Star Taverna* and *New Harbour* are also recommended. For bars, try *Nikos* near the *Agra* and the upmarket bar-club *Skouna*.

For **accommodation**, try the Anglo-Greek NSK UK Travel (☎0663/63 471, fax 63 274; UK office ☎01792 790662), which offers a wide range of rooms, villas and apartments, and also rents cars. Nostos Travel on the seafront (☎0663/64 601, fax 64 602; ③) rents basic rooms and handles car rental, as does Spitias Travel (☎0663/63 014, fax 63 974). The large *Hotel Afroditi* (☎0663/63 147, fax 63 125; ④) has decently priced en-suite rooms with sea views, and the English-run *Roda Inn* (☎0663/63 358, UK ☎01332/776 353; ③) is also on the seafront and remarkably good value. The one campsite, *Rodha Beach Camping* (☎0663/63 120 or 63 209, fax 63 081) has had a new lease of life after a change of management; the main disadvantage to its otherwise ideal shady setting on the east of Ródha is that it is the best part of a kilometre gently uphill from the beach. Yuko and Myron's by the crossroads rent bicycles, useful for exploring this relatively flat region.

Sidhári and Avliótes

The next notable resort, **SIDHÁRI**, is expanding rapidly under the influence of travel companies such as Thomson and First Choice. It has a small but pretty town square, with a bandstand set in a small garden, but this is lost in a welter of bars, snack joints and some very well-stocked shops. It's extremely popular with British package visitors, whose presence makes it a busy and fairly noisy party resort most nights.

The main beach is sandy but not terribly clean, and many people tend to head west to the various coves near Sidhári's star attraction, the direly named **Canal d'Amour**. This area is noted for its coves walled by wind-carved sandstone cliffs, which give the coastline a curious, almost science fiction landscape. One of these coves was once almost enclosed as a cave, and local legend claimed that if a woman swam its length she would win the man of her dreams. Erosion has completely reshaped the channel, but it has become known as the Canal d'Amour, and many local tour operators offer "romantic" evening cruises there. The nickname may have something to do with its reputation – at least in local rumour – as the setting for some fairly scandalous late-night parties in recent years. A more functional, and probably more enjoyable watery experience is provided by Sidhári's much-advertised water slide (2500dr), away from the beach off the main road.

There is little about Sidhári that will captivate the first-time visitor, although it gets its fair share of returnees. The main reason the independent traveller would probably want to visit or stay is en route to the **Dhiapóndia islands** to the northwest. Day-trips to Mathráki, Othoní and Erikoússa (see p.115) tend to leave weekday mornings at around 9am, so unless you're able to catch the 5.30am Sidhári bus from Corfu Town, your only option is to stay in the area. The boats are run by Nearchos Seacruises (☎0663/95 248) and cost around 5000dr return per person.

Practicalities

Kostas Fakiolas at the *Scorpion* café-bar at the west end of the main road (☎0663/95 046; ②) and Nikolaos Korakianitis' mini-market on the main road (☎0663/95 058; ③) are the best sources of **rooms**. Princess Travel (☎0663/95 667; ② and up) and Alkinoos Travel (☎0663/95 012 or 95 550; ② and up) also have good-value rooms in town, while Dhimitris Vlasseros can offer larger self-catering apartments, with a snack bar and pool (☎0663/95 313, fax 95 737; ④). The biggest accommodation agency in Sidhári is run by can-do young tycoon Philip Vlasseros, whose Vlasseros Travel (☎0663/95 695 or 95 062) also handles car rental and a boggling range of excursions, including horse-riding. Sidhári's **campsite**, *Dolphin Camping* (☎0663/31 522), is quite a walk inland from the T-junction at the western end of the main drag. The site is small and pleasant, with cleaning facilities and a shop, and is positioned to avoid the worst of Sidhári's night-time noise. An even quieter alternative, about 2km east near **Karousádhes**, a sizeable but unspoilt village with shops and a few cafés and tavernas, is *Karoussades Camping* (☎ & fax 0663/31 415), which has ample shade and some bungalows (②).

Eating in Sidhári is often an event for which people dress up, but more to flash their tanned bodies than to look smart: most restaurants are pitched at those looking for a great night out rather than a quiet meal in a taverna. The *Olympic* is the oldest taverna in Sidhári, but has sold out and provides ersatz folk entertainment most evenings. Quieter are the traditional *Diamond* and *Sea Breeze* tavernas, while the *Romana* pizzeria is recommended for simple refuelling, a function also supplied by numerous *souvláki joints*. The British influence means that full cooked breakfasts are dirt cheap in many of these and other snack bars. It also means that English ale, though too chilled and questionably kept, is easy to come by, although Sidhári is certainly not the place to go for a quiet drink. If you have the urge to join in raucous choruses of "Three Lions" though, it's just the ticket. Among the **nightclubs** that vie for your custom, the *Remezzo* and the dodgily named *Ecstasy* have been surpassed in popularity by the trendy *Caesar's*.

Avliótes

The Sidhári bus usually continues to **AVLIÓTES**, a handsome hill town with bars and tavernas but few other concessions to tourism. Avliótes is noteworthy for two reasons, however: its accessibility to the quieter beaches below Perouládhes just over a kilometre away, which make a welcome alternative to the rather cramped sandstone coves of Sidhári; and the fact that Áyios Stéfanos (see p.101) on the west coast is under half an hour's walk from here, downhill through lovely olive groves.

Paleokastrítsa and the west coast

The northwest of Corfu conceals some of the island's most dramatic coastal scenery and, in the interior, violent mountainscapes jutting out of verdant countryside. Its resorts are fairly developed, though not on the same scale as the north and east coasts, probably because the craggy northwestern landscape just doesn't have much accessible terrain. Further down the west coast, the landscape opens out to reveal long sandy beaches such as delightful Myrtiótissa and the backpackers' haven of Áyios Górdhis. Given the structure of the bus system, travel along the west coast is at best haphazard: virtually all buses ply dedicated routes from Corfu Town, only rarely linking resorts.

Paleokastrítsa

PALEOKASTRÍTSA is the honeypot of the west coast, with hotels
spreading so far up into the surrounding area that some are a taxi ride
from town. The village itself is small, surrounded by dramatic hills and
cliffs – an idyllic setting which led British High Commissioner Sir
Frederic Adam to popularize Paleokastrítsa in the nineteenth century.
It has been suggested as a possible site of the Homeric city of Scheria,
where Odysseus was washed ashore, discovered by Nausicaa and her
handmaidens and welcomed by her father King Alcinous, although
this is a claim shared by a number of other sites in the islands. The
thirteenth-century **Paleokastrítsa monastery** overlooks the town,
and a circuitous 6km or so north is the **Angelókastro** castle, one of
the most impressive ruins on the island.

Unfortunately, these days – at least in high season – Paleokastrítsa
has a mean and even grasping air about it. This is probably due to the
intensity of commerce in such a confined space, but there's an attitude about parts of Paleokastrítsa that is almost hostile. Some businesspeople are plainly contemptuous of visitors, although this is
counterbalanced by displays of *filoxenía* elsewhere.

Accommodation

Accommodation is at a premium in Paleokastrítsa, both in terms of price

*If you opt to
stay in
Paleokastrítsa,
you may find
room owners
reluctant to let
for less than
a week,
especially in
high season.*

and sheer availability. However, there are good-value independent
rooms for rent above Alipa beach on the road down into Paleokastrítsa:
try at the *Dolphin Snackbar* (☎0663/41 035; ④), Spyros and Theodora
Mihalas (☎0663/41 485 or 41 643; ③) or George Bakiras at the *Green
House* (☎0663/41 311 or 41 328; ③). Above the centre, past Nikos'
Bikes, the friendly Korina family also have rooms (☎0663/44 0641; ④),
while *Villa Grigoris* (☎0663/41 260; ③) is nice quiet alternative, but
some way removed from the sea at the start of the Lákones road.
Alternatively, some room owners have formed the misleadingly named
Paleokastritsa Tourism Information Office (☎0663/41 673), which
rents out a wide range of accommodation in and around town, from an
office on the road outside Paleokastrítsa. The town's **campsite**, imagi-
natively named *Paleokastritsa Camping* (☎0663/41 204, fax 41 104),
is just off the main road into town, a ten-minute walk from the centre, but
has a restaurant, shop and bike rental.

Hotels in Paleokastrítsa tend to be in the upper grades, and to
cater for package tourism. A reasonable independent exception, easily accessible from the town, is the small, family-run *Odysseus*
(☎0663/41 209 or 22 280, fax 41 342; ⑤), a mid-range hotel with
pool, restaurant and sea views. The first-class *Akrotiri Beach Hotel*
(☎0663/41 237 or 41 275, fax 41 277; ⑦) has rooms aside from its
block bookings, is friendly and unpretentious for such a large, modern hotel and is accessible on foot. The more modest *Paleo Inn*
(☎0663/41 101–2 or 41 204; ④), with simple but comfortable
rooms, may also be able to fit you in.

The beaches and boat trips

The focal point of modern Paleokastrítsa is a large car park on the seafront, which backs onto the longest and least attractive of three town **beaches**, home to sea taxis and *kaïkia*, and plagued by flurries of wind-borne sand. The second, to the right of the main beach and signed by flags for Mike's Ski Club, is preferable, a stony beach with clear water. The best of the three, however, is Ambelákia a small, relatively secluded strand reached along the path from the *Astakos Taverna*. Protected by surrounding cliffs, it's undeveloped apart from the German-run Korfu-Diving Centre (☎0663/41 604) at the end of the cove. The centre runs daily trips (bar Saturdays) for beginners and advanced divers to more than twenty sites, taking in reefs, arches, canyons and caves. It can also offer night dives, cave diving and advanced training.

From the beach in front of the main car park, **boat trips**, starting at around 2000dr per person for half an hour, leave for the Blue Grottoes, a trip worth taking for the spectacular coastal views alone. These trips also serve as a taxi service (3000dr for drop-off and later pick-up) to three neighbouring beaches, Áyii Triánda, Platákia and Alípa, each a pebbly strand over blue water, and served by beach bars and snack bars on the slopes above.

Paleokastrítsa monastery

On the rocky bluff above the beaches, the beautiful, whitewashed **Paleokastrítsa monastery** (also known as the Theotókos monastery) is believed to have been established in the thirteenth century, though the current buildings date from the eighteenth. It's a favourite with coach parties and, despite being within walking distance of the town's main car park below, has had to have traffic lights installed to ease the flow of vehicles up and down the bluff.

Paleokastrítsa monastery is open daily 7am–1pm & 3–8pm; free, donations welcome. Go early or near either closing time to avoid the crowds.

The small monastery church, set amidst an attractive complex of courtyards, archways, monks' cells, oil presses and storerooms, has a number of impressive **icons**, including depictions of St George and the dragon and an atmospheric Last Judgement, while the ceiling features a woodcarving of the Tree of Life. There's also a museum, resplendent with further icons, most notably a beautiful Dormition of the Virgin Mary, jewel-encrusted silver-bound Bibles and other impedimenta of Greek Orthodox ritual, as well as a curious "sea monster", with very large vertebrae and tusks, said to have been killed by fishermen in the last century. The real highlight, however, is the beautiful paved gardens, which afford spectacular views over the coastline.

The Angelókastro

Paleokastrítsa's castle, the **Angelókastro**, perched dramatically on an impossibly abrupt if diminutive peak, is in fact around 6km from town, up the coast. There are short-cut paths through open country

*At the time of
writing
Angelókastro
was closed for
repairs. Check
that it has
reopened to
avoid a long
hike only to view
it from afar.*

from Paleokastrítsa, but the main approach, and certainly the only one by car, involves doubling back to the Lákones turning and heading for the village of Makrádhes, a route with some of the finest views in the region, and cafés such as the *Bella Vista* to enjoy them from. **Makrádhes** itself is a pleasant little village built in the Venetian style, with a curious tradition of roadside stalls whose energetic owners could probably sell refrigerators to Eskimos. The route to the *kástro* leaves the smaller, dead-end hamlet of Kríni. Angelókastro is only approachable by path (the walk from the car park takes about 30min), but the ruined castle has stunning, almost circular views of the surrounding sea and land – presumably why its Byzantine builders and later Venetian developers chose the site. Indeed, the Angevins of Naples held out here for the best part of a year when the Venetians took over the rest of the island in 1386, and the fortress remained unbreached during the brief but destructive Turkish invasions of 1537, 1571 and 1716. On a clear day, it's possible to see Corfu Town some 25km away; however, little remains of the fort except for parts of the main walls. The only structures left within are a vaulted underground cistern, the small church of the Archangels Michael and Gabriel and the tiny cave chapel of Ayía Kyriakí, which still has some original frescoes.

Eating and nightlife

There isn't a huge choice of **restaurants** in the centre of Paleokastrítsa, considering the number of visitors the town entertains. The *Astakos Taverna* and *Corner Grill* are two traditional places, the former with the rather unusual habit of closing early in the siesta. *Il Pirata* has a raised balcony with sea views and offers a wide range of Italian and Greek dishes, including local seafood. Beachside restaurants tend to suffer from the same problem of windborne sand as the beach itself, but the largest, the curiously named *Smurfs*, has awnings to beat the winds and an excellent, if expensive, fish menu, featuring live trout and salmon, which you can choose from tanks. Also recommended are the very smart *St Georges on the Rock*, and the restaurant of the *Odysseus Hotel*.

Nightlife hangouts include the restaurant-bars in the centre, and those straggling up the hill towards Lákones. By the Lákones turning is Paleokastrítsa's one nightclub, *The Paleo Club*, a small disco-bar with a garden, which opens and closes late.

Áyios Yeóryios and Aríllas

ÁYIOS YEÓRYIOS is reached by road via the village of Troumbétas and, before that, the hill town of **Skriperó**. One of the largest settlements in the interior, it has few facilities beyond the shops, tavernas and bars used by townspeople; it is worth a stop, however, to see how island life proceeds away from the tourism racket. Like many of the west coast resorts, Áyios Yeóryios isn't actually based around a village (it's not to be confused with the Áyios Yeóryios near the island's southern tip). The resort has developed in response to the popularity of its three-kilometre sandy bay, which cuts deep into the land between Cape Aríllas to the north and Cape Falákron to the south. It's a major **windsurfing** centre, with schools and rental companies on the beach, and tends to be quite busy even in low season. There are several good **hotels**, among them the *Alkyon Beach Hotel* (☎0663/96 222; ⑤), the *Chrisi Akti* (☎0663/96 482; ④) and the slightly cheaper *San Giorgio* (☎0663/96 213; ④), some rooms, such as *Studio Elena* (☎0663/96 366; ③), and *San George* campsite (☎ & fax 0663/51 759), back towards Kavvadhádhes, but unless you're after a watersports holiday, with little to do at night, Áyios Yeóryios is best visited as a day-trip. The village of Afiónas at the north end of the bay has been suggested as the likely site of **King Alcinous' castle** – there are vestigial Neolithic remains outside the village – and the walk up to the lighthouse on Cape Arílas has excellent views both over Áyios Yeóryios and Arílas bay to the north.

ARÍLLAS, a small settlement in the neighbouring bay, has a long beach of pebble and firm sand, inferior to the great sweep of sand at Áyios Stéfanos in the next bay but less crowded. It is an up-and-coming resort nonetheless, and has reached the balance between lack of development and choice of facilities that some find just right. Of the increasing **accommodation** options, the *Akti Arilla* (☎51 201 or 51 206, fax 51 221, email *aktiaril@otenet.gr*; ⑤) is a smart modern hotel whose rooms have sea-facing balconies, the *Villa Mitsis* (☎0663/51 943; ③) is a more modest pension, while Arillas Travel (☎0663/51 280 or 51 380, fax 51 381) has a fair range of rooms and apartments. The *Lambada* taverna and *Arilas Inn* provide tasty waterside dining possibilities, while inland the *Calypso*, *Brouklis* and *Rainbow* restaurants all have wide menus of fish, meat and favourite starters. Laid-back cocktail sipping is encouraged by the presence of the *Coconut* and *Malibu* bars, adjacent to each other just off the front. The barren rocky **islets** of Kraviá, Yinéka and Sykiá out to sea are yet another on the list of places claiming to be the petrified remains of Odysseus' ship.

Áyios Stéfanos

The most northerly of the west coast's resorts, and the most distant from Corfu Town, **ÁYIOS STÉFANOS** is a family-oriented resort that's still very low-key, even in high season, despite a tourist presence going back some decades. It takes its name from the beautiful eighteenth-century **chapel** dedicated to that saint at the southerly end of the village. Gentle hills give onto a large sandy beach, although there's a small marshy area at the centre of the beach with a stream running into the sea; given Corfiot farming techniques, this might spell chemicals. The terrain militates against too much development; the bay is tucked into an amphitheatrical hillside that precludes any further building. There is not much to do here, which is probably one of the place's strengths, and it would make a quiet base from which to explore the northwest and the Dhiapóndia islands, visible on the sea horizon. Day-trips to Mathráki, Othoní and Erikoússa (see p.115), run regularly in season, and cost around 5000dr per person.

Its distance from any major settlements – and hence from any major traffic flow – makes Áyios Stéfanos a particularly good base for walking. As well as Avliótes and Perouládhes to the north, Magouládhes – which boasts one of the area's finest village tavernas – 3km to the east and other small villages in the gently rolling hinterland are well within hiking distance of Áyios Stéfanos.

Practicalities

Áyios Stéfanos's longest-standing **hotel**, the *Nafsika* (☎0663/51 051, fax 51 112; ④), is a pleasant, purpose-built structure with en-suite rooms and balconies overlooking the sea. It has a large restaurant on the ground floor, a favourite with villagers, and gardens with a pool and bar. In recent years, it has been joined by the twinned *Thomas Bay* (☎0663/51 353 or 51 767, fax 51 913; ⑤) and *Romanza* hotels (☎0661/22 873, fax 41 878; ⑤), upmarket places with pools, cocktail bars, tennis courts and, in the *Romanza*, self-catering apartments. Both take block bookings from package operators, but keep some rooms free throughout the season.

For those on a tighter budget, the gift shop of Peli and Maria, on the northern edge of the village, offers bargain purpose-built **rooms** (☎0663/51 424; ②), as does the Margarita supermarket (☎0663/51 910; ③), while the *Restaurant Evnios* (☎0663/51 766; ③) and *Hotel Olga* (☎0663/71 252; ③) have apartments on a rise above the village with excellent views over bay and open sea. A number of travel agencies handle accommodation, among them San Stefanos (☎0663/51 771, fax 51 910) and Mouzakitis Travel in the centre (be warned, however, that virtually everyone in Áyios Stéfanos is called Mouzakitis).

Besides the *Nafsika*, good options for **eating** include the large, varied menu at the *Golden Beach Taverna*, and the *Waves Taverna*, which is ideal for lunches on the beach. The *Taverna O Manthos*, with a garden above the beach, serves Corfiot specialities such as *sofríto* and *pastitsáda*, and has a barbecue. *Margarita's* restaurant in the village has good snacks, sweets and ice cream as well as standard meals. For **nightlife**, there's a pair of lively music bars, the *Condor* and the *Athens*, in the centre of the village, plus the small but smart *Enigma* nightclub, towards the chapel.

Érmones

ÉRMoNES, the first major settlement south of Paleokastrítsa, is one of the busiest resorts on the island. Its lush green bay is backed by the mountains above the Ropa river, which empties into the sea here.

The beach is a mix of gravel and sand, often hectic with water-sports activities, and the seabed shelves quite steeply, making it ideal for good swimmers but not for children or uncertain swimmers.

The resort is dominated by the extensive grounds of the upmarket *Ermones Beach* **hotel** (☎0661/94 241; ⑦), which was the first place in the archipelago to provide its guests with a small funicular railway down the cliff to the beach (it rather scars the view). More reasonable accommodation can be found near the beach at the *Pension Katerina* and *Georgio's Villas*. Further back from the shore, it is also possible to stay at the *Athena Ermones Golf* (☎0661/94 226; ⑤), attached to the Corfu Golf and Country Club, the only golf club in the archipelago, and said to be the finest in the Mediterranean. Head for *George's* **taverna** above the beach for some of the best Greek food here: the *mezédhes* are often enough for a meal in themselves. For a drink, you can't beat the *Morrison Café*, with its spacious garden by the sea and an appealing mix of rock, ethnic and jazz music.

Myrtiótissa and Vátos

Far preferable to Érmones are the sandy beaches just south, at Myrtiótissa and Glyfádha. Half a century ago, in *Prospero's Cell*, Lawrence Durrell described **Myrtiótissa** as "perhaps the loveliest beach in the world" – though he qualified that by adding that the sand has the consistency of tapioca. Difficult to reach down a path from Vátos (see below), it's been a long-guarded secret among aficionados, a shallow, safe strand with rollers, spotted with vast boulders and overlooked by tall, tree-covered cliffs. Nowadays, however, the secret has been passed on to more than enough people to fill the beach on a summer's day. Nudists and freelance campers now have to share the sand with the increasing numbers who risk the steep clamber down, or invade from the sea on day-trip boats from nearby resorts such as Glyfádha. There are also a couple of refreshment stalls and sunshade concessions. The charm of the place hasn't been entirely swamped, but it's best visited at either end of the day or out of high season entirely. Above the beach is the tiny whitewashed **Myrtiótissa monastery**, dedicated to Our Lady of the Myrtles, which is open in the daytime and has a curious little gift shop attached.

The small village of **VÁTOS** has a couple of tavernas, a disco and rooms, and is on the Glyfádha bus route from Corfu Town. Spyros Kousounis, owner of the *Olympic Restaurant and Grill* (☎0661/94 318; ③), has rooms and apartments, as does Prokopis Himarios (☎0661/94 503; ②), who is next to the *Dhoukakis* café-minimarket in the traditional centre of the village. The steep, half-hour path to Myrtiótissa beach is signposted just beyond the extremely handy, if basic, *Vatos Camping* (☎0661/94 393).

Glyfádha and Pélekas

GLYFÁDHA is thoroughly dominated by the *Louis Grand* (☎0661/94 140–5, fax 94 146; ⑦), a large A-class hotel in its own spacious grounds, with a residents-only pool and a bar and restaurant open to non-residents. The hotel, which takes up a good quarter of the available beachfront, is used by the major package-tour operators, but has rooms for independent travellers throughout the season. There's another hotel at the far north end of the bay, the *Hotel Glifada Beach* (☎0661/94 258; ⑤), an upgraded but still family-run affair with en-suite rooms and balconies overlooking the beach, and set away from the action to avoid most of the noise. Its owners, the Megas family, also have a fine traditional taverna attached to the hotel. Most of the other accommodation at Glyfádha is block-booked by tour operators – this is a very popular family beach – but the *Gorgona* pool bar and *Restaurant Michaelis* might have rooms. There's another, unnamed, family taverna midway along the beach, while nightlife centres on two music bars, the *Kikiriko* and *Aloha*, both of which open onto the beach and have a habit of pumping loud rival music out all day. At night, however, Glyfádha begins to look slightly tacky, and with a five-kilometre hike uphill just to reach tiny Vátos, you really are stuck here.

The attractive hilltop village of PÉLEKAS, 2km inland from Glyfádha, has long been popular for its views – particularly at sunset – and for its welcome summer breezes. A thirty-minute walk along the Glyfádha road is the **Kaiser's Throne**, a small viewing tower with sweeping views of the coast in both directions, that was Wilhelm II's favourite spot on the entire island. However, Pélekas is fast getting spoilt, with new developments beginning to swamp the town. There are still some good **hotels**, including the elegant, upmarket *Pelekas* (☎0661/94 230; ⑥) and the friendlier, more budget-oriented *Nikos* (☎0661/94 486; ③), as well as rooms at the *Alexandros* taverna (☎0661/94 215; ③). Lina's Travel (☎0661/94 580, fax 94 694) can also help find accommodation, including the economical *Villa Natassa* (②). Out towards the Kaiser's Throne, the *Sunset Hotel* (☎0661/94 230; ⑦) is a top-class establishment, with views out over the sea and coastline which are unlikely to be bettered anywhere else on the island. Its restaurant, whose balcony shares the view, is open to non-guests. Among **tavernas**, the *Alexandros* and *Roula's Grill House* are highly recommended. Just above Pélekas towards Kaiser's Throne, the cosy *Vavel* bar is reckoned by knowledgeable musicophiles to be the best place on the island for jazz and eclectic rock.

Pélekas's long, sandy **beach** can be reached down a small path; quieter neighbouring Kondós Yialós beach is down another path, signposted off the road to Corfu Town. At the former, *Maria's Place* is an excellent family-run **taverna** with a reputation for the fish caught daily by the owner's husband, Costas. There are **rooms** above the taverna (☎0661/94 601; ③), and at *Tolis Rooms* (☎0661/94 059; ②), 50m back from the beach. Sadly, the scenic nature of the beach has been rather spoilt by the monstrous new *Pelekas Beach* hotel that now looms over it.

Sinarádhes and around

The mountainous interior behind this central stretch of the west coast conceals some picturesque villages, well worth touring if you have your own wheels or a passion for walking. Places such as **Kouromádhes** and **Varypatádhes** are full of character, with arche-typal country churches, stone houses crowded into narrow streets, the odd old-time *kafenío* and a sense of Corfiot life long lost at the coastal resorts. This atmosphere of days gone by is best reflected in **SINARÁDHES**, which has the **Folk Museum of Central Corfu**. The museum comprises an authentic village house, complete with original furniture, fittings and decoration and full of articles and utensils that formed an intrinsic part of daily rural life. South of Sinarádhes, at a high point in the road that winds south to Áyios Górdhis, the bright *Aerostato* café is a great spot at which to enjoy a drink or snack while admiring the sweeping coastal views its name (Air Balloon) promises.

The Folk Museum of Central Corfu is open Tues–Sat 9.30am–2.30pm; free.

Áyios Górdhis and Áyii Dhéka

Around 7km south of Pélekas, **ÁYIOS GÓRDHIS** is one of the key play beaches on the island, largely because of the activities organized by the startling **Pink Palace** complex (☎0661/53 103 or 53 104, fax 53 025, email *pink-palace@ker.forthnet.gr*; ①) which fairly dominates the resort. The beach itself is one of the finest on the island, a long, sandy strand backed by pine-clad hills. The *Pink Palace*, covering much of the hillside, has swimming pools, games courts, restaurants, a shop and disco, and some seventy staff to run beach sports and other activities. It's hugely popular with backpackers, who cram into communal rooms for up to ten (although smaller rooms, and singles, are also available) for a bargain 6000dr a night including breakfast and evening meal. People booking for four or more days also get free scooter hire. Other accommodation is available on the beach, notably at the quieter *Pension Dandidis* (☎0661/53 232, fax 53 183; ④) or *Michael's Place* taverna (☎0661/53 041; ③) at the end of the beach road. Rooms can also be found here and elsewhere on the island through the large and efficient Karoukas Travel (☎0661/53 909, fax 53 887), which also handles excursions and vehicle rental. Apart from *Michael's Place*, the neighbouring *Alex-in-the-Garden* **restaurant** is also a favourite.

Inland from the resort, about half way to Benítses on the east coast, is the south's largest prominence, the humpback of **Áyii Dhéka**, at 576 metres officially a mountain. Reached by path from the hamlet of Áno Garoúna (signposted at Káto Garoúna on the inland road between Áyios

Górdhis and Paramónas), the mountain is the island's second largest after Pandokrátor. The lower slopes are wooded, and it's possible to glimpse buzzards wheeling on thermals over the high slopes. Its peak affords panoramic views across the south and to the mainland. Those with the stamina – and a good map and a compass – might consider following the path that leads from the summit down into the village of Áyii Dhéka and on to Benítses, whose regular bus connections to Corfu Town make this a viable, if taxing, day's hike from Áyios Górdhis.

Pendáti, Paramónas and Áyios Mathéos

Around 2km south of Áyios Górdhis as the crow flies, but reached by a country lane skirting around the hills for 5km, the fishing hamlet of **PENDÁTI** sits on a narrow coastal plateau 200m above sea level. Small, winding tracks north and south of the hamlet lead down to tiny inlets from where the local fishermen ply their trade. There is hardly any accommodation in the village, but *Angela's* café and minimarket and the *Strofi* grill cater to villagers and the few tourists who stray here.

Walkers and careful drivers are recommended the four-kilometre coastal road between here and **PARAMÓNAS**, which is still only partially surfaced but affords excellent views over the coastline. Paramónas itself is slightly larger than Pendáti, but still has only a few businesses geared to tourism. Situated on sandy Makroúla Bay, the hamlet is, however, beginning to develop an infrastructure: the *Paramonas* (☎0661/76 595–6, fax 75 686; ⑤) is a smart modern **hotel** a little way back from the beach; the *Paramonas Bridge* restaurant (☎0661/75 761; ②), by the small ford through the stream that bisects the beach, has **rooms and apartments** to rent, as does Dina Merianou (☎0661/75 185; ③) at various locations around the village; finally, the *Areti Studios* (☎0661/75 838; ③) on the road in from Pendáti are quiet and reasonable. For eats, the *Sun-set* taverna has a wide menu and specializes in freshly caught fish.

The town of **ÁYIOS MATHÉOS**, 3km inland and shadowed by Mount Prasoúdhi, is chiefly an agricultural centre, and has little truck with tourism. Its narrow main road is often thronged with local traffic – so much so that visiting motorists have had their vehicles manhandled aside to allow the Corfu Town bus to pass. There is still no noticeable accommodation in the town, although a number of **kafenía and tavernas**, still unused to tourism, offer a warm if bemused welcome to passers-by: head for the *Mouria* snack bar-grill, or the modern *Steki*, which maintains the tradition of spiriting tasty *mezédhes* onto your table unasked.

On the other side of Mount Prasoúdhi, 2km by road, is the **Gardhíki Pýrgos**, the ruins of a thirteenth-century castle built in this unlikely lowland setting by the Despots of Epirus. Little remains of the castle apart from its outer walls and traces of frescoes in the southernmost of the eight towers that constituted the whole, but at the time of writing work was in progress to open the building to the public. Just off the road south of the castle, a large cave, now empty, was the site of some of the oldest archeological finds on the island, dated back to the Paleolithic age. The road continues on to the northernmost tip of the beach on the sea edge of the Korissíon lagoon (see p.112). Paleokastrítsa and the west coast

Benítses and the south

Corfu's southeast coast was the first to develop tourism on the island back in the 1960s, and became synonymous with some of the worst excesses of package tourism, in terms of both tacky development and the behaviour of some visitors. There are still echoes of this at **Kávos**, which is almost entirely given over to beach, bar and (if you're lucky) bonking, but the early-1990s slump in tourism wrought many changes. Ten years ago, the idea of casting even a sympathetic eye at **Benítses** would have been unthinkable. Yet the crowds of drunks and people screwing in the streets have vanished (or moved to Kávos), and the second half of the 1990s has seen the resort spruce itself up and regain popularity as a family destination. Towards the southern tip, **Lefkími**, Corfu's second largest town and capital of the south, is a functional but not unappealing place that is sadly often overlooked.

Rooms are plentiful thoughout the lower half of the island, although at the time of writing there was, unfortunately, no operational campsite south of Corfu Town. **Beaches** along this stretch of coast, at least as far as Messongí, tend to be narrow pebble or stone and, near the centres of habitation, water quality can be doubtful. Unfortunately, the best beach on this side involves running the gauntlet of Kávos for its two-kilometre stretch of sand. Beyond Messongí, the road south turns inland, and is more or less equidistant from the coasts, putting spectacular beaches such as Íssos and those bordering the **Korissíon lagoon** on the southwest-facing shore within easy reach. The lagoon itself provides the south's natural highlight.

Benítses

Heading south from Corfu Town, there's little point in recommending anything much before **BENÍTSES**: accommodation in the suburb of Pérama and on the edge of the swamps around the Halikópoulou lagoon is just too close to the airport and its approach paths. Once you reach Benítses, you'll still see signs of its grim heyday – the southern end still boasts music bars such as *B52s* and *Alcoholics Anonymous* – but the old town at the north end has reverted to a quiet, whitewashed, bougainvillea-splashed Greek village with a long landscaped square cushioning much of it from the busy thoroughfare. A few minutes' walk through the alleys of the old town and you're in thick woodland with streams. Benítses' beach, however, is at best serviceable; most people congregate on the small spit of land below the *Hotel Corfu Maris* at the southern end of town.

There's little to see in Benítses, beyond some small, and rather disappointing, Roman remains, a small corner of a bathhouse buried in weeds behind fences at the back of the village and the curious **Shell Museum**, on the main road north of the village (daily 10am–9 pm; 1000dr). This contains over two thousand items of shell, coral and skeleton, and is a little tacky, but worth a quick peek.

Practicalities

Rooms are plentiful in Benítses, but often rented through agencies. Bargain Travel (☎0661/72 137, fax 72 031; ③ and up) and All Tourist (☎0661/72 223; ③ and up), both in the heart of the village, have decently priced options in and around the village. With visitor numbers still not back to the levels of yore, however, some **hotels** are almost as cheap. The *Corfu Maris* (☎0661/72 035 or 72 129; ④), on the beach at the southern end of town, has modern en-suite rooms with balconies and views, while the *Hotel Benitsa* and neighbouring *Agis* in the centre (both ☎0661/39 269 or 92 248; ③) can offer quiet rooms, also en suite, set back from the main road; the *Benitsa* was the first hotel in the resort, and is still owned by the friendly, Anglophone Spinoulas family. Another cheapie is the *Eros* (☎0661/72 083 or 72393; ③), whose name harks back to days when youth arrived in search of erotic adventures. Seemingly conceived as an ironic tilt at the nearby Achillíon, the larger *Hotel Potamaki* (☎0661/71 140 or 72 201, fax 72 451; ⑤) revels in eye-popping Neoclassical detail in its large courtyard bar-restaurant and interior halls, although the en-suite rooms, most with views, are more demure.

Above the coast road 2km north of Benítses is one of the smartest hotels on the island, the *San Stefano* (☎0661/71 117 or 71 123, fax 72 272; ⑦), a vast, international ziggurat-style hotel with pools, restaurants and its own kilometre-long access road, as well as a patch of private beach ten minutes' walk below. Also worthy of note, on the road to the Achillíon just north of the *San Stefano* – though a steep 2km from the sea – is the quiet *Hotel Montagnola* (☎0661/56 205 or 56 789; ⑥), with pool, tennis court, restaurant and en-suite rooms with sea views.

Benítses always catered to a free-spending crowd, and it has its fair share of decent if not particularly cheap **tavernas**, notably *La Mer de Corfu* and the Corfiot specialist, *Spyros*, as well as the plush *Marabou*, which specializes in steaks, seafood, pasta and north European dishes. There's also a curiously popular hybrid of Chinese, Indian and Greek in the extravagantly decorated *Flower Garden*, and decent pizzas and pasta at *Bravo*. The **bars** at the southern end of town are still fairly lively at night, despite new rules controlling the all-night excesses, and the *Stadium* **nightclub** still opens most nights. If you're looking for a quiet drink, head for the north end of the village, away from the traffic.

Moraïtika and Messongí

The coast road south of Benítses is speckled with rooms and small hotels above scraps of beach, although negotiating any length of this road on foot can be a nightmare due to the traffic. The next two resorts of any note, Moraïtika and Messongí, have now more or less merged into one. **MORAÍTIKA'S** main street is an ugly strip of bars, restaurants and shops you could find anywhere in the islands, but the beach behind it is the best between Corfu Town and Kávos, a mixture of shingle and sand, and very busy in high season. The usual range of wind sports is on offer, as well as a small water slide, with chutes made of soft plastic, which charges an exorbitant 3000dr per hour.

Much accommodation is block-booked for families on package tours, but there are **rooms** for independent travellers between the main road and beach, and up above the main road, all within a minute or two of the centre: try Alekos Bostis (☎0661/75 637; ③) or Kostas Vlahos (☎0661/55 350; ③), both near the beach, or the smarter *Golden Keys* (☎066175 598, fax 76 404; ④) above the main road. For a wider range, it's worthwhile trying the G & S Moraitika Tourist Centre (☎0661/75 723 or 30 977, fax 76 682) and Budget Ways Travel (☎0661/75 664 or 76 768, fax 75 664), which both offer rooms from 8000dr upwards. Reasonable beach-side **hotels** likely to have space for the independent traveller include the *Margarita Beach* (☎ & fax 0661/76 267; ⑤) and the *Three Stars* (☎0661/92 457; ④), both of which have comfortable en-suite rooms with balconies, some with sea views. Much of the main drag is dominated by souvenir shops and minimarkets, as well as a range of **bars**: flash joints like *Scorpion, Crocodile, Rainbow* and *Cotton Club*, and the village's oldest surviving bar, *Charlie's*, which opened in 1939. *Islands* **restaurant** on the main drag is recommended for its mix of good vegetarian, Greek and international food, as is the beach restaurant named, with charming innocence, *Crabs*, where the seafood and adventurous salads are excellent.

Áno Moraïtika

The garish main drag is by no means all there is to Moraïtika: the village proper, **ÁNO MORAÍTIKA**, is signposted a few minutes' hike up the steep lanes inland, and is virtually unspoilt. Among its tiny houses and alleys, practically drowning in bougainvillea, you'll find two **tavernas**: the *Village Taverna*, with a catholic range of island specialities, and the *Bella Vista*, which offers a contrastingly limited blackboard menu, but which justifies its name with a lovely garden and view out over the coast – on hot days, it's a great place to park yourself in front of a breeze. There's little **accommodation** in the village, apart from *Corifo Apartments* (☎0661/32 891; ④) on its southern edge.

Messongí

Barely a hundred metres on from the Moraïtika seafront, **MES-SONGÍ** is disappointing even in comparison to its larger northerly neighbour: large parts of the resort are sadly moribund, and the beach is minor, a narrow tract of gravelly sand, bisected at the north end by a small river. The sand is dominated by the vast *Messonghi Beach* hotel complex (☎0661/76 684–6, fax 75 334; ⑦), one of the plushest on the island, with pools, bars and extensive grounds. Both the cheaper *Hotel Gemini* (☎0661/75 211–2, fax 75 213; ⑤) and *Pantheon Hall* (☎0661/76 906 or 75 268, fax 75 801; ④) also have pools and gardens, and en-suite rooms with balconies. *Christina's* (☎0661/75 294, fax 76 515; ④) is very popular with British tourists, who get a special deal, if booked independently, on weekly and fortnightly rates. There are good, cheap **rooms** right on the beach: contact Dinos Ramos (☎0661/75 695; ②) or the village travel agency, Pandora Travel (☎0661/75 329), which has a range of apartments and villas.

Despite several closures, Messongí still has a number of good **restaurants**, notably the *Memories Taverna*, which specializes in Corfiot dishes and serves its own barrel wine, and the upmarket *Castello*, which mixes local dishes like *sofríto*, with seafood (including mussels) and – a rarity on Corfu – asparagus. *Christina's Hotel* and the neighbouring *Rossi's* taverna have bars that open onto the beach, but a better option at night, offering seafood under the stars, is to head for the two popular beachside tavernas, *The Almond Tree* and *Sparos*, a short walk south on the road to Boúkari.

*Aryirádhes
and Perivóli
are both good
watering holes
for those
heading south,
but have few
amenities.*

Boúkari and around

The road from Messongí to **BOÚKARI** is barely used by traffic even in high season, and follows the seashore for about 3km, often only a few metres above it. The few available plots of land here have been snapped up by wealthy Greeks, whose discreet villas testify to the appeal of the area. It is out of the way, but an idyllic little strip of unspoilt coast for anyone fleeing the crowds elsewhere on the island. Inland from here is the unspoilt wooded farming region around Aryirádhes, rarely visited by tourists and a perfect place for undisturbed walks. The hamlet of Boúkari itself comprises little more than a handful of tavernas, a shop and a few small, family-run hotels. The *Boukari Beach* is the best of the **tavernas**, though it tends to attract *kaïkia* tour parties, who moor at its tiny jetty. The very friendly Vlahopoulos family who run the taverna also manage two small, smart hotels nearby: the *Boukari Beach* and *Penelopi* (☎0662/51 791 or 51 269, fax 51 792; ④), as well as good rooms attached to the taverna (③). Just back from the *Karidis Taverna* is the *Helios Hotel* (☎0662/51 824; ③), which also has a taverna.

Back on the coastline, the friendly, seemingly prosperous village of **PETRITÍ** fronts a small but busy dirt-track harbour, but in general is mercifully free of noise and commerce. In its setting among low olive-covered hills, with tree-covered rocks in the bay, Petrití would be perfect if you wanted to disappear somewhere quiet for a while. Maps claim that it has a beach, but this is a cartographic fancy: the littoral is variously bulldozed rock, thick mud and a small stretch of sand above more mud – though local children do swim in the sea

The *Pension Egrypos* (☎0662/51 949; ③) has **rooms** and a **taverna**, set back a hundred metres or so from the harbour, among trees near a beautiful white church with a large free-standing campanile. At the harbour, which is the departure point for yacht flotilla holidays, three tavernas serve the trickle of sea traffic: the smart waterfront *Limnopoula*, guarded by two handsome caged parrots, with a wide range of locally caught fish and seafood, and the more basic but friendly *Dimitris* and *Stamatis*. Some way back from the village, moored in the middle of woodlands near the hamlet of Vassilátika, is the elegant *Regina* **hotel**, with gardens and pool (☎0662/52 132, fax 52 135; ④), which specializes in full-board holidays for German tourists, but also has room-only availability.

Áyios Yeóryios and around

With its beach spreading as far south as Méga Hóro point, and north to encircle the edge of the Koríssion lagoon, **ÁYIOS YEÓRYIOS** (not to be confused with the Áyios Yeóryios just north of Paleokastrítsa) can lay claim to around 12km of uninterrupted and fairly unspoilt sand. The village itself, however, is an unprepossessing sprawl that's in danger of becoming a real mess. British package-tour operators have arrived in force, with bars and tavernas competing to present bingo, quizzes and video nights.

The *Golden Sands* (☎0662/51 225, fax 51 140; ⑤) can offer a pool, open-air restaurant and gardens, but the best **hotel** bargain, for its setting and size, has to be the smaller *Blue Sea* (☎0662/51 624, fax 51 172; ③). Much of the resort's accommodation is block-booked, even in those places that advertise rooms on street signs (no doubt hedging against the possibility of the package-tourism business going pear-shaped). The most likely place to head for in search of good **rooms** is the *Barbayiannis* taverna-bar (☎0662/52 110 or 52 377; ③) at the southern end of the strip. The Status travel agency in the centre of the main strip (☎0662/51 661) also has rooms, apartments and villas, as well as car rental. This far from Corfu Town's banks, a number of local agencies, notably the St George, offer bank-rate exchange.

Besides the *Barbayiannis*, Áyios Yeóryios has a number of good **restaurants**: *La Perla's*, mixing Greek and north European in a walled garden; the *Napoleon psistariá*; and the *Florida Cove*, a grill and barbecue taverna with a beachcomber sea theme. **Nightlife** centres around music and pool bars like the *Gold Hart* and *Traxx*, although the best bar in Áyios Yeóryios is the sea-edge *Panorama*, which has views as far south as Paxí.

Marathiá and Ayía Varvára

Approached from the interior via various access roads, the long stretch of beach south of Áyios Yeóryios is labelled either **Marathiá** or **Ayía Varvára**, depending on which sign you follow or where you come out. Burgeoning touristic settlements are in constant growth at both points, with the usual hotch-potch of characterless apartments, restaurants and bars. Both places are still quieter than Áyios Yeóryios though, so if you want to stay you could try the *Pansion Gerasimos* (☎0662/51 610 or 52 673, fax 51 602; ③) at Marathiá or the *Pension Santa Barbara* (☎0662/22 200, fax 24 941; ④) at Ayía Varvára, which has a lot of German groups and its own taverna.

Íssos beach

For further information on the Issos Beach Windsurfing School, contact, in winter in the UK, ☎015396/ 25385.

A few minutes' walk north of Áyios Yióryios, **Íssos** is by one of the best beaches in the area, a largely deserted stretch of sand and dunes; it's so quiet that the dunes that continue north of Íssos remain an unofficial nude bathing area. Further on, the beaches towards the channel that cuts into the Korissíon lagoon (which makes it impossible to circumnavigate on foot) also see very few visitors. Parts of Íssos and the Korissíon beach are turtle nesting grounds, so should be treated with due care. Avoid nests, stay off the beach at night, don't dig or use spiked beach furniture in the day and never approach a turtle, young or old, if you see one.

Facilities around Íssos are drastically limited: one **taverna**, the *Rousellis Grill* (which sometimes rents out rooms), a few hundred metres from the beach on the lane leading to Línia on the main road, and the *Friends* snack bar in Línia itself. An English-run **windsurfing school**, operating from a caravan on the beach, has a wide range of boards of different sizes for rent (starting at 3000dr an hour), as well as a beach simulator and rescue craft, and offers tuition for beginners and upwards – prevailing cross-beach winds make it a safe place to learn.

The Korissíon lagoon

Over 5km long and 1km wide at its centre, **KORISSÍON LAGOON** is in fact man-made, excavated, with a channel to the sea, by the Venetians. Now a nature reserve, Korissíon is home to turtles, tortoises, lizards and numerous indigenous and migrating birds, including ducks, waders, herons and other species that feed on wetlands. Migratory birds are more often observed towards the end of the season (even though rifle-hunting of birds is allowed in the autumn), but they can also be seen in early season as well.

The lagoon is most easily reached by walking from the village of Línia (on the Kávos bus route) via Íssos beach. An alternative route is from the north, via Khlomatianá, which brings you to an isolated inland shore at the lagoon's widest point. The best approach, however, especially if you have transport, is to the northernmost end: follow the Áyios Mathéos signs from Áno Messongí, then two left turns bring you via the Gardhíki Pýrgos (see p.106) to **Halikoúna beach**, a glorious thick wedge of sand backed by wind-blown dunes, which is even more deserted and beautiful than the southern edge of Korissíon towards Íssos.

It is possible that the south's only campsite, formerly named *Agios Matheos* (☎0662/75 069), will be up and running again by the year 2000; the site is over a kilometre inland but would make an excellent base. Some freelance camping does take place on the beach, but potential campers should make sure they stay at the very northern end of the lagoon, away from the turtle nesting grounds. Comfortable and isolated **accommodation** is available at *Marin Christel Apartments* (☎0661/75 947; ⑤), on a cliff above tiny Alonáki beach, just north of Halikoúna, and at *Logara Apartments* (☎0661/76 477; ⑤), 500m inland. There are no facilities at either beach, but a couple of tavernas on the access road provide staple meals at very fair prices.

Lefkími

Most guides either ignore or dismiss **LEFKÍMI**, but anyone interested in how a Greek town works away from the bustle of tourism should not miss it. The charm of the place, where donkeys are still occasionally used as transport and some women retain traditional costume, lies in its almost perverse resistance to tourism.

Maps distinguish between Áno Lefkími and Lefkími proper, but in fact the two flow into each other. The second largest town after Corfu, Lefkími is the administrative centre of the south of the island. While it's hardly Amsterdam, the canal that carries the Himáros river through the centre of town and the facades of the main street and surrounding alleys are very attractive. There's some fine architecture, including two striking (but usually locked) churches: **Áyios Theodóros**, whose beautiful campanile sits on a mound above a small village square, and **Áyios Arsénios**, with a vast orange dome that can be seen for miles around.

Lefkími is also the major commercial port in the south, fitted up with a startling new stretch of sodium-lit four-lane highway – once you get to the harbour, however, you'll find no facilities apart from a coffee stall that opens to serve lorry drivers awaiting boats. The half-dozen or so daily **ferries** to Igoumenítsa only take an hour to make the crossing.

There are some **rooms** at the *Cheeky Face* taverna (☎0662/22 627; ②) and the *Maria Madalena* apartments (☎0662/22 386; ②),

*Using Lefkími
as an
alternative
link with the
mainland
is worth
considering,
especially if
you're staying
in southern
Corfu; check
with the Port
Authority
(☎0662/23
277) for
timings.*

both by the bridge over the canal, but little other accommodation. A few **bars and restaurants** sit on the edge of the canal – try the *River Psistaria*. Away from the centre, the *Hermes* bar has a leafy garden, and there are a number of other good local bars where tourists are rare enough to guarantee you a friendly welcome, including the *Mersedes* and *Pacific*, and tavernas, notably *Kavouras* and *Fontana*.

Kávos and around

The mayhem of Kávos is reflected in the fact that there are no fewer than four 24-hour first aid clinics: two numbers are (☎0662/61 555 and 61 161).

The very name **KÁVOS** can make most regular island visitors – and not a few islanders – cross themselves in dread. There are no ambiguities here: either you like 24-hour drinking, clubbing, bungee-jumping, go-karts, video bars named after British sitcoms and chips with almost everything, or you should avoid the place altogether. The resort is sizeable, stretching over 2km of decent, if not particularly clean, sandy beach, with water sports, pedalos, ringoes and serried sunbeds. Sport at night consists of several goals set up in the streets for penalty shoot-out competitions and less innocent pursuits in the bars. The bulk of tourism here is package, but if you want independent **accommodation**, Britannia Travel (☎0662/61 400) and Island Holidays (☎0662/23 439) have decent, cheap rooms and apartments. The nearest to genuine Greek **food** you'll find is at the *Two Brothers Psistaria*, well away from the crowds at the south end of town. The emphasis here is on shoving down a quick hamburger or portion of fish'n'chips and hitting the bar trail. Well before midnight and for hours after it, even walking along the main drag is something of an obstacle course, so legion are the drunken bodies cavorting outside the unbroken chain of noisy rival bars. *Future* is still the biggest **club**, with imported north European DJs mixing techno and house, and these days jungle and Goa trance, followed by the ironically named *Whispers*. *JCs*, *Jungle* and *The Face* are among the more enduring **bars**, while *Wet Knickers* and *Hard On* typify the sort of cheap thrill joints that have closed up by next season. The bars are usually self-policed, but still prone to the off-their-face antics of Britons unused to Greek licensing hours. Away from the core, the hip *Jazz Bar* at the southern end of town adds a welcome note of cool.

Beyond the limits of Kávos, where few visitors stray, a path leaving the road south to the hamlet of Sparterá heads on through unspoilt countryside; after around thirty minutes it reaches the cliffs of **Cape Asprokávos** and the crumbling monastery of Panayiás, which retains its bell tower and supporting walls. The cape looks out over the straits to Paxí, 19km away, and down over deserted **Arkoudhílas beach**. The beach, however, is inaccessible from here, though it can be reached from Sparterá, 5km by road but only 3km by the signed path from Kávos. Even wilder is the beach of **Áyios Górdhis Paleohoríou** (to avoid confusion with the resort of Áyios Górdhis further north), 2km west of Sparterá, one of the least visited beaches on the island.

Corfu's satellite islands

Corfu's three (barely) inhabited satellite islands, **Erikoússa, Othoní**
and **Mathráki**, in the quintet of **Dhiapóndia islands**, are situated a
good 20km off the far northwest coast. Each is distinct in character
from the others: Erikoússa is flat and sandy, Othoní rocky with a hilly
interior, Mathráki, the most attractive for island collectors, a green
hill surrounded by almost volcanic sandy beaches. Some travel agencies, for example in Aharávi, offer **day-trips** to Erikoússa only, often
with a barbecue thrown in – fine if you want to spend the day on the
beach. A trip taking in all three from Sidhári or Áyios Stéfanos is
excellent value, if a little hurried: the islands are between thirty and
sixty minutes apart by boat, and most trips allow you an hour on each
(though usually longer on sandy Erikoússa).

It's now possible to **stay** on all three islands, although travel
between them is difficult. Islanders themselves use day-trip boats, so
it's possible to hitch (or offer to pay for) a lift if the craft is going
your way: out of Sidhári, from where day-trips are most frequent,
kaïkia usually travel Mathráki–Othoní–Erikoússa. There is also a
twice-weekly **ferry** from Corfu Town, the *Alexandros II*, which
brings cars and goods to the islands, but given that it has to sail
halfway round Corfu first, it's the least attractive option for reaching
them.

Mathráki

Hilly, densely forested and with a long, deserted beach, beautiful
MATHRÁKI is the least inhabited of the three islands. Its tiny harbour is on the east coast, facing Corfu, and at present sports little
more than a taverna. The beach begins at the edge of the harbour,
and extends south for 3km of fine, dark-red sand. A single road rises
from the harbour into the interior and the scattered village of Káto
Mathráki (walkable with time for refreshments on most day-trip
stops), where just one friendly taverna-*kafenío*-shop overlooks the
beach and Corfu. The views are magnificent, as are the sense of isolation – few day visitors make it even this far – and the pungent smell
of virgin forest. The road continues to the small settlement of Áno
Mathráki, but this is beyond walking distance on a day visit.

Sadly, the population on Mathráki has dwindled: about 700 people
used to live here, but many have moved away to America, Australia
and elsewhere, leaving mainly the elderly behind. Most homes are
only used in the summer, when the diaspora or their children return.
Construction work above the beach suggests this may be about to
turn, however, and islander Tassos Kassimis (☎0663/71 700; ②) is
already renting **rooms**. Apart from the village *kafenío* with its basic
provisions, there are no shops on Mathráki, so if you plan to stay be
prepared for limited taverna menus.

Othoní

Six kilometres north of Mathráki, **OTHONÍ** doesn't come with the
same recommendation as its southerly neighbour. The island has a
handful of good tavernas and some rooms for rent in the main village, Ámmos, on the southern coast, but the reception from islanders
who aren't in the tourism trade is rather unfriendly, an observation
shared by regular visitors from Corfu's north coast.

The island's interior is dramatic, and a path up out of the village
leads through rocky, tree-covered hills to the dwindling central hamlet, Hório, after about half an hour. Paths also run to the telecom-
munications station at the north end of the island, and the lighthouse
at the south, journeys of around an hour, although the distances
mean these would be accessible only to those staying on the island.
The main village has two beaches, both pebbly, one of them part of
the harbour, which is used by fishermen and visiting yachts. The village *kafenío* serves as a very basic shop, and there's one smart
restaurant, *La Locanda di Sogni*, which also has **rooms**
(☎0663/71 640; ④) – though these tend to be prebooked by Italian
visitors. Three tavernas, *New York*, *Mikros* and tiny *Rainbow*, offer
decent but fairly limited menus; Alex Katehis, owner of the *New
York*, offers rooms for rent (☎0663/71 581; ③).

Erikoússa

East of Othoní, **ERIKOÚSSA** is the most populous of the Dhiapóndia
islands, and the most frequent destination of day-trips from the northwestern resorts. It's invariably hyped as a "desert island" trip, although
this is a desert island with a medium-sized hotel, rooms, tavernas, a year-
round village community, a paved road and an ugly aggregates plant
overlooking its small harbour. In high season, it's far from deserted:
Erikoússa has a large diaspora living in America and elsewhere, who
return to family homes in their droves in summer, so you may find your
yiá sou or *kaliméra* returned in a Brooklyn accent.

Erikoússa has an excellent golden sandy beach right by the harbour, with great swimming off it, and another, quieter, beach
reached by a path across the wooded island interior. Even when
the day-trip craft arrive in high season, the main beach is rarely
busy and, when they depart in mid-afternoon, Erikoússa reverts to
something approaching the "desert island" promised by the tour
companies. The island's small cult following keep its one **hotel**,
the *Erikoussa* (☎0663/71 555 or 71 110; ④), fairly busy through
the season; it has a good restaurant and bar, and rooms are en
suite with balconies and views. Simpler rooms are available from
the main **taverna** on the beach, *Anemomilos* (☎0663/71 647; ③).
If you're hoping to stay, phoning ahead is essential, as is taking
anything you might not be able to buy on an island where there are
no conventional shops, only a snack bar selling basic groceries.

Travel details

BUSES

Green KTEL buses run from about 6am to 8pm. The following summer timetable will be reduced on most routes during the winter:

Corfu Town to: Aharávi (5 daily, 1 Sun; 1hr 15min); Aríllas (4 daily, not Sun; 1hr); Athens (4 daily, 1 via Lefkími; 11hr); Áyios Górdhis (7 daily, 3 Sun; 45min); Áyios Mathéos (4 daily, 1 Sun; 1hr); Áyios Stéfanos (on the west coast; 6 daily, 1 Sun; 1hr 30min); Áyios Yeóryios (in the south; 5 daily, 3 Sun; 1hr 15min); Áyios Yeóryios (in the northwest; 3 daily, 2 Sun; 1hr); Érmones (3 daily, not Sun; 55min); Glyfádha (9 daily, 7 Sun; 40min); Ípsos (9 daily, 1 Sun; 30min); Kassiópi (9 daily, 1 Sun; 1hr); Kávos (11 daily, 4 Sun; 1hr 30min); Lefkími (11 daily, 4 Sun; 1hr 15min); Messongí (8 daily, 3 Sun; 40min); Moraïtika (8 daily, 3 Sun; 35min); Paleokastrítsa (10 daily, 8 Sun; 1hr); Pélekas (9 daily, 7 Sun; 30min); Petrití (4 daily, 1 Sun; 50min); Pyryí (9 daily, 1 Sun; 35min); Ródha (5 daily, 1 Sun; 1hr); Sidhári (9 daily, 1 Sun; 1hr 15min); Thessaloníki (2 daily; 15hr); Vátos (3 daily, not Sun; 45min).

Blue town buses run from about 6am to 10pm. The following summer timetable will be reduced on most routes during the winter:

Corfu Town to: Achilleion (6 daily, 4 Sun; 15min); Aqualand/Áyios Ioánnis (10 daily, 5 Sun; 20min); Benítses (13 daily; 25min); Dhassiá (every 20 to 30min; 25min); Kanóni (every 30min; 10min); Pélekas (14 daily, 8 Sun; 30min).

FERRIES

Corfu Town (New Port) to: Igoumenítsa (at least one hourly from 5.15am to 10pm; 1hr 30min–2hr); Pátra (3–5 daily; 8–9hr); Paxí (2–3 daily; 2–4hr); Sámi on Kefalloniá (1 weekly, summer only; 7hr). Also in season roughly daily departures to the following ports in Italy: Ancona (17–19hr); Bari (11–12hr); and Brindisi (10–11hr). Most services are reduced off season (for further information, see p.16 and p.31).

Lefkími to: Igoumenítsa (6–8 daily; 1hr). Less frequent off season.

HYDROFOIL

In season there is a once or twice daily *Flying Dolphin* from Corfu Town to Igoumenítsa (45min) and Paxí (1hr 30min).

FLIGHTS

Corfu Town on Olympic to: Athens (3–5 daily; 1hr); Thessaloníki (1–2 Mon–Sat; 1hr). Air Greece has one daily flight to Athens (1hr).

Chapter 2

Paxí

Small, unusually green and still surprisingly underdeveloped, **Paxí (Paxos)** has established a firm niche in Greece's tourist hierarchy and draws crowds out of proportion to its attractions. It has the least to offer of all the major Ionian islands – no sandy beaches, no historical sites, only two hotels and a serious water shortage – yet it undeniably has an air of mystique that makes it one of the most sought-after destinations in the archipelago. Despite the aforementioned privations, Paxí draws a high proportion of return visitors, who can make its three harbour villages rather cliquey. It's also very popular with yachting flotillas, whose shopping, eating and drinking habits have brought a certain sophistication to shops and tavernas with a long tradition of telling their customers to be thankful for what they're given.

It's the most expensive place to visit in the Ionian – just about everything consumed on Paxí has to be ferried in from Corfu or the mainland – yet so popular in high season that casual visitors are warned to book ahead before boarding a ferry to the island. Most accommodation is block-booked by upmarket north European travel companies – though there are local tour operators whose holidays might cost half the price. To make matters worse, the one official campsite is rather remote and has been experiencing closures due to

---

Accommodation price codes

Rooms and hotels listed in this book have been price-coded according to the scale outlined below. The rates quoted represent the cheapest available double room in high season. Out of season, rates can drop by as much as fifty percent or more, especially if you negotiate for a stay of three or more nights. Single rooms, where available, cost around seventy percent of the price of a double. For further information, see p.36.

① up to 6000dr
② 6000–9000dr
③ 9000–12,000dr
④ 12,000–16,000dr

⑤ 16,000–20,000dr
⑥ 20,000–30,000dr
⑦ 30,000dr upwards

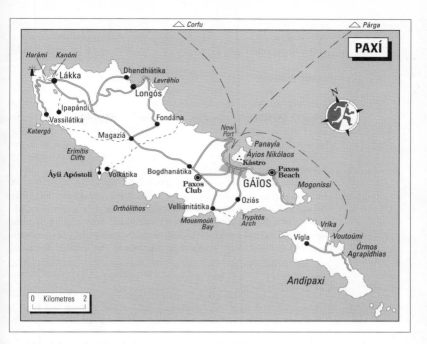

ownership wrangles, although there are pockets of freelance camping. On the plus side for independent travellers, Italians have been deserting the Ionian for Sicily and points west in recent years, freeing up rentable rooms.

Although it gets only a fraction of the bad weather that is regularly visited on neighbouring Corfu, Paxí is remarkably verdant. Its abundant **flora** and **bird life** make it a favourite haunt of ornithologists, botanists, walkers and watercolourists, particularly in spring. Drenching winter rains produce carpets of dwarf cyclamen in spring; daffodils and antirrhinums flower in February, and by Easter the island's woods and olive groves are full of wild lilies, irises and orchids. Despite the unwanted attentions of hunters, the island is home to numerous native and migratory species of birds. Barn owls and the tiny Scops owl are heard at night, and peregrine falcons nest on remote hilltops.

Barely 12km long by 4km wide, Paxí has only three villages of any size, all of them ports: its capital, **Gáïos**, towards the southern end, **Lákka**, at the northern tip, and tiny **Longós**, 2km south of Lákka. Gáïos is where most visitors will arrive, although many immediately head off to quieter Lákka and Longós. The island's best bathing is around Longós and Lákka, or further afield in the desert island coves and beaches of **Andípaxi**, Paxí's sibling 2km south. Many of Paxí's

Walking routes on Paxí are detailed on the comprehensive map produced by cartographers Elizabeth and Ian Bleasdale and sold by most tourism businesses on the island (3000dr). "Exploring Paxos and Andipaxos" by Susan Valeria Omar is also informative.

beaches are not accessible by road or foot, which is where a boat with outboard motor comes in handy. Most village travel agencies and some of the larger international companies offer boat rental by week or day.

Some history

There are two overlapping myths about Paxí's origins. In one, Poseidon needed a place to hide his lover, Amphitrite, and struck the sea with his trident – now Paxí's emblem – to create an island. In the other, the sea god simply wanted somewhere to rest while travelling between islands (odd, given that Homer credits the gods with the power to traverse the Med in a flash), and so created this hideaway between Corfu and Itháki.

Ancient history seems to have passed the island by, apart from a walk-on role in a few key moments. In the third century BC, Paxí was the site of a sea battle between Corcyreans, as Corfiots were then known, and the Illyrian fleet, which resulted in Corcyra becoming the first Greek state to surrender to Roman rule. Antony and Cleopatra are believed to have dined on Paxí on the eve of the ill-fated Battle of

---

Párga

Spread over three wooded, hilly coves, **PÁRGA** is the most attractive coastal resort in mainland Epirus. Its jumble of low, red-tiled buildings faces out towards Paxí, over vegetation-tufted rocks and islets a short swim off some of the best beaches in the region. Unfortunately, Párga is also Epirus's most popular resort: even in low season it can be hectically busy, and in high summer it heaves. All the same, it can be a welcome change of scene on one of the **day-trips** that leave Gáïos most days of the week (from around 4500dr per person).

As a stopover on the way to or from the islands, however, it can be problematical in season, when accommodation is hard to come by. Thankfully, you should not get stuck there unless you arrive late, as the twice daily excursion **kaïki** (9.30am and 5.20pm) is happy to take one-way passengers. There is no proper ferry, however, so out of season you can only reach Paxí from the mainland from Igoumenítsa, 70km north. **Buses** to Igoumenítsa (4 daily; 1hr 30min) and Préveza (5 daily Mon–Fri, 3 daily Sat–Sun; 1hr 30min) leave from near the crossroads in the centre of town, on Odhós Skoufá. This crossroads is the commercial heart of the town, with post office, banks, shops and travel agencies.

Of Párga's **beaches**, the pebble strand immediately below the quay is probably the poorest; the smaller **Kryonéri** and **Píso Kryonéri** beaches just to the north are cleaner and quieter; best, however, is the long, sandy **Váltos beach**, beyond the massive *kástro* that towers above the town. Sea taxis connect Váltos and Párga every fifteen minutes from 9am onwards for those reluctant to face the twenty-minute slog over the headland. Another long strand is **Lýkhnos**, 3km southeast of town. The **kástro** (open all day; free) is the ruined skeleton of a major Venetian fort, built when Párga was Venice's sole mainland settlement during its rule of the Ionians from the fourteenth to eighteenth centuries. It has excellent views, as well as some rather dangerous unguarded precipices, and makes a good stroll or picnic destination.

Actium in 31 BC, when they were decisively defeated by Octavian's fleet. Paxí is also associated with a piece of Christian mythology, retold by Plutarch in his *Moralia* and interpreted by Spenser and Milton, which cites the island as the place where the death of paganism and the birth of Christ were announced. An Egyptian captain taking his craft north through the Ionian found himself becalmed off Paxí, when a mysterious voice called him by name from the island and told him to shout out to the inhabitants of a mainland port as he passed that "the great god Pan is dead". The captain reluctantly obeyed, and reported an unearthly wailing from the mainland at this news.

Paxí is believed to have first been settled by shepherds from the mainland in the sixth century AD; a ruined chapel near the hamlet of Oziás in the south of the island has been dated back this far. Shortly afterwards, it was subsumed into the Byzantine empire along with Epirus and the rest of the northern Ionian. The Venetians, after their invasion of the region from 1386 onwards, proved to be more forward-thinking rulers. They planted olive trees throughout the archipelago, including an estimated quarter million on Paxí alone, and as well as

---

Accommodation in Párga is notoriously difficult to find, except at a price. Phoning ahead is near obligatory, but anyone who finds themselves here without accommodation should first try the friendly *Souli* taverna on the seafront (☎0684/31 658; ③), which has **rooms** in town, or some of the rooming houses in the whitewashed lane leading past the *kástro*, such as Kostas Pappas (☎0684/31 301; ③). More upmarket are the purpose-built *Magda Apartments* (☎0684/31 332, fax 31 690; ④) out near the Váltos turning. The only three **hotels** not block-booked are the *Ayios Nektarios* (☎0684/31 324, fax 32 150; ③), on the edge of town at the corner of Livadhá and the road in, the mostly German-patronized *Galini* (☎0684/31 581, fax 32 221; ③), set in a nearby orchard, and the *Paradise* (☎0684/ 31 229, fax 31 266; ④), which is in a rather noisy location on Spýros Livadhá, opposite the school. Two **travel agencies** on the seafront with access to a variety of accommodation are *Kryoneri Travel* (☎0684/32 488, fax 32 400) and *IYS Travel* (☎0684/31 833 or 31 683, fax 31 834). **Campers** should head for either *Parga Camping*, just behind Kryonéri beach, or *Elea Camping*, fifteen minutes' walk from the centre on the main road into Párga.

Párga is overrun with mostly touristic **restaurants**. Two of the most notable exceptions are secreted in the lane ascending towards the *kástro*: the smart, and fairly expensive, *Kastro*, near the fort itself, and in a courtyard nearer the town, the cheaper, but if anything superior *Kastello*, whose reputation has spread to Paxí and even Itháki. In town, as well as the traditional *Souli* taverna, the *Tzima* restaurant at the far end of the quay is recommended for its vast range of vegetarian-friendly Greek and north European food, as is *To Kantouni*, at the rear end of the market. The seafront **bars** tend to fill quickly at night, but some of the best drinking spots are to be found at the upper end of the lane leading up to the *kástro*, including the aforementioned *Kastro*, with stunning views down over the town.

---

producing a bumper crop, the trees helped to bind the topsoil, allowing the cultivation of fruit, vegetables and vines. Islanders were paid the equivalent of a drachma for each tree planted, and under Venetian auspices produced the extraordinary terracing and intricate dry-stone walling that covers much of the island. The invaders also initiated the construction of basic civic amenities: a harbour at Gáïos, various official buildings and several small water reservoirs still seen, and some still in use, around the island. The distinctive Venetian architectural style can be observed on the seafront at Gáïos, and as ruins in a few isolated parts of the island's interior.

More than four hundred years of Venetian rule finally came to an end with the arrival of the French, but not before Paxí had suffered a particularly brutal maritime raid in 1537, when the Turkish admiral **Barbarossa** enslaved most of the islanders in a revenge attack, after failing in a siege on Corfu. When the **British** took over in 1809, they improved on the Venetians' building schemes, as well as instituting the basis of a government infrastructure and education system. Britain ceded the Ionian islands to the Greek government in 1864, at which point Paxí slipped into the mainstream of Greek history. During **World War II**, garrisons of German troops were stationed in Gáïos and Lákka, and, it's claimed, the Luftwaffe used Paxí for practice bombing runs from Corfu. Along with the rest of Greece, the island was liberated in 1944 – a popular local story has German troops in Lákka attempting to arrest arriving British troops, only to be told it was they who were being arrested.

Arrival and getting around

Most **ferries** arrive at Gáïos, with larger vessels from Corfu Town and Igoumenítsa on the mainland docking at the new port, 1km north of Gáïos. There's no bus connection at the new port, so people either walk into Gáïos (15min) or take a taxi (700dr). Smaller boats and hydrofoils, when they are running, moor a hundred metres or so along the quayside from Gáïos's tiny town square.

Buses shuttle between Gáïos and Lákka seven or eight times a day (35min), with most departures travelling via Longós. Timetables are posted in each village and in most travel agencies. Gáïos's bus stop is at the back of the village, 150m from the square, in a small dirt car park where the village alleys meet the island's one main road. In Lákka buses stop by the *Petrou kafenío* at the back of the village; in Longós on the quay. There are **taxi** stands in Gáïos (by the church in the main square) and Lákka (by the *Petrou kafenío*); an average one-way fare between Lákka and Gáïos is 2500dr. Both buses and taxis, which are often shared, can be flagged down anywhere.

There are at least two **motorcycle** rental outlets in all three villages: by the dock in Gáïos, 50m back from the ferry ramp behind the *Dionysus* taverna in Lákka and on the northern end of the quay at Longós. Rental starts at around 3000dr a day. However, riders should

There is no tourist office on Paxí, but local travel agencies in the three ports are usually happy to help with information, even if you're not travelling or staying with their company.

beware Paxí's treacherous gravelly roads, which are often slicked with oil from the olive trees – accidents are a daily occurrence in season.

A limited number of **cars** can be rented in Gáïos and Lákka, with established companies such as *Planos* and *Gáïos Travel* getting first choice of what's available. It's also fiendishly expensive: between 80,000 and 110,000dr a week for a saloon, depending on season, and between 130,000 and 160,000dr for a four-wheel drive. British-based travel companies such as CV Villas and Greek Islands can hire cars ahead for clients; an alternative for independent travellers is to rent a car on Corfu or the mainland and bring it to Paxí by ferry.

Gáïos and around

Named after St Gaius, who is said to have brought Christianity to the island, and whose tomb is to be found in the plain church of Áyii Apóstoli next to the post office, **GÁÏOS** is the one of most attractive villages in the Ionian. Known to locals simply as Gáï, it's extremely compact, consisting of little more than a crescent-shaped quay, a small Venetian town square – the hub of village life – and a few narrow alleys leading away from it. It's the island's administrative centre (three banks, one magistrates' court, Paxí's sole police station), its major port of arrival and shopping centre, including several minimarkets, two delis and a pharmacy.

The town is protected from the open sea by two islands, **Áyios Nikólaos** and **Panayía**. The former is little more than 20m across from the harbourfront and crowned by a magnificent stand of pines. Beyond the pines stands a ruined Venetian fortress built in 1423 and renovated by the French in the eighteenth century. Panayía is named after a white-walled church dedicated to the Virgin Mary (*Panayía*), the site of a major festival every August 15. Both islands are well worth exploring: a sea taxi (there's a desk on the seafront) will take you to either for around 1000dr. Smoking is discouraged on Áyios Nikólaos to prevent fires on its tinder-dry pine forest floor.

The island's only museum is the **Folk Museum** (May–Oct 11.30am–1.30pm and 7pm–midnight; 500dr), housed in an old school building on the seafront about 200m south of the square. One room is set up as an eighteenth-century bedroom with some period furniture and several dummies dressed in the garb of that time. Other items on display from different epochs are kitchen implements, musical instruments, china, stationery and guns.

If you are here on August 4, it's worth checking out the annual *Neroladhiá* festival, during which the islanders recall hard times of the past, when they were forced to share out stale bread dunked in water and smeared with olive oil and whatever leftovers remained. There is live music on the quay and free food (yes, bread dunked in water with a few tidbits and covered in oil) and a glass of wine is handed out to anyone who gets in the queue.

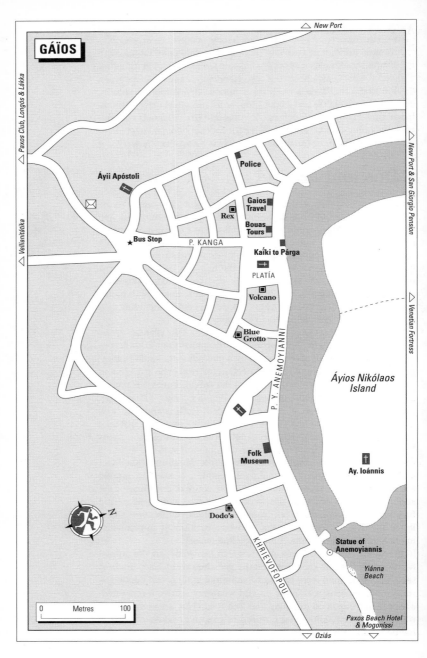

GÁIOS

New Port

Paxos Club, Longós & Lákka

New Port & San Giorgio Pension

Velliánátitka

Police

Áyii Apóstoli

Gaios
Travel

Rex

Bouas
Tours

Bus Stop

P. KANGA

Kaíki to Párga

PLATÍA

Volcano

Venetian Fortress

Blue
Grotto

P. Y. ANEMOYIANNI

Áyios Nikólaos
Island

Folk
Museum

Ay. Ioánnis

N

Dodo's

KHRIEVOTOPOU

Statue of
Anemoyiannis

Yiánna
Beach

0   Metres   100

Paxos Beach Hotel
& Mogoníssi

Oziás

Accommodation

Much accommodation in Gáïos – and elsewhere on Paxí – is block-booked by British and other northern European travel companies, and the range of freelance accommodation dwindles near high season, when a call ahead is essential. However, a few villagers offering **rooms** meet ferries arriving at the quay in season, and a few metres from the ferry is one of the biggest Paxiot-run tourism and accommodation companies, *Gaïos Travel* (☎0662/32 033, fax 32 175). The company shares an office with *CV Villas* and can also help with money exchange, trips and other business. Another travel agency worth contacting for accommodation is *Bouas Tours* (☎0662/32 401, fax 32 610), also situated on the seafront. Or you can try the *San Giorgio* pension (☎0662/32 223; ③) just above the coastal road to the new port.

Paxí's two seasonal **hotels** are both near Gáïos. They are heavily used by package companies in high season, but will often have rooms available to independent travellers. The secluded *Paxos Beach Hotel* (☎0662/31 211; ⑥) is sited on a hillside above a small pebbly beach 2km south of Gáïos. Accommodation is in bungalows, spread out through the trees, though the place has an unfriendly and rather regimented air. The hotel has its own irregular minibus service into Gáïos; otherwise access is by taxi or on foot.

The newer *Paxos Beach Club* (☎0662/32 450, fax 32 097; ⑦), 2km outside of Gáïos on the main road towards Bogdhanátika, is fairly luxurious. On an island with a severe water shortage, it boasts a large fancy-shaped pool which, along with its bar and restaurant, welcomes non-residents. Rooms are en suite with balconies, and some large, suite-style apartments are also available. However, the hotel currently has a fairly short season, and has been known to close in early September.

Eating and drinking

Eating out is not one of Paxí's strong points, although it has been improving in recent years. For a long time many tavernas operated on the basis that on a small island customers were a captive audience, and most islanders would have been embarrassed to serve in their own kitchens the sort of food that got served in the village squares. When the large number of return visitors to the island started switching to self-catering in the early 1990s, the taverna owners' response to the fall in business was simply to raise their prices. More recently, however, increased competition has forced most restaurateurs into seeing the wisdom of upping the quality and variety of their fare

Consequently, in Gáïos itself there are a number of decent **tavernas**, best of them *Carcoleggio's*, 1.5km out of town on the main road to Bogdhanátika. The menu and wine list are limited, and opening hours unpredictable, but it fills up with islanders who flock

for its *souvláki*. Tucked away to the left at the back of the village
square, the long-standing *Blue Grotto* is a good second choice for
its grills and pan-cooked meat and fish dishes. *Spiros*, to the right
at the top of the square, opposite the alley leading to the *Blue
Grotto*, offers friendly service and excellent meat, fish and veggie
dishes in a pleasant, arcaded Venetian square. Another no-
nonsense *estiatório* in a side-street off the square, particularly
good for oven food is *Rex*, while the *Gaïos Grill* nearby provides a
conventional range of lamb, chicken and fish dishes. *Dodo's*, a little
way inland from the Anemoyiannis statue, is a welcoming taverna
with outdoor seating, serving pizza, pasta and indigenous food, The
one traditional taverna in the line of eating houses running down to
the quayside, the *Volcano* has been family-run for decades, with
vegetarian-friendly alternatives such as stuffed vegetables as well as
conventional taverna dishes. As is often the case, the establishments
on the seafront itself are uninspiring and overpriced.

For self-caterers, the picture is rosy. Thanks to the demands of
picky yacht crews, Gáïos now offers as sophisticated a range of
foodstuffs as you're likely to encounter in the Ionian islands. The
deli at the top left of the town square offers the widest range of
cured meats, dairy products, wines and other delicacies, while the
supermarket directly opposite the ferry dock (nicknamed Harrod's
by some expats) also stocks a wide range of alcohol and deli/dairy
foodstuffs. The spread of high-class *zaharoplastía* has now
reached Gáïos, with a mouthwatering **cake shop** a stone's throw
from the ferry dock, and a larger, even fancier store opposite *Spiros*
taverna in the arcade to the right at the top of the town square. The
bakery a few doors uphill on the main road out of the square is the
only one on the island to stock a daily supply of brown as well as
white bread.

Nightlife

As on most small Greek islands, visitors soon discover that evening
entertainment on Paxí consists largely of lotus-eating outside tavernas and bars. The *Carnayo* on Gáïos' seafront, a source of much
amusement and scandal over the years, has again reopened after various vicissitudes and seems to be on good behaviour with a standard
mix of Greek and foreign sounds. Another popular hangout for
drinks and sweets is *Red Chairs* on the square, while *Alter Ego* on
the way to the new port is a fairly smooth rock-oriented bar.

There are two **discotheques** outside Gáïos: the *Castello*, a moribund barn that opens only fitfully, on the first turning out of town on
the main road; and the *Phoenix*, out of harm's way just past the new
port, a lively and popular late-night venue with a terrace for sub-
lunar fun, dodgy music policy and pricey bar list. The most likely
dancing venue right in town is *Tango*, by the post office.

Listings

Banks and exchange The branches of the National Bank of Greece, the Agricultural Bank and the Commercial Bank in Gáïos, the only banks on the island, are primarily for domestic accounts but handle foreign exchange too. The last has a cash dispenser. Most travel companies will change travellers' cheques at rates checked daily with banks, although with a commission.

Doctors and medical emergencies The island's surgery (☎0662/31 466), in the village of Bogdhanátika, 3km west of Gáïos, opens weekday mornings – attendance avoids the doctor's call-out fee of around 10,000dr. The two doctors both speak English. Serious injuries are taken to Corfu by sea taxi or helicopter. There are no dental services on Paxí.

Ferry agent A tiny caravan at the new port is the only dedicated ferry office on Paxí, although any travel agency (see p.125 or p.131 for examples) will be able to make reservations.

Police station Two blocks inland about 100m north of the square (☎0662/31 222).

Post office The only proper post office and OTE on the island is by the bus stand at the back of the village (Mon–Fri 8am–1.30pm).

Beaches around Gáïos

When it comes to beaches, Gáïos is the least well-endowed of the island's villages. Apart from a tiny pebble strand dynamited a few years back just south of the town, the only true beach is at the micro-resort of **Mogoníssi**, 3km south of Gáïos. Mogoníssi is in fact an island, attached to Paxí by a short causeway, set in the dullest landscape on the entire island – flat, part scrubby and part rocky. At the time of writing, local wrangling over ownership had led to the closure of its facilities and rendered it, in effect, out of bounds. However, it was anticipated to be up and running again for the new millennium, so check what the current situation is. Before the closure it had a small **campsite** set in trees above a beach of imported sand, watersports and a **taverna**, which used to hold "Greek nights" in season, for which it provided a free sea-taxi service. Other than that, however, there is no bus service south of Gáïos, so it's either foot or taxi.

There are, however, numerous rocky coves between Gáïos and Mogoníssi, popular with those staying in the capital; the large slabs of rock sloping into the sea make them ideal for swimming and sunbathing. One bay south of Gáïos, the taverna *Klis* overlooks a bay with safe swimming and sometimes, in season, a floating bathing platform with its own bar. Further bays are accessible from the road north beyond the new port, but they're a good few kilometres' walk through a landscape akin to a building site. They're also uncomfortably close to the island's eco-unfriendly municipal dump, a hill of smouldering garbage that glows orange at night while slipping slowly into the sea.

Southwest Paxí

The comparative flatness of the landscape around Gáïos makes the
surrounding countryside easy walking terrain. A circular two-to
three-hour route leaving the southern end of Gáïos takes in some of
the oldest hamlets on the island: through Ozías, Vellianitátika, neighbouring Zenebissátika and on to **Bogdhanátika** on the main road.
The chief interest in these hamlets is the architecture, much of it dating from Venetian times and before, but there are hardly any facilities along the way – only Bogdhanátika has a *kafenío* and bar.

The walk can be augmented by taking a path leading from near the
church in **Vellianitátika**. This cuts across fairly rough country to the
cliffs above Mousmoúli bay and on to the dramatic **Tripitós arch**, a
hundred-metre limestone sea-stack attached to the island by a walkway.
It's a strenuous and even dangerous trip, with vertiginous drops, and
should only be attempted by the sure-footed (and never in bad weather).

Longós and around

The smallest of the island's three ports, **LONGÓS** is also the most
picturesque and, for its size, blessed with the best ratio of amenities.
Its pocket-sized, east-facing harbour is perfectly sited to catch the
morning sun (making alfresco breakfasts idyllic), the handful of tavernas are among the best on the island, and the nightlife is lively. The
one drawback to staying here, which should be taken seriously in
high and shoulder seasons, is the lack of space and noise at night,
with bars, restaurants and other tourists right on your doorstep.
Indeed, the extent of Longós's facilities can be taken in simply by
looking around its harbour: with the exception of one minimarket, a
bakery, a bike rental shop and a restaurant tucked into an alleyway,
the village's few amenities, including another well-stocked minimarket and all the other bars and restaurants, are here on the quay.
There is no bank or post office – exchange transactions are dealt
with by the travel agencies.

Longós's seclusion has made it a favourite with upmarket villa
companies such as CV and Simply Ionian, whose properties are
located in the hills above the port. The village has a small and
scruffy beach, but most people swim from pebbly **Levréhio beach**,
around ten minutes' walk away in the next bay south. The cove also
has some excellent, gently sloping slabs of smooth rock with good
access to the water, to sun yourself on and swim from. Above the village to the north, reached by steps rising above the disused factory
on the beach, is the small Venetian hamlet of **Dhendhiátika**. While
there are no tavernas or *kafenía* here, it has excellent views over
the port. The trek up there makes a diverting short walk: follow the
Dhendhiátika road, signposted off the Lákka–Longós road, and then
carry on down into Longós.

Accommodation

Like Paxí's other two ports, Longós has little accommodation for independent travellers, and in the high season months of July and August the supply all but dries up. You should be prepared to move on to Lákka if Longós is full or, as has happened in at least one drought year, has been forced to "close" because of water shortages.

The bulk of villas and apartments here are controlled by companies such as Greek Islands and CV Villas, though Planos Holidays, now the island's largest local accommodation agency, with its main office in Lákka, has an increasingly large stake. Planos's office in Longós (☎0662/31 530, fax 31 010) is probably the best place to start looking for accommodation hereabouts, from village **rooms** to country **villas**, especially if phoning ahead. Paxos Sun Holidays (☎ & fax 0662/31 341) also have an office in the resort. It's possible to rent rooms from the Dendias minimarket (☎0662/31 597 or 31 158; ④) or from the proprietor's relative A. Dendias (☎0662/ 31 610 or 32 580; ④). Julia's bike rental, 100m back from the harbour, also has a few rooms (☎0662/31 330; ②). A certain amount of unofficial **camping** takes place on Levréhio beach, but it's nowhere near as hidden as at Lákka – it's best to ask for advice at the beach taverna.

Eating and drinking

The **restaurants** in Longós are good, but there aren't many of them, so people often head for Lákka by bus, taxi or, in daylight, on foot (taxis run until well after midnight). The *Nassos* is probably the best restaurant in Longós, with a wide variety of fish and seafood dishes, including things like prawns with a side order of mayonnaise (unusually for Greece, they'll bring hot water and lemon finger-bowls, if you ask). The seafront *Vassilis* is immortalized in thousands of holiday tales as the restaurant where those sitting at outside tables have to squeeze in off the street to make way for the island bus when it rumbles by; it has a basic taverna menu, but done with imagination and more veg than you'll ever find in Lákka. Both establishments are definitely overpriced, however. Tucked behind the *Vassilis*, *Kakarantzas* offers a range of fish, meat and vegetarian dishes far more adventurous than the majority of tavernas on the island, while *O Gios* is another reasonable standby. The cheap and cheerful *Iy Gonia* grill in the corner of the harbour is the best value in the village, with a small selection of starters and vegetable dishes as well as excellent meat.

Nightlife is very low-key and largely limited to the few bars facing the seafront, of which the most pleasant for an early evening drink is the relaxed *To Taxidhi*, with seating on both sides of the quay. The most popular late bars are *Malia* (also known as Nikos's) and *Ores*, both featuring the standard mish-mash of Greek and English hits. For more energetic entertainment you'll have to head for Lákka or Gáïos.

Lákka and around

LÁKKA is the coolest and friendliest of the island's ports, attracting a large crowd of loyal return visitors, as well as a fair share of roustabouts, although locals affirm that it is quieter now than in the past, and it doesn't begin to compare with the rowdiness to be encountered on some of the larger Ionian islands. The sea approach into the horseshoe bay has to be one of the most magnificent views in Greece, though arriving from elsewhere on Paxí is disappointing: you're greeted by a jumble of half-built apartment blocks at the back of the village. Beyond these, however, a compact grid of narrow alleys around the village's small main square, lined with two-storey houses in the Venetian style, comprises the village's charming centre. It's full of surprising details and strange corners and turns – not least Platía Edward Kennedy, commemorating, probably with tongue in cheek, a visit by members of the Kennedy clan (including, rumour insists, Jackie O) in the 1960s. The *platía* is in fact only a tiny, triangular alley, signalled by a blink-and-you'll-miss-it wall sign.

Lákka is so compact that you'll trip over most of what there is here in the first five minutes. Shops are based around the back of the village, bars along the seafront and restaurants along the front and around the village square. Taxis and buses stop metres from each other near the *Petrou Kafenio* at the back of the village. There's no bank or post office, but the two main travel agents, Planos and Routsis, both on the quayside, change money, sell stamps and operate quiet payphones, as well as renting watersports equipment; Planos also offers car rental. The village houses the office of Dive and Fun (☎ & fax 0662/30 004), a German-run **scuba-diving** operation, and **horse-riding** is offered beside the taverna around east end of the bay. The only place to visit is the small and rather costly **Aquarium** (daily 10am–2.30pm and 7–10.30pm; 1000dr) with its motley collection of local fish, lobsters, crabs and octopus (who actually have a feeding time), all kept in none-too-shiny tanks.

Lákka and its bay offer the best swimming and watersports on Paxí, with its two public **beaches** on the western side of the bay – **Kanóni** and **Harámi**, which has a snack bar-taverna – and a small beach by the schoolhouse opposite. As elsewhere on the island, the beaches are pebble, with occasional tar deposits, but shelve into sand at the edge of the clear, shallow water. In recent years, however, questions have been raised about the quality of the water at high season. Eye and ear infections, stomach upsets and infected cuts and abrasions have led some to suspect that untreated sewage is finding its way into the bay. Take local advice on whether to swim or not.

Paxí olive oil

Paxí's prize-winning **olive oil** is regarded by some as being on a par with, or even superior to, Italian brands. The olive trees originally planted by the Venetians still dominate the island's economy and landscape; olive oil remains the largest business after tourism, and the trees cover around eighty percent of the island.

Unlike crops elsewhere, Paxí's olives are allowed to fall before being harvested, and until nets were introduced a few decades ago, this was done by hand. The biennial crop would be hand-picked, winnowed, bagged and carried to olive presses in each village. The traditional stone mills were driven by donkeys and sometimes by women and children: a generation of islanders still remembers this back-breaking work. Mechanization of the mills and the introduction of nets has transformed the industry, and most of the stone presses have fallen into disuse, their overgrown masonry and machinery visible at points throughout the island.

Mechanized presses operate in Gáïos, Fountána and, most visibly, Lákka. The olive oil sells at barely more than 2000dr a litre, but it is rarely seen in shops, less still in restaurants. However, it's a staple in the kitchens of the islanders, most of whom have a stake, if only a few trees, in the crop. The oil is sold chiefly in the presses themselves, which only open when deliveries from the olive groves require processing. If you're planning to take some home, buy early to avoid finding the press closed on your day of departure.

Accommodation

Accommodation is marginally easier to come by in Lákka than either Gáïos or Longós, although even here rooms are scarce at the height of the season. The village has a large number of return visitors, many of whom book the same accommodation year after year. Rooms in the village itself are generally noisy, especially as some bars stay open until dawn.

The growth of the two main village travel companies has resulted in a healthy choice of accommodation that directly benefits the islanders rather than anonymous multinational corporations. Planos (☎0662/31 744 or 31 821, fax 31 010) is the larger of the two, and can offer anything from a village room the size of a cupboard to a villa with pool up in the hills. It also offers complete holiday packages from its British office (see p.6), inclusive of flights and transfer. Routsis (☎0662/31 807 or 31 162, fax 31 161; ②–④) is fast catching up, and also has a wide range of rooms, apartments and villas in the village and outlying areas. It now also offers bonded flight and holiday deals through its British agents (see p.60). Of the two, Routsis is friendlier, and more likely to have some basic options for the independent traveller, whereas Planos presells much of its accommodation.

Between them, these two companies and several overseas operators have sewn up much of the accommodation in and around Lákka; even the "hotels" *Ilios* and *Lefcothea* (in fact basic rooming houses) are run by Routsis. Some self-contained apartments above Kanóni are rented out at Marigo's food store (☎0662/30 087 or 31 458; ④) at the landward

end of the main square, or ask for directions to Maria's rooms, set in a
paradisiacal garden, but difficult to find in a lane rising out of the west
end of the village.

Camping

The locals' tacit acceptance of **freelance camping** has been reinforced by the removal of a once prominent "No Camping" sign on the
way to the beach, and a constant trickle of backpackers happily pitch
tent in the terraced olive grove above Kanóni, the smaller beach
reached a few minutes before Harámi. This practice goes undisturbed provided that campers take care with litter and fires: there's
no fire brigade on Paxí, and islanders are understandably anxious
about the threat to the olive groves.

Eating and drinking

In recent years, **tavernas** have proliferated in Lákka to a capacity
beyond the numbers of tourists arriving: bad news for the restaurant-
owners, good news for customers. Restaurants are sited in the central
square or visible two or three minutes' walk away. There is also a fair
range of late night **bars**, some well-established, others opening and
closing according to the vagaries of their clientele's preferences.

Restaurants

Butterfly. In the square, this is one of the best conventional tavernas, with
friendly family service and plenty of veggie alternatives to taverna staples.

Dionysus. This specializes in grills – chicken, chops, *souvláki*, even whole
baby lamb – for the flotilla crowd; tell-tale signs of when the fleet's in (tables
lined up for twenty or more) should warn you to eat elsewhere.

Nautilus. Under a blue-striped awning on the far side of the bay, this has the
most breathtaking view of any taverna on Paxí. It specializes in seafood
(expensive), salads and conventional fare prepared with effort and imagination, not least a classic bean soup.

Nionios. Right next to *Butterfly* and possibly even better for genuine home-
style cooking. Try the pork in lemon sauce, mussels and shrimps in red sauce
or spinach and cream pot.

Pergola. Tucked in a secluded alley and rather upmarket, this has an imaginative menu, including some dishes with a spicy Asian touch.

Rosa di Paxos. The most stylish restaurant on the island, with prices to match
(which is why they're left off the menu outside). Good choice of designer
Greek and international cuisine, especially strong on lasagna and pasta dishes.

To Steki. Unpretentious taverna with grilled and oven food and standard
starters, next to the steps leading towards Harámi.

Bars

Spyros Petrou's *kafenío*, by the bus stop at the back of the village, has
been the hub of Lákka society since anyone can remember, and remains
the place to eavesdrop on village life. It's perhaps the friendliest *kafenío*

in the whole archipelago, with none of the usual macho atmosphere. Another genuine and cheap *kafenío* on the waterfront is *O Xenikhtis*. Among the new generation of venues, *Akis's* seafront bar is a smart cocktail bar overlooking the harbour. It's noisy but popular with younger islanders and visitors. Not far along is *Harbour Lights*, the liveliest bar in town, which opens late and provides a decent soundtrack that hovers between pop and rock. The village's premier cocktail joint, the *Romantica*, is also on the seafront, and offers the biggest nightcap list in town, as well as cool jazz music. *Serano's*, in the square, serves home-made sweets and cakes to induce sugar shock, and is a favourite among long-term visitors, who park their tape collections behind the bar.

Around Lákka

Lákka is perfectly sited for the finest walking on the island. For a simple, short hike, take the track leaving the far end of Harámi beach. This mounts the headland and leads on to the **lighthouse**, where a goat track descends through tough scrub to a sandy open-sea beach with rollers best left to confident swimmers.

Another good walking route heads west into the hills above the village to **Vassilátika**, high on the west coast cliffs, which has stunning views out to sea. From here, the path to the left of the blue-painted stone archway leads on to the most dramatic cliff-edge views (vertigo sufferers beware) and continues to **Magaziá** in the centre of the island, where you can flag down a bus or taxi.

The best walk on Paxí, however, especially good under a clear early evening sky, is to the church at **Áyii Apóstoli**, almost halfway down the west coast, next to the hamlet of Voïkátika. The rough track is sign-posted a few hundred metres south of Magaziá, and takes less than half a hour on foot. The church and surrounding vineyards overlook the sheer 150-metre **Erimítis cliffs**, which at sunset are transformed into a seaside version of Ayers Rock, turning from dirty white to pink and gold and brown. If you visit Áyii Apóstoli at sunset, take a torch and prepare to return from the trailhead by bus or – more likely – taxi, either of which can be waved down on the main road. Tourism agencies in Lákka and the other ports organize coach trips to the cliffs involving "Greek night" meals in a Voïkátika taverna afterwards.

Andípaxi

The neighbouring island of **Andípaxi** is a flawed paradise, with the clearest blue coves in the entire archipelago – and some of the best snorkelling in Greece – but some rather indifferent beaches. Unfortunately, even the quieter low-season afternoons will invlove your sharing the two most popular bays with large numbers of day-trippers from Paxí and various resorts on Corfu. Even so, this does-n't entirely dent the charms of Andípaxi, and the island still has space to accommodate its invaders. The trick is to head south away from the crowds to find the quieter spots. Sunny Octobers can leave you with a small cove to yourself and a clear sea as warm as a bath.

High-speed sea taxis and more leisurely *kaïkia*, which take in the sea-stacks and blue-water caves of the west coast as well as the east coast bays, leave all three of Paxí's ports for Andípaxi each morning in season. Some craft try to charge substantially more than others and the best deals are to be found in Gáïos, where you should get a round trip for 1000dr, just to be dropped off and picked up later. The **sea caves** are the finest in the Ionian, and large enough to be entered by pleasure craft; according to local legend, one even concealed an Allied submarine during World War II. The sea taxis tend to buzz in and out, while *kaïkia* enter and cut their engines to scare faint hearts.

The first of the two main beaches where the tour boats and shuttle craft deposit their passengers is sandy, family-oriented **Vríka**, which has a taverna at each end – try *Spiros* for a tasty snack in the shade. From the side of *Taverna Vrika*, at the other end of the beach, a path winds up to the sprawling ghost settlement of **Vígla**, which is strung along the northern spine of the island. There are no facilities and, sadly, the wild and deserted west coast is inaccessible thanks to the thick rocky scrub, so the sweaty climb is barely worth the effort.

The island's ridge can also be reached from the other main beach, the longer but pebbly **Vatoúmi**, which has gorgeous turquoise sea but whose only taverna, the aptly named *Bella Vista*, is a stiff climb up the cliff at the southeastern end. If you find Vatoúmi too crowded, you can take the wide track on the west side, which hairpins round the valley behind before ascending the other side to join another path. Turn left here towards some villas; a path immediately to their right leads down steps to the first of two coves, collectively known as **Agrapidhiá**. A path on the far side joins the road down to the second, larger bay, which has a concrete jetty for the highly infrequent car ferry to dock at. Both coves have fine rock formations, make for excellent snorkelling and remain near deserted even in high season.

Accommodation is scarce on Andípaxi, and what little there is only caters for those wishing to stay by the week rather than the odd night. The limited number of **villas** can be booked mainly through tourism agencies in Gáïos such as Gáïos Travel (see p.125), although *Spiros* taverna (☎0662/31 172, daytime only; Paxí contact ☎0662/32 417 or 32 677) has a couple of large, well-equipped houses too. Although the level of comfort is high, prospective residents must be prepared to transport provisions with them and cater for themselves. There's little on Andípaxi apart from a smattering of summer houses owned by Paxiots – no shops or bars, and the three beach **tavernas** mentioned above only open during the day in season, closing once the day-trip craft depart

Travel details

BUSES

The reliable island bus service runs 7 or 8 times daily (30–40min) between Lákka and Gáïos from 9.15am until midnight. Most detour via Longós.

FERRIES

Ferry services have stabilized again after a couple of disrupted years. The *Pegasus* travels every day except Sunday (twice on Mon and Sat) between Gáïos and Corfu (1hr 30min), calling at Lákka on the way 3 times a week. The *Theologos* departs Gáïos daily at 7.30am for Igoumenítsa (1hr 45min) and Corfu (4hr 15min). At least one of these should be running all year. Check with the Port Authority (☎0662/ 32 259).

There is no proper ferry to Párga but *kaïkia* leave Gáïos at 9am and 4pm (2hr) during summer months. In season there is also a hydrofoil service to Corfu twice daily; Mon–Sat 8.30am direct, 4.20pm via Igoumenítsa; Sun 10.30am and 5.45pm, both via Igoumenítsa.

Chapter 3

Lefkádha

Although it is home to two very busy resorts, Nydhrí and Vassilikí, **Lefkádha (Lefkas)** is the least developed of the larger Ionian islands. The uninhabited parts are as wild and unspoilt, and the settlements as quintessentially Greek, as you'll find anywhere. Its terrain provides little land on which tourism might develop: almost ninety percent is mountainous or semi-mountainous, and just ten percent lowland. Its typically Ionian geography – cliffs on the west coast and flat land to the east – leaves a mixed endowment of beaches: the best, though splendid, are difficult to get to, while the more accessible are stony or pebbly, and sometimes rather scruffy.

Much of the island's tourism straggles along the east coast road heading south from Lefkádha Town. **Nydhrí**, overlooking Lefkádha's satellite islands, is a popular package destination, and has been commercialized to meet this demand. **Vassilikí**, set on the vast bay of the same name at the south of the island, is not far behind, and has some of the finest windsurfing in Europe. The mountainous **west coast** is less developed, but shelters some of the most attractive smaller resorts, notably the pretty village of **Aï Nikítas**, and the sandy beaches of **Káthisma**, **Pefkoúlia** and **Yialós**, as well as the phenomenally scenic bay of **Pórto Katsíki**.

Accommodation price codes

Rooms and hotels listed in this book have been price-coded according to the scale outlined below. The rates quoted represent the cheapest available double room in high season. Out of season, rates can drop by as much as fifty percent or more, especially if you negotiate for a stay of three or more nights. Single rooms, where available, cost around seventy percent of the price of a double. For further information, see p.36.

① up to 6000dr	⑤ 16,000–20,000dr
② 6000–9000dr	⑥ 20,000–30,000dr
③ 9000–12,000dr	⑦ 30,000dr upwards
④ 12,000–16,000dr	

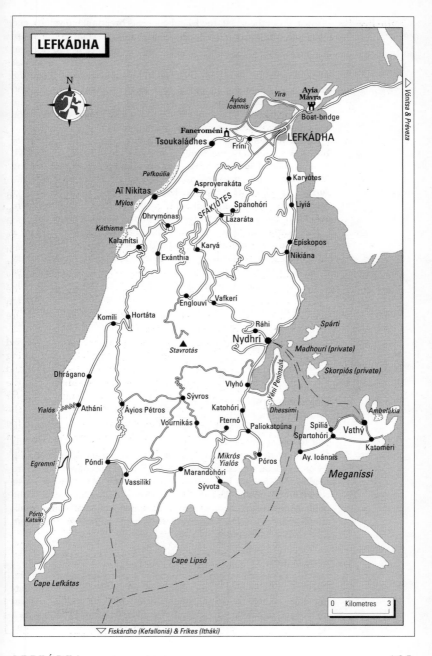

LEFKÁDHA

Away from the coast, the island conceals breathtaking valleys and hill ranges, offering some of the best **walking** terrain in the entire archipelago. Serious hikers should base themselves in **Karyá**, dead centre of a whole network of easily walkable villages set in an almost alpine landscape. Similarly, the road to Vournikás and Sívros in the south has fine mountain views, and the west coast route beyond Káthisma is also recommended, although probably in sections; the walk from Atháni to Cape Lefkátas is particularly fine, with primeval mountainscapes and empty arable land.

Lefkádha is also notable for its **satellite islands**. The proximity of the main quartet gives Nydhrí the finest sea views on the island, but only two of these – **Spárti**, and the larger and more interesting **Meganíssi** – are accessible to visitors. Some 20km away are the further satellites of **Kálamos**, **Kástos** and **Átokos**, all nowadays inaccessible from Lefkádha and, in the case of the latter two, reached only by occasional ferries from the Greek mainland.

The northernmost tip of Lefkádha, at Lefkádha Town, is barely a hundred metres from the mainland region of Akarnanía, and connected to it by a **causeway** that incorporates a boat bridge, raised every hour on the hour to allow yachts and small boats to pass through. This makes the island very accessible to Greeks from the mainland, who invade in high summer, and it's also very popular with Italian drivers arriving in the region by ferry. Buses connect Lefkádha Town to the Áktio **ferry** (for Préveza), half an hour's drive north, and there are also ferries to Itháki and Kefalloniá (from Nydhrí and Vassilikí).

These connections have given an unusual configuration to tourism on Lefkádha. In high season, especially now that the **international cultural festival** has been extended throughout the summer, the place can become as packed as anywhere, and rooms can be almost impossible to find in the main resorts. Outside these resorts, however, Lefkádha remains the least Anglophone of the Ionian islands, and even in the four-star hotels in Lefkádha Town staff may rely on you to speak Greek. As if to emphasize this ambivalence towards tourism, some years ago the island took the unusual step of closing its only official tourist information office, and the tourist police are unable to offer any more assistance than the phone numbers of rooms in the town. That said, after Corfu, **Lefkádha Town** is the most sophisticated of the island capitals, with a cinema, clubs, bookshops and a main shopping street where you can buy anything from a cowbell to a computer.

Some history

Lefkádha's **history** largely follows that of the archipelago as a whole. Excavations have produced evidence of settlement on the island dating back to the Neolithic, around 8000 BC. According to local mythology, Lefkádha was given to Arcadius, father of Penelope, as a gift from Laertes, on her marriage to his son Odysseus. It is this, along with a close geographical reading of Homer's *Odyssey* and the discovery of Mycenaean remains in the hills above Vassilikí, that led archeologist **Wilhelm Dörpfeld** (Heinrich Schliemann's assistant at the excavations of Troy and Mycenae) to spend many years in the late nineteenth century vainly attempting to identify Lefkádha as the home of Odysseus. Some of Dörpfeld's excavations are still visible on the roads just south and north of Nydhrí, but amount to little more than rather forlorn collections of architectural details fenced into small gardens which are locked to the public.

The island's **name** derives from the ancient Greek for "white", referring to the colour of its cliffs and barren mountain ranges. There has been much pedantic debate over whether it is a real island at all. Lefkádha appears to have been originally joined to the mainland by a narrow isthmus, through which the Corinthians excavated a channel in the sixth century BC – although those who argue in favour of its island status suggest that the Corinthians may simply have been clearing a pre-existing channel that had silted up.

Under the Corinthians, Lefkádha became a major seat of power, and played an important part in the Peloponnesian War in the fifth century BC; however, much of the archeological detail from this period has disappeared beneath farmland and more recent settlements. During the Byzantine period, the island fell into the same Byzantine "theme", or regional administration, as Kefalloniá and Zákynthos. Venetian rule on Lefkádha was shorter than elsewhere in the Ionian, lasting just over a hundred years from 1684 to 1797, and was interrupted, briefly, when the Turks captured the island – not for the first time – in 1715.

Like other Ionian islands, Lefkádha developed an extensive olive industry under the Venetians, but it also built its wealth on currants and wine grapes. The island's other **specialities** include honey (often produced by bees fed on thyme), *mandoláto* nougat, almonds and strong island wines and retsina. Lefkádha also has its own tradition of **kandádhes** and other folk-song forms, which can only be heard in village festivals and in certain tavernas in Lefkádha Town.

Arrival and getting around

Most visitors arrive via **Préveza (Áktio) airport**, 40km to the north on the mainland and only 2km west of Préveza town across the narrow entrance to the Amvrakikós Gulf (see box on p.140). There are no dedicated buses from the airport to the town of Préveza or to Lefkádha, although a minibus meets Olympic flights from the airport to the Áktio–Lefkádha ferry and the bus from the ferry to Lefkádha Town passes the end of the airport slip road five times daily (4 on Sun). The bus can be flagged down at the end of this road, barely 300m from Arrivals. Taxis to Lefkádha Town from the airport are negotiable, but expect to pay 4000–5000dr.

Préveza

Though the majority of tourists visiting Lefkádha use its airport, few ever see the town of **PRÉVEZA**, 2km to the east. The airport actually stands on, and takes its name from, the sandy peninsula of Áktio, off which the Battle of Actium was fought in 31 BC, when the fleet of Octavian decisively defeated that of Antony and Cleopatra. Anyone wishing to stay in Préveza itself is advised to walk (about 15min) or take the Olympic minibus (at Olympic flight times) or a taxi from the airport only as far as the ferry across the entrance to the Amvrakikós Gulf; after the ten-minute crossing (90dr), everything in Préveza is within short walking distance of the ferry quay.

Préveza can boast a pleasant seafront and a newly renovated centre, and is very popular with Greek holidaymakers, even though there are no beaches beyond a thin strip of imported sand. It's also a useful base for visiting either Nikópolis, the ancient city whose scattered walls and foundations can be seen 7km north of town, or the Amvrakikós wetlands skirting the Gulf of Amvrakikós which extends 20km inland from the town. The wetlands are one of the biggest wildlife sanctuaries in Greece, but are only really accessible with your own vehicle.

The town is built on a grid system, with most facilities – tavernas, bars, shops, hotels – a few minutes' walking distance from the quay. It's bookended by two large medieval forts, the castles of St George and St Andrew, but both are in use by the armed forces (who have quite a presence in Préveza) and off limits to the public.

Buses from other mainland towns arrive at the KTEL station on Ioannínon, the first true road reached through the grid of alleys behind the seafront. Services are basic: three daily from Athens (6hr); two daily from Igoumenítsa (3hr); ten daily (8 Sun) from Ioánnina (2hr 30min); five daily (3 on Sat and Sun) from Párga (2hr); and one daily from Thessaloníki (not Sat or Sun; 7hr). The five daily buses from Lefkádha Town (30min) terminate at the Áktio ferry (see above). The tourist office (Mon–Fri 8am–1pm) is in the government building at the west end of the seafront, next to the post office. There are various banks on Odhós Ethnikís Antistásis, the

It's worth pointing out that Préveza airport is still largely a military base, home to SEAC early-warning planes, with their distinctive disc-like radar, and the high-tech jets that streak through the islands on training runs. The authorities are particularly sensitive about security; the armed guards are extremely strict with queues for outbound flights and even people chatting to friends through the fences that bound the tiny airport building. Photography is banned, as at other Greek airports. Beyond a small bar and exchange kiosk, there are no other services at the airport.

Lefkádha Town's **bus station**, on Odhós Dhimítri Golémi opposite the small yacht marina, has connections from Athens and Thessaloníki, and is the hub of island transport. The station's new computerized system issues tickets with numbered seats, which you should use to avoid potential confusion, although outside the town it's normal to pay on board and sit anywhere. The bus station is the pedestrian precinct two alleys back from the seafront, plus a 24-hour money exchange machine on Ioannínon.

Because Préveza is very popular with Greek tourists, there are no cheap hotels and no rooms in the centre. The nearest rooms are in the suburb of Pantokrátoras, 3km northeast of town: try Evyenia Peroni (☎0682/27 745 or 26 640; ②) or Ilias Katsimbokis (☎0682/24 227; ③). The best-value hotels are the newly renovated apartment-hotel *Urania*, at Irínis 33, the diagonal thoroughfare through the centre of town (☎0682/27 123 or 24 307; ③), and the simple but pleasant *Minos*, in an alley off 21 Oktovríou in the centre of town (☎0682/28 424 or 27 424; ③). The large, modern *Preveza City* (☎0682/27 370 or 27 365, fax 23 872; ④) is away from the hubbub of the seafront, although on busy Ioannínon, but not particularly good value. More upmarket again are the *Dioni* on Platía Papayeoryíou (☎0682/27 381–2, fax 27 384; ⑤), a small, comfortable hotel tucked away from the crowds in the centre of town, and the smart *Hotel Avra* (☎0682/21 230, fax 26 454; ④), across the road from the ferry quay in the middle of the action. Two travel agencies offer a wide variety of accommodation and other services: Kiss Travel (☎0682/23 753 or 23 157, fax 28 846) and Elias Stamatis (☎0682/23 003 or 21 025), both on the seafront.

There are at least a dozen tavernas scattered around the inland market lanes in central Préveza, with cafés and bars on the pedestrianized portion of the waterfront boulevard Venizélou. Good eating choices inland include *Psatha*, Dhardhanellíou 2 (west of the main shopping strip), for standard oven food, and the long-standing favourite *Amvrosios*, a budget spot specialising in grilled sardines and good local wine, on the lane leading seaward from the Venetian clocktower. Other decent restaurants nearby are *Stavraka* or *Trata*; alternatively you could try the even more basic *Ouzeri Ousies*, one block inland from the front. By night, these bazaar alleys around the clocktower come alive with an assortment of bars, ouzeris, cafés (including an Internet one at Vasilíou Bálkou 6–8) and shops. In terms of organized culture, a range of musical and theatrical events is held at Nikópolis July and August as part of the Nikópolis Festival.

---

most efficient and friendly in the islands, although the more remote services sometimes vary wildly from the handy printed timetable (summer only). It's worth remembering that services to remote destinations such as Atháni stop early, and last buses frequently turn round immediately, with no later return service. There's also a smaller ticket office and bus stop where Golémi turns into Odhós Merarhías, but this is favoured by locals using longer-distance island buses to get to the suburbs, and often resembles a small-scale riot.

Taxis are easy to find outside the siesta, and even the smaller villages in the interior have at least one resident taxi driver; they don't come cheap, however, and a cab from Lefkádha to Vassilikí, a distance of some 38km, may cost up to 8000dr, unless your bargaining skills and Greek are well versed. In emergencies, bars, shops and travel agencies will usually telephone a cab for you. Cars and motorbikes can be rented in Lefkádha Town and the main resorts.

Lefkádha Town and around

LEFKÁDHA TOWN is compact, squeezed between a seawater lagoon – the *Ikhthyotrofrío*, quite literally "fishery" – and the foothills on the north side of Mount Stavrotás. Like neighbouring Kefaloniá and Itháki, it was devastated by the 1953 earthquakes, and little remains of the original town beyond a number of small private chapels. Sitting on a stunted peninsula, the town comprises one central thoroughfare, **Ioánnou Méla** (becoming **Dörpfeld** at the northern end), a trio of seafront roads (Golémi, Panagoú and Sikelianoú), and a warren of minor streets and mainly pedestrian alleys that vein the heart of the town. As a precaution against further earthquake damage, few buildings are above three storeys. The dormitory area of the town, west of Dörpfeld, took even greater precautions: most houses are built of stone only on the ground floor, and wood on the second, often with wooden balconies. The closely built houses with their small, elaborately planted gardens give this district the look of lanes you might find on Romney Marsh or Fire Island, perhaps even the flatter parts of old San Francisco. You can walk the length of the whole town in fifteen minutes, and traverse it in around ten, but despite its size Lefkádha Town is surprisingly cosmopolitan, with a spanking new cultural centre, a cinema, some excellent tavernas, cocktail bars, clubs and a small but hectic souvenir bazaar.

Accommodation

There's no campsite in Lefkádha Town; head for the bus station where you can catch a bus 4km south to Kariotes Beach Camping at Karyótes (see p.150)

The few **rooms** that are available in Lefkádha Town tend to be in the dormitory area on the west side, between Odhós Dörpfeld and the lagoon. Few houses have telephones, so most accommodation has to be found on foot. If your Greek isn't up to negotiating a room, householders are usually happy to find an English-speaking neighbour to translate. Rooms still tend to be cheap and very basic, with wooden floors and walls, spare furnishing and shared bathrooms, although some have been given a facelift. To book ahead, try the Lefkádha Room-owners Association (☎0645/21 266; ②–③) or either of these smarter operations: *Pinelopis Rooms* (☎0645/24 175; ②), Odhós Pinelópis, a small alley off the seafront two blocks from the pontoon bridge, or the nearby *Filion* (☎0645/25 326; ③), Odhysséos 6, a new set of apartments further back from the coast road.

As there is little space for expansion on the outskirts of Lefkádha, building has remained static in the town for several years, with no new **hotels** built in over a decade. The half-dozen or so that do exist are all at the northern tip of town, from Platía Ayíou Spyridhónos upwards.

Byzantio, Dörpfeld 40 (☎ & fax 0645/21 315). Small and basic old-style hotel with a lovely wooden spiral staircase. Located above its own taverna in the busiest section of town, with shared facilities. Good value. ②.

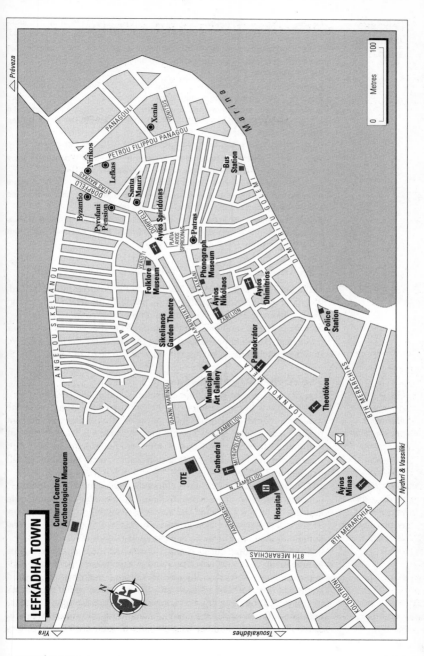

LEFKÁDHA TOWN

- Préveza
- Yíra
- Tsoukaládhes
- Nydhrí & Vassilikí

Cultural Centre/ Archeological Museum

PANAGOULÍ
Xenia
PETROU FILIPPOU PANAGOU
VÓNITSIS
Nírikos
Lefkas
AYÍAS MAVRAS
DORPFELD
Santa Maura
Byzantio
Pyrofáni Pension
Ayíos Spiridónas
DÖRPFELD
Bus Station
Patras
PLATÍA AYÍOS SPIRIDÓNAS
VERIÓTI
Phonograph Museum
Folklore Museum
FILARMONIKÍS
Áyios Nikólaos
KALKÁNI
Áyios Dhimítrios
Sikelianos Garden Theatre
ZABELÍOU
Police Station
IOANNI MARINOU
Municipal Art Gallery
Pandokrátor
IOANNOU MELÁ
Theotókou
D. DHIMÍTROU GOLEMÍ
8TH MERARCHÍAS
E. ZAMBELÍOU
OTE
Cathedral
MITRÓPOLIS
N. ZAMBELÍOU
FANEROMÉNIS
Hospital
Áyios Minas
8TH MERARCHÍAS
VOLKÓKHRONI

Marina

N

0   Metres   100

Lefkas, Panagoú 2 (☎0645/23 916, fax 24 579). In a prime location overlooking the lagoon, with excellent rooms and facilities, though rather overpriced. ⑤.

Nirikos, Ayías Mávras (☎0645/24 132–3, fax 23 756). Very comfortable modern hotel, with its own restaurant and bar, and en-suite rooms overlooking the causeway. ④.

Patras, Platía Ayíou Spyridhónos (☎0645/22 359). Best bargain after the *Byzantio*, with clean, basic rooms, shared hot-water facilities and cold water in rooms. Some rooms have wonderful views of the *platía*, which can be a mixed blessing, especially in high season, when you can forget about getting any sleep before 2am. ③.

Pension Pirofani, Kendrikí Agorá (☎0645/25 844 or 23 530, fax 22 270). Smart, newly renovated place above separately owned taverna of the same name on Dörpfeld. All rooms have air-conditioning and TV. ⑤.

Santa Maura, Spyridhónos Viánda 2 (☎0645/21 308–9, fax 26 253). Tucked in an alley off the top of Dörpfeld, smart en-suite rooms, with air-conditioning and double-glazing to fight the town's heat and noise. ④.

Xenia, Panagoú 2 (☎0645/24 762–3, fax 25 129). Large, modern B-class hotel, now privately owned, with restaurants and bars. Not bad value, but rather characterless and impersonal. ④.

The Town

Lefkádha Town is the most walkable of all the island capitals. Indeed, given the difficulty of actually getting a vehicle into the centre, walking is almost obligatory. Nightlife and tavernas are mostly clustered around Dörpfeld, and most of the churches and museums are either on or near Dörpfeld or Ioánnou Méla, the street it runs into south of the Italianate Platía Ayíou Spyridhónos at the heart of town.

The Archeological Museum

The Archeological Museum's opening hours given here were still under review at the time of writing, and may have changed by the time you read this.

The brand new **Archeological Museum** (daily 8am–2.30pm; free), which opened in the summer of 1999 at its new location inside the modern cultural centre, ten minutes' walk west along the seafront towards the lagoon, is now second only to Corfu's in its collection of antiquities. It is well laid out in four air-conditioned rooms, with interesting background explanations and clear labelling of all exhibits in English.

The largest gallery, **room A**, immediately in front as you enter, contains displays on weaving, fishing, the monetary system, trade and the techniques of wine, oil and bread-making in ancient times. There is a range of original artefacts on each subject, backed up by tasteful modelling. The loom is particularly impressive.

To the left, **room B** has a theme of cults and the worship of deities in ancient Leucas and contains various figurines of gods and goddesses, as well as votive objects. The bronze mirror on a caryatid stand and terracotta of a female sitting on a swan, which represents the myth of Zeus ravishing Leda, are the most noteworthy. The adjacent **room C** comprises a display of cemeteries and funerary procedures. There are a number of grave *stelai*, some inscribed, others sculpted, a casket complete with skeleton and numerous objects found at burial sites, including some delicate gold wreaths.

Room D, to the right of the entrance, is the prehistoric collection of Wilhelm Dörpfeld, dedicated to the work of the famous German archeologist. There is a concise history of the Paleolithic, Neolithic and Bronze Ages, with an array of mostly broken pottery plus tools, jewellery and photographs of various digs.

The Folklore Museum and Municipal Art Gallery

Located on Filarmonikís in the warren of streets to the west of Platía Áyiou Spyridhónos, the **Folklore Museum** houses a modest collection of traditional artefacts, but its series of photographs of the town before the 1953 earthquake is fascinating, and it contains some interesting models of Dörpfeld's excavations on the island (see p.139). The displays of domestic items – furniture, beds, cookware and clothes, including some beautiful women's costumes for island festivals – take up three rooms and could, at a pinch, provide an hour's diversion from the heat or rain. For a different slant on Lefkadhan life, you might check out the **Municipal Art Gallery** (daily 10am–1pm and 7–10pm; free) on Amaxikís, which is dedicated to Theodoros Stamos and features the work of local artists.

The Folklore Museum was closed for long-term renovations in 1999; its reopening date, opening hours and entry price are uncertain.

The Phonograph Museum

More of a junk shop than a museum and comprising a single room, the **Phonograph Museum** (daily 9am–1pm and 7–11pm; free) at Kontandínou Kalkáni 14, one block east of Ioánnou Méla, contains a dazzling, occasionally bizarre battery of bric-a-brac and paraphernalia such as electrical equipment, household utensils, ornaments, toys, photos, paintings, clothes and some books from the house of poet and politician Aristotelis Valaoritis on the family island of Madhourí (see p.166). They also sell cassette recordings of the old 78rpm records in the collection, featuring various *kandádhes*, *rembétika* and other folk music.

Churches

A number of small private **churches** dotted around the town, mostly dating from the eighteenth century, have so far survived the earthquakes. Modest in size, their architecture is atypical of the region in abandoning Byzantine design for simple, single-aisled rectangular buildings that would withstand earthquakes, with free-standing bell towers built of iron as an additional precaution.

The interiors of these churches are opulently decorated with screens and icons by painters of the **Ionian School**, including its founder, **Panayiotis Dhoxaras** (see box on p.77). Dhoxaras, who also painted the original ceilings of Áyios Spyrídhon in Corfu which were destroyed by damp, was responsible for the paintings in the church of **Áyios Dhimítrios** on Zabélion, his son Nikolaos for the

*Most of
Lefkádha
Town's
pre-quake
churches are
privately
owned by
island families,
and open and
close erratical-
ly; before and
after morning
and evening
services are the
best times to
visit.*

ceiling paintings of **Áyios Minás**, at the crossroads of Méla and Merárhias. The latter church has a striking metal clocktower and some of the best examples of the Ionian School, including work by Nikolaos Koutouzis and Lefkádha's most famous pupil of the school, Spyridhon Ventouris (see p.77).

The church of the **Pandokrátor**, on Ioánnou Méla, is owned by the family of the poet and politician Aristotelis Valaoritis (1824–79), who rivals the Zakynthian poet Solomos for the title of father of modern Greek literature, and is entombed behind the altar of the church. Further down Ioánnou Méla is the church of the **Theotókou** (or Presentation of the Virgin), which has ceiling paintings copied from the work of Raphael by Lefkadhan painter Spyridon Gazis, and the only remaining stone bell-tower in Lefkádha.

Eating and drinking

Much of Lefkádha's evening entertainment is centred on Dörpfeld and its surrounding streets and alleys, and in particular the small elegant square of Áyios Spyrídhon church. Surrounded on three sides by bars and restaurants, busking musicians, jugglers and even fire-eaters sometimes perform here on summer evenings. However, with the exception of old-fashioned *Ouzeria Thalassina* in the square itself, establishments in this area are the priciest in town. The north end of Dörpfeld is as hectic as London's West End in high season, with garish souvenir shops and tourists spilling out of cafés and bars onto the streets.

Less expensive **bars** are to be found away from the centre, particularly along the southerly end of Ioánnou Méla. One of the best is *Cafe Karfakis*, an old-style *kafenío* with straw-upholstered wooden seats, and ancient phonographs and 78s decorating the interior. Staff are helpful and in the evenings provide generous servings of *mezédhes* (often resembling miniature meals) with drinks, a tradition that has all but died out in most tourist bars. Another stylishly modernized *kafenío* is *Theofilos* with tables in the stone interior and under the colonnade outside. The hippest watering hole on Lefkádha is the difficult-to-find *Vengera Club*, tucked away on tiny Odhós Maháïra (signposted up an alley one block down Dimítriou Golémi from the bus station). This little-known hangout has a cool jazz and soul music policy, reasonably priced drinks and snacks and a quiet walled garden away from the crowds on Dörpfeld. Some of the town's most trendy bars like *Excess* and *Coconut Groove* are on the seafront road Sikelianoú, which is closed to traffic in the evenings. Further out towards Ayiánni, the *Atmosfera* club is a big disco with foreign sounds, while *Cosmos* is the place to shake your stuff to Greek hits.

Lefkádha Town's best local **restaurants** are hidden away in the alleys west of Dörpfeld by Áyios Spyridhón. *Taverna Reganto*, on tiny Dhimárhou Venióti and signposted by the church, is the favourite here: island cuisine at its best, in a simple, friendly setting that's always full of locals. In high season its opening hours can be erratic,

The Lefkádha Festival of Music, Arts, Literature and Dance

Each summer, Lefkádha hosts a wide-ranging cultural festival, which attracts performers and visitors from around the world. This has been extended throughout the summer from its original three-week spot in August, with events now being staged from June to September. It still peaks in August, adding to the usual high-season demand for accommodation. Troupes come from eastern and western Europe, South America and elsewhere, performing mainly in Lefkádha Town, but also in villages around the island. The island and mainland Greece respond with troupes of their own musicians and dancers, as well as concerts and theatre performances: the 1999 festival, for example, featured theatrical performances of Aristophanes' *Thesmophoriazouses* by a Greek company and Euripides' *Medea* by a Japanese one, jazz and classical concerts and dance groups from Slovakia, Thailand, Egypt, Georgia and South Africa. There were also art exhibitions and special cinema showings. For details, call ☎0645/23 352.

so if it's closed head for the *Lighthouse*, on Filarmonikís, which has its own small garden and a range of succulent, freshly prepared starters and taverna dishes. Larger and more tourist-oriented is the *Romantika* on Mitropóleos, with eyebrow-raising, almost postmodern decor, a small garden at the rear, and a vast menu of grills, seafood, salads and oven-baked staples. In season, the *Romantika* hosts nightly performances of Lefkadhan *kandádhes*; so if you'd prefer a quieter evening, try the *Bitsounis* opposite, which specializes mainly in grills. The smartest restaurant in town is the *Adriatica*, at the corner of Faneroménis and Merarhías, a rather barn-like establishment with a mixture of Greek and international dishes, where people tend to dress up. There are also a couple of upmarket restaurants facing the yacht quay on Golémi, the international-style *Sto Molo*, and the more traditional *psistariá O Karavoulias*. Both are favoured by the yachting fraternity, although the view is marred by incessant traffic and, in summer, the smell of drains. If the melée of Dörpfeld is your preferred backdrop for a lively evening meal, the *Eftihia* by the *Hotel Santa Maura* is recommended. For a pastry or breakfast, try the *Gustoso zaharoplastío* at the south end of Méla.

Listings

Banks Both the Ionian Bank and the National Bank of Greece have branches on Ioánnou Méla, the former at the southern end, the latter midway down. The Agricultural Bank of Greece is situated in the corner of Platía Ayíou Spyridhónos. Banks only open mornings (Mon–Thurs 8am–2pm, Fri 8am–1.30pm); outside these hours the larger hotels and travel agencies will change travellers' cheques, but not always at bank rates.

Bookshops There are no dedicated English-language bookshops on the island, although some Greek bookshops stock foreign-language guides and paperback fiction in English, German and Dutch. Most accessible are the *Katopodis*, *Konidaris*, *Mataragas* and *Tsiribasis* stores, all of them on Ioánnou Méla.

Car/motorbike rental EuroHire, Golémi 5 (☎0645/267 76), a few doors from the bus station, is a good bet for car and motorbike hire. The oddly named I Love Santas (☎0645/25 250), next to the *Xenia* hotel, is reliable for two-wheelers.

Cinema The *Cinema Eleni*, on Faneroménis, is an outdoor cinema set in a small, overgrown garden with a large screen attached to a handy block of flats. Its fare is mostly subtitled English-language films, with programmes changed daily (9pm & 11pm; 1800dr); as well as the usual parade of American block-busters, it can also startle with the occasional art-house movie. Be sure to wear long clothes and/or mosquito repellent.

Hospital Corner of Mitropóleos and Zambelíou (☎0645/22 336).

Laundries There are two laundries/drycleaners on Ioánnou Méla, but laundry doesn't come cheap; you can expect to pay 200dr and upwards per item, more if you want it ironed.

Library Ioánnou Marínou (Tues–Sat 8.30am–1.30pm).

OTE Corner of Zambelíou and Faneroménis (daily 7am–2pm).

Police Golémi 1 (☎0645/22 100). Tourist Police (☎0645/26 450).

Post office Ioánnou Méla (Mon–Fri 7am–2.30pm).

Around Lefkádha Town

The main point of interest in the immediate vicinity of Lefkádha Town is the impressive semi-ruined **castle of Ayía Mávra** (Santa Maura) squatting on the other side of the causeway to the mainland, a ten-minute walk from the north end of Dörpfeld. The fort, which now comprises three structures – Ayía Mávra itself, and the George and Alexander forts built during the Russian occupation – was start-ed in the fourteenth century by the Orsini family, and was extensive-ly rebuilt by the Venetians in the eighteenth century. However, much of the interior was destroyed when an explosives magazine acciden-tally blew up in 1888, and bombing during World War II further dam-aged the structure. Parts of what remains of the fortifications are open to the public daily, and are used as a spectacular backdrop to performances during the arts festival (see box on p.147).

Yíra beach

Lefkádha Town has an excellent boomerang-shaped beach, **Yíra**, on the seaward side of the lagoon. You can catch a bus there during high season from the bus station (hourly 10am–2pm), or it's a pleasant forty-minute walk from town, heading out westwards along Sikelianoú; alternatively, you can walk there along the sea road on the opposite side of the pontoon bridge, perhaps combining it with a visit to Ayía Mávra castle.

Roughly 4km long, the shingle and sand beach is often virtually deserted even in high season, save for the occasional cuddling cou-ple or nudist bather hiding in its most secluded spots – which, para-doxically, are in the centre (look out for the flagpole with an anemometer on top). The beach is bookended by two **tavernas**, of which the *Yíra* at the town end is recommended, and at the western end there are a couple of **bars**: one is housed in the first of four renovated windmills, while the larger *Club Milos* also serves as a restaurant by day and a club by night, where the local kids and the odd windsurfer while away afternoons and nights to the accompaniment of nosebleed techno and other rave culture imports. The presence of the windmills attests to the power of the prevailing winds here, which can produce small, choppy surf, although few windsurfers seem to have caught on to Yíra, opting for the flatter bay of Vassilikí instead.

Faneroméni monastery

Easily accessible on foot from Lefkádha Town, or from the south end of Yíra beach, the picture-postcard **Faneroméni monastery** (open daily 8am–2pm & 4–8pm; free) is the major ecclesiastical attraction on the island. From the outside, it resembles a large Swiss ski chalet, but this effect disappears once inside the spacious courtyard, which houses a chapel with beautiful stained-glass windows, a museum crammed full of ecclesiastical accessories, small and austere monks' cells, a bookshop and even public toilets. The monastery was originally built in the seventeenth century, but was destroyed by fire and rebuilt in the last century. During the German occupation of the island in World War II, the monks were forbidden to sound bells lest this be used as a code. They resorted to sounding a large wooden log, which hangs in the main entrance; nowadays, a solitary monk tends the building. Skimpy clothing is frowned on, though women can borrow capes (hanging on hooks by the entrance) to cover their shoulders. Near the main entrance to the monastery are some excellent shady walks along signed paths through the pine woods.

The quickest way to reach Faneroméni monastery from town is to walk along Faneroménis and up the lane from the hamlet of Fríni, which gives excellent views over town, lagoon and mainland (30min).

The east coast to Vassilikí

Lefkádha's **east coast** is the most accessible part of the island, and in parts is beginning to resemble Corfu's east coast, as the small resorts strung along the coast road expand and merge into one another. The road itself, largely due to the bridge link to the mainland, resembles a noisy motorway during the summer months. Most people head for, or find themselves deposited in, the major settlements of **Nydhrí** or **Vassilikí**, but there are the constantly expanding resorts of **Liyiá** and **Nikiána** nearer to Lefkádha Town and also a number of more remote spots, such as **Sývota** and **Mikrós Yialós**, as well as some fine walking routes around **Mount Stavrotás**.

Karyótes and Liyiá

Travelling south out of Lefkádha Town, the first village you'll arrive at, barely 3km from town, is **KARYÓTES**, now more of a satellite suburb and with no seafront beyond the *alykés* (salt pans) outside the village – which, like their namesakes on Zákynthos, are as fascinating as, well, watching salt dry. Karyótes does, however, have the best **camp-site** on Lefkádha: *Kariotes Beach*, also known as *La Pissina*, a small site hard by the coast road south of the village, but set back beneath olive trees, with washing facilities, a shop, bar, restaurant and a small pool (☎0645/71 103); the island buses stop just outside. There's little else immediately around it, besides *To Katoyi*, an ouzerí serving meat and fish in a lush grassy garden right next door. Less than ten minutes' walk further south is a small square with a supermarket, a couple of cafés and the excellent and friendly *To Syntrivani* taverna, situated, as the name suggests, beside a refreshing fountain.

The first stop of note on the route south is **LIYIÁ**, a working fishing harbour, with views across to the ruined castle of Áyios Yeóryios on the mainland, and a couple of narrow but clean shingle beaches on its outskirts – the best bet is **Tembéli**, just south of the port, with a beach bar and shady pines. There's little here to detain the independent traveller, though the choice of **accommodation** is reasonable, including the pricey *Konaki* (☎0645/71 127 or 71 397, fax 71 125; ⑥), a smart B-class hotel on the northern edge of the village with pool and gardens. Another, newer upmarket hotel is the *Porto Ligia* (☎0645/71 441 or 72 000, fax 71 900; ⑥) behind Tembéli beach. If you prefer an apartment (all ③) try *Marios Messinis* (☎0645/71 333), *Mavra* (☎0645/22 649 or 24 587) or *Verde Apartments* (☎0645/22 536) or contact Katina Gourzi (☎0645/71 105). Another source of accommodation is the Salt Lakes tourist agency (☎0645/71 820, fax 71 810) on the way in from Karyótes. The fishing trade supplies a number of excellent **tavernas**, such as the extremely popular *O Yiannis* on the seafront, *O Xouras* on the quay, *Paradisos* above Tembéli beach and *Marios* on the road out of town, and there are a couple of **bars**, *Polyxenis* and the oddly named *Art Club*, which features live football as well as loud music.

Epískopos and Nikiána

Two kilometres on is the shallow pebbly bay of **EPÍSKOPOS**, which shelters *Episcopos Beach* (☎0645/71 388), a basic but shady **campsite** with a shop, restaurant, grill and bar, and wash facilities. It shares the beach with the *Dukato* (☎0645/71 122, fax 71 852; ⑥), a stylish **hotel** with gardens overlooking the bay, and *Villa Thomaïs* (☎064571 985, fax 72 220; ⑦), a posh new place affiliated to the Best Western chain, but having the disadvantage of being on the opposite side of the road to the sea.

Epískopos may shortly become a suburb of the port of **NIKIÁNA**, which is smaller than Liyiá but shows more signs of development. It too has a working harbour, with a beach just beyond. The beach is another narrow strand of shingle, with rocky outcrops; far better is the strand on the other side of the bay, accessible from the main road but with no facilities. Nikiána has several **hotels**, among them the family-run *Pegasos* (☎0645/71 766, fax 25 290; ⑥), with gardens and en-suite rooms that have sea views, and the smaller, better-value *Ionion* (☎0645/71 721; ⑤). There are also a number of apartment developments: *Philigros* (☎0645/24 310; ④) has studios built around an overgrown garden off the main road; *Vicky Apartments* (☎0645/71 555; ④) is a small, upmarket establishment, with its own gardens and bar, but overlooking the road; while *Porto Fino Pension* (☎0645/71 389; ③) is about the best deal here. There are three **tavernas** overlooking the small harbour, of which the best is the *Pantazis Psistaria*, which also has rooms to let (☎0645/71 211; ③). Heading south, the *Lefko Akroyiali* taverna is good for fish. Nikiána is also home to the Lefkas Diving Centre (☎0645/72 105).

Nydhrí

Beyond Nikiána, sporadic development has now spread along the coast road pretty much all the way south to Nydhrí. The road climbs a fair way above sea level at some points, meaning that most of these places leave you with an awkward walk down to the nearest beach and some distance from any restaurants. Some of the new hotels are rather plush, however, most notably the *Sunrise* (☎0645/71 400, fax 71 868; ⑤), set on a bluff affording sweeping coastal views. From here a series of small coves leads on to the hamlet of Periyiáli, where the sprawling resort of **NYDHRÍ** begins.

Nydhrí is where most package holidaymakers to Lefkádha will find themselves, and offers boat trips to Meganíssi and the satellite islands. Although it has some fine pebble beaches and a lovely setting, at the mouth of a three-kilometre-long inlet, facing out towards the Yéni peninsula and the islands of Madhourí, Spárti and Skorpiós, the resort has been ruined by untrammelled development. Sadly, just as breathtaking as the sea views in Nydhrí are the car fumes. Some high-season mornings and evenings, when whistle-wielding traffic cops are fielded to massage traffic flow, the town actually develops its own smog problem. And, on top of the traffic congestion, the centre is scarred by the ugly, unchecked development along the main road, with many hotel rooms just metres from the traffic, which is busy day and night.

Fortunately, there's a tailor-made escape in the form of Nydhrí's very own **waterfall**, about a 45-minute walk inland (5min by car). From the road beyond the hamlet of Ráhi, a signposted track leads beyond the summer canteen to a small waterfall on the left, which shouldn't be mistaken for the main fall, further along the path. Depending on the preceding months' precipitation, the waterfall's pool can be big enough for a refreshingly cool swim, and makes a great place for a picnic. Unfortunately the area can get very crowded in high season, so don't expect too much of a peaceful idyll then. The walk from Nydhrí is pleasant and on level ground, through a rocky gorge with overhanging rocks and a floodstream strewn with snowy-white boulders. There's some shade en route, but the walk is best attempted in the cool of early morning or late afternoon.

Much of the accommodation in and around the village is run by travel agents, who can offer a wider choice of rooms, apartments and villas than the individual room owners – see "Listings" opposite for details.

Accommodation

Those **hotels** not already block-booked tend to fill up fast in Nydhrí and are not generally cheap, but the town does boast one of the best places to stay on the island: the *Hotel Gorgona* (☎0645/92 197 or 95 634, fax 92 268; ④), which offers an unbeatable combination of position (away from the busy main road), price and welcome. It's set in its own lush, subtropical garden, signposted two minutes' walk along the road to Ráhi, and offers good, modern en-suite rooms with balconies at decent rates, and the owner and her staff are unfailingly friendly and helpful.

Nydhrí also has a number of hotels on the beach, notably the twin *Nidrion Beach*, the second of which is in fact an extension of the first (☎0645/92 400 or 92 401, fax 92 151; ⑥). They offer modern, air-conditioned B-class comfort in en-suite rooms, some with good views of the islands. To the north of town, the smart *Bel Air* apartment hotel is air-conditioned and double-glazed against the noise and has its own pool, bar and other facilities (☎0645/92 125, fax 92 238; ⑤). Of the **rooms** to let, Emilios Gazis (☎0645/92 703; ③) and Athanasios Konidharis (☎0645/92 749; ④), both in the centre of Nydhrí, provide some of the best.

Eating and drinking

Nydhrí's core is the dozen or so tavernas and bars that line its quay, the grandly named **Aktí Aristotéli Onási** – now mostly used as a car park, but the view just about compensates for this sorry waste of one of the island's prime sites. At night, the quay comes alive: day-trip boats string lights in their rigging and there's usually a street market offering anything from books and toys to palmistry and tarot readings. Some of the most popular restaurants have queues for tables; others have hired greeters to lure punters off the pavement.

The *Barrel* **taverna** here dishes up an interesting variety of local dishes and north European food, especially fish, with exotica such as bream (a local speciality) cooked in a whisky sauce, but is pricey and typically tourist-oriented. The *Ionion*, on the front south of the quay, is cheaper and more genuine. *Il Sappore* lays on a vast range of pizzas and pasta, but if you want a quieter meal head for the beachfront *Agra Beach* taverna, under the hotel of the same name, which specializes in traditional dishes like *pastítsio* and is very popular with Greeks. Of the many places on the main drag, which are invariably better value if you can put up with the traffic, two that stand out are *Agrabeli*, whose menu includes unusual touches like cumin sauce, and *Ta Kalamia* grill, with a pleasant garden out back. Nightlife is limited to **bars** like *Status*, *No Name* and *Byblos*, and the *Sail Inn Club*, a music bar-disco which claims to stay open 22 hours a day.

Boat trips

The east coast to Vassilikí

Most people staying in Nydhrí seem to spend a lot of their time trying to leave it, if only on the myriad **boat trips** heading out to the islands of Madhourí, Spárti, Skorpiós and Meganíssi. Some tours go further afield to Itháki and Kefalloniá. The boats line up along the quay each morning, ready for departure between 9 and 10am, returning late afternoon. Tickets are around 3500dr per person for the local trips, 5000dr for the longer distances. Most craft to the nearby islets are interchangeable: small fibreglass *kaïkia*, with small bars and toilets, and open seating areas on the top deck or aft. Where they do differ, however, is in their itinerary – some will take in the sea caves of Meganíssi, others not, so it's advisable to check. The islands are all close to each other, so the journeys between them are short and sheltered. One of the best alternatives to these fibreglass buckets is the large wooden *Motor Sailer Panagiota*, a handsome old-fashioned *kaïki* run by and moored behind the *Barrel* taverna; the *Barrel* also offers day-trips on yachts that can take up to sixteen people. Another vessel with character is the wooden *Odysseas*, modelled on an ancient trireme, whose captain/guide is an enthusiastic old salt to boot. Athos Travel just south of the Ráhi turning (☎0645/92 185) organizes unusual night-time star-watching excursions, as well as other themed boat trips.

For more on Lefkádha's satellite islands, see p.166.

Listings

Car/motorbike rental As well as from the travel agencies mentioned below, car rental is available from branches of Eurohire (☎0645/26 776), Avis (☎0645/92 136), Budget (☎0645/92 008) and Hertz (☎0645/92 289), all in the centre of Nydhrí. Of the numerous bike outlets, I Love Santas (☎0645/92 668) is one of the most reliable.

Doctor Surgeries by the town hall (Mon–Fri mornings only) and next to the *Lefko* hotel.

Exchange The only proper bank in Nydhrí is a small branch of the National Bank of Greece on the main road. There is also a cash dispenser booth, most travel agencies offer bank rates, and the post office (see below) changes travellers' cheques.

Laundrette The island's sole self-service laundry, *Sunclean*, is situated at the southern end of town, opposite the *Athos Hotel*, and opens till late.

Port Authority For up-to-date information on all sailings (☎0645/92 509).

Post office There is now a small permanent post office building in the centre of the village (Mon–Fri 9am–2pm).

Travel agents Nydhrí's travel agencies are all close to each other on the main road. Biggest is the island-wide *Samba Tours* (☎0645/92 658 or 92 035, fax 92 659), which offers rooms as well as the usual range of travel, car rental and exchange services. Similarly, *Nidri Travel* (☎0645/92 514, fax 92 256) offers rooms and apartments, car rental and tickets, and can also arrange sailing-boat charters and jeep safaris to the more inaccessible parts of the island. *Homer* (☎0645/92 554, fax 92 627) rents out rooms, apartments and a wide range of cars and bikes (motor or pedal).

Vlyhó and the Yéni peninsula

When Nydhrí finally peters out, the country reverts to flat olive
groves. Just outside the village limits, near the hamlet of Stenó, are
the main set of **excavations** by Dörpfeld, a small circle of
Mycenaean burial chambers, which produced some of the finds displayed in the Archeological Museum in Lefkádha Town. A kilometre beyond the Dörpfeld site is the turning for the small hamlet of
Haradhiátika, which is one of the main routes up onto the island's
highest mountain, **Mount Stavrotás**. Haradhiátika is erratically
served by the Vassilikí bus, has just one taverna, but is a favourite
with walkers, who use the road to the even smaller hamlet of Áyios
Ilías to reach the 1100-metre summit.

About 3km from Nydhrí, the main road comes to **VLYHÓ**,
which looks out over the marshy flats at the bottom of the inlet
– a veritable mosquito incubator in summer. Vlyhó is popular
with freelance and bareboat yacht sailors, but has no hotels and
little to detain the traveller, apart from a few rooms and a handful of tavernas such as *O Thalassolikos* on the seafront by the
village's tiny square.

From Vlyhó, a minor road leads round to the **Yéni peninsula**,
where those who want to enjoy the view of the inlet but escape
the madness of Nydhrí can find **accommodation**: *Villa Maria
Rooms* (☎0645/95 153; ④) and *Australis* apartments
(☎0645/95 521;④) are near the bend at the bottom of the peninsula, while *Ilios Club* apartments (☎0645/95 612; ③) are up in
the village of Yéni itself. The road ends after 3km at the tiny
chapel of **Ayía Kyriakí**, where Dörpfeld is buried under a simple
stone memorial, and which has excellent views of Nydhrí and the
hills beyond.

Over the saddle of the Yéni peninsula, **Dhessími bay** is a large
expanse of blue water cutting deep into high green hills, behind
which it loses the sun early. It is flanked by two neighbouring **campsites** which, confusingly, are reached by two different (and steep)
lanes, even though they are separated by no more than a few metres.
Santa Maura Camping (☎0645/95 007 or 95 270, fax 26 087),
the further and larger of the two, is a basic site with washing facilities, shop, bar and a simple taverna-snack bar, but it's shady, with a
fair sprinkling of olive trees. The beach in front is narrow, pebbly
and, in high summer, tangled with the lines from innumerable pow-
ered inflatables in the water. The similar *Dessimi Beach Camping*
(☎0645/95 374 or 95 328), which gives onto a wider and cleaner
stretch of beach, has a better taverna, but in high season is packed
bumper to bumper with large 4-wheel-drive vehicles. There are
plenty of watersports available and, when you've worked up an
appetite, the mid-beach *Pyrofani* taverna offers a wide selection of
tasty meals.

Póros and Mikrós Yialós

From Vlyhó the main road south winds sharply up into the hills, passing through the quiet hamlets of Katohóri and Paliokatoúna, where a turning leads down to the attractive village of **PÓROS** and on to the small resort of Mikrós Yialós. Don't mistake Póros's presence on the map as a sign of tourism development – it's quiet even at the height of the season, and its few tavernas and bars close during the daytime.

MIKRÓS YIALÓS is a 4km trek downhill (the twice-daily bus from Lefkádha Town turns back at Póros), and the number of cars using the road is a sign that this isn't the quiet beach you may have hoped for. The small bay boasts an increasing amount of **accommodation** and number of **tavernas**. Most facilities are behind the main beach to the right as you hit the seafront. The best-value place to stay is *Oceanis Studios* (☎0654/95 095–6, fax 95 095; ③) or there are the more upmarket new *Rouda Bay* apartments (☎0645/95 634), which have sprung up from the eponymous taverna, formerly the *Mermaid*. Spreading up the hill in the corner of the bay, the well-kempt *Poros Beach Camping* (☎0654/23 203) has self-contained bungalows (④), shops and a pool. The pebble beach is clean, and the lack of any waterborne traffic in the long Rouda Bay that leads out to the open sea keeps the water clear. On the east side of the bay there is a concrete quay and tiny sandy beach in front of several more establishments, including the good-value *Hotel Ionio Sea* (☎0645/95 110; ③) and fine *Zolithros* taverna.

Inland to Sývros

About 2km on from Paliokatoúna, a right turn off the main road leads up into the hills, shortly passing the untouched village of **FTERNÓ**. The village *kafenío* and the *psistariá*, *O Haris*, are good spots to break your journey, though the sight of a tourist is still enough to draw a small crowd of bemused children and the odd inquisitive adult.

Fternó itself is quite literally a dead end, but further on from the Fternó turning, along spectacular and sometimes vertiginous mountain roads, are the neighbouring villages of **VOURNIKÁS** and **SÝVROS**. The former sports a pretty town square and fountain, one taverna and two cafés. There's no advertised accommodation, but rooms are sometimes available through the taverna or the cafés. Similarly, Sývros, which has stunning views down over the farming plain behind Vassilikí, is a quiet hill town with one taverna, one café and no visible accommodation. There are some private rooms here, but they're difficult to find: enquire in the taverna or café, or ask for the village taxi driver, who might be able to help. There are few facilities in either village, but either could make an excellent walking base, perhaps after an initial investigative trip, away from the hubbub of Vassilikí. One pleasant stroll is up the road to the church of

Áyios Ioánnis, formerly a monastery and before that a temple of
Artemis. The English-speaking priest may be willing to show you the
disused monastic cells and fragments of the ancient walls. A path
that branches right off the road before the church leads through pine
forest to the small mountain lake of Bísa.

Sývota

The next bay round from Mikrós Yialós – though 14km away by
road – is **SÝVOTA**, a long, crooked and beautiful inlet where the
open sea is not actually visible from the village. Already, however,
apartment developments are appearing on the hills around the harbour, and Sývota has become a favourite with yachties, visited by
flotillas of the British tour op Sunsail. Nights can be lively, but during the day, even in high season, the place tends to remain fairly
quiet, making it a good spot to come for a swim, even though there
is not much in the way of beach. Thomas Skliros (☎0645/31 151
or 31 347; ③), at the first supermarket on the right of the harbour,
has a few **rooms**, as do Yiannis Fatouros (☎0645/31 180; ③) at the
taverna *Delfinia* and Spyros Ktenas (☎0645/31 115, fax 32 337),
above the *Pavan* café round the harbour. There is an unofficial
campsite by the bus stop at the edge of the village. The list of facilities extends to several shops, bars, bike and car rental, a pizzeria
and a number of excellent **tavernas**: the *Ionion* is the most popular, but the *Delfinia* and *Kavos* are also good. Sývota has no real
beach, just a thin pebbly strand that can be reached by taking an
overgrown path along the north side of the harbour and a recently
imported strip of sand in the corner of the harbour. Only two **buses**
a day (6am and 1.15pm) thread their way down from Lefkádha
Town; beyond that you're stuck here, unless you're prepared to
negotiate the two-kilometre hike up to the main road to wave down
the Vassilikí bus.

Vassilikí and around

*There are no
banks in
Vassilikí, but
the post office
at the back of
the village and
the travel
agencies listed
below will
change trav-
ellers' cheques.*

Visitors tend either to love or loathe **VASSILIKÍ**. It's nightlife and
watersports make it very popular with a young crowd, but island-
hopping purists shudder at the intensity of commercialization along
its narrow streets and quayside. Nevertheless, the crowds and traffic congestion – eased a little by a one-way system around the village
– can't entirely obliterate the charm of its waterfront bars and tavernas, or the view out over its huge bay and spectacular mountains.
It is certainly an improvement on Nydhrí. Be warned, however, that
in high season Vassilikí can simply overload with tourists, to the
extent that frustrated visitors sometimes have to take a taxi to elsewhere on the island to find a bed for the night. Here, even more than
at Lefkádha Town or Nydhrí, it's crucial to phone ahead to book
accommodation.

Accommodation

Much of Vassilikí's **accommodation** is on or around the one-way system at the centre of the village, which tends to be both busy and noisy. A better bet is to go **beyond the ferry dock** on the northern spur of the harbour, along the road that leads along the back of the beach towards Póndi. The *Paradise* (☎0645/32 156; ③), a basic but friendly hotel overlooking the small rocky beach beyond the dock, is the best bargain here. Also good value for its class is the upmarket *Hotel Apollo* (☎0645/31 122 or 31 141, fax 31 142; ④). Rooms and apartments are available along the beach road to Póndi: *Billy's House* (☎0645/31 418 or 39 363; ③), Christina Politi's rooms (☎0645/31 440; ③) and the *Samba Pension* (☎0645/31 555; ④), also bookable through *Samba Tours* (see below), are all smart and purpose-built. In the opposite direction from the dock, left towards the wooded headland, the most reasonable of the few places to stay is *Pension Holidays* (☎0645/31 011 or 31 426; ④). Vassilikí's only **campsite**, the large *Camping Vassiliki Beach* (☎0645/31 308 or 31 457, fax 31 458), is about 500m along the beach road. It has its own restaurant, bar and shop, but is comparatively expensive.

In the **centre of town**, the two main hotels are the *Vassiliki Bay Hotel* (☎0645/31 077, fax 23 567; ⑤), whose prices are commensurate with its stylish, modern en-suite rooms with balconies and views; however, it is probably a better bet than the *Hotel Lefkatas* (☎0645/31 801–3, fax 31 804; ⑤), a large, modern building with bar, restaurant and disco, overlooking the busiest road in town.

Rooms in the centre of town tend to disappear into the maw of the package companies who bring clients here. With such a premium on accommodation, few private room owners are prepared to rent for just one night; many refuse to negotiate for less than a week. Worth trying, preferably in advance, are Yioryios Khrisovitsanos (☎0645/31 002; ③), Yioryios Politis (☎0645/31 455; ③) and the upmarket *Pension Kalas* (☎0645/31 003; ④). Alternatively, get in touch with one of the local **travel agencies**, which keep a range of accommodation on their books, plus **car rental**, exchange facilities and a variety of other tourism services: Hortis Travel on the Póndi road (☎0645/31 414, fax 31 127); Samba Tours, who are open all year, on the road running down to the quay (☎0645/31 520, fax 31 522); and nearby Star Travel (☎0645/31 833, fax 31 834, email: *startrvl@lefkada.hellasnet.gr*), where you can also use Internet facilities. Cars can also be rented from GM Rental (☎0645/31 650–1, fax 31 651) and Chris and Alex's (☎0645/31 580), both near the Póndi turn.

The beaches

Vassilikí's **beach** is a disappointment, at least for those hoping to spend time on it, as opposed to windsurfing off it. Much of it is gritty, although it improves towards Póndi. The deep bay, protected by an eight-kilometre promontory leading to Cape Lefkátas and by Cape

In any medical emergency, Vassilikí has a Health Centre, which can be contacted 24 hours on ☎0645/31 065.

Lipsó on its eastern side, is ideal for **windsurfing,** and forms the venue for regular top-quality tournaments. The prevailing north-westerly winds and local topography produce a fairly stable pattern of onshore winds in the morning, and increasing cross-shore winds in the afternoon. Three windsurfing centres now ply their trade on the beach, including Club Vassiliki, which claims to be the largest in the world. It offers boards, equipment and tuition from beginner to advanced levels, with simulator boards and video tuition in its club house. Half-day board hire costs 7000–8000dr in the morning (9am–1pm) and around 8000–9000dr in the afternoon (2–6pm), depending on the season.

*Club Vassiliki
and Fanatic
Board Centre
can offer
complete
windsurfing
packages to
Vassilikí
through agents
in Britain –
see p.6.*

The number of boards on the water at Vassilikí makes swimming slightly hazardous, so most people join the morning queues for the *kaïkia* that ply between the quayside and the excellent sandy beach-es of Egremní and Pórto Katsíki, on the wild, uninhabited west coast of Cape Lefkátas (see p.162).

Eating, drinking and nightlife

Vassilikí's quayside **tavernas** are difficult to differentiate, but stand-outs include the *Dolphin Psistaria*, near the bus stop on the quay, which offers a large selection of fish and seafood; *Alexander*, whose menu includes Chinese dishes in addition to Greek staples; and the *Penguin* in the centre, which specializes in lobster, swordfish and steaks served with exotic sauces. If you're looking for somewhere more peaceful, head for the *Sapfo* taverna-grill near the *Vassiliki Bay Hotel*, or southeast round the quay to the *Apollo*, which has a lovely leafy setting on the wooded headland.

Vassilikí's **nightlife** has developed along with its fashionability among high spenders, although a cynic might diagnose style out-stripping content. Where to drink tends to depend on the size of crowds and your taste in music: bars along the front specialize in terms of music policy and develop faithful followings. Amazingly, one of the cheapest places to drink on the entire island is in the cen-tre of the L-shaped quay: the *Livanakis kafenío* next to the bakery, with tables on the edge of the harbour, which is much favoured by savvy Greeks. Two decent bars on the road down to the harbour are *Abraxas Tunnel*, a cosy hole-in-the-wall place with imported beer, and the similar but less attractive *After Eight*. For those wishing to dance to Greek disco, the *Center Club* is a modern *ellinadhikó* and there's one club on the beach, *Remezzo*, which gets more than its fair share of poseurs and designer beefcakes. Flyers sometimes advertise raves on the beach at Pórto Katsíki.

Póndi

Barely a twenty-minute walk along either the beach or the road, the micro-resort of **PÓNDI** has become a quieter alternative to Vassilikí. It has a better, less crowded section of beach, which even has some patches of sand on the foreshore. There is still not that much **accommodation** here, though construction works suggest that will soon change, and only a handful of tavernas. About a five-minute walk up from the beach, the *Ponti Beach Hotel* (☎0645/31 572–5, fax 31 576; ⑤) is very popular with Greek visitors. It has en-suite rooms with excellent views of the bay, a tiny pool, and a bar and restaurant that are open to non-residents. Cheaper rooms are available on the beach at the *Pondi* (☎0645/31 888; ③), which is used by the tour operator Manos Holidays, and the comfortable *Nefeli* (☎0645/31 515; ④). The most appealing restaurant is *Panorama*, which offers specialities like garlic prawns and steak Diana. A horse-riding club, *Hippokambos*, is tucked in the fields behind the beach.

The west coast

The mountainous and often sheer west coast is the least developed part of Lefkádha, but is blessed with the most attractive resort in picturesque **Aï Nikítas**, the best beaches, such as **Pefkoúlia**, **Káthisma** and **Yialós**, as well as some of the island's most interesting villages clinging to the high mountain roads. It is worth making the effort to travel down the west coast at least once, as it offers some of the most splendid vistas of rugged mountains tumbling into startling blue seas to be found anywhere in Greece. **Buses** from Lefkádha Town travel as far as the small, remote village of Atháni, from where a newly metalled road continues 14km to Cape Lefkátas, but it is advisable to procure your own wheels to get the most from this exquisite part of the island.

Tsoukaládhes and Pefkoúlia beach

TSOUKALÁDHES, just 4km from Lefkádha, is beginning to develop a roadside tourism business, with some tavernas and bars, a small, basic **campsite**, and two sandy beaches a couple of kilometres' hike below the hamlet. Given its proximity to Lefkádha Town, however, and its dull appearance, there's very little reason to stay here.

Four kilometres on, the road plunges down to the sand and pebble **Pefkoúlia beach**, one of the longest on the island. The *Jorelos* taverna towards the southern end is the best place to eat, and there are some rooms above it – unfortunately, however, they are owned and rented by the unpleasant proprietor of the adjacent establishment. Back at the north end, about 2km away, there is unofficial camping. Buses to points further down the west coast stop at either end.

Aï Nikítas

Jammed into a gorge between Pefkoúlia and the next beach, Mýlos, is **AÏ NIKÍTAS**, the prettiest resort on Lefkádha, its wood-clad buildings jumbled together claustrophobically. The beach is small and

Aï Nikítas is
within walk-
ing distance of
both Káthisma
(3km) and
Kalamítsi
(5km), along
the dramatic
coastal road.

pebbly, and loses the sun before 6pm even in high season, but it's blessed with crystal-clear water last seen in a David Hockney painting. Small boats ply from here to the difficult-to-reach, kilometre-long sandy beach at Mýlos (800dr return). The back of the village, however, has been left as an ugly, dust-blown car park, which rather detracts from the appeal of the pleasant, if basic, *O Aï Nikitas* **camp-site** (☎0645/97 103, fax 21 173), set in terraced olive groves.

Accommodation

In between the car park and beach is a long pedestrianized lane of shops, bars and tavernas; most **accommodation** is situated in the alleys that run off this lane. Tourism here is determinedly upmarket, and consequently there are few bargains to be had. The best bets are the *Pansion Aphrodite* (☎0645/97 372; ③), the small *Hotel Selene* (☎0645/97 369; ④), the *Hotel Kalypso* (☎0645/97 332, fax 97 333; ④) and the purpose-built wooden apartments owned by Spyros Verikios (☎0645/97 380; ③). A quieter option and one of the most reasonable places is the *Olive Tree* (☎0645/97 453; ③), tucked away on the south side of the village, a friendly, wood-clad hotel with en-suite rooms and balconies, accessible either from the village or the road above it. In the middle of the village, the modern *Hotel Nefeli* (☎0645/97 400, fax 97 402;⑤) and plush new *Odyssey* (☎0645/97 351–2, fax 97 421;⑥), complete with pool, offer some of the smartest accommodation, while the *Hotel Agios Nikitas* (☎0645/97 460, fax 97 462; ⑥), which has rooms spread through three small balconied buildings built around beautiful gardens, has been usurped at the top of the range by the huge new *Santa Marina* (☎0645/97 455 or 97 111, fax 97 113; ⑦) on the hill up behind the campsite. By far the most attractive upmarket option, however, has to be the *Pension Ostria* (☎0645/97 483 or 25 318; ⑤), a beautiful blue and white building above the village with a restaurant-bar overlooking the bay, decorated in a mix of beachcomber and ecclesiastical (driftwood, stones, church relics). The rather small en-suite rooms have similar views of garden and sea, and the bar and restaurant are open to non-residents, making this a good spot to relax if you're just passing through. It is worth noting that, somewhat unusually for Greece, the price of all the upper-range hotels includes a mandatory buffet breakfast.

Aï Nikítas has
a Europcar
rental agency
at the top of
the village
(☎0645/23
581, fax 23
282), which
shares an
office with the
general tourist
agency Travel
Mate.

Eating and drinking

Teetering just above the beach, the **taverna** *Sapfo* offers the best views in Aï Nikítas and a choice of seafood, pasta, grills and salads. Tucked up an alley on the west side of the village is the quieter and cheaper *T'Agnantia*, with an extensive menu and views over village and sea. Of the numerous restaurants lining the village's high street, *Taverna Portoni* also juggles a wide range of fish, pasta and traditional Greek dishes; *Milos*, halfway down, offers a wide menu of inexpensive standards; while *Zorbas* is a cheap and cheerful grill. Wicked ice creams can be sampled at *Mr Gel*, while a fine selection of sweets and pastries is to be found at the *zaharoplastío Elena* opposite.

Nightlife is fairly low-key, with *Captain's Corner* at the seaward end of the main street being the liveliest, followed by the gentler ambience of *Café Ambali*, right on the beach, and the adjacent *Barbarossa*, which actually juts out over the water.

Káthisma beach and Kalamítsi

Beyond Mýlos beach is the first of this coast's magnificent beaches, **Káthisma**, served by five daily buses from Lefkádha Town, one of which originates in Nydhrí. Viewed from the cliffs above, the beach is stunning, a perfect line of gold sand and dazzling blue sea with a creamy turquoise wash at the water's edge. Close up, the reality is a little more prosaic, and in high season the main section of beach can be scruffy, with no likelihood of improving until the winter storms hoover the Ionian. Few people, however, wander far beyond the craggy rocks that mark the southern end of the busiest strip, and yet there is a huge stretch of much more appealing sand in this direction, right along to below Kalamítsi. There are several canteens and two **tavernas** on the beach, the vast, barn-like *Kathisma Beach* at the north end, which boasts a huge menu and has some first-class apartments (☎0645/97 050, fax 97 335; ⑥) available all year, and the quieter *Akroyiali* towards the rocks. On the winding road above the beach there are two more tavernas with **rooms**, the *Balcony* (☎0645/97 491; ④) and the slightly cheaper *Sunset* (☎0645/97 488 or 97 474; ④). A large sign on the beach insists "Camping strictly forbidden", although there remain pockets of discreet freelance camping at the far end of the beach. Káthisma has little natural shade but there are enough sunbeds and umbrellas to relax an army, and the *Kathisma Beach* offers free showers and a range of watersports and paragliding.

From here the coast road takes a series of spectacular hairpin bends on the way to the mountainside village of **KALAMÍTSI**, the last tourist-oriented settlement on the coast before distant Atháni. Most of the houses here are the barely modernized shells of cramped peasant cottages, although tourist **accommodation** tends to be in purpose-built two-storey houses. Basic rooms are available through Spyros Karelis (☎0645/99 214; ②) and Spyros Verginis (☎0645/99 411; ②); larger rooms and apartments are at *Hermes* (☎0645/99 417; ②), the *Blue and White House* (☎0645/99 413; ②) and the smart new *Pansion Nontas* (☎0645/99 197 or 99 451; ③). There are a few shops and bars, as well as three **tavernas**: the *Paradisos*, in its own garden with fountain, the more basic *Ionio* and the small *Steki* grill. Just outside the north end of the village, the aptly titled *Panorama View* restaurant offers a good selection of decently priced seafood, pasta, grills and taverna staples. Three kilometres down a recently paved road is the village's quiet sandy **beach**, in effect the southern end of Káthisma. The *Avali Beach* taverna sits at the end of the road, while a dirt track beforehand leads to some smaller rocky coves.

South to Atháni and beyond

Beyond Kalamítsi, the road first climbs the mountainside then dips into a valley behind the cliffs. The first settlement you reach is the workaday, yet appealing village of Hortáta with an attractive plane-shaded square and a few shops, restaurants and cafés. On the way in, look out for the excellent *Lygos* taverna, which serves a lot of fresh home produce and also rents comfortable rooms at a snip (☎0645/33 395; ②). Just before Komíli, a turning skirts the mountains of the interior and leads all the way to Vassilikí bay, via the lively village of **Áyios Pétros** with its charming little square and fine tavernas such as *O Faros* and *Ta Madzanakia*.

Komíli itself is more mundane, with just one taverna and a smattering of houses. Beyond it, the landscape becomes eerily empty, although the four-kilometre stretch before Dhrágano, with its magnificent near-deserted wheat-farming landscape, makes for an excellent walk. As the road winds on south through the continually captivating landscape, there are ample opportunities to take home a sweet memento in the form of the pure local honey, made by bees fed on wild thyme, that is sold at roadside trestle tables.

Take care if visiting Atháni on public transport – the last bus back to Lefkádha Town leaves early in the afternoon.

Some guides speak misleadingly of **ATHÁNI** as a centre for this region of the island. In fact, it's a bit of a dead end – three tavernas, two shops and a public phone – albeit a very pleasant one. Most visitors head for the *Panorama* (☎0645/33 291 or 33 476; ②), which, as well as a **restaurant** with balcony, has an upstairs cocktail bar and very cheap **rooms** with, as the title justifiably claims, panoramic views over the sea as far as Cape Lefkátas and, on clear days, Kefalloniá in the south. You may even find your self being serenaded by the friendly musical proprietor. *O Alekos* (☎0656/33 484; ②) is a more traditional taverna, also with rooms, but if you want a quieter lunch or dinner, head for the family-run *Lefkatas* taverna on the edge of town.

Directly west of Atháni, a newly asphalted road winds 4km down to the splendid beach of **Yialós**, which is several kilometres long, rarely at all crowded and has a couple of seasonal canteens for refreshment. Meanwhile the main road south – now decently surfaced too – continues for about 2km along the barren Lefkátas peninsula to a signpost for the steep track, unpaved for the last 2km, down to **Egremní beach**, and a further 5km to the beach at **Pórto Katsíki**. Sandy and shady, these are two of the most picturesque beaches on the island, though any dreams of solitude will be shattered as hundreds of *kaïkia* full of day-trippers come puttering in mid-morning from Vassilikí. Pórto Katsíki is particularly comely with chalky turquoise sea near the shore, deepening to deep violet, and dramatic overhanging cliffs, upon which perch several well-stocked snack bars.

Cape Lefkátas

Cape Lefkátas is a shadeless 14km from Atháni and, while the terrain is suitably rugged and majestic, you'll find little to celebrate here beyond a lighthouse and a sense of achievement for actually having made it this far. The cape, which can be quite fearsome in bad weather, rises an almost sheer 60m on its west coast, and is little gentler on the protected east side. It has numerous mythological associations, not to mention a barely recognized role as one of the key sites in early queer history.

The rocks have been identified as the site of human sacrifices as long ago as 1200 BC. By the fourth century BC the ritual victims were criminals, with feathers and even live birds tied to them to help ease their descent, and boats at hand in the sea below; if the victims survived the plunge, their lives were spared. By this time, the promontory was the site of a temple of Apollo, who was believed to take care of seafarers and whose cult promoted the idea of leaping from the cliff to cleanse mind and body – not only from the stain of crimes, but also from the torment of unrequited love. Aphrodite is said to have been the first to go over the edge, in response to the death of her lover, Adonis. Byron describes the cape in *Childe Harold's Pilgrimage* as "the lover's refuge, and the Lesbian's grave" – a reference to **Sappho** (born on Lésvos), who according to local myth threw herself off Cape Lefkátas out of frustrated love for a man, Phaon. Nineteenth-century engravings of her suicide tend to figure the iconic lesbian in a state of bliss, lyre clasped to her bosom, eyes closed and raised to the heavens, fearless on the western precipice and about to jump. Perhaps the greatest irony, however, is that despite the untold number of tavernas and bars that sport her name, Sappho probably never actually visited Lefkádha at all: the suicide is inferred from literalist readings of the few remaining fragments of her poetry, and the boyfriend was written into the story by historians mortified at the fact that she dated girls. Still, with all the testosterone wafting over from Vassilikí, the island could do with the odd coachload of carousing dykes.

Karyá and the interior

No one should leave Lefkádha without venturing into its **interior** at least once. Whereas the interiors of the other Ionian islands are either too easily accessible or just plain dull, inland Lefkádha can startle with panoramic hillscapes or hidden valleys which nurture the island's wheat industry. The elephantine humps of **Mount Stavrotás** and its neighbour Mount Eláti block communication across the island, so that communities such as Sývros and Vournikás (see p.155) have to be approached from the south, though the majority of the inland villages can be easily reached from Lefkádha Town itself (buses visit most villages at least once a

day) and the road from Karyá via Vafkerí is now paved most of the
way to Nydhrí. Cross-island jaunts may soon be made even easier
by the projected construction of a direct link from Hortáta to the
Sývros–Nydhrí road.

Karyá

The road south from Lefkádha Town forks at the urban limits, the
right-hand prong rising into the hills to enter the district of
Sfakiótes, a conglomerate of some half a dozen tiny villages. A couple of these merit a break in your journey: **Lazaráta**, 8km south of
Lefkádha Town, has a handful of cafés and restaurants huddled
around the small square, marred only by its proximity to the main
road, upon which stands the comfy *Pension Filoxenia* (☎0645/61
533 or 61 427; ③); 2km further on, the pretty vine-growing village
of **Asproyerakáta** also offers a couple of **hotels**, *Iy Zoí* (☎0645/61
136; ②) and *Villa Karidia* (☎0645/61 196; ③), and a number of
tavernas around a small town square, as well as a bizarrely named
duo of hangouts – *Café Stewart* and *Fryas Cosmic Centre*.

About 3km beyond Asproyerakáta is **KARYÁ**, which boasts an
extremely scenic main square, shaded by plane trees, with excellent
views out over the Liyiá/Nikiána coast to Akarnanía on the mainland.
As well as a post office and petrol station, the village is noted for the
number of shops selling carpets and other woven goods, and **lace
embroidery**. This timeworn tradition is celebrated in the fascinating
folklore museum on the edge of the village, run by the family of one
of Karyá's greatest lacemakers (daily in summer 9am–10pm; 600dr).
Even if the notion of lacemaking causes your eyes to glaze over, this
renovated peasant home is worth a visit for its wealth of social detail,
with eating, sleeping and living quarters carefullly reconstructed,
and clothing, implements and lacework artfully arranged around the
house. The museum has recently been expanded into a weaving
school, where visitors can see young apprentices being trained in
these traditional skills.

Practicalities

The *Karia Village Hotel* (☎0645/51 030; ④), tucked away 200m
along the first lane rising above the village, is a surprisingly large and
modern **hotel** for its setting, with balconied en-suite rooms, a swimming pool, bar and restaurant. **Rooms** are available from Haritini
Vlahou (☎0645/41 634; ②), the Kakiousis family (☎0645/61 136;
②), Olga Lazari (☎0645/61 547; ③) and Michael Halikias
(☎0645/61 026; ③).

Karyá's square, which also serves as the village bus stop, is an
excellent place for lunch or dinner, or just chilling out. As well as a
number of *kafenía*, it has two popular *psistariés*, *Ta Platania* and
O Rousos, while just off the corner of the square is the smarter
Klimataria taverna, with the widest choice of food and best views.

Curiously, the village also boasts a German-style beer cellar, the *Alt Kelerei*, hidden away on the northern edge.

Around Karyá

To the south of Karyá, rising up the slopes of Stavrotás' smaller but nonetheless impressive northern neighbours, are two of the oldest villages on the island, with architecture dating back to the sixteenth century. The one most worth visiting is **ENGLOUVÍ**, the highest village on Lefkádha, with spectacular views, and the centre of the island's lentil crop. The name means "encaged", which makes perfect sense when you stand looking out from the pretty village square or sit at one of the cafés, surrounded by mountains on three sides. Unfortunately, the nearest peak is dominated by ugly military instalments, adding an ominous edge to the otherwise pristine natural surroundings. Less than a kilometre outside the village, a small cave, barred to the public, is claimed to have been the cave of the *Odyssey*'s one-eyed giant, Polyphemus, although only a liberal reading of the tale would identify it as the place. From Englouví, a track, signposted at the south end of the village, leads circuitously up to the 1182-metre summit of Mount Stavrotás – a good half-day's round walk there and back.

The road to Englouví branches off from the much improved road to the other old settlement of **VAFKERÍ**, which is nearly deserted today, but still has some fine island architecture and is worth a halt if you are continuing along the useful road linking it to Nydhrí on the east coast. There is no accommodation but sustenance is available at the *Dhyo Adherfia* and *O Platanos* taverna/grills. On the way between Karyá and Vafkerí, the small village of **Platýstomos** is less appealing architecturally, but it has a grill, affords fine views across the eastern valleys and offers fine local wine for sale at the well-advertised family vintners. Beyond Vafkerí the road winds gradually down towards the east coast, passing close by the waterfalls (see p.151) before reaching Nydhrí.

On the opposite side of Karyá, recently paved roads skirt the lesser peak of Mount Méga to reach the two main west coast mountain villages, **DHRYMÓNAS** and, 3km further, **EXÁNTHIA**, high above the beaches of Káthisma and Kalamítsi. Clinging to the side of the mountain, both villages have a few shops and cafés, primarily to serve local people, and spectacular views of the sunset out at sea. In Dhrymónas the *psistariá O Memis* is located in a shady spot with views down the valley below, but Exánthia is more picturesque overall. Note the ornate metal framework of the campanile of Áyios Stéfanos, the church that dominates the centre of the village. *Iy Rahi* café/grill is the best spot to stop for refreshment and sweeping coastal vistas.

Lefkádha's satellites

Lefkádha's four main satellite islands lie a short way off its east coast and can be reached – or at least viewed – by day-trip boat from Nydhrí (see p.153). **Meganíssi**, the largest and most interesting, can also be reached by regular ferry. The nearest, tiny **Madhourí**, is owned by the family of nineteenth-century poet and political hero Aristotelis Valaoritis, and is off limits to visitors. **Spárti** is deserted and covered in scrub. **Skorpiós**, purchased in the 1960s by Aristotle Onassis, is held in trust for Athina Onassis, daughter of the late Christina, and is patrolled by armed guards. Daily tours pass close by – some even stop to let you swim off the boat in a sheltered bay – and you can spot a few buildings through the trees from the Meganíssi ferry, but the island, where Onassis and Jackie Kennedy were married, is virtually a ghost estate. Over fifteen different *kaïkia* circle the islands daily, which must make life for the inhabitants rather like living in a zoo.

Lefkádha's more distant satellites, the near-deserted islands of Kálamos, Kástos and Átokos, are in fact closer to the Greek mainland. Nowadays, none of them can be reached from Lefkádha, and only **Kálamos** has a regular ferry service, from Mýtikas on the mainland (south of Vónitsa on the coast road between Préveza and Astakós). **Kástos** has a small village and harbour, but can only be reached by finding a lift with an independent yacht heading in that direction or by hiring a *kaïki* to take you – enquire in Mýtikas or Kálamos. **Átokos**, to the southwest of Kástos, is now deserted, and attended by rumours of forced evacuation after an outbreak of disease.

Meganíssi

Almost barren **MEGANÍSSI** has remained a well-kept secret for many years, kept quiet by visitors who like their islands nearly deserted. Little has changed over the decades, although there are the first small signs of development, suggesting that Meganíssi should be visited before it's sucked into the mainstream of Greek tourism. An excellent, year-round (weather permitting) **ferry** service connects Nydhrí with the small port of **Spiliá** and the main port of **Vathý**. The ferry takes under half an hour (single 435dr) and exists to serve the inhabitants of Meganíssi, which is why the first services leave Meganíssi, and the last Nydhrí (see also p.169).

Spiliá and Spartohóri

The first port, **SPILIÁ**, is little more than a landing stage and a pebble beach, though it does have three **tavernas**, a very basic semi-official **campsite** and a public telephone. The campsite is behind the *Star Taverna*, the best of the restaurants by the quay, which also has a basic shop and shower facilities, for which there is a nominal charge. Five minutes' walk around the bay is a longer, sandier beach with a couple of snack bars and the recommended *Spilia* taverna.

Five minutes up the hill from Spiliá is the small, whitewashed village of **SPARTOHÓRI**. Unspoilt for decades, Spartohóri now has a souvenir shop and a couple of more touristic **restaurants**: a pizza place, the *Tropicana*, which can direct you to **rooms** (☎0645/51 486; ②–③), and the *Rooftop Cafe*, which serves up a wide range of Greek and international dishes on a balcony with panoramic views over the satellite islands and Lefkádha. The two more traditional **tavernas**, both in the centre of the village, are *Lakis* and *Gakias* (☎0645/51 050; ③), which also acts as an outlet for rooms. Other accommodation possibilities are through Yiannis Tsolakis (☎0645/ 51 409; ②) or Massos Kavvadhas (☎0645/51 644; ②). Apart from a few shops, this is all there is to this quiet, pretty village – walk too fast and you'll find yourself out in open country in minutes.

The up and coming part of the island most likely to be developed is its finest beach at **Áyios Ioánnis** on the west coast, twenty minutes' walk from Spiliá. A newly paved road already leads to it and, though there is currently just one taverna, there is talk of an official campsite, and the addition of apartments would seem to be only a matter of time.

Katoméri and Vathý

The island's oldest road rises over the hills to the east of Spartohóri, giving panoramic views, notably of the wild, narrow peninsula to the south. Traffic is rare, and the silence and sense of isolation at the centre of the island are to be savoured, especially if you've just escaped the craziness of Nydhrí. After about an hour's walk, you'll reach the main village of **KATOMÉRI**, which can lay claim to a couple of bars and *kafenía*, and the island's one **hotel**, the *Meganisi*, a small and comfortable place with en-suite rooms and balconies, a restaurant, bar and terraces (☎0645/51 240, fax 51 639; ③), and – surprisingly – open year round.

The port of **VATHÝ** is a ten-minute walk down from Katoméri and can also be reached direct from Spiliá by the new coast road. While unremarkable, and lacking any swimming facilities, it's still a very attractive place, with a deep bay and very little development beyond a handful of tavernas and bars, and one or two villas on the surrounding hills. There's now **accommodation** in Vathý at the waterfront *Different Studios* (☎0645/22 170; ③). The *Rose Garden Taverna*, with a surprisingly varied menu, vies for custom with the basic *Restaurant Greco*, but the favourite among Greek visitors – where Lefkadhans flock for Sunday lunch – is the waterside *Porto Vathi*, which serves vast portions of locally caught seafood. The most popular of Meganíssi's beaches is **Ambelákia**, to the east of Vathý, but still accessible only by the path which heads east and then north out of Katoméri.

Kálamos

KÁLAMOS is another drowned mountain, mostly bare but with some evergreen woods reaching down as far as its pebbly beaches. It's mainly seen as a stopping-off point for bareboat sailors, some of whom favour it above any other small island in the region. A **ferry** leaves mainland Mýtikas – which sports several hotels, among them the *Kymata* (☎0646/81 258; ③) and the *Simos* (☎0646/81 380; ③) – twice a day (three times in high season) for the voyage to the island.

Kálamos has just one village, HÓRA, with some **rooms**, although these are often booked through the summer. Try calling Dhionyssis (☎0646/91 279; ①). Hóra is spread out above the small harbour, and is one of the few villages in the area that survived the 1953 earthquake, whose epicentre was quite close by. Beside the harbour there's the large taverna *Akroyiali* (0646/ 91 358; ②), which has rooms and an extensive menu, an old-fashioned grocer's shop and a café/snack bar, while up the hill you can find several more shops and a post office (which will change money), as well as a couple more snack bars and cafés and the village butcher's, which doubles as a basic grill. There are passable beaches within ten to fifteen minutes' walk either side of Hóra and the westerly one has a sporadically opening taverna. **Freelance camping** is quite acceptable on these or any of the island's other coves, many of which are only really accessible by sea.

With just one road winding around the 920m top of Mount Vouní, Kálamos provides an excellent, if limited, walking terrain. The fortified former capital, **Kástro**, now deserted and overgrown, is near the summit, a ninety-minute walk from Hóra. The five-bastioned castle is surrounded by derelict buildings. The road also goes to the monastery of **Áyios Yeóryios**, which is open to visitors. The island's most attractive beaches are to be found on the north coast, between Hóra and Episkopí, although almost all involve a hair-raising scramble down through the woods. The longest walk on the island, to the deserted village of **Pórto Leóni** (abandoned due to water shortages, hence the expansion of Hóra) is a two-hour hike across the mountainside with fantastic views over Kástos. If you had a vessel for easier access or were prepared to cart provisions along the path, the eerie uninhabited buildings and adjacent patch of beach would make a fine spot for the hardy to live out post-apocalyptic fantasies.

Travel details

BUSES

Lefkádha Town to: Aï Nikítas (5 daily; 45min); Áktio (for Préveza, 5 daily, 4 on Sun; 30min); Atháni (2 daily, ex Sun; 1hr 45min); Athens (5 daily, 4 on Sun; 7hr); Englouví (3 daily, ex Sun; 1hr 15min); Kalamítsi (2 daily, ex Sun; 1hr 15min); Karyá (7 daily, 2 on Sun; 1hr); Káthisma (5 daily; 1hr); Katohóri (2 daily, ex Sun; 1hr); Nydhrí (18 daily, 7 on Sun; 40min); Póros (2 daily, ex Sun; 1hr 30min); Sývota (2 daily; 1hr 45min); Sývros (2 daily, 1 on Sun; 1hr 30min); Thessaloníki (3 weekly; 12hr); Vassilikí (5 daily, 3 on Sun; 1hr 45min); Vlyhó (18 daily, 7 on Sun; 45min); Yíra (5 daily; 15min). This is the summer timetable; many services may be reduced at other times.

FERRIES

During the summer months (July–Sept), the services listed below connect Lefkádha to Kefaloniá and Itháki. These are gradually scaled up and down on either side of high season but at least one triangular route of Nydhrí–Fiskárdho–Fríkes–Nydhrí runs all year:

Nydhrí to: Fiskárdho, Kefaloniá (1 daily; 2hr 30min); Fríkes, Itháki (1 daily; 1hr 30min); Meganíssi (7 daily; 30min).

Vassilikí to: Fiskárdho, Kefaloniá (2 daily; 1hr); Sámi, Kefaloniá (2 daily; 2hr); Pisaetós, Itháki (2 daily; 1hr 30min).

Chapter 4

Itháki

Odysseus' legendary homeland, **Itháki (Ithaca)**, is described thus in Homer: "There are no tracks, nor grasslands... it is a rocky, severe island, unsuited for horses but not so wretched, despite its small size. It is good for goats." In some ways not much has changed; the island's landscape, much of it almost vertical, precludes any significant development. Like its larger neighbour, Kefalloniá, Itháki is essentially a series of drowned mountains – here three of them, joined by a tall, narrow isthmus, with human settlements on a number of plateaus around the peaks. In C.P. Cavafy's splendid poem *Ithaca*, the effort to reach the island symbolizes man's journey through life:

> *Always keep Ithaca in mind.*
> *Arriving there is your destiny.*
> *But do not hurry the journey in any way.*
> *Better that it lasts for years,*
> *so you are old when you reach the island,*
> *enriched by all you have gained along the way,*
> *not expecting Ithaca to make you wealthy.*

Itháki is, however, well worth visiting for its own sake, not just on a classical whim, influenced by those ancient myths, and once you've decided to go, you should certainly be able to get there a lot more quickly and easily than Odysseus. It is the **least spoilt** of all the major Ionian islands, but precisely because of that it is also the most difficult for visitors to get settled into during the busy summer months. Accommodation is scarce (there are only two small hotels on the entire island outside Vathý), much of it prebooked by overseas travel operators, which only increases competition for the remaining beds. There is no official campsite, though there's a semi-official site at Déxa beach and, as usual, the discreet pitching of tents is ignored in select spots.

The Homer/Odysseus industry has led to an orgy of theming, but otherwise there are few signs of the commercialism that has blighted

other islands. There are no burger joints on Itháki, no pubs or video
bars named after British sitcoms, yet it is very Anglophone – much
more so than Lefkádha, for example – and welcoming to foreigners.
The preponderence of English speakers is due to the statistic that
around eighty percent of Ithacans have lived at some time in the diaspora, mostly in Australia and the US. Many have returned to take up
full-time residence, while others spend the summers in the land of
their fathers.

The capital, **Vathý**, is separated from the three outlying villages,
Stavrós, **Fríkes** and **Kióni**, by a journey of over 20km along the one
main road, making getting around surprisingly difficult for such a
small island. Ease of movement is not helped by the fact that the
ghost port of **Pisaetós**, the island's best connection with neighbouring Kefalloniá, has no bus connections at all.

Itháki's **beaches** are almost entirely pebble, with some sand
deposits and sandy seabeds. The best are in the south, around Vathý,
although there are some decent stretches between Fríkes and Kióni,
and others accessible by boat.

Some history

Itháki is known to have been inhabited since at least 3000 BC from
Neolithic finds in the north of the island. One local history suggests
more than half a dozen possible origins for the island's **name**; from
the ancient mythical figure Ithacus, son of the sea god Poseidon,
through a variety of possible Phoenician, Turkish and Venetian
roots, although this seems fanciful given the clear references in
Homer. The first settlers lived in the north, but by 1500 BC the south
was also inhabited. During the Mycenaean period, Itháki became the
seat of power for the Kefallonian state, which extended over the
other Ionian islands and parts of the Akarnanian mainland as well.
The peak of this period, prior to 1000 BC, probably coincides with
the composition of the much-disputed **Odyssey** (see box on p.180);
archeological finds from this period, which have been used to support a reading of the epic as a literal description of historical events,
can be seen in Vathý's archeological museum.

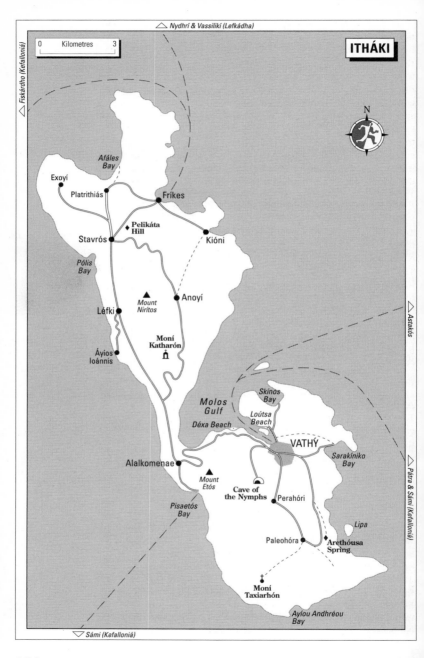

In 1000 BC Itháki fell under Dorian rule and slipped from its position of power. Under Corinth (800–180 BC) it became a political backwater, and was similarly undisturbed when power transferred to Rome. During the Byzantine era (395–1185 AD), Itháki was annexed to Kefalloniá, and from then on shared much of its larger neighbour's history. However, the smaller, unprotected island fell prey to repeated attacks by pirates and Turkish invaders, and in the 1470s was sacked by Turkish forces. Most survivors abandoned the island, and the new Venetian rulers were forced to offer land and tax exemptions to lure settlers back. By the 1570s, the island had a new, fortified coastal capital, **Vathý**, set on a generous natural harbour from which it derives its name (meaning "deep" in Greek). Under Venetian rule, the population on the island rose from only sixty families in the 1560s to an estimated 12,000 people in the 1790s.

Ithacans were prominent among the activists who, led by the Friendly Society, fomented the War of Independence against the Turkish rulers on mainland Greece in 1821. In the early part of the nineteenth century, growing emigration saw Ithacans travelling around the world and gaining a widespread reputation for their **seafaring** skills. This in turn transformed Itháki into a wealthy and powerful island. As well as building the Neoclassical mansions that can be seen in Vathý today, Itháki's middle class financed a strong and vibrant social and cultural infrastructure. However, maritime success abroad ultimately led to further emigration, initiating an economic decline that only began to bottom out in recent decades. During World War II, Itháki was overrun by Axis forces, first the Italians (1941–43), and then the Germans (1943–44). Like neighbouring Kefalloniá, Lefkádha and Zákynthos, the island was devastated by the earthquakes of 1953 (see box on p.197).

Arrival and getting around

There isn't a flat piece of ground on Itháki that's long or straight enough to land anything other than a helicopter, so everyone visiting the island arrives by sea. Package tourists will frequently find themselves **flying into Kefalloniá**, where they are bused, rather tediously, to Fiskárdho in the north, and then transported by ferry to **Fríkes** at the northernmost point of Itháki. With bus journey, embarkation and transfers to accommodation, this can add at least three hours to your journey. If you're flying to Kefalloniá independently, it's better to sail from Sámi, where ferries are more frequent, to the capital, **Vathý**, a sensible place to stop and get your bearings on Itháki. Unfortunately, the shortest and most frequent link from Sámi to **Pisaetós** is complicated by lack of public transport on the Itháki side.

Island-hoppers have the choice of arriving at Vathý (from Sámi on Kefalloniá), Fríkes (from Fiskárdho on Kefalloniá, or Nydhrí or Vassilikí on Lefkádha), or Pisaetós (from Sámi). The only other options, short of parachuting in, are the connections with Pátra and Astakós (see box on p.174) on the mainland.

If you find yourself being bused to Fiskárdho to transfer to Itháki, sit on the left of the bus for the best views

In high season, only two **buses** run daily between Vathý, Stavrós, Fríkes and Kióni. A **taxi** from Vathý to Fríkes costs around 4500dr, while to Pisaetós the standard fare is 2500dr; since there is no bus, despite the regular ferries, this is the only means apart from walking or trying to hitch. Travel agencies in all three villages can arrange moped or bike **rental**, and larger agencies car rental, although given the size of the island this is of questionable value: there are relatively few navigable roads – to Perahóra and Pisaetós in the south and Anoyí and Exoyí in the north – and it would probably be cheaper to go by taxi. In any case, apart from the journey between Vathý and Stavrós, most points on the island are within reasonable walking distance of each other.

Vathý

Itháki's capital has the most idyllic setting of any port in the archipelago. Ships approaching **Vathý** have to turn into a large outer bay, and again into a smaller one, then pass between headlands into an interior bay, where the town sits at the crux. Vathý is entirely hidden from the open sea, in such convoluted folds of terrain that visitors sometimes fail to realize that the mountains in the distance are in fact the northern half of the island. It was for this reason that islanders chose the bay as the site of their first major sea port in the sixteenth century, when the threat of piracy had been largely eliminated with the help of the Venetians.

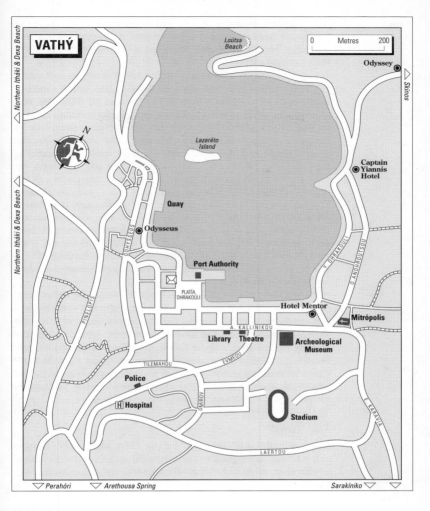

▽ Perahóri   ▽ Arethousa Spring   Sarakíniko ▽   ▽

Accommodation

Except at the very height of the season, townspeople still meet ferries offering **rooms**. Most are in the quieter backstreets rising into the hills above the town, and in this large pedestrian warren of alleys, they can be hard to find if you're by yourself. There are also a few, rather pricey rooms within stumbling distance of the ferry ramp on the south side of the harbour, amidst the yacht moorings. Especially worth seeking out are the rooms owned by Vassilis Vlassopoulos (☎0674/32 119; ③) – surrounded by pleasant gardens, they're clearly visible from the bay on the Venetian steps leading from behind the ferry quay towards the church. Also within easy access are those owned by Sotiris Maroulis at Odysseus 29, near the Peráhóri road (☎0674/28 300; ③).

Vathý now has four **hotels**, with the addition of two new establishments round the bay towards Loútsa; the smart *Captain Yiannis Hotel* complex (☎0674/33 173, fax 32 849; ⑤), with large comfortable rooms and a pool, just off the seafront, and the smaller *Odyssey*(☎0674/32 268, fax 32 668;④), a short way up the new road to Skínos beach. The two older places are on the quay at either end of town. Nearer the ferry dock and cheaper is the *Odysseus* (☎0674/32 381; ③), a good, basic hotel with en-suite rooms above its own taverna, set back from the street but slightly troubled by traffic on the nearby main road out of town. Topped by a big neon sign at the far end of the quay, the *Mentor* (☎0674/32 433, fax 32 293; ③) has en-suite rooms with balconies, some with full-on sea views, but is a little overpriced these days. At least it's open year round, but even out of season, it's a favourite with walking-tour companies, and can sometimes fill up. The hotel has its own restaurant and bar, much favoured at night for its illuminated patio.

Vathý's two main travel agencies, Polyctor Tours and Delas Tours (see p.179), offer a range of rooms, apartments and villas in town and across the island. If none of the above have space, or can make alternative suggestions, the town's taxi drivers, lined up along the quay by the bus stop, may be able to help. More accommodation is becoming available in the way of private rooms up in the suburb/village of Peráhóri above Vathý, but it's a long way to go to be disappointed. One snazzy new place with fantastic views is the *Calypso* (☎0674/33 138; ③), just below the main settlement.

The Town

Much of Vathý was destroyed by the 1953 earthquake, leaving only a few of its magnificent Neoclassical mansions and a number of churches, including the small **cathedral** and the church of the **Taxiárhi**, which contains an icon of the Crucifixion believed to be the work of El Greco. However, the modest size of the town and the comparative wealth of its seafaring population seem to have worked in its favour after the earthquake: it was reconstructed far more sympathetically than either Zákynthos Town or Argostóli. And a preservation order passed in 1978, forbidding unsightly development, has protected the town from excessive commercialization. Its boutiques, souvenir shops, tavernas, *kafenía*, cafés and cocktail bars are all discreetly housed in vernacular architecture.

The focal point of the town is the large **Platía Dhrakoúli**, which occupies the southwest corner of the elongated seafront and has many of the town's facilities on or around it. The alleys behind are an atmospheric jigsaw of swish new shops, small shiny banks and old *kafenía* or packed *pandopolía*, but they soon give way to quiet residential streets. Sections of the seafront on either side of the square have been suitably gentrified, mostly with smart eating and drinking establishments or tourist shops, but long stretches further away are unutilized, a surprising waste of such scenically situated property. This does, however, add to the impression of Vathý being a functioning port, with fishing still a major source of income and only limited pretensions to being anything else.

Vathý Archeological Museum

While many of the best finds have been taken to Athens, or simply looted by unscrupulous north European archeologists, Vathý's **Archeological Museum** maintains a decent collection of exhibits related to the *Odyssey* myth. Mainly domestic wares, they include Mycenaean tripods that support the theory that Odysseus' home was indeed on Itháki. The museum is linked to the **Library**, which has an extensive and often bizarre collection of editions of Homer, including one in Chinese.

The Archeological Museum is opposite the bus stop and is open Tues– Sun 8am– 2.30pm; 500dr.

Beaches

If you're staying in Vathý or, perhaps more importantly, visiting from Kefalloniá with only a few hours to spare, it's good to know that there are decent beaches within fifteen minutes' walk in either direction around the bay. The biggest, and busiest, is **Déxa** on the western side of the bay, over the hill along the main road rising above the ferry quay. This long pebble strip offers watersports and a snack bar, and has been claimed as the site of Phorcys (it's actually signposted "Forkinos Bay"), the beach where the Phaeacians deposited the sleeping Odysseus. The snack bar does simple meals and allows those camping in the semi-official site in the adjacent field to shower for a small fee.

The nearest and smallest beach is at **Loútsa**, on the opposite side of the bay to the ferry quay, a sandy cove with a snack bar in season. Loútsa is also the site of one of the few surviving Venetian fortifications, whose cannon emplacements are visible on a low bluff above the beach. A very narrow path leads on from Loútsa past some microscopic coves towards the headland.

The newly paved road that strikes off to the right and uphill before Loútsa leads over the headlands towards the superior deserted pebble beach in **Skínos bay**. An even longer track, leaving the centre of town, trails over the hills to **Sarakíniko bay**, which is a good hour's hike but, like Skínos, worth the effort for the swimming. The one drawback to this part of the coastline, though, is the noisy industrial plant overlooking Sarakíniko, which fills the area with an insistent drone that can be heard as far as the Arethóusa Spring.

Eating and drinking

Vathý's nightlife unfolds around its tightly packed seafront and the few short streets behind it. There is little to differentiate between the **cafés and bars** on the main drag facing the fishing quay – here it's perhaps best to follow the locals to the *kafenío* in the middle of the strip. For a yet more traditional atmosphere, seek out the ancient *kafenío* tucked behind the seafront near the National Bank – though unaccompanied women may find the predominantly male atmosphere unwelcoming. An excellent alternative is the magnificent Neoclassical mansion on the seafront that's recently been transformed into the *Drakoulis* café. The grounds, with a curious seawater pond connected to the bay by a tunnel under the road, are spread with tables during the summer, and the large bar inside, though it looks like some sort of swank gentlemen's club, is open to all. For louder music and dancing, the two night haunts are the *Oktapodi Club*, an indoor disco near the square, and *Maribou*, a large outdoor club towards Loútsa.

For dinner, you are surprisingly spoilt for choice in such a small town. Many visitors head off around the bay to one of a trio of **tavernas**: *Gregory's*, popular for its lamb and fish, and the more traditional *Tziribis* and *O Vrachos* nearby. The views back across to Vathý are excellent, but bills usually reflect the setting. On the way you'll pass the *Mylos Creperie*, a hip music, booze and snacks hangout that's popular with townies and visitors alike.

In town, *O Nikos*, tucked behind the strip of cafés, is an excellent point-at-what-you-want-to-eat taverna, and its few tables fill early, although it's not as cheap as it looks. A few doors away, the *Sirenes Itháki Yacht Club* takes a similar menu upmarket in a nautical theme restaurant: Smyrna meat balls with a red sauce, fish in rosemary and raisins, shrimps in lemon and mustard sauce, and others. The food is good and the price reasonable for the slightly outlandish setting. Of the row of half a dozen or so restaurants lining the front between the dock and the square, by far the best is *To Kohili*; on offer at decent prices is a range of specialities like lamb *kléftiko* and other meats in original sauces.

Listings

Banks The National Bank of Greece is visible from the junction of the two quayside roads; the Commercial Bank and the Agricultural Bank are just behind it (all Mon–Thurs 8am–2pm; Fri 8am–1.30pm). Hotels and travel agencies will change currency and travellers' cheques, but shop around for the best deal or, if possible, the "Bank rates offered" sign.

Car hire As well as the travel agents listed below, AGS on the seafront is a reliable outlet (☎0674/32 702).

First aid As well as the 24hr clinic in the hospital on Evmeïou, 350m back from the seafront (☎0674/32 222), the pharmacy on the quay by the bus stop is able to give advice on minor ailments.

OTE On the seafront (Mon–Fri 7.30am–2pm).

Police station On Evmeïou, just before the hospital (☎0674/32 205).

Port Authority On the seafront corner of the square (☎0674/32 909).

Post office On the square (Mon–Fri 8am–2pm).

Shopping Vathý has many well-stocked minimarkets, a bakery, fish and meat stores, as well as other shops, including a couple of excellent local art galleries and craft outlets.

Travel agencies There is no tourist information office in Vathý or elsewhere on Itháki, but commercial travel agencies and hotels are usually happy to provide information. Polyctor Tours in the town centre (☎0674/33 120, fax 33 130) has a range of rooms and apartments and is the agent for most ferries (as well as for Olympic Airways, useful if returning to Athens via Kefalloniá). Polyctor's smaller neighbour, Delas Tours (☎0674/321 104, fax 33 031, email *delas@otenet.gr*) offers accommodation as well as other travel services.

Odysseus sites

The **Odysseus sites** at this end of the island – the Arethoúsa Spring, the Cave of the Nymphs and Alalkomenae, suggested location of Odysseus' castle – are all within reach of Vathý, the first two on foot, the third by bus or taxi. Trips to either (but not both) the Cave of the Nymphs and Arethoúsa Spring can be fitted into a day-trip from Kefalloniá, Alalkomenae only if you take a cab (a return fare should be no more than 5000dr).

The Arethoúsa Spring

The walk to the **Arethoúsa Spring** – allegedly the place where Eumaeus, Odysseus' faithful swineherd, brought his pigs to drink – is a three-hour trip there and back, setting off along a signposted track out of Vathý next to the OTE. The isolation and the sea views along the way are magnificent, but the walk crosses some slippery inclines and might best be avoided if you're nervous of heights. The route, particularly where it turns off the rough track onto a narrow path, is shadeless, so take a hat and plenty of liquids in summer. When the weather's fine it's worth taking a picnic, but the route shouldn't be attempted in poor weather and isn't recommended for lone walkers.

Near the top of the lane leading to the spring path, a signpost points up to what is said to have been the **Cave of Eumaeus** – if you're tempted, the tortuous path zigzags up to just below the bluff high above, and the cave is a large single hollow with a tree growing up through a hole in the roof.

The route to the spring continues along the track for a few hundred metres, and then branches off on to a narrow footpath through the maquis that covers the sloping cliffs. Parts of the final downhill track involve scrambling across rock fields (follow the splashes of green paint), and care should be taken around the small but vertiginous ravine that houses the spring. The geographical features around the spring, which is sited at the head of the ravine below a

Homer, the Odyssey and Itháki

Anyone travelling in the Ionian will soon become either confused or cynical about the sheer number of places – from Paleokastrítsa in northern Corfu to Alalkomenae on Itháki – competing to be accepted as the actual sites of events in the **Odyssey**. Classical authorities still take a dim view of arguments for placing so much of Homer's epic in Greece, preferring the traditional reading, which identifies sites as far afield as Gozo, the Messina straits between Italy and Sicily, Italy's Aeolian islands and Tunisia. Indeed, some interpretations of the story have taken it entirely outside the Mediterranean basin, to such improbable locales as Iceland. The safest interpretation is that Homer – whose single authorship is itself questioned by theories that hold the *Odyssey* to be a group effort put together over the centuries – was mixing myth and legend with actual historical and geographical detail. The most probable answer to the authorship debate is that Homer was the first to commit the formulaic oral tradition to writing, embellishing it and imbuing it with his own muse in the process

Explorer Tim Severin, however, in his book *The Ulysses Voyage: Sea Search for the Odyssey*, comes down in favour of siting Odysseus' adventures around Itháki, the island the epic names as his home – even if German archeologist Wilhelm Dörpfeld (see p.139) tried unsuccessfully to cart it off to Lefkádha. In 1985, following earlier expeditions to reconstruct Jason's search for the Golden Fleece, Severin and a group of fellow explorers set off in a full-scale model of a Bronze Age galley to retrace Odysseus' journey home from Troy. Using estimated times of journeys described in the *Odyssey*, and matching descriptions of landscape and astronavigational details, Severin pieced together Odysseus' adventures around Itháki and neighbouring islands.

Among Severin's key propositions is that King Alcinous' castle was probably sited at Paleokastrítsa on Corfu, and that Odysseus was washed ashore at Érmones. Severin cites Paxí, in particular Harámi beach in Lákka bay, as the likely position of Circe's home of Aeaea, which concurs with the local nickname of Circe's Grove for a glade at nearby Ipapánti. He speculates that Scylla and Charybdis may have been natural features in the landscape at the northern tip of Lefkádha, and further suggests Déxa bay on Itháki as the likely site of the Cave of the Nymphs, Pelikáta as Odysseus' castle and Arethóusa as the site of the spring where Eumaeus watered his swine. Ultimately, however, even Severin concedes to the many ambiguities surrounding the text, and Homer's tale resists the attempt to moor it definitively to dry land.

crag known as Kórax (the raven), compare to Homer's description of the meeting between Odysseus and Eumaeus, lending themselves to literalist claims. However, the spring itself is distinctly underwhelming – in summer it's just a dribble of water sounding like a kitchen leak in a shallow cave. It's worth pointing out that the spring is a dead end – the only way out is back the way you came. A small pebble beach a short way down from the spring, reached by a steep, narrow path, is good for a swim if time allows.

If you feel a little uneasy about the gradients involved in reaching the spring, it's still worth continuing along the main track that runs above it, a journey up through woodlands that affords some excellent sea views. The track loops round and heads back into the village of **Perahóri** above Vathý, which has views as far as Lefkádha to the north and is actually the island's second largest settlement. There are several places to stop for a bite here, including the *Ovenos* and *Kaliora* grills, both of which have stunning views. On the way, you'll pass **Paleóhora**, the ruined medieval capital abandoned centuries ago, but with vestiges of houses fortified against pirate attacks and some churches still retaining details of Byzantine frescoes of the saints. Around 3km southwest of Paleóhora, through densely forested highlands, is the site of the sixteenth-century **Moní Taxiarhón**. The monastery was destroyed in the 1953 earthquakes, but its small church has since been rebuilt.

The Cave of the Nymphs

The **Cave of the Nymphs** (known locally as *Marmarospíli*), is about 2.5km up a rough track signposted on the brow of the hill above Déxa beach. The cave is atmospheric but nothing like as impressive as the caverns of neighbouring Kefalloniá, and these days is illuminated with coloured lights. The claim that this is the *Odyssey*'s Grotto of the Nymphs, where the returning Odysseus concealed the gifts given to him by King Alcinous, is enhanced by the proximity of Déxa beach (see box opposite), although there is some evidence suggesting that a cave above the beach, which was unwittingly demolished during quarrying many years ago, was the "true" Cave of the Nymphs.

Alalkomenae and Pisaetós

Alalkomenae, Schliemann's much-vaunted "Castle of Odysseus", is signposted on the Vathý–Pisaetós road, on the saddle between Déxa bay and Pisaetós, with views over both sides of the island. The actual site, however, some 300m uphill, is little more than foundations spread about in the maquis. Schliemann's excavations unearthed a Mycenaean burial chamber and domestic items such as vases, figurines and utensils (to be seen in the archeological museum), but sections of Cyclopean wall and the remains of what has been suggested is a temple to Apollo date from three centuries after Homer. In fact, the most likely contender for the site of Odysseus' castle is above the village of Stavrós in the north, and intriguingly close to the site of the ruined ancient capital of Pólis.

The road (though not buses) continues to the harbour of **Pisaetós**, about 2km below, with a large pebble beach that's good for swimming, though popular with local rod-and-line fishermen. Other than that it's pretty much a non-event, with a snack bar on the quay to serve the ferries from Sámi on Kefalloniá and Astakós on the mainland, and a taverna that rarely seems to open at all.

Northern Itháki

The road to the north of the island rides high on the side of **Mount Nírito**, affording breathtaking views of neighbouring Kefalloniá. At the hamlets of Agrós and Áyios Ioánnis, new roads are continually being upgraded to allow access to small remote beaches along this hitherto wild stretch of coastline. The only facilities along this road are the shops and *kafenía* of **Léfki**, halfway to Stavrós, which was a notable centre of Resistance organization in the Ionians during World War II. If you fancy a scenic base for a longer stay, you can't do any better than contacting Ilias Vassilopoulos, whose house for four commands views across to the larger neighbour (☎0674/31 395).

Stavrós and around

STAVRÓS is the second largest town on the island, discounting Perahóri as being separate from Vathý, and the administative centre of the north, although its inland position and distance from any decent beaches – the nearest, a steep 2km below the town, shares Pólis bay with a small fishing harbour – make it a less than ideal place to stay. It's a pleasant enough town nonetheless, with *kafenía* and tavernas edging an elongated *platía* that doubles as the main thoroughfare. The square is crowned by a modern but imposing yellow and white church and hosts a rather fierce statue of Odysseus – the only such public monument dedicated to him in the islands. The small **museum** (Tues–Sun 9.30am–2.30pm), displaying local archeological finds, is situated just above the main road to Platrithiás about 500m from the centre. Stavrós's Homeric site is on the side of **Pelikáta Hill**, where remains of roads, walls and other structures have been suggested as the possible site of Odysseus's castle. Items from the site, including part of a mask engraved *"EFHIN ODHYSSEI"* (Dedicated to Odysseus), can be seen at the museum.

Stavrós is probably only useful as a base if both Fríkes and Kióni are full up, and is an obvious stopping-off point for exploring the northern hamlets and the road up to the medieval village of Anoyí on Mount Nírito. Both Polyctor and Delas (see p.179) handle **accommodation** in Stavrós, and a number of the town's traditional tavernas, including the *Petra* (☎0674/31 596; ③), offer rooms. The *Tritsarolis* studios (☎0674/31 393; ③) and *Porto Thiaki* (☎0674/31 245 or 31 712, fax 31 638; ③) above the pizzeria are also options. Of the tavernas, *Fatouros* is the oldest and best, while the *Petra* and *Polyphemus*, with its garden and upstairs bar, are also worth trying. For a drink, *Soris' Ways* café and the *Margarita zaharoplastío*, which specializes in the local sweet *rovaní*, provide pleasant surroundings.

Anoyí

A mountainous and highly scenic road leads some 5km southeast from Stavrós to **ANOYÍ**, whose apt name roughly translates as "upper land". It was once the second most important settlement on the island, but is almost deserted today. The centre of the village is dominated by a free-standing Venetian campanile, built to serve the (usually locked) church of the **Panayía**; enquire at the one *kafenío* about access to the church and its frescoes and striking reredos, originally painted in Byzantine times but mostly replaced after earthquake damage over the intervening centuries. The village only comes alive when it hosts a major Panayía festival on August 14, the eve of the Virgin Mary's big day. On the outskirts of the village are the foundations of a ruined **medieval prison**, and in the surrounding countryside, some extremely strange **rock formations**, the biggest being the eight-metre-high Arakles (Heracles) rock, just east of the village.

The **monastery of Katharón**, 3km further south along the road, has stunning views down over Vathý and the south of the island. The monastery houses an icon of the Panayía discovered by peasants who were clearing scrubland in the area. Local mythology claims that a temple to Artemis stood on the site, and suggests a link to the medieval Cathar sect. Byron is said to have stayed at the monastery in 1823, during his final voyage to Messolóngi. Every year the monastery celebrates its own festival on September 8, when the icon is displayed and everyone sings and dances.

North of Stavrós

Two roads leave Stavrós heading north: one, to the right, heads 2km directly down to Fríkes, while the main road, to the left, loops round via **Platrithiás**. Just over halfway to Platrithiás, a road branches up to Exoyí, which has a basic *kafenío* and incredible views from the bell-tower of Ayía Marína church. A short way from the main road on the way to Exóyi, a motorable track leads 1km to the unfenced **School of Homer**, where excavations continue apace. Apart from the usual foundations, a well and a fine set of stone steps have already been unearthed. Mycenaean graves and buildings establish that the area was inhabited at the time of Homer. It is also a fine spot to sit and survey **Afáles bay**. The bay itself, the largest on the entire island, with an unspoilt and little-visited pebble beach, is reachable down a partly paved road from the edge of Platrithiás. Among a group of tiny settlements above Platrithiás are the abandoned hamlet of Kálamos, 3km north, and Koliéri just a kilometre away, with its curious folklore monument – a towering column of millstones, next to a stone mill with wheels and grinding channel intact. The landscape around here, thickly forested in parts and dotted with vineyards, makes excellent walking terrain.

Fríkes

Viewed from the daily ferries that leave Lefkádha or Kefalloniá, or from the island bus as it trundles through en route to Kióni, **FRÍKES** doesn't appear to have much going for it. You could sprint around its tiny harbourfront in under a minute, and find yourself in open country towards Stavrós in five. Wedged in a valley between two steep hills, Fríkes was only settled in the sixteenth century when the threat from pirate raids had diminished. Waves of emigration in the nineteenth century have further capped its size – as few as 200 people are estimated to live here today – but its maritime prowess and proximity to other islands have made it a natural trading post and year-round port. Consequently, it stays open for tourism far later in the season than its neighbour Kióni, and at present has a better range of tavernas. There are no beaches in the village, but plenty of good, if small, pebble strands a short walk away towards Kióni. When the ferries and their cargoes have departed, Fríkes falls quiet, and this is its real charm: a downbeat but cool place to lie low from the touristic rat race.

Fríkes' one **hotel**, the rather pricey *Nostos* (☎0674/31 644, fax 31 716; ⑤), is a small but smart family-run affair, with en-suite rooms, a bar, restaurant and small garden; it's about 150m from the quay, along the first turning of the two roads leaving town. Just before it the new *Aristotelis Apartments* (☎ & fax 0674/31 075; ④) has comfortable rooms, some with sea views, at lower rates. The seafront Kiki Travel (☎ & fax 0674/31 726; ③) has **rooms** and other accommodation, and also offers vehicle rental and other travel services. Next door, the friendly proprietor of the souvenir shop, Panos (☎0674/31 735; ②) has contacts with basic rooms and rents out bikes, while the *Ulysses* taverna (☎0674/31 733; ④) can arrange for smarter apartments. None of the places listed above is likely to have space on spec during the early to mid-August peak. Arriving without a reservation at that time means you probably have to sleep in one of the nearby coves. A more secluded and acceptable freelance **camping** spot is among the olive groves at a lovely little pebble beach fifteen minutes' walk along a footpath that starts just beyond the last seafront houses on the left side of Fríkes, as you face the sea.

For such a small place, Fríkes has a wealth of good seafront **tavernas**. *Symposeum* has a variety of grill and oven dishes, seafood and some unusual vegetarian options, such as baked beetroots and potatoes. The *Rementzo* is a straightforward taverna with a few extras like pizza and spicy Mexican dips, while the *Ulysses* specializes mostly in meat and fish. The quartet is completed by the *Penelope*, marginally the most upmarket of the cluster, with a varied menu covering north European and Greek. The anonymous and most of the time innocuous bar in the corner of the quay jerks into action after midnight as the prime venue in northern Itháki, and often develops into quite a raucous affair till the wee hours.

Kióni

KIÓNI sits at a dead end in the road, 5km southeast of Fríkes (although a rough path ascends towards Anoyí from the back of the village). It too was only established in the sixteenth century, when settlers from Anoyí felt it was safe to move down from the hills. On the same geological base as the northern tip of Kefalloniá, it avoided the very worst of the 1953 earthquakes, and so retains some fine examples of pre-twentieth-century architecture. It's an extremely pretty village, wrapped around a tiny harbour, comparable in prospect and features to Longós on Paxí and Fiskárdho on Kefalloniá. Tourism here is dominated by British blue-chip travel companies, and by flotilla and bareboat sailors, so it does exude a rather forced and claustrophobic air.

Kióni's bay has a **beach** of sorts, 1km along its south side, a small sand and pebble strand below a summer-only snack bar. Better pebble beaches can be found within walking distance northwards towards Fríkes, where bizarre rock formations along the roadside are stacked upright in places like matchsticks. You can also hire a boat from the Moraitis boat rental agency (from around 8000dr – see below) to explore quiet nearby bays and coves, and larger *kaïki* trips to further beaches are occasionally organized.

There are two major dates in Kióni's summer calendar: June 24 when the church of **Áyios Ioánnis** celebrates its saint's day, and anyone called Yiannis has his name day; and July 20, the festival of Áyios Ílias, when the village's 200 or so inhabitants set off in boats to attend a service at a small chapel that sits on Kióni bay's southern promontory.

While the best **accommodation** has been snaffled by the Brits, some local businesses have rooms and apartments to let, among them *Maroudas Apartments* (☎0674/31 691, fax 31 753; ③), near the harbour, *Apostolis* (☎0674/31 072; ③), friendly *Dellaportas* (☎0674/31 481, fax 31 090; ④) and a range at Kioni Vacations (☎0674/31 668). A quieter option, just a short walk uphill on the main road in the tiny hamlet of Ráhi, are the rooms and studios run by Captain Theofilos Karatzis and his family (☎0674/31 679; ③), with panoramic views over the area. Alternatively, seek out or phone the very helpful Yioryios Moraïtis (☎0674/31 464, fax 31 702), whose boat rental company has access to accommodation in Kióni.

For all its blue-chip tone, Kióni's **restaurants** do not compare favourably with Fríkes. There are four waterfront tavernas: the traditional *Avra*, which is the best value, the *Kioni*, which mixes European and Greek, and the distinctly upmarket duo of *Galatis*, specializing in fish, and *Calipso*, which offers gourmet dishes such as artichoke polita. There is also a pizzeria and a couple of bars that do snacks – *Spavento*, just behind the front, plays the most interesting sounds. Apart from that, village facilities stretch to two well-stocked shops, a post office and a couple of cafés.

Travel details

BUSES

Vathý to: Kióni (2 daily; 1hr).

FERRIES

The frequencies of the ferry services given below apply in season, from May to September; out of season, there is usually only one daily service on each route, unless otherwise specified. All the ferries carry vehicles.

Fríkes to: Fiskárdho, Kefalloniá (1 daily; 1hr); Vassilikí, Lefkádha (1 daily; 2hr 15min); Nydhrí, Lefkádha (winter only; 1 daily; 1hr 30min).

Pisaetós to: Sámi, Kefalloniá (5 daily; 45min) (winter 2 daily); Astakós (1 daily; 2hr 45min).

Vathý to: Sámi, Kefalloniá (2 daily; 1hr); Pátra (2 daily; 4hr 30min).

Chapter 5

Kefalloniá

R ugged, mountainous and blessed with some of the most dramatic scenery in the region, **Kefalloniá** is the largest Ionian island, but has resisted the sort of development that has overtaken Corfu and some of the other islands. The island is variously known as Kefalloniá, **Kefallínia** and **Cephalonia** – the first is the phonetic transliteration of the present Greek name, the second the modern version of its ancient moniker (which is also used for its airport) and the third the anglicized version. Like its tiny neighbour, Itháki, it's little more than a series of mountain tops piercing the waves – **Mount Énos**, which looms over the south of the island, is one of the highest in Greece – with towns and villages sheltering in the valleys and on the lower slopes. Despite its area, there are only three towns of any size: the handsome and spacious capital, **Argostóli**; the main ferry port, **Sámi**, a quiet and under-used base on the eastern coast; and **Lixoúri**, virtually a suburb of Argostóli but, because of the convoluted landscape, 35km away by road yet only thirty minutes by ferry.

Until well into the 1980s, the islanders resisted mass tourism and the only foreign visitors were independent travellers who were not too fussed about levels of comfort. Indeed, Kefallonians had quite a reputation amongst other Greeks as being rather eccentric and

---

Accommodation price codes

Rooms and hotels listed in this book have been price-coded according to the scale outlined below. The rates quoted represent the cheapest available double room in high season. Out of season, rates can drop by as much as fifty percent or more, especially if you negotiate for a stay of three or more nights. Single rooms, where available, cost around seventy percent of the price of a double. For further information, see p.36.

① up to 6000dr	⑤ 16,000–20,000dr
② 6000–9000dr	⑥ 20,000–30,000dr
③ 9000–12,000dr	⑦ 30,000dr upwards
④ 12,000–16,000dr	

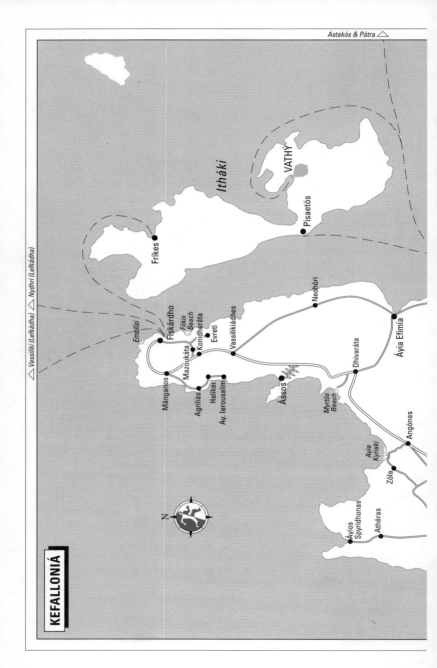
△ Vassilikí (Lefkádha) △ Nydhrí (Lefkádha)

KEFALLONIÁ

Ithákí

VATHÝ

Pisaetós

Frikes

Neohóri

Emblísi

Fiskárdho
Fókis Beach
Konidharáta
Evretí
Vassilikiádhes
Ávia Efimía

Mánganos
Mazoukáta
Dhivaráta

Agriliás
Halikéri
Av. Ierousalím
Ássos
Myrtós Beach

Angónas

Ávia Kyriakí

Zóla

Áyios Spyridhonas
Athéras

N

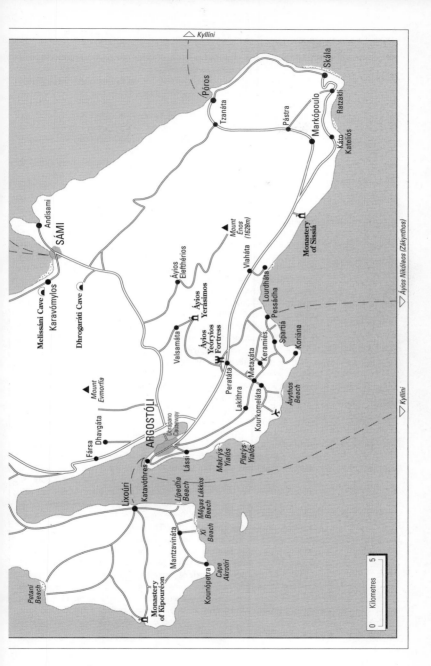

Pátra

The busiest mainland port after Pireás, **PÁTRA** is a major stopping-off point for travellers moving between the islands and mainland. There are ferries to Kefalloniá and Itháki and a direct bus service via Kyllíni to Zákynthos. It also has train (9 daily; 4hr–5hr 30min; OSE ☎061 221 311 or 277 441) and bus (28 daily; 3hr 30min) connections with Athens and services to the rest of the Peloponnese and some northern destinations – though, oddly, no civil airport. It is also a major terminal for ferries to Italy, many of which call at Igoumenítsa and Corfu. Pátra itself has little to detain the traveller, although if you find yourself in between connections it's not an unattractive city. There are no beaches or major historical sites in the immediate vicinity, but Pátra is handy for ancient **Olympia**, 2hr away by regular bus or train.

Buses and **trains** arrive within a few hundred metres of the ferries on Óthonos & Amalías, in an area that resembles a rail shunting yard. The only **tourist office** (Mon–Fri 7am–9pm; ☎061/620 353) is in the ferry terminal building, and keeps local maps and accommodation info. If you're passing through with time to spare, the railway station has a handy **left luggage** office.

Pátra is built on a grid system, much of it one-way. The long cross-streets are very busy, so it's best to try for accommodation off the main roads and away from the seafront. **Hotels** are often booked out, even in low season, so expect to have to shop around. Handy mid-range places include the *Galaxy*, Ayíou Nikoláou 9 (☎061/278 815 or 275 981; ④), the *Mediterranee*, nearby at no. 18 (☎061/279 602 or 279 624; ④), and the *Adonis*, Kapsáli 8 (☎061/224 213 fax 226 971; ④). There is also a **youth hostel** at Iroón Polytekhníou 68 (☎061/427 278; ①). **Banks** and exchanges abound, and there are 24-hour foreign exchange machines at the corner of Óthonos & Amalías and Patréos, and on Ayíou Nikoláou next to the *Galaxy* hotel.

Patra's two main sights, visible from most parts of the city, are the **Kástro**, some 193 steps up from the top of Ayíou Nikoláou, whose ruins are set in a quiet park, commanding stunning views north to Messolóngi, and sometimes feature outdoor concerts; and the giant jelly-mould **basilica of Ayíou Andhréou** at the far end of town, which opened in 1979 and house the relics of St Andrew, said to have been martyred on this spot.

Much of the town's eating is uninspired, like the cheap *souvláki* joints around Platía Trión Symáhon and better places well hidden or in the flashier suburbs. Try the seafront *Faros*, corner of Óthonos & Amalías and Sakhtoúri, an excellent-value fish taverna or *Krini*, Pandokrátoros 57, a local favourite up by the Kástro. The *Majestic* and *Nikolaras*, both on Ayíou Nikoláou, are old style *estiatória* with a good range of fare but neither is particularly cheap. While the seafront and central Platía Trión Symáhon have cafés, bars and a few shops, most of Pátra's **nightlife** goes on some blocks back from the port. The town centre is Platía Yioryíou, which houses the city's main Apóllon Theatre. Town youth congregates around Platía Ólgas; families and couples among the many bars and tavernas around the pleasant Psilá Alónia park, some ten blocks from the sea. Odhós Yerokostópoulou, north of Yioryíou, also has a number of **music bars** and restaurants and around the foot of the steps at the top of Ayíou Nikoláou there is the most concentrated conglomeration of loud and trendy bars. For a drink away from the obvious places, try the popular and curiously titled *Beer Society*, tucked in an alley off Ríga Ferréou near Ermoú and Kolokotróni.

xenophobic, and it is only recently that Greeks without family connections here have been attracted in any numbers too. This has gone hand in hand with the creation and constant upgrading of the **seaside resorts**, which has continued apace since the locals decided that the money-making potential was too great to be ignored. That is not to say that the attitude is predominantly mercenary; most Kefallonians come across as genuinely welcoming, and the island can boast a noticeable proportion of distinct characters. Its other great virtue is its size, so it can comfortably absorb the larger numbers now arriving without seeming overcrowded or unduly compromised.

Kefalloniá's seaside resorts are all based around small villages and ports. The **beaches** in the south tend to be sandy, those in the north, pebbly, including the exquisite white crescent of **Mýrtos**, one of the most famous and most photographed beaches in the entire Ionian. Below the thumbnail of limestone around the popular port and resort of **Fiskárdho**, much of the northern coastline is sheer cliff, with the most terrifying mountain roads in the archipelago and some of the most breathtaking views. Kefalloniá also conceals two unmissable geological quirks, the **Dhrogaráti cave system** and the **Melissáni underground lake**, as well as some minor archeological sites and some more locations said to be associated with the Odysseus myth.

The island sits close to the fault line that has given this area of the Ionian a history of cataclysmic **earthquakes**. The most violent ever recorded, in 1953, levelled its graceful capital, Argostóli, destroyed almost all of its outlying villages, and in some places killed up to eighty percent of the population (see the box on p.197). Argostóli was rebuilt with overseas help, not quite to its former elegance, though it remains a pleasant town. Most of the interior villages were rebuilt, often beside earthquake ruins which can still be seen today. Many Kefallonians were forced or chose to live abroad after the earthquake, but a large number have returned, bringing languages and a sophistication absent in some other parts of the Ionian.

Kefalloniá's **bus** system is basic but expanding, and with a little legwork it can be used to get you almost anywhere on the island. Key routes connect Argostóli with Sámi, Fiskárdho, **Skála**, a small development with a long sandy beach and pine woods, and **Póros,** a slightly shabby resort built around a fishing port. There's also a useful connection on from Sámi to the tiny resort of **Ayía Efimía**, which attracts many package travellers. The island has a plethora of **ferry** connections, principally from Fiskárdho to Lefkádha and Itháki, and from Sámi to Lefkádha, Itháki and the mainland, as well as links to Zákynthos, Kyllíni and Pátra.

Some history

Remains excavated around Kefalloniá, and now on display in Argostóli's archeological museum, have established that there were settlements on the island as long ago as 50,000 BC – before the modern Mediterranean began to take shape. Kefalloniá was once covered in fir trees – **abies cephalonica**, named after the island – which formed a large part of its trade in ancient times: *cephalonica* wood has been discovered in the structure of the Minoan palace at Knossós on Crete. The island is believed to have acquired its name from legendary king Cephalus, whose escapades were recorded by Hesiod, Ovid, Apollodorus and others. Son of Hermes and Herse, he was known above all as a hunter – an activity keenly pursued by modern Kefallonians, to the chagrin of animal lovers and walkers harassed by hunting dogs.

By the seventh century BC, the island had split into four democratic cities; the most famous of them was Same (modern-day Sámi), named in Thucydides and Homer, who records that Odysseus sailed for the Trojan War with twelve ships from the city. During the Peloponnesian War (431–404 BC), Kefalloniá was overrun by Athens which, although an ally, distrusted the island and seized it to use as a base for attacks on Corinth to the east – to no avail, as the Ionian islands fell to Sparta at the end of the war. In the Byzantine period, Kefalloniá became the seat of the "theme", or administrative district, of the islands. Out of the mainstream of Byzantine politics, however, it – like the rest of the Ionian islands – fell prone to attack by pirates and other opportunists. In 1082, the Ionians were attacked by the Normans, under Robert Guiscard. When his son failed to take Kefalloniá, Guiscard and his forces sailed from Corfu to back him, but within weeks of reaching the island the Norman leader had succumbed to plague. The port where he died, Fiskárdho, derives its name from his.

The island was handed over to Venice in 1204, and for some time was administered by the powerful Orsini dynasty of Rome, who imported their own aristocrats and introduced a feudal system. Over the following centuries, Kefalloniá ricocheted between the Turks, the Venetians, the French and the Russians, until in 1809 the **British** took over in a bloodless invasion. Kefalloniá became a focus for the widespread resentment of the British in the Ionian: in 1848, this erupted in open rebellion, with violent clashes in Argostóli, followed by heavy jail sentences for activists. A brief period of liberal parliamentary reform followed, but was overturned by a new British administration, which exiled the editors of radical island newspapers. Britain finally ceded Kefalloniá and the other Ionian islands to Greece in 1864.

Kefalloniá was taken over by the **Germans** in World War II in a particularly gruesome fashion. The island had been seized by the Italians, who controlled it briefly prior to the fall of Mussolini and Italy's capitulation in September 1943. At this moment of administrative confusion, with contradictory orders both to surrender and to repel the Germans, the Italians were left helpless and hopelessly outnumbered. Rather than herd them into POW camps, the Germans, according to Ionian historian Arthur Foss, "decided in cold blood to massacre their former allies". In villages on the slopes of Mount Énos, and out near the sea mills of Katovóthres at Argostóli, over 5000 Italian soldiers were shot and their bodies burnt. The massacre is a key event in Louis de Bernières' novel, *Captain Corelli's Mandolin*, a tragicomic epic spanning the start of Greece's involvement in World War II up to the present day.

Argostóli and around

Despite the 1953 earthquakes, **ARGOSTÓLI** is a very attractive town, with some remaining pre-quake architecture, a large and airy main square and a busy waterfront facing east across the Koútavos lagoon to the wooded slopes of Mount Evmorfía. The waterfront doubles as a working quayside used by fishermen and freighters, and an illuminated promenade at night. Day and evening tour craft line the parts of the quay not used by working boats. The lagoon is traversed by the Dhrápano bridge, a remarkable feat of engineering overseen by the Swiss-born soldier and politician, Charles Philippe de Bosset, British governor of Kefalloniá from 1810 to 1814. Originally built of wood, the bridge caused some controversy among islanders, who feared that it might help potential invaders. Although most package tourists to Kefalloniá will find themselves based along the Lássi peninsula (a twenty-minute walk from Argostóli) or at outlying resorts such as Skála, Póros, Ayía Efimía or Fiskárdho, there is still a high level of tourism based in town, with restaurants and bars catering to both townspeople and visitors.

Arrival and information

Argostóli's shiny new **Kefallínia airport** lies 11km south of town. There are no airport buses, although Olympic is considering introducing one in 2000, and suburban bus routes to nearby villages like Svoronáta are so infrequent there is little point in recommending that you try to connect with them. As with every airport in the Ionian, expensive taxi rides into town (around 3500dr) have become an unofficial tourism surcharge. Negotiate a price beforehand and *always* feign disbelief. Apart from a bar-café and an exchange booth which opens to meet international flights, there are no other facilities at the airport.

Those arriving in Argostóli by bus from other parts of the island will wind up at the new KTEL **bus station**, a minute from the Dhrápano causeway, which sports a café-bar and modern toilets. Unless you're booked into a hotel or travelling straight on from Argostóli, it's best to head for the main square, **Platía Metaxá**, if only to get your bearings, or to dump your bags at a bar and look for a hotel or room. This is easiest done by heading along the seafront, now renamed Andoníou Trítsi after the popular leading PASOK politician from here, who died prematurely not long ago.

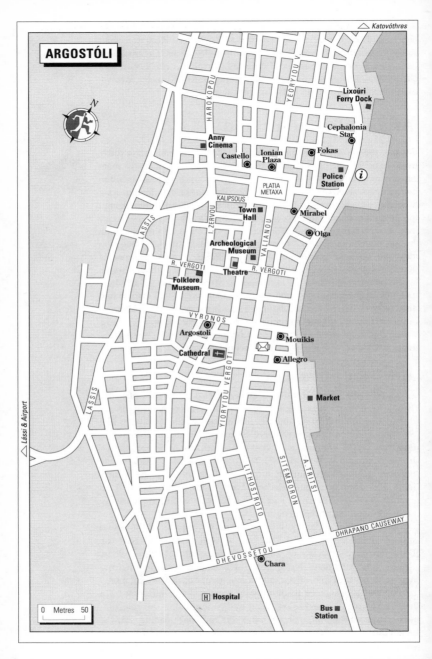

△ Katovóthres

ARGOSTÓLI

N

YEORYIOU V

**Lixoúri
Ferry Dock**

**Cephalonia
Star**

HAROKOPOU

**Anny
Cinema**

Castello

**Ionian
Plaza**

◉ **Fokas**

**Police
Station**

i

PLATIA
METAXA

KALIPSOUS

I. ZERVOU

**Town
Hall**

◉ **Mirabel**

VALIANOU

◉ **Olga**

LASSIS

**Archeological
Museum**

R. VERGOTI

R. VERGOTI

Theatre

**Folklore
Museum**

VYRONOS

◉

Argostoli

Cathedral ✠

YIORYIOU VERGOTI

◉ **Mouikis**

✉

◉ **Allegro**

■ **Market**

LASSIS

△ *Lássi & Airport*

LITHOSTROTO

SITEMBORON

A. TRITSI

DHRAPANO CAUSEWAY

DHEVOSSETOU

◉ **Chara**

[H] **Hospital**

Bus ■
Station

0 Metres 50

Argostóli's **tourist office**, one of the friendliest in the Ionian, is right in the middle of the quay, in a one-storey building opposite the police station. The office has information about rooms, and can advise on transport and other resorts around the island (☎0671/22 248 or ☎ & fax 24 466; Mon–Fri 7.30am–2.30pm and 5–10pm).

Accommodation

Argostóli never seems a particularly busy town, but its **accommodation** can fill up even at the dead end of the tourism season and in the winter, when some of the hotels around Platía Metaxá remain open. This is partly due to business clientele. Unfortunately for the budget traveller, all the cheap hotels bar one have closed down or gone upmarket, leaving only upper mid-range to expensive establishments.

In a working town with a large permanent population, **private rooms** aren't too plentiful, but the tourist office has a list of what's available. Some of the best bargains can be found through waterfront tavernas, such as the *Kalafatis* (☎0671/22 627; ②–④), near to the Dhrápano bridge on the A. Trítsi waterfront, the *Tzivras* (☎0671/24 259; ②) on Vandórou, just off the centre of the waterfront, or *Spyros Rouhotas* taverna (☎0671/23 941; ③), opposite the Lixoúri ferry ramp. A number of travel agencies also offer rooms, apartments and villas: try Myrtos (☎0671/25 895 or 25 023, fax 24 230) on A. Trítsi, towards the main quay, or Filoxenos Travel (☎0671/23 055–6) on R. Vergóti, near the square.

The town's one **campsite**, *Argostoli Camping* (☎0671/23 487), lies 2km north of the centre, just beyond the Katovóthres sea mills. The site has only patchy shade and basic amenities; a shop, restaurant-bar and, surprisingly, what it describes as a "music hall". Despite the presence of a bus stop, there's only an infrequent service in high season, so you'll probably have to walk. Campers, however, are strongly recommended to head for the campsite at Sámi (see p.210), unless they particularly want to be close to Argostóli.

Allegro, Andréa Hoïdha 2 (☎0671/22 268). A block from the front, in an alley off the middle of A. Trítsi, newly renovated and now decidedly upmarket with classy en-suite rooms. ⑤.

Argostoli, Výronos 21 (☎0671/28 358 or 28 272). Fairly plain mid-range hotel with functional en-suite rooms. Set further back from the hubbub of seafront and shopping areas and better value than most. ④

Castello, Platía Metaxá (☎0671/23 250–1, fax 23 252). Small but stylish hotel with en-suite rooms overlooking the *platía*. Café and bar. Open year-round. ④.

Cephalonia Star, A. Trítsi 50 (☎0671/23 181–3, fax 23 180). Large waterfront hotel, with spacious en-suite rooms whose balconies overlook lagoon and hills, all with TV and a/c. Restaurant and bar. Tends to be heavily booked by British travel companies, but rooms should be available throughout the season. ⑤.

Chara, Devossétou (☎0671/22 427). A small and drastically simple rooming house with shared bathrooms, but close to the Dhrápano bridge and the bus station, with a friendly manager who offers coffee in the leafy courtyard. The only budget option, open all year but often full with local workers. ①.

Fokas, Yeroulánou 1–3 (☎0671/22 566 or 28 100, fax 23 109). Large modern low-rise hotel a block back from the front. Tastefully decorated en-suite rooms. One of the better-value mid-range places. ④.

Ionian Plaza, Platía Metaxá (☎0671/25 581–4, fax 25 585). One of the ritziest hotels in the archipelago, and surprisingly cheap for what it is – designer decor down to its swagged curtains and chic bathroom fixtures. If it's in your budget, this is a pampered capitalist's bargain. ⑤.

Mirabel, Platía Metaxá (☎0671/25 381–3, fax 25 384, email *mirabel@compulink.gr*). Tucked into the southwest corner of the main square, with large and comfortable air-conditioned en-suite rooms. Reasonable value for its position, open year-round and takes credit cards. ⑤.

Mouikis, Výronos 3 (☎0671/23 455–6, fax 24 528). Anonymous decor but very comfortable en-suite rooms with air-conditioning, balcony, phone and TV. Comparable to *Mirabel* but in a quieter setting. Now one of the priciest hotels in town, takes credit cards. ⑥.

Olga, A. Trítsi 82 (☎0671/24 981–4, fax 24 985). Imposing upmarket seafront hotel with a/c and TV in all rooms but rather overpriced. Breakfast included. ⑥.

The Town

The mansions on the palm-lined boulevard of V. Yeoryíou leaving the north side of Platía Metaxá give an idea of the elegance and wealth of Argostóli before the 1953 earthquakes. The *platía* is the focus of town life, although, typically, its restaurants and bars are the most expensive in town. The square's southwest corner, next to the small park, makes a useful landmark as it leads off both towards Lássi and the nearest beaches. Argostóli's main retail and administrative streets, where you'll find shops, banks and the post office, run south of the square.

The Archeological Museum

*Argostóli
Archeological
Museum, on R.
Vergóti, was
closed for
refurbishment
at the time of
writing so any
new displays,
opening times
and entry cost
cannot be
given here.*

Modest if compared to Corfu Town's, the **Archeological Museum** at Argostóli nevertheless runs to two spacious rooms containing a plethora of artefacts excavated on the island, mainly pottery, jewellery, glassware and other domestic items, some dating from the Mycenaean period. There are also fragments of architectural details, funerary relics and some statuary, including a ribald Pan figure found at the Melissáni cave shrine, who was once obviously priapic but is now in a state of blunt detumescence. The collection, if underwhelming, does suggest that prehistoric Kefalloniá was culturally advanced compared to the neighbouring islands.

The Folklore Museum

The **Korgialenío History and Folklore Museum**, on Ilía Zervoú behind the Municipal Theatre, is rich in detail of domestic life and island culture over the centuries. Its collection of furniture, clothing

Earthquakes in the Ionian

Three **tectonic plates** meet in the region of Kefalloniá, Itháki and
Zákynthos: the Eurasian Plate, which carries Italy, parts of northern
Greece and the Balkans; the Turkish–Hellenic Plate, which carries southern Greece and the Aegean, as well as Turkey and Cyprus; and the African
Plate, which supports most of the southern Mediterranean. These plates
are in constant, minute motion, part of a process called subduction which
is causing Greece to sink slowly into the Aegean. The tension between the
plates causes continual, usually minor, **seismic activity**. Major earthquakes occur only a few times each century, and the twentieth seems to
have had its quota, notably in the violent upheavals of 1948 and 1953.

The worst quake on record, in **August 1953**, wreaked destruction
across Kefalloniá, Itháki, Lefkádha and Zákynthos, and inspired an international aid campaign by America, Britain and France. No fewer than 113
distinct tremors or aftershocks hit the islands over a period of five days
from August 9 to 14. Argostóli and Zákynthos Town were virtually razed to
the ground, with roads piled up like waves and huge vents opened up in the
landscape. Over six hundred islanders died and thousands more were
injured. The toll would have been higher if the main quake had not struck
on a summer afternoon, when many people were outdoors. An estimated
seventy percent of buildings throughout the islands were destroyed, and
some communities were wiped out altogether. Argostóli's Archeological
Museum exhibits some remarkable photographic records of the event.

Tremors are common throughout the Ionian every year, but are normally so minor that they go unnoticed. Islanders are generally phlegmatic
about the threat of another major earthquake; beyond limiting the height
of buildings and reinforcing foundations, there is nothing else they can do.
Your chances of experiencing a tremor, less still an earthquake, while on
holiday here are very slim.

and other memorabilia is presented in a series of mock rooms from
various eras and social strata: from a peasant kitchen to the drawing
room of a wealthy family's mansion. The mock chapel contains some
glorious icons, a tomb and several carved marble *stelai*. Another
quaint feature is two flat stand-up oxen labouring under the yoke.
Most fascinating is its extensive collection of photographs of the
island before and after the 1953 earthquakes, which record both the
sophistication of Kefallonian architecture and culture, and the extent
of the devastation after the tremors.

*The
Korgialenío
History and
Folklore
Museum is
open Tues–Sun
9am–2pm;
500dr.*

The Focas-Cosmetatos Foundation

Housed in a beautiful old mansion on Valiánou, opposite the
Nomarhía, this small museum and cultural foundation was set up by
the two noble families whose name it shares. It is arranged as a family
house of the old ruling classes, with an array of fine furniture and ornaments, as well as a selection of paintings and lithographs, including
original works by English nineteenth-century artists Edward Lear and
Joseph Cartwright. There is also an interesting display on the history
of money and a couple of flowery but confusing family trees.

*The Focas-
Cosmetatos
Foundation is
open Mon–Sat
9am–1.30pm
and 6.30–9pm;
500dr.*

The sea mills

The disused **sea mills** at Katovóthres, an intriguing geological oddity forty minutes' walk north through pine woods from the centre of Argostóli, have become something of a tourist trap, dominated by a large, multi-roomed taverna and music hall to which coachloads of tourists are bused in shifts starting at 6pm. During the day, though, anyone can walk into the concreted-over complex of pools and (disused) waterwheel. The view of Lixoúri, the Gulf of Argostóli and the mountains is magnificent, as are the sunsets. The sink holes at the tip of the peninsula into which seawater drains were first discovered in the 1830s, and before World War II were harnessed to provide electricity. However, it took until the 1960s for scientists to discover where the water went: they dumped green dye into the sink holes, and two weeks later the traces started to appear in the Melissáni cave and in springs along the Sámi–Áyia Efimía coast. Moving at something like 1km a day, the water seeps under the mountains to reappear 20km away on the other side of the island.

There are some small, pebbly coves towards and around Katovóthres, but most Greeks and tourists based in town either walk or take the bus to the beach at Lássi.

Nearby is the **Áyios Theódoros lighthouse**, no more than a small Doric rotunda with a light on its roof. It was built by Charles Napier, governor of the island from 1822 to 1830, and resident during Byron's brief visit prior to his fateful journey to Messolóngi (the original was in fact destroyed by an earthquake in 1875, but rebuilt to the same design). Curiously, it resembles a smaller version of the Maitland rotunda in Corfu Town, built only a few years before, which might suggest a certain rivalry between the two men.

Eating and drinking

If you want to eat with the Greeks, your first destination should be either the *Tzivras* or *Kalafatis* **restaurants**: the former, a daytime-only *estiatório* (closes 5pm) has an impressive range of staples from the oven with a lot of vegetarian options such as *briám* (potato and courgette bake), helpings of which tend to be large and should probably be ordered on their own. *Kalafatis* has a more conventional taverna menu, but succulently done. Either is the likely place to find a bona fide Kefallonian meat pie, a traditional dish with a pudding-like crust, and meat stuffing mixed with rice and vegetables. Both are extremely popular, so if thwarted head for the neighbouring *Anonymos* or *Sapfo* tavernas. Further along the seafront, *Portside* has a good, inexpensive selection of grilled and baked meals and salads.

Eating in Platía Metaxá is an altogether different matter, usually done to the accompaniment of tinkling stemware under candlelight. The *Ionian Plaza Hotel*'s *Palazzino* restaurant has a good, if not particularly cheap, range of exotic pasta dishes, and the *Kefalos* opposite is recommended for decent breakfasts and lunch, and evening staples like spaghetti, steak and salads. *The Captain's Table*, the smartest in town – it actually has a greeter – is recommended for a splurge and for anyone keen to experience the little-heard Kefallonian style of *kandádhes* singing (nightly from 9pm). Another place with live music, a folk guitar duo and more reasonable prices is the *Demosthenes* garden taverna, opposite the *Mirabel* hotel.

Zaharoplastía around the square and on the waterfront serve continental breakfasts, but at a price. The best is the *Igloo* on Andréa Hoïdha, a few blocks south of the *Mouikis Hotel* and a block from the waterfront, which is also good for a quiet evening drink. Alternatively, the waterfront fruit and veg **market** is a great place to assemble your own breakfast or lunch, with provisions from the bakeries and supermarkets opposite.

Platía Metaxá is the main attraction in the evenings, for a meal, drink or just a *vólta*, but it's also prone to overspill from two loud and competing music **bars** – fab if you like your Human League remixes laced with blasts of grunge, not so great if you don't. Local poseurs prefer to loll at the *Da Cappo* café-bar, the *Flonitiko* café and the *Koukos* club-bar, on V. Yeorgíou near the square – all very stylish but none of them cheap. The *Farcus* bar, just off the square above Filoxenos Travel, plays more eclectic indie sounds, while at *Space Girls*, near the *Mirabel*, you can expect the unexpected. You'll find a quieter and cheaper drink on the waterfront in the bars towards the Lixoúri ferry – *Spyros Rouhotas'* is ideal – or, in the opposite direction, head for the best-sited bar in the whole of Argostóli, the modest but welcoming *kafenío* right by the Dhrápano bridge, with a view other bar-owners would kill for.

Listings

Banks and exchange The Ionian Bank, A. Trítsi 73; the Bank of Greece on Valiánou; the National Bank, corner of Konstandínou and Sitebórou (all Mon–Thurs 8am–2pm, Mon–Fri 8am–1.30pm). The post office also changes travellers' cheques, and the *Hotel Mouikis* offers bank rates.

Car and bike rental Recommended is the island-wide Sunbird agency, which has an office at A. Trítsi 84 (☎0671/23 723). Budget can be found at Lássis 3 (☎0671/24 232), and Ford car rental has offices in Argostóli on A. Trítsi (☎0671/22 338) and on the main drag at Lássi (☎0671/25 471–2), as well as Skála and Póros.

Cinema The surprisingly costly (2500dr) but pleasant open-air *Cine Anny* is on Harokópou, three blocks northwest of Platía Metaxá.

Email Full Internet facilities are available at *Excelixis*, just off Lithostrotoú by Áyios Spyrídhon church (☎0671/25 530; Mon–Sat 9am–2.30pm and 6–10pm) and the *Bibis* Internet café on Platía Metaxá.

Ferries The *Bartholomos* agency by the Lixoúri ferry dock (☎0671/28 853) is the main agent for Greece–Italy lines. The *Vassilatos* agency, A. Trítsi 54 (☎0671/22 618 or 28 000), also handles international ferry bookings.

Hospital On the corner of Devossétou and Souidhías (☎0671/22 434 or 24 641).

Laundry There's a self-service laundromat on the Lássi road, three blocks up from the Napier Gardens (daily 8am–1pm); the minimarket opposite sells tokens for the machines and individual one-wash bags of powder.

Olympic Airways Y. Vergóti 1 (☎0671/28 808). Airport (☎0671/28 881).

OTE R. Vergóti (daily 7am–2pm).

Performing arts The imposing blue and white *Municipal Theatre* on Y. Vergóti opens occasionally for special performances of music and drama. It also has eclectic film showings.

Police A. Trítsi, by the main ferry jetty (☎0671/22 300 or 22 200). Tourist Police (☎0671/22 815).

Port Authority On the quay (☎0671/22 224).

Post office Konstandínou (Mon–Fri 8am–2pm).

Taxi ranks (☎0671/28 505 or 22 700).

Lixoúri and the Lixoúrion peninsula

LIXOÚRI was flattened in the 1953 earthquake, and little of it has risen above two or three storeys since. The waterfront it presents to ferries arriving from Argostóli is uninspiring: a smattering of tavernas and bars on either side of the town square, Platía Petrítsi, but all of it rather dowdy. It has many fans, however, who use it as a base for the quiet sandy beaches on the way to Cape Akrotíri, and for exploring the mountainous central and northern sections of the peninsula by car or motorbike.

Like its larger neighbour, Lixoúri consists of a long, narrow grid of alleys stretched along the seafront, with little beyond apart from a few hotels in the dormitory area at the back of town. The beach immediately to the south is narrow but sandy, and popular with families. Better beaches can be found 2km south, at **Lépedha**, with its rich red sand and unusual sandstone rock formations. While there are rooms within a kilometre of Lépedha (see below), the only facilities so far at this embryonic resort are two beach bars.

Lixoúri practicalities

Ferries run between the northern end of Argostóli's quayside and Lixoúri in half an hour (every 30mins in summer, hourly in winter; 5am–midnight; 300dr per person, 1000dr per vehicle).

Lixoúri has a small strip of beachside **hotels** a few hundred metres south along the coast road leaving the waterfront. The two main establishments here, the *Poseidon* (☎0671/92 518 or 92 519, fax 91 374; ④) and *Summery* (☎0671/91 771 or 91 871, fax 91 062; ⑤), are both reasonable value and, though heavily booked by British tour operators, should have rooms free through most of the season for independent travellers. Both have en-suite rooms with balconies and views; the former has gardens giving on to the beach, the latter a pool and tennis courts. The best bargain for accommodation in Lixoúri, however is the *Giardino* (☎0671/92 505 or 92 382, fax 92 525; ③), four blocks back from the front – take the road leaving the right-hand corner at the back of Platía Petrítsi – which has en-suite rooms, pool, restaurant and bar. This too is used by package tours, but if you phone ahead you'll often find that it has availability.

Perdikis Travel (☎0671/91 097 or 93 077, fax 92 503; from ③) on the ferry quay is an agent for **rooms** in Lixoúri and outside town, as is the very friendly A.D. Travel (☎0671/93 142, fax 92 663; from ③), on the main road through town just north of the square. An attractive if out-of-the-way alternative is the *Taverna Apolafsi* rooms and studios (☎0671/91 691, fax 91 572; ③). Blissfully quiet except on music nights, the taverna is a twenty-minute walk south from Lixoúri towards Lépedha beach.

If you're **eating** in Lixoúri, the first place to head for is the *Akrogiali* on the seafront. This authentic and friendly island taverna has an extensive menu and attracts customers from all over the island. Food prices are very reasonable, and the local wine is not only excellent but must be the cheapest in the Ionian. Nearby *Antonis* mixes traditional dishes with a line of steaks and European food, and there's an identically named grill on the main street, while *Maria's*, a block back and behind the square to the south, is a large, cheap and basic family taverna. One block behind the seafront and south of the square, *Iy Avli* is a nice garden restaurant. Also south of the square but back on the front, the *Archipelagos* restaurant-*ouzerí* has a good range of seafood and pasta, and doubles as a bar in the evenings. At night, drinkers tend to congregate in the square and in the pricey seafront **bars** such as *Sousouro* (Whisper) and *Pame* (Let's go), but the funkiest place to drink in Lixoúri is the small and friendly *kafenío* facing the ferry dock. There is a small Internet café called *Factory* in an alley southwest of the square.

The south coast of the peninsula

The flatter southern part of the peninsula, known locally as **Kátoï**, still bears some of the most dramatic scars of the 1953 earthquake. This farming region was one of the worst hit on the island, and in places there remain eerie landscapes of subsided fields and orchards, and small hills shunted up out of the earth. Flocks of bell-laden sheep graze on the weird tumuli left by the quake, sending crazed gamelan music drifting across the countryside. The only bus service on the peninsula connects Lixoúri with Xi beach, 6km away to the south, three times a day. On the way it detours to **Mégas Lákos**, whose name means "big hole", where the narrow beach is a rich, almost silky, red, set below stunted cliffs and served by a couple of tavernas – try the *Oasis*. The price at the smart *Kefalonia Beach* bungalows (☎0671/92 679 or 92 409; ⑤) includes half-board. You can walk along the beach to Xi in a quarter of an hour.

Xi itself has a beach bar, a couple of tavernas, *Ocean View* and *Ta Delfinia*, and serried ranks of sun loungers on the beach in front of the *Cephalonia Palace* **hotel** (☎0671/93 112 or 93 190, fax 92 638; ⑥), whose price includes breakfast and an evening meal. Popular with British tourists, this has all the typical facilities of a large, self-contained resort hotel – vast pool, restaurants, bars, shops, gardens – which is just as well, because the landscape between it and the nearest village, Mantzavináta, 2km north, is a desert-like moonscape, if you can imagine the moon with rudimentary vegetation.

A road also leads from Mantzavináta 4km southwest to the quieter beach at **Kounópetra**, site of a curious rock formation. Until the 1953 earthquake, this rocking stone had a strange rhythmic movement that could be measured by placing a knife into a gap between the rock and its base. However, after the quake the rock became motionless. Kounópetra is really a headland with a tiny harbour and beach, neighbouring the beach of Agrosykiá, which hosts *To Meltemi* restaurant. Development is gradually creeping in here, though it would still make a peaceful base for those with their own transport; try staying at the *Villa Carina* (☎0671/93 604; ④) or *Kounopetra's Studios* (☎0671/93 252 or 93 772; ⑤), both comfortable purpose-built apartment blocks, or the larger *Hotel Ionian Sea* (☎0671/92 280, fax 92 980; ④), about a kilometre inland.

The west coast of the peninsula

The peninsula has one of the finest vantage points for sunsets on the entire island: the **monastery of Kipouréon**, hefted up on the cliffs above the wild west coast some 14km from Lixoúri. The views are magnificent, but the monastery itself is minor, most of it having been rebuilt in the 1970s. Like the rest of the west coast of the peninsula, Kipouréon is only really accessible by private vehicle, although the roads have been improved in recent years.

If you do have your own transport, you could also reach the magnificent beach at **Petaní**, 14km northwest of Lixoúri, a dramatic two-kilometre stretch of smooth pebbles that's possibly the finest, and certainly the remotest, on the island. Even this haven is in the process of being discovered; two seasonal snack-bars provide refreshments, and there are signs of accommodation being built. The **Áyios Spyrídhon** inlet, also known as Pórto Athéras as it serves the traditional village of Athéras a short way inland, 18km from Lixoúri at the north of the promontory, has a sandy beach with shallow water that's safe for swimming, though it seems to be unfortunately positioned to catch seaborne garbage. There is an *ouzerí* and the *Yialós* taverna, whose garden acts as home for families with camper vans and would probably be all right for camping.

Lássi

LÁSSI, a twenty-minute walk south from the centre of Argostóli, is an unattractive package resort that sprawls along the edge of a busy four-lane highway and suffers from being right under the flight path to the airport. The beaches, to be fair, are well maintained, although their modest size and the concentration of tourism in the area means they are very busy even in low season. Lássi's ribbon development has a number of good **restaurants** – the *Il Gabbiano* pizzeria, the *Panorama* taverna, the *Olive Press* garden taverna, the huge *Lassi* restaurant with a full Chinese menu as well as Greek, and the upmarket *Trata* and *Sirtaki psistariés* – to serve those holidaying here, but given that there are far superior beaches around the southeastern tip of Kefalloniá, the independent traveller would be wasting time staying here. Immediately beyond Lássi, **Makrýs Yialós** and **Platýs Yialós** are good sandy beaches for a day out if you're staying in Argostóli, with snack bars and restaurants in the hotels overlooking the beach.

The Livátho peninsula

The **Livátho hills** to the southeast of Argostóli, beyond and inland from the beaches at Makrýs Yialós and Platýs Yialós, are ideal for gentle walking. This lush green range of rolling farmland and tree-shaded country roads slopes down to some fine beaches, most notably at Ávythos. The pretty little villages that dot the hills between Lakíthra and Pessádha are home to many wealthy islanders, which gives places such as Kourkomeláta the air of chintzy suburbs – though there is surprisingly little in the way of facilities. The walking hereabouts is excellent, except in the hunting season (Sept 25–Feb 28), when the threat of attack by off-leash hunting dogs has to be taken seriously (take a walking stick). Three **buses** a day run to Kourkomeláta, stopping at Lakíthra, Metaxáta and Svoronáta. On the road out of Svoronáta the *Dum Spiro(s) Spero* taverna deserves a refreshment stop for the name alone.

Ten kilometres southeast of Argostóli, the well-preserved village of **Metaxáta** boasts a number of large, pre-earthquake mansions shaded by ancient palm trees. In the small, deserted town square, a bust of Byron marks the site of a house where the poet stayed. Substantially rebuilt after the 1953 earthquake, **Kourkomeláta**, 1km to the southwest, sits on a bluff overlooking the coast. The *Marina* café-bar here, with a garden and excellent views, is virtually the only such establishment between Lakíthra and Spartiá. Kourkomeláta also has a large, impressive church, Áyios Yerásimos (usually locked), and a Neoclassical cultural centre, used occasionally for special events. Just downhill from Kourkomeláta is **Kaligáta**, dominated by a beautiful blue and white campanile attached to its Baroque church. The village is home to the Calliga winery, which produces some of the island's excellent Rombola wines. **Ávythos beach**, a gentle two-kilometre walk south of Kaligáta, is in fact two large coves, with a solitary beach taverna and views out to Dhías island. It's the last sign of sand before the pebbles of Lourdhá bay to the east and offers good, safe swimming.

East of Metaxáta, the terrain alters from green woodland to flat farmland and, north towards Peratáta, the scrubby lower slopes of Mount Énos. Two kilometres on, **Keramiés** is a working country town, with a large square and fountain. It's an oddly quiescent place: the population still seems to get by with just one *kafenío*. On the coast at Lourdhá bay, **Spartiá** sits above a small harbour with a smattering of holiday bungalows and a taverna. **Pessádha**, further round the bay, is equally uninspiring: apart from a couple of tavernas, it's notable solely for its daily summer ferry connection with Zákynthos. Note that the two daily buses from Argostóli pointedly miss the two ferry crossings and leave you up in the village about a kilometre from the dock. There is a small canteen near the quay and a decent beach round the corner to while away time. *The View* (☎0671/69 991; ④) has adequate rooms – useful if you're planning to catch the morning ferry or arrive on the evening one.

Áyios Yióryios fortress

Áyios Yióryios fortress was closed for restoration in 1999 but usually opens Tues–Sat 8am–8pm, Sun 8am–2pm; 500dr.

Although an earthquake destroyed much of its interior detail in the seventeenth century, the Venetian fortress at **Áyios Yióryios** is one of the best-preserved structures of its kind in the archipelago. The *kástro* is reached by a steep one-kilometre walk up the lane signposted at the centre of the town of Peratáta, 7km from Argostóli and on the bus routes to both Skála and Póros. The remaining walls and battlements command spectacular views out over the entire Livátho region, Argostóli itself and Mount Énos to the east.

It's estimated that a defensive structure has existed on the rocky pinnacle since the fourth century AD, and the fortress was established as the island's capital by the Normans in the twelfth century. It was extensively expanded by the Orsinis in the thirteenth, and remained the centre of island life for several centuries, with a population of as many as 15,000, as a bulwark against repeated Ottoman attacks.

While much of the interior is ruined, the walls, towers and subterranean features such as dungeons remain. Most remarkable is a secret **tunnel**, some 9km long, leading from the *kástro* to a point on the road around the south of the Koutávos lagoon. Now disused, the tunnel was dug as an escape route in case the *kástro* were ever overrun. It was last used in 1943, when a group of Italian soldiers, besieged inside the *kástro* by German troops, were spirited out of it by sympathetic islanders.

Mount Énos

Mount Énos, the vast hogback mountain that dominates the south of the island, has been declared a national park, more to protect wildlife than to attract visitors. Facilities are nonexistent and walking to the summit, 15km from the Argostóli–Sámi road, isn't much of an option.

Minor routes lead up onto the mountain from the south, at Astoupádhes and Áyios Yióryios, and from the north at Dhigaléto, but the most direct approach is to take the signposted turning some 14km from Argostóli on the main Sámi road. From the turnoff, it's 3km to the hamlet of Áyios Elefthérios, and 12km further by rough road to the highest peak (1628m). It's worth detouring from the Sámi road, 4km before the Mount Énos turn, to the village of **Frangáta**, where you can visit the main Rombola factory for wine tasting (☎0671/86 301 for current opening times). A little further

> **Mountain safety**
>
> It's essential to take local advice on weather before setting out for Mount
> Énos, particularly out of season, when conditions can deteriorate very
> quickly. Take some warmer clothing and waterproofs, let someone know
> you're going and when you expect to be back, and allow plenty of time for
> the descent.

on, nestling in the lower folds of the mountain, is the renowned
monastery of **Áyios Yerásimos**, which is open to visitors and hosts
two of the island's most important festivals; on August 15 the saint's
death is commemorated, and on October 20 the removal of his relics.

As well as being one of the highest mountains in Greece, Énos is
also unusual for the amount of vegetation, notably the indigenous
Abies cephalonica firs. Despite vast fires and animal deforestation
over the centuries, the mountain remains one of the largest areas of
forest in the archipelago. A herd of a dozen or so wild horses forages
in the woodlands, but they tend to avoid humans. Falcons, eagles and
other raptors are commonly sighted. The views are the best in the
entire Ionian, reaching as far north as the mountains of Corfu, across
to the Peloponnese, and to nearby Zákynthos, Lefkádha and Itháki.

Southeast Kefalloniá

The main coast road to the east of Peratáta yields few places to stay,
although there are some pleasant dining and swimming spots to
which you could make a detour, while the vast **Kateliós bay** to the
west of Skála has the finest sandy beaches on Kefalloniá. The resort
of **Skála** is the best package destination at this end of the island, as
its neighbour **Póros**, with a narrow pebble beach and crumbling concrete seafront, has begun to look a little careworn recently.

Vlaháta and Lourdháta

The first stop of any note beyond Peratáta is the village of **VLAHÁTA**,
which is slowly blending with the micro-resort of Lourdháta on the
coast below, although a turning at tiny Mousáta, 2km before Vlaháta,
leads down to the excellent beach of **Trapezáki**, whose only development is a popular taverna. Vlaháta has some rooms such as *Maria
Studios* (☎0671/31 055; ③) or *Madison Studios* (☎0671/31 294;
③) and a good taverna, the *Dionysus*, but you would be better off
continuing to **LOURDHÁTA**, 2km south. This growing seaside hamlet has a fine shingle beach, a kilometre or so long, with a couple of
tavernas (try the *Blue Sea*), canteens and a few rooms. There are two
more established **tavernas** on the tiny plane-shaded village square –
the *New World* and the *Diamond*, which has a large range of vegetarian alternatives to standard fare – as well as the smarter *Spiros*
steak and grill house just above the village. *Adonis* (☎0671/31 206;

④) and *Ramona* (☎0671/31 032; ③) have **rooms** just outside the village, on the road down, while the one **hotel**, the *Lara* (☎0671/31 157, fax 31 156; ⑤), down by the beach, has comfortable en-suite rooms with sea views, a pool, a restaurant and bar. Most of its clientele are British package tourists, booked by the week or fortnight, but it also has rooms for independent travellers at most times in season. Beyond this, Lourdháta's facilities stretch only as far as a couple of shops, a bike rental place, *Yamaha* (☎0671/31 311), and the *Adonis* cocktail bar.

Sissiá and Markópoulo

Beyond Vlaháta, the road passes beneath the peak of Mount Énos, through primeval mountainscapes and boulder fields veined with flood drains to channel the sometimes apocalyptic winter storms. Four kilometres from Vlaháta, a lane leads 1km down towards the sea and the ruins of the thirteenth-century **monastery of Sissiá**, associated in myth with a visit by St Francis of Assisi, who is said to have been forced ashore here in a storm. The original building was abandoned centuries ago, and devastated in the 1953 earthquakes. A new and rather nondescript monastery was built after the quake.

Three kilometres on, the main road forks – left to Póros, right to Skála. The villages in this region are small and mostly resistant to tourism, although **MARKÓPOULO**, 5km along the Póros road, is noteworthy for two curious reasons. On the one hand, it is claimed by local wags to be the birthplace of the eponymous adventurer. More importantly, every August 15, for the festival of the Dormition of the Virgin Mary, its church of the **Panayía of Langouvárdha** is the site of a bizarre **snake-handling ritual**. The church stands on the site of the monastery of Our Lady of Langouvárdha, destroyed in the earthquake, which in turn had been first established as a nunnery. The story goes that when the nunnery was attacked by pirates, the nuns prayed to be transformed into snakes to avoid being taken prisoner. Their prayers were answered, and each year the "return" of a swarm of small, harmless black snakes is meant to bring the villagers good luck. As Mother Nature is unlikely to keep such a schedule, some discreet snake-breeding on the part of the village priests must be suspected.

Kateliós

Along the Skála fork of the coast road, the mountain landscape opens out into a wide valley around **KATELIÓS** and the neighbouring resort of **KÁTO KATELIÓS**, which are undergoing continual expansion. Manos Holidays already brings clients here, and a number of other enterprises are now capitalizing on the long sandy beaches. Of the new **hotels**, the smart, modern *Odyssia* (☎0671/81 615, fax 81

614; ⑤) and sprawling *Galini Resort* (☎0671/81 582; ⑤), complete
with pool and mini-golf course, are typical. There is also a small
development of self-contained **apartments**, available through the
stylish *Arbouro* **taverna** (☎0671/81 192; ③) and beachside *Faros*
taverna (☎0671/81 355; ③). The seafront now has half a dozen tavernas, bars and cafés in a row: of the restaurants, *Sirines* and *Ostria*
have the best selection and ambience, while the *Cozy* bar is the
choicest spot for a drink. The beaches looping around eastwards to
Kamínia, below the village of Ratzaklí, are loggerhead turtle nesting
grounds, so care should be taken to avoid nests and the usual guidelines followed (see box on p.245). Because of the turtle presence,
freelance camping isn't advisable; you would, in any case, face a
strenuous hike to Ratzaklí to find water, toilets or shops.

Skála

The popular resort of **SKÁLA** attracts a sizeable return clientele, who
keep it busy into October when other resorts (including its neighbour
Póros) have all but closed down. It can boast the finest beaches at this
end of the island, running away for several kilometres in either direction
and backed by a sweep of native Kefallonian pines, which give the place
an oddly un-Mediterranean feel, more akin to parts of the Scottish or
New England coastline. A small **Roman villa**, signed on a path above
the beach just by the *Golden Beach Palace* rooms, was excavated in
the 1950s to reveal a pair of well-preserved mosaics, one of a man being
attacked by wild cats, the other a scene around a sacrificial altar. The
mosaics are protected in a modern wood and glass structure, and a
modest entrance fee (300dr) is charged.

Rebuilt after the 1953 earthquake, the compact village spreads out
from a small square, with the main action on the short high street
that runs down to the beach. Much **accommodation** is prebooked
well in advance, and private rooms are scarce, although Dennis
Zapandis has studios and apartments at his *Dionysus Rooms*
(☎0671/83 283; ③), a block south of the high street, and rooms can
be found at the *Golden Beach Palace*, 100m south of the seafront
square (☎0671/83 327; ④). The more upmarket *Tara Beach Hotel*
(☎0671/83 250 or 83 341–3, fax 83 344; ⑥) can offer comfortable
en-suite rooms or individual bungalows in lush gardens on the edge
of the beach. If all else fails, try Skalina Tours (☎0671/83 175 or 83
275) or Etam Travel Service (☎0671/83 101, fax 83 142), two of a
number of agencies that offer accommodation and car/bike **rental** in
the village; Sunbird car rental has an office just off the main drag
(☎0671/23 723).

Skála falls behind neighbouring Póros in terms of seafood restaurants, but it does have a number of good eating options. Try the
Pines, which is split between the beach (serving snacks and salads)
and the road above the beach, where it becomes a fully fledged
restaurant veering between north European and local dishes; or the

adjacent *Flamingo*, which offers a mix of seafood, steaks and island dishes such as Kefallonian meat pie. The beach also has two conventional tavernas, the *Paspalis* and *Sunset*, both good for lunches. On the main drag, the *Siroco* has a wide selection of pastas and Greek fare, while the slightly upmarket *Noufara* offers a refreshing choice of soups and mushroom dishes in a leafy garden setting. *The Loft* is a hip late-night cocktail **bar** near the town square, and the beachside *Pikiona* pool and music bar stays open until the small hours.

Póros

With stamina and three or four hours to spare, it's possible to reach **PÓROS** on foot from Skála, along 13km of coastal road through fairly wild undeveloped countryside; 1km out of Skála, you'll pass the vestigial remains of a Roman temple. Only three buses a day (Mon–Sat) run between the resorts, so the journey is most easily covered by car or motorbike, over the final hump of Mount Énos, through the hill towns of Áyios Yióryios and **TZANÁTA**. The latter is worth a halt (at 4km – uphill – it's also walkable from Póros) to visit the large Mycenaean burial chamber unearthed outside the village. The chamber, a lined circular underground vault with entranceway, was only excavated in 1991, and is believed to be the last resting place of a local Bronze Age chieftain. Archeological investigations are continuing, as this is another site contending for the crown of Homer's "real" Ithaca. Beyond here, the road to Póros plunges down through a small but dramatic gorge which carries a river (usually dry) through the town.

Póros in fact comprises two bays: the larger, northerly one is the centre of tourist activities; the second, a five-minute walk over the small headland to the south, is the port proper, which has ferry connections with Zákynthos Town and Kyllíni on the mainland. After the three main towns, Póros is the largest development on the island, and there's certainly plenty to do and consume. Away from high and mid-season, however, when the bus services dwindle, Póros is geographically isolated, and anyone holidaying here without their own transport may feel they've picked the short straw.

These days, Póros looks distinctly frayed at the edges, with a scruffy concrete seafront in the first bay, which is where most package tourists will find themselves billeted, and a narrow, kilometre-long pebble beach stretching to the north. Paths off the road south to the port lead down to inviting blue-water swimming off rocks. Most of the action takes places in the main street running down to the seafront, and along the seafront itself.

Practicalities

Póros has plenty of **rooms**, **apartments** and a few **hotels**, although many of these places are block-booked by tour operators. The *Hotel Kefalos* (☎0674/72 139 or 73 140; ④) has good-value en-suite rooms on the seafront, while the elegant new *Odysseus Palace*, on the crossroads at the back of town (☎0674/72 036, fax 72 148; ⑥), has very stylish en-suite rooms with balconies, and has offered bargain discounts of sixty percent to British visitors in recent summers (August excluded). Nearby the *Santa Irena* (☎0674/72 017, fax 72 117; ③) throws in breakfast despite the cheap rate. Rooms and apartments tend to cluster around the bridge crossing the riverbed: best value is *Pension Elena* (☎0674/72 407; ②) or you could try *Blue Bay* apartments (☎0674/72 500, fax 72 550; ③), *George's Studios* (☎0674/72 508; ③) or the *Macedonia Studios* (☎0674/72 840–2). Among **travel agents**, *Poros Travel* by the ferry dock (☎0674/72 476 or 72 284) offers a range of accommodation, as well as services such as car rental and ferry bookings. Ford car rental has an office on the main drag (☎0674/72 675).

The main seafront has the majority of the **restaurants**, the best of which for setting and value is *Fotis Family*, tucked into the corner of the headland. At night, however, the old port is quieter and has more atmosphere, with tavernas such as *Tzivas* and the *Dionysus* that are strong on locally caught seafood. **Nightlife** centres around *J & A's*, overlooking the sea on the main bay, which also hosts the *Bad Boys Club*, whose clientele seem remarkably well behaved, and *Mythos*, an Internet café.

Sámi and around

The former capital, **SÁMI**, is where the majority of island-hoppers will arrive on Kefaloniá. It's the only surviving settlement of the island's four ancient city-states, although little remains from this time beyond fragments of foundations dotted about the hill above the modern town. The town itself is not particularly attractive, but has a pleasant seafront, a range of facilities and a long sandy beach that becomes more attractive the further it stretches towards Karavómilos. The fact that it has been largely abandoned by the British tour companies means it does not easily get overcrowded. There is a fine pebble beach 2km east at **Andísamis** and, more importantly, Sámi is the natural jumping-off point for the two major tourist attractions on the island, the **Drogharáti** cave system and the underground lake of **Melissáni**. Given the frequency of ferries between Sámi and Itháki, day-trips to the latter's capital, Vathý, are also easily manageable.

Sámi comprises a long, L-shaped seafront with a small harbour to the east and a compact grid of dormitory roads behind it. Most bars and restaurants are close to the crossroads – rather grandly dubbed Platía Kyproú – at the centre of the seafront. Hotels and rooms tend to be in the streets behind the seafront, and on the roads out of town: the main road to Argostóli, and the coast road north towards Ayía Efimía.

Daily **ferries** arrive in Sámi from Vathý and Pisaetós on Itháki, and Astakós on the mainland, and there are connections from Italy and Pátra (Strintzis Lines has an office on the waterfront). The *Ithaca Star* does full-day cruises daily except Sunday to Vathý, Kióni and a couple of quiet beaches for 5000dr. **Taxis** meet ferries and congregate on Platía Kyproú. There are daily **bus** services between Sámi and Argostóli, although the last leaves at 5.30pm. In season, there are also two buses a day (Mon–Sat) from Sámi to Fiskárdho via Ayía Efimía. Buses stop on the seafront not far from Platía Kyproú. For renting a car the handiest agency is Karavomilos Hire by the crossroads (☎0674/23 066), while two wheelers can be hired from Sami Center on the front (☎0674/22 254). In medical emergencies, there is a health centre (☎0674/22 222), also on the harbour.

Accommodation

Sámi has a good, though not particularly cheap, range of accommodation. Conveniently, the two *periptera* on the front handle basic **rooms** in town, and Sami Travel (☎0674/23 051, fax 23 052; ⑤) has more luxurious apartments. If you arrive in high season and find these full, head for the miniature suburb just north of the town centre, which has walk-up signs for rooms in private homes. It's also worth considering the small, if rather dull, suburb of Karavómilos, around the bay from Sámi itself, for rooms: try the purpose-built *Calypso Apartments* (☎0674/22 933; ④) attached to the pottery workshop.

Given the prices of rooms in Sámi, you might just as well opt for a **hotel**. The *Ionion* (☎0674/22 035 or 22 412; ③) has simple but modern en-suite rooms at the best rates, while the *Kyma* (☎0674/22 064; ④) on Platía Kyproú is very basic, old-fashioned and rather overpriced, but within spitting distance of the quay. For the same outlay you can stay in the far more comfortable *Melissani* (☎0674/22 464; ④), a small, friendly modern hotel signposted behind the main parade of quayside tavernas. The more upmarket *Kastro Hotel* (☎0674/22 656 or 22 282; ⑤) has small but plushly decorated air-conditioned rooms, as does the new *Theodora Studios* (☎0674/22 650, fax 23 109; ⑤), a little way past and behind it. Sámi's largest establishments are all out of town: the *Pericles* (☎0674/22 780–5, fax 22 787; ⑤), over a kilometre along the road to Argostóli, is popular with British tourists and has extensive grounds, with two pools and sports facilities, restaurant, bar and entertainment; while the *Sami Beach* (☎0674/22 802 or 22 824, fax 22 846; ⑥), with pool, bar, restaurant, and rooms overlooking the hotel gardens and the beach and the slightly smaller *Athina Beach* (☎0674/23 067 or 22 779, fax 23 040; ⑤) are both actually in Karavómilos

Sámi's one **campsite**, *Camping Karavomilos Beach* (☎0674/22 480, fax 22 932), is a short walk along the path behind the beach towards Karavómilos, with an exorbitant taverna, bar and shop. The site, however, is excellent, with over 300 pitches on flat, shady ground, and its gate leading directly on to the beach.

Grape-picking, Stavrós, Itháki

Exoyí, Itháki

Fríkes harbour, Itháki

Cove near Fríkes, Itháki

Selling fish from a boat, Zákynthos

Fókis Bay, Kefalloniá

View over Kefalloniá

Icon painter at work in the Monastery of Áyios Yerásimos, Kefalloniá

Shipwreck Bay, Zákynthos

Goats exploring pick-up truck, Itháki

Ayía Kyriakí, Kefalloniá

Eating and drinking

Sámi doesn't have a great many **tavernas** beyond those on the seafront. The most genuine and reasonably priced is *O Faros*, a classic *estiatório* with a good range of oven-cooked food, including Kefallonian meat pie. Most of the others on the main strip are adequate but somewhat touristic, like the *Delfínia*. The best taverna, however, on the quieter stretch of seafront out towards the campsite, is the partly British-run *To Karnayio*, which serves delicious grilled meat and fish as well as casserole dishes, washed down with fine barrelled Rombola wine.

The *Riviera* and *Aqua Marina* are among the favourite **bars** in the evenings, pumping out nondescript Euro faves. The former's *zaharoplastío* is great for after-dinner sweets or **breakfast**. The best place for a snack breakfast, however, is *Captain Jimmy's*, which is also recommended to anyone who has to feed a Häagen-Dasz habit.

Melissáni and Dhrogaráti caves

These two small but dramatic cave systems are both within walking distance of Sámi. At **Melissáni**, 3km away off the Ayía Efimía road, there's an underground lake, illuminated by sunlight falling through a large hole in the ceiling. **Dhrogaráti** is a conventional cave tunnel system, but with a large central cavern. If you're stuck for time and have to choose, Melissáni is the more spectacular of the two.

Melissáni

Melissáni cave is at least 30,000 years old, with stalactites that have been dated at around 20,000 years. Although it was only opened to tourists in the 1960s, it is known to have been used as a shrine to Pan in prehistoric times; artefacts from the shrine, including a risqué Pan figure, are displayed in Argostóli's archeological museum. From the entry in a small car park off the Sámi–Ayía Efimía road, stairs lead down to a short tunnel sloping to a small balcony overlooking the underground lake, which is filled with water from the sinkholes at Katovóthres on the other side of the island (see p.198). Water exits Melissáni into the so-called Karavómilos Lake, which is actually a salt-water duckpond at Karavómilos beach, 500m away. The roof of the cave collapsed during the 1953 earthquake, providing a light that turns the water brilliant turquoise. Boatmen take groups out into the middle of the lake, and through to an interior electrically-lit chamber, where the Pan shrine is believed to have been. They give a curt and hurried commentary in Greek and English, pointing out amusing features such as the "duck's head" stalactite and "diving dolphin" stalagmite. The lake is best seen around midday in high summer, with the sun overhead filling the cave with light, but it's just as impressive on a sunny October afternoon.

The Melissáni cave is open daily 8am–8.30pm; 1200dr. Carry a windcheater or lightweight waterproof – the cave can be chilly even on hot days.

*The
Dhrogaráti
caves are open
daily
8am–9pm;
1000dr.*

Dhrogaráti

The **Dhrogaráti** caves are a good 2km along the main road to Argostóli and then just under 1km along a signposted road to the right. You can enter on your own or guides take small groups through a series of illuminated cave sections, leading to the stunning, cathedral-like central chamber. As well as an impressive array of illuminated stalactites and stalagmites, the chamber has extraordinary acoustics, and is still occasionally used for musical performances. Past events include a concert by Maria Callas. Care should be taken not to slip on the floor, which is treacherous in some parts, and again you might need clothing to protect against the cool damp air, especially if you intend to hang out and drink in the subterranean atmosphere.

Ayía Efimía

Built around a small port, 9km northwest of Sámi, **AYÍA EFIMÍA** is an amiable little town in which to lie low, although its beaches are among the worst on the island. The main one – laughably called Paradise – is a pebble cove barely 20m in length; those who find Paradise too tiny to squeeze onto will, however, find quieter coves along the road to Sámi. One of these, Ayía Paraskeví, boasts an excellent eponymous taverna, which serves a marvellous mussel marinade on spaghetti. The town itself comprises an L-shaped quay around a tiny harbour, with a handful of backstreets and terraced alleys mounting the hillside above. Virtually all the action takes place on the quay, or just behind it.

In low season, Ayía Efimía isn't a place to get stuck in without wheels, although it makes a fairly convenient base if you do have your own transport. In summer, however, there are two **buses** a day to Sámi and to Fiskárdho, timed to enable you to spend the day in either. It is also a prime base for scuba-diving and is home to Aquatic World (☎0674/62 006), which can issue certification or take you on simple introductory dives.

Practicalities

The *Dendrinos Taverna*'s **rooms** (☎0674/61 392; ③), at the northern end of town, are the bargain stay in Ayía Efimía, although (as with all taverna rooms) they're prone to the heat and noise of the establishment. Both Dionysios Logaras (☎0674/61 202 or 61 349; ⑤) and Gerasimos Raftopolous (☎0674/61 233, fax 61 216; ③) have comfortable modern rooms and apartments available in the centre. Of Ayía Efimía's two small **hotels**, the seafront *Pilaros* (☎0674/61 800, fax 61 801; ⑥) is completely air-conditioned, with TV in all rooms, but *Moustakis* (☎0674/61 030; ③), a couple of blocks back from the quay, has a cosier feel.

The *Dendrinos* **taverna**, above Paradise beach, is the best place to go for authentic island cuisine and barrel wine; the long-established *Pergola Restaurant* in the centre also has a wide range of island specialities and standard Greek dishes. Its neighbour, the newer *Finikas* taverna, offers a costlier mix of fish, steaks and international cuisine, and the owners may be able to help with accommodation. Hipsters head straight for the *Music Café Irida* at night, died-in-the-wool philhellenes to the *Asteria Kafenio*, while those intent on more active headbanging flock to the *Paranoia Music Club*, 700m along the road north. The *Strawberry zaharoplastío* is the place for a decadent breakfast, and Gerolimatos Rentacar (☎0674/61 036, fax 61 516) can supply a getaway vehicle.

Northern Kefalloniá

Kefalloniá's northern tip is most easily reached along the main road north from Argostóli, which provides some jaw-dropping views (the link road from Ayía Efimía on the east coast to Dhivaráta sees fewer buses, though it's easily manageable if you're making a loop by car or motorbike). Heading out of the island capital, the road climbs above the Gulf of Argostóli into a series of small mountain villages. The first, **FÁRSA** (which has a *kafenío* and snack bar), was rebuilt after the earthquake; the ruins of the original village can be seen just above. A detour before Fársa can be made to **Dhavgáta** to visit the recently opened Museum of Natural History (daily 9am–1pm, Mon–Sat 6–8pm; 500dr), which chronicles the island's land and marine life and has educational displays on environmental issues. Between Fársa and Mýrtos beach there is little else of note apart from the hamlet of Agónas, which leads off to the village of Zóla and the long, sandy beach of **Ayía Kyriakí** below it. This fine strand now has a couple of canteens and draws a fair few sun-seekers in high summer, so further development is to be expected.

If heading north by bus from Argostóli, sit on the left to get the best sea views.

Mýrtos

From the near-sheer cliffs above it, **Mýrtos** appears as a dazzling crescent of white pebble next to a turquoise sea, and is one of the most photographed spots in the Ionian – though if you have to make the four-kilometre trip down from Dhivaráta on foot it loses a little of its sparkle. Buses only stop at Dhivaráta, although with your own transport you can drive all the way down to the beach. There's just one **restaurant** and a snack bar on the beach, which, along with a cave in the cliffs, provide the only shade for most of the day unless you hire one of the myriad umbrellas – for the beach is heaving with visitors in summer and not the place for a quiet swim. The west-facing beach is, however, a great place to catch the sunset, although given the bus times this is the preserve of the motorist or biker – or anyone prepared to stay in the **rooms** at the no-name taverna in Dhivaráta.

Mandolin wind

Kefalloniá is the setting for most of the action in Louis de Bernières' novel *Captain Corelli's Mandolin* (which for some inexplicable reason loses the word "Captain" in the American edition). The prose is stunning, the vocabulary rich with vivid similes, and the characters lovingly crafted and artfully brought to life. The story chronicles life immediately before and during the Italian and German occupation of the island during the World War II, and briefly skims over events in the lives of the surviving characters up to the present day. The detailed evocation of island life in the middle of the twentieth century, and the references to many places you are likely to visit, can certainly enhance your stay. The historical detail, which appears to be thoroughly researched, is shocking in places, and reminds us that we are not so far removed in time from such horrible events as we sometimes believe.

What will be interesting to see is whether the book itself starts to impact on the island's tourism in the way that *The Big Blue* has done in Amorgós, especially now that a big-budget film of the story is in the pipeline. Word during the writing of this edition was that the *Pericles* hotel near Sámi was already booked out for filming in spring 2000, and that Tom Cruise and Antonio Banderas were among the cast. If this scheme goes ahead and it turns out to be a blockbuster, apart from an increase in visitors blown in by the winds of fame, we may well expect a proliferation of restaurants and bars with names like *Corelli's* or *Pelagia*, no doubt with resident mandolin players.

Ássos

ÁSSOS should not be missed, even if you have to visit it on one of the coach trips that swing through nearly every afternoon. The most atmospheric village on the island, it clings to a tiny isthmus leading to a huge fortified rock, which protects the pocket-sized harbour and pebbly beach. Ruined walls of pre-quake mansions surround the plane-shaded village square, dubbed "Paris" by villagers in honour of the French, who financed its reconstruction after the 1953 earthquakes. A path, zigzagging up through woodland and terraces, leads into the ruins of the **Venetian fortress**, which itself contains the ruins of three small churches, including the Catholic church of Áyios Márkos. Until 1815, part of the fortress was Kefalloniá's version of Alcatraz, a virtually inescapable prison whose foundations are visible today.

Unfortunately, Ássos is also one of the most difficult places on the island to get to. Only one 2pm KTEL **bus** from Argostóli visits the village every week, and that is reduced to two or three days a week out of season. Otherwise, Fiskárdho buses stop at the Ássos turning if you ask, and the early afternoon bus from Argostóli sometimes detours down to the village if it has school students to drop off. Early (10am) buses out of Argostóli and the afternoon (4.30pm) bus back from Fiskárdho make it easy to spend a day in Ássos if you allow time and energy for the walks down and up (a good hour each way).

Getting there on your own wheels is decidedly less dicey than it used to be now that the road has been resurfaced and widened, but care is still in order on the sharper hairpin bends.

Practicalities

Staying in Ássos is not easy, as much of the **accommodation** is block-booked throughout the season. The best place to start is with Andreas Rokos (☎0674/51 523; ②), whose good-value rooms are on the right-hand side entering the village, with a telltale NTOG plaque outside (enquiries in the village are often directed towards him, anyway). Almost directly opposite, the *Kanakis Apartments* (☎ & fax 0674/51 631; ⑤) offer far more luxurious surroundings at a price. Further down towards the bridge the *Linardos Apartments* (☎0674/51 563; ⑤) are also pretty smart but rather less costly. Any of the harbour tavernas or shops may also be able to help with accommodation.

Ássos is cut off from the rest of Kefalloniá and charges accordingly. It has a number of good but pricey **restaurants**, including *Nefeli's Garden* on Platía Páris, and the *Platanos Grill*, whose wide menu includes oven food. The *Assos*, set a little way back from the front, also offers a good range of tasty fare at slightly less inflated prices. For a drink or light snack, you can't do a lot better than the anonymous blue and white café situated scenically at the end of the quay. There are a couple of shops for basics, and fruit and vegetables can be bought from a small truck that stops in the village most afternoons. It's likely that staying for any length of time here might begin to feel like living in a goldfish bowl, but Ássos lacks the development of somewhere like Fiskárdho, and in low season it can be truly idyllic.

Fiskárdho

Beyond Ássos, the road heads inland and the terrain begins to alter. The northern tip of the island around **FISKÁRDHO** sits on a bed of limestone which buffered it against the worst effects of the 1953 earthquakes, and the coastline here is reminiscent of the tree-lined pebble coves of Paxí. Fiskárdho is the island's premier resort, a small fishing port built around a horseshoe bay lined with handsome old houses – most of them restaurants, bars or boutiques – with *kaïkia* and yachts moored at the quay. Day or night, the scene is picture-postcard pretty, its only drawback the lack of a beach other than one poor patch of shingle. After Sámi, Fiskárdho is Kefallonia's busiest passenger port, with daily **ferry** connections to Itháki and Lefkádha (the ferry from Vassilikí also connects with Sámi to the south). If you arrive by boat, the village does not look as impressive from the sea as it does once you've disembarked and start to wander its characterful seafront and side-streets on foot.

Fiskárdho has an upmarket reputation, with prices to match, and its boutiques teeter on the edge of flat-out chi-chi. As one restaurateur proudly boasts, "we attract mainly middle- and upper-class English people", which could either hasten your step or send you screaming in the opposite direction. At night it's a very vibey place, even in low season, though it tends towards claustrophobia: village rivalries run very close to the surface, and some visitors love playing doll's house with the Greeks and with other tourists. Although the village remains small and development is fairly contained, it's also the busiest resort, and remains so up until the last days of October. Much of the prime accommodation was snapped up years ago by blue-chip travel companies such as Greek Islands Club and Simply Ionian, though everyone and her sister seems to have rooms to rent in Fiskárdho.

Accommodation

The best bargain for **private rooms** in Fiskárdho is *Regina's* (☎0674/41 125; ③), at the back of the village just below the car park: rooms are decent but basic, the owners friendly, and *Regina's* has the benefit of being some distance from the village's night-time revels. For slightly more, the central *Theodora's Cafe Bar* has six rooms in two whitewashed houses at the far end of the quay (☎0674/41 297 or 41 310; ④), and old-style *Erissos*, just behind the quay, has small clean rooms in a friendly atmosphere (☎0674/41 327; ④), while the *Koria* handicraft shop in the centre of the village has rooms on the seafront (☎0674/41 270; ④). Moving up the price range, *Fiskardhona* (☎0674/41 436; ⑤), opposite the post office, and *Philoxenia* (☎ & fax 0674/41 319; ⑤), next to Nikos's bike rental, offer rooms in renovated traditional island homes in the village. On the north side of the harbour, the large *Nicolas* taverna has good, modern rooms, also away from the front and with the best views of the village (☎0674/41 307; ⑥), which explains the fact that their prices have escalated in recent years.

Around the bay and towards Fókis beach, there are a number of **apartment** buildings, although some of these are for three, four or more people. *Stella Apartments* (☎0647/41 211, fax 41 262; ⑤) have kitchens and lounge/dining areas, and balconies with views of Lefkádha; *Kiki* (☎ & fax 0674/41 208, fax 41 278; ⑤) can offer studios and apartments overlooking a small beach.

Pama Travel (☎0674/41 033, fax 41 032), on the southern quay opposite the lighthouses, is the main **travel agency** in town, run by Dhimitris Patrikios and co-owned by the impeccably well-connected Tassos Matsoukis, an elder statesman of Fiskárdho's tourism industry and owner of the village's oldest tourist restaurant, *The Captain's Cabin*. *Pama* handles rooms in Fiskárdho, and also offers accommodation in the Matsoukis family village, Mazoukáta, a

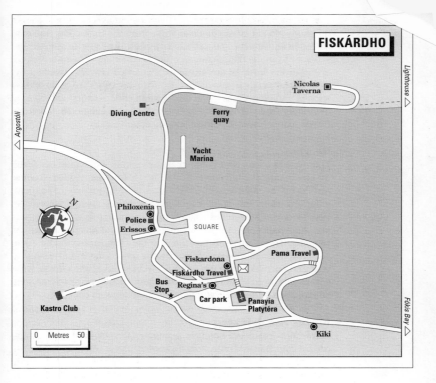

short walk or drive into the hills above town. Fiskardho Travel, just back from the quay (☎0674/41 315, fax 41 352), also has rooms in Fiskárdho, among a wide range of services, including yacht charter, car and boat rental, ferry tickets, tours and excursions. Typical of the day-trips on offer are those by large motor cruiser to Itháki, Lefkádha and satellite islands for 6000dr. For those wishing to do some scuba-diving, the Fiskardo Dive Club (☎0674/41 004) has offices back towards the main ferry dock.

The Town

The northern tip of Fiskárdho bay is guarded by the remains of a Venetian **lighthouse**, and above it on the headland are the crumbling ruins of what is believed to have been a Norman **church**. Arthur Foss, in his *The Ionian Islands*, speculates that the structure might be a relic of Norman invader Robert Guiscard's plans for a settlement here in the eleventh century. Guiscard, however, died of the plague a few weeks after arriving, and the settlement was probably abandoned, although the port derives its name from his. Below the church on the north shore of the bay, a Friends of the Ionian **nature trail**, reached through a low gate below the *Nicolas* taverna, runs through the shady woods, where you can bathe from the rocks. The trail can be followed with an FOI self-guide leaflet, available in the village shops or from the Simply Ionian office on the quay. The only church in Fiskárdho itself is the attractive Panayía Platytéra, reached by steps from various points on or behind the harbour. The plain white-washed building dates from the seventeenth century and was a monastery from 1676 to 1911. One of the icons inside, *The Birth of Christ*, dates from the monastery's inception.

Beaches

There are two excellent pebble **beaches** within a few minutes' walk on either side of the village. To the north **Émblisi**, signed down a turning off the main road into Fiskárdho, is slightly marred by a humming electricity sub-station at the back of the beach, where the island's power line comes ashore. It is a pleasant spot nonetheless, with flat white rocks for sunbathing and signs of discreet freelance camping. The eponymous taverna near the turning above provides a standard range of food and drink. On the other side, **Fókis** is set in a beautiful fjord-like cove ten minutes' walk south of the village, with a summer taverna above the beach and plenty of olive-tree and tamarisk shade on the pretty patch of land between the two.

Eating and drinking

Fiskárdho's **restaurant** culture seems to have achieved the ecological balance that has disastrously eluded places such as Lákka on Paxí: no two are alike and, while menus overlap, all are distinct from each other. The **seafront** is dominated by the *Tassia estiatório*, which has to have the widest choice of fish on Kefalloniá, ranging from lobster and red mullet to fish in Kefallonian garlic sauce, squid and fish soup. It's popular and busy at lunchtime and evenings, but not cheap – be sure to specify what weight of fish you want. *The Captain's Cabin* is the other major waterside eating house, with Greek and Kefallonian specialities such as *keftédhes* succulently done. This too can be terrifically busy, even in low season: it's a favourite with British tourists, and the place where flotilla folk knock back incendiary sambuca cocktails into the small hours. The only other quayside restaurant of note is *Nefeli*, which is not cheap but also has a wide range of food, including such dishes as curry.

Away from the front, the *Alexis* bar-restaurant strays off the conventional Greek menu with chicken and other meats in a variety of sauces, and has the best prices. Set in its own small square, it also has a cheap and quiet bar independent of the restaurant. The *Lagondería* specializes in grills but also cooks food in trays, and is fairly secluded at the back of the village. *Nicolas*, alone on the north side of the bay, is a noisy, barn-like taverna with a vast menu and a balcony blessed with a stunning night-time view of the village.

The best place to **drink** has to be the quayside *kafenío*, which produces magnificent *mezédhes* – miniature meals of fish, vegetables or meat – in the evening. Carousing tends to end late in Fiskárdho: most popular are the *Captain's Cabin* and the louche *Sirene* music bar, from where those with enough energy and co-ordination left to dance can head up to the *Kastro Club* disco, mercifully located out of ears' reach off the main road. Hidden at the back of the alley containing the post office, *Iy Folia tou Peirati* is a quiet and friendly bar away from the hubbub, though it's not cheap.

Around Fiskárdho

Kefallonia's slim northern tip offers some interesting diversions away from the focal point of Fiskárdho. There are some **walks**, outlined below, as well as the administrative capital of the north, **Vassilikiádhes**, which can provide useful accommodation overspill. The west coast of the peninsula also hides some coves, which are among the least visited beaches on the island.

Walks from Fiskárdho

Fiskárdho sits at the knot of three pleasant **walks** along the lanes circling the limestone northern peninsula, with excellent sea views on either side of the promontory. The easiest, heading beyond Fókis beach, cuts up into the hills overlooking Itháki to Mazoukáta (4km; taverna and *kafenío*), before rejoining the main Argostóli–Fiskárdho road at Mánganos 1km further on. The second follows the same route to begin with, before veering south after 2km at the partly ruined village of **Tselendáta**, where there are some fine old stone buildings and the smart and spacious *Loula* rooms (☎0674/51 808 or 51 857; ⑥) for groups of four or more; after another 2km you'll reach the dead-end hamlet of Evretí, which has views over the Daskalía island, claimed to be the place where Penelope's suitors set their ambush for the returning Odysseus. The third heads up the main road from Fiskárdho to Mánganos (5km), before veering off southwest to the villages of Agriliás (1km on) and Halikerí (2km on), above small coves on the west coast. You'll reach the main road again at **Konidharáta** (3km on), where if you time it right you can catch a bus back to Fiskárdho; otherwise it's around 8km (downhill) on foot. Konidharáta also has good-value alternative accommodation in the shape of the new *Donados Apartments* (☎0674/51 502; ③).

Vassilikiádhes

Surprisingly perhaps, the seat of local government for Érisos, the northermost municipality of Kefalloniá, is not Fiskárdho but the more mundane village of **VASSILIKIÁDHES**, some ten kilometres to the south. The tiny town hall and other facilities straddle the main road and are mostly unappealing modern constructions, although there are some fine old traditional stone buildings dotted around the old village on the hill to the west. What the place does have to offer is a real sense of life in a functional island community, with its mixture of old and new customs, as opposed to the rather forced quaintness and downright commercialism of Fiskárdho.

It is also a viable alternative to Fiskárdho for **accommodation**, when all the rooms there have reached capacity. Of the several options, the brand new *Nicolas Studios* (☎0674/51 231; ③) and *St Ferentinos Studios* (☎0674/51 281; ④) are both on the main road and recommended. For eating there are several choices: *Makis* grill does tasty meat with a few salad and veggie options, while *Iy Enosis* offers pizza and pasta dishes and *Café Ektos* serves snacks.

Less than a kilometre away, the small village of **Mesovoúnia** – the name means "amidst mountains" – certainly has a lazy mountain feel, and is a good place to drink in the soporific atmosphere from a seat at *Iy Synandisi* café-snack bar or the old *kafenío* opposite. The diminutive church of Ayía Paraskeví boasts a stylish pre-seismic campanile.

The west coast

The northern section of Kefalloniá's **west coast** does not offer grand sweeping views like those around Ássos and Mýrtos, largely because the road does not run along the edge of such a precipitous drop, but it does conceal some charming seaside nooks and crannies, which can provide welcome relief from midsummer crowds. The access point is a turning off the main road at the village of **Mánganos** down through hedgerow-lined fields and past Agriliás, beyond which there are two appealing options.

The first turning, by the tiny settlement of Halikerí, leads down a reasonable track to **Alatiés**, where a tiny beach is tucked in between folds of impressive white lavic rock. It has the advantage of being sheltered and safe for swimming even in quite rough weather, and you can pick your way across the rock, which turns to black on the seaward side, past drying salt-pools (hence the name), to the exhilarating point where the waves crash in, sending plumes of foam high into the air and misty spray into the faces of onlookers.

Alternatively, you can continue south from Halikerí and follow the road as it winds down to the larger bay of **Ayía Ierousalím**. Although less scenic, the beach here is wider, the sea shallower and you may have the place to yourself even in August, although it would seem to be only a matter of time before it becomes more popular. Currently, there are no phone connections, and the only development is the *Odysseus* taverna, which has rooms (③) and allows camping in its spacious grounds at a small fee for the use of facilities.

Travel details

BUSES

Argostóli to: Ayía Efimía (Mon–Sat 2 daily; 1hr); Áyios Yerásimos (3 daily, 1 on Sun; 30min); Ássos (Mon–Sat 1 daily; 1hr 15min); Athens (3 daily; 7hr); Fiskárdho (Mon–Sat 2 daily; 1hr 45min); Kateliós (Mon–Sat 2 daily; 50min); Kourkomeláta (Mon–Sat 3 daily; 30min); Lássi (9 daily; 10min); Pessádha (Mon–Sat 2 daily; 40min); Platýs Yialós (9 daily; 15min); Póros (4 daily, 2 on Sun; 1hr); Sámi (3 daily, 2 on Sun; 45min); Skála (2 daily, 1 on Sun; 1hr).

Lixoúri to: Athens (1 daily; 8hr); Xi beach (3 daily; 30min).

Póros to: Athens (1 daily; 6hr); Kateliós (Mon–Sat 3 daily; 30min); Skála (Mon–Sat 2 daily; 1hr).

Sámi to: Athens (1 daily; 6hr); Fiskárdho, via Ayía Efimía (Mon–Sat 2 daily; 1hr).

Note that all these services are for summer and may be reduced during other months.

FERRIES

Argostóli to: Kyllíni (2 daily; 1hr 45min); Lixoúri (every 30min, hourly in winter; 30min).

Fiskárdho to: Fríkes, Itháki (1 daily; 1hr); Nydhrí, Lefkádha (2 daily; 1hr 30min); Vassilikí, Lefkádha (2 daily; 1hr).

Pessádha to: Áyios Nikólaos, Zákynthos (2 daily; 1hr 30min).

Póros to: Kyllíni (3 daily; 1hr 15min).

Sámi to: Astakós (1 daily; 3hr 30min); Kérkyra (1 weekly; 4hr); Pátra (2 daily; 5hr); Pisaetós, Itháki (5 daily; 40min); Vassilikí, Lefkádha (1 daily; 3hr); Vathý, Itháki (2 daily; 1hr).

The summer services listed above may be reduced out of season. Connections to the mainland remain much the same, while those to other islands should retain at least one daily service.

FLIGHTS

Kefalloniá airport to: Athens (1–2 daily; 1hr).

Zákynthos

T hird largest of the Ionian islands after Kefalloniá and Corfu, **Zákynthos** has three distinct landscapes: the deserted, mountainous north and west coasts, the undulating central plain which with its green rolling hills and red-roofed hamlets resembles parts of Tuscany, and the extremely busy southern coasts which in parts could be Blackpool or Coney Island without the rides. Its tourism industry, based in a few resorts in the south, is one of the most developed in Greece and second in the Ionian only to Corfu's, yet large parts of the island are untouched by commerce. Indeed, while **Laganás** is the most commercialized resort in the entire archipelago, a few kilometres away there are ancient hill villages as pristine as any to be found on Paxí or Kefalloniá. The capital, **Zákynthos Town**, rebuilt after the disastrous 1953 earthquakes, has lost almost all of its Venetian architecture, but remains pleasant to visit or to stay in. The **Vassilikós peninsula** south of the town has some fine countryside and beaches, culminating in exquisite **Yérakas**, one of the best beaches in the entire Ionian. Virtually all the accommodation is confined to the busier centres, so those seeking a quiet retreat should consider the island's northern neighbours instead, although discreet pockets are appearing in the less visited northern half.

Accommodation price codes

Rooms and hotels listed in this book have been price-coded according to the scale outlined below. The rates quoted represent the cheapest available double room in high season. Out of season, rates can drop by as much as fifty percent or more, especially if you negotiate for a stay of three or more nights. Single rooms, where available, cost around seventy percent of the price of a double. For further information, see p.36.

① up to 6000dr	⑤ 16,000–20,000dr
② 6000–9000dr	⑥ 20,000–30,000dr
③ 9000–12,000dr	⑦ 30,000dr upwards
④ 12,000–16,000dr	

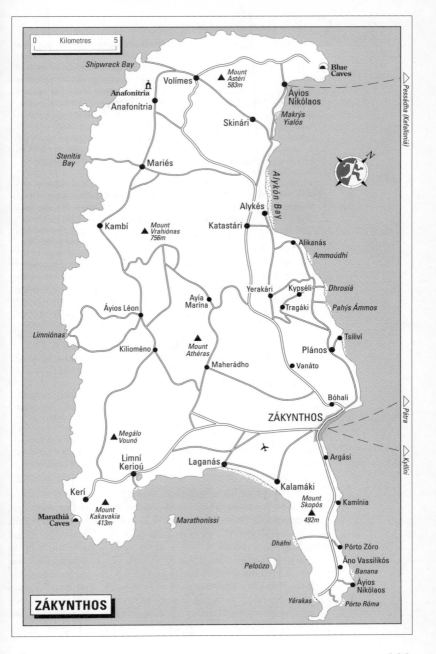

A taste of Olympic spirit

If your whole stay in Greece is on Zákynthos or a combination of Ionian islands and you are contemplating one visit to the mainland, then the most obvious and interesting choice from here is a trip to the site of **ancient Olympia** in the Peloponnese. Even the least classically minded person is aware that the Olympic Games were born in Greece, and their original home is up there with Delphi and Mycenae as some of the most moving and atmospheric remnants of the ancient heritage. For well over a millennium the **Panhellenic Games** were held at the sanctuary, and it is well known that a truce was called in all conflicts for their duration. Since the modern games were revived and first held in Athens in 1896, it has been the custom to rekindle the Olympic flame here every four years to be carried to each new venue in turn.

The setting of the site is remarkably beautiful: a luxuriant valley of wild olive and plane trees, spread beside the twin rivers of Alfiós (Alpheus) and Kládhios, and overlooked by the pine-covered hill of Krónos. The site itself (daily: May to mid-Oct 8am–7pm, 9pm in Aug & 8pm in Sept; mid-Oct to April 8am–5pm, Sat & Sun 8.30am–3pm; 1200dr) is a little jumbled and leaves a lot to the imagination. The games were originally held in the **Altis**, along whose walls you enter the site. On the right are the remains of the **Gymnasium** and **Palaestra** (wrestling school), where the competitors were obliged to train for a month before the contests. Other impressive structures are the **Theokoleion** (Priests' House), a colonnaded building whose southeast corner was later converted into a Byzantine church, and the **Leonidaion**, a large hostel for important festival guests, but the most important edifices were the two principal temples: the great Doric **Temple of Zeus**, built between 470 and 456 BC, was almost as large as the Parthenon, while the earlier **Temple of Hera** behind it is the most complete building on the site, with thirty odd columns surviving to some extent, along with parts of its inner wall. The remains and foundations of numerous lesser structures are dotted around.

Pride of place for most visitors, however, goes to the huge **stadium**, where the competitions were held as the games expanded. You enter through a long arched tunnel at the back of the site to the confines of the 200m track, surrounded by seating ridges, now grassed over, where the 20,000 spectators used to sit. The starting and finishing lines and judges' thrones are still there. Many awed visitors can't resist doing a lap or at least a length in the hope of being rewarded with a makeshift laurel leaf by

Like the rest of the archipelago, Zákynthos owes much of its history to the Venetians, who after their invasion in the fourteenth century planted the olive trees that are such a conspicuous feature of the island's landscape. The main agricultural produce, however, has traditionally been **raisins**, to which, at the peak of the industry in the eighteenth century, two-thirds of the island's cultivated land was devoted, creating fortunes for its aristocracy. The central plains are still blanketed in a stunning canopy of vineyards, stretching for miles in all directions, contrasting sharply with the abysmal concrete suburbs of workshops and factories you have to pass on the way to them. The Venetians called the island **Zante**, dubbing it *fior di Levante*, their travelling companions. Behind the southern slope is the site of the **Hippodrome**, where the chariot races were held.

The **Archeological Museum**, some 200m to the north of the site across the road, is also not to be missed – opening hours are roughly the same except it is closed on Monday mornings; entry 1200dr. It contains some of the finest Classical sculpture in existence, both Greek and Roman, all superbly displayed. The two most famous pieces are the **head of Hera** and the **Hermes of Praxiteles**, both dating from the fourth century BC and found in the Temple of Hera. There are many other fine sculptures and objects in bronze and terracotta, as well as finds from the workshop of **Pheidias**. The centrepiece, however, occupying the grand central hall, is a brilliantly reassembled set of statuary and sculpture from the Temple of Zeus. This includes a frieze of the **Twelve Labours of Hercules**, the east pediment of Zeus presiding over a **chariot race** and the **Battle of Lapiths and Centaurs** from the west pediment. Other rooms display objects connected with the games. For more detailed descriptions of the site and museum, see the *Rough Guide to Greece*.

The modern village of **Olymbía** has grown up to service the excavations and has no real character. It does, however, have an abundance of accommodation to put up transient visitors, and competition keeps prices low. The *Hercules* (☎0624/22 696; ②), by the church and school off the main street, and *Praxiteles* (☎0624/22 592; ③) are typical of the small, functional hotels available. Food is equally easy to come by, as most hotels have a restaurant and there is a plethora of independent tavernas, all bashing out the usual Greek staples. Coming from Zákynthos by public transport is a little convoluted, so an overnight stay is really required. Olymbía is well connected to the town of **Pýrgos** – there are five trains a day and hourly buses, both taking around 40mins – but to get there you will first have to catch the ferry to Kyllíni and then take a bus up to the national road to connect with another one coming down to Pýrgos. You could make the trip in a hired car, of course, but the ferry crossing is not especially cheap and you should first check that the vehicle is allowed off the island. Not surprisingly, most people go for the easy option of an organized day-trip. **Tours** run at least twice a week in summer and can be booked at agencies all over the island for around 8500dr per head. Check what is included in the way of site/museum entry, guides or lunch. These bus tours usually leave on the first ferry and return on the last, making quite a tiring day of it, but at least you get a reasonable amount of time amid the ancient glories.

"flower of the Levant", because of the luxurious vegetation, and even today islanders slip between either name. The island has in effect two springs: early in the year, and again between October and November, when autumn rains revive cyclamen, irises, lilies and wild orchids. Some local **wines**, such as the white Popolaro, Calliniga or Solomos, compare with the best in the archipelago, and Zákynthos produces its own brand of the sticky, white *mandoláto* nougat, commonly sweetened with sugar but also available in its superior honey-sweetened variant. The best local **cheese** is the pungent *grapéria*, which may be a little too strong for milder northern palates, and *ladhotýri* is another favourite.

Two things have shaped modern-day Zákynthos: an **earthquake** and an airport. This area of the Ionian Sea is a site of fairly constant seismic activity (see box on p.197), most of it minor and largely indiscernible. However, on August 9, 1953, an earthquake comparable to that of 1992 in San Francisco hit the region at midday. Two hundred died on Zákynthos, thousands were seriously injured, and in some rural areas whole communities were wiped out. The force was such that an estimated seventy percent of buildings on the island were destroyed. Zákynthos Town, which had won the nickname of "Venice of the South" for its elegant architecture, was further damaged by fires that spread from wood- and gas-burning stoves and raged for ten days; contemporary photographs in the Zákynthos Museum show the town's streets heaped up like waves.

After the earthquake, Zákynthos had to rebuild itself from the ground up, and this has had a curious effect on the island's **maps**. Many villages had to be abandoned and rebuilt away from the quake ruins, so few places now stand where they were originally built (Zákynthos Town is the obvious exception). Village names are now officially held to refer to "areas" rather than specific places, but the disorientation is only increased by haphazard road signs. Anyone planning trips on the island should bear this in mind, as some maps imply a settlement where the visitor will find only desert or forest.

The earthquake also left Zákynthos clear to rebuild itself for the tourism boom, which in the last decade has taken hold of parts of the island with a vengeance. Thanks to the presence of the busiest international **airport** in the Ionian islands outside Corfu, over 360,000 Britons alone visited Zákynthos in 1995 – compared to an indigenous population of roughly 30,000. This has given rise to certain unspoken cultural tensions, but many islanders seem to be profiting from the building explosion that is threatening to engulf the southeast and much of the central plain as well. Despite the seasonal invasion – a fair number of Dutch, German and Scandinavian visitors add to the British crowds – much of Zákynthos remains relatively unspoilt. The party resort of Laganás and its more refined neighbour, **Kalamáki**, as well as eastern resorts such as **Tsiliví**, are all fairly self-contained. The local bus system is poorly developed outside the main resorts and – combined with some of the most hair-raising driving in Greece – doesn't encourage mobility among visitors (indeed, walking anywhere on the roads of southern Zákynthos might count as an extreme sport). Some of the beaches aren't served by public transport at all and don't even have a taverna or a beach bar, but **Áyios Nikólaos** on the Vassilikós peninsula has cleverly launched its own free bus service, luring tourists away from other resorts.

Some history

Zákynthos was first settled by Achaeans from what is now the northern Peloponnese in the Mesolithic era (12,000–3000 BC), and earned a brief mention in the *Odyssey*: Homer refers to "woody Zákynthos" and includes twenty young men from the island among the small army of doomed suitors who proposed marriage to Penelope. Zantiots fought alongside the Athenians in the Peloponnesian War (431–404 BC), but the island was subsequently overrun by the victorious Spartans, who were themselves supplanted by successive waves of invading Macedonians and Romans. The Byzantine empire, heir to Rome's eastern provinces, retained its hold on the region until the twelfth century. In 1185, Zákynthos and neighbouring Kefalloniá broke away to form a semi-independent palatinate, ruled by a succession of regional aristocrats sanctioned by Rome. In a complex game of regional politics, the islands frequently changed hands between Rome, Venice, Naples and Ioánnina, capital of the northern mainland region of Epirus. After years of skirmishes, the Turks took the region in 1479, but were expelled by the Venetians in 1485. One local history describes the Turkish onslaught on Zákynthos as a "holocaust". Few islanders survived, and the Venetians began a campaign of settlement.

Under Venetian rule, Zákynthos expanded beyond the port to establish settlements elsewhere on the island. The Venetians imported their own stratified social system, with the names of the nobility inscribed in the *Libro d'Oro* (Golden Book), which became the social register of Zákynthos society and a despised symbol of privilege and power. This caste system created great wealth for Zákynthos's dynasties, but was clearly hated by the impoverished majority, who staged an uprising in 1628 that was bloodily put down by the Venetians. When they were finally unseated by the French in 1797, the *Libro d'Oro* was burnt by jubilant crowds in Platía Ayíou Márkou. The French were ousted by a Russian–Turkish alliance in 1798, and in 1800 the Russians and Turks signed a treaty to establish the Eptánissos (Seven Islands) state of the Ionian islands. The new constitution still favoured the island's elite, however, and the Zakynthians once again rebelled, unsuccessfully, raising the Union Jack on the Venetian fort as an appeal to the expansionist trading partner from the north. In 1807, the island was briefly handed to the French again, but in 1809 the British took Zákynthos. The island remained a British protectorate until the archipelago was ceded to Greece in 1864. Zákynthos was overrun by the Italians and then by the Germans in World War II, although it didn't suffer as badly as neighbouring Kefalloniá.

Arrival

Most visitors arrive at the island **airport**, equidistant from Laganás and Kalamáki in Kólpos Laganá (Laganás Bay) on the southern coast. It has recently been enlarged and improved, so waiting is more comfortable, although there is still a shortage of seating and no facilities beyond a snack bar, gift shop and several car rental outlets. There's no dedicated bus service from here, although the

Laganás–Zákynthos Town bus does pass the bottom of the road leading away from the airport at least once an hour. Taxis into Zákynthos Town or to Laganás cost around 2000dr; it is possible to haggle, but the drivers know you're stuck without them. It's just about feasible to walk to either Zákynthos Town, 5km or so to the north, or Laganás, 4km south, but most independent travellers tend to give in to the taxi drivers.

Ferries from the mainland port of Kyllíni (the main year-round point of access) arrive at **Zákynthos Town**. Oddly, there is no regular ferry connection between Zákynthos Town itself and the rest of the Ionian islands to the north, except via Kyllíni/Pátra. A twice-daily ferry sails between Pessádha on Kefalloniá and the port of **Áyios Nikólaos** in the north of Zákynthos (not to be confused with the beach complex of the same name in the south) in the summer, and is met by a KTEL bus to Zákynthos Town.

Local transport

The island's skeletal **bus** system radiates out from Zákynthos Town to serve the larger resorts and some outlying villages, but little else. The KTEL bus station is on Odhós Filíta, one block back from the seafront, and buses usually run on time, though the timetable is subject to change without notice. A printed timetable is available for peak season and is reliable. It includes information on KTEL's 2000dr island tour, which compares favourably with more expensive private equivalents.

There are **taxi stands** in Zákynthos Town and some of the larger resorts; taxis also cruise the smaller resorts when they're in the area (but tend to disappear during the siesta). You could try phoning for a taxi (see p.237) from a bar or hotel, but this is more expensive than flagging one down; drivers often charge for the journey to pick you up.

Zákynthos Town and around

ZÁKYNTHOS TOWN is a small, busy working port that has made few concessions to tourism. However, it is the only sensible place to base yourself if you want to explore the island by public transport, and is certainly more authentic than the resorts. Its principal squares are grand enough, and its backstreets quite interesting to meander in. There are sufficient hotels, a few private rooms, bars and restaurants for visitors who do choose to stay, as well as a number of museums and historic buildings – notably the **Kástro** that towers above the town. The seafront restaurants and bars give onto a busy main road, and are prone to its noise and fumes. A further drawback to this part of Zákynthos Town is its one-way system, which has the novel effect of speeding up the already crazy traffic. After school and in the evenings bored teens race each other on bikes and mopeds around the town centre until late, giving even the

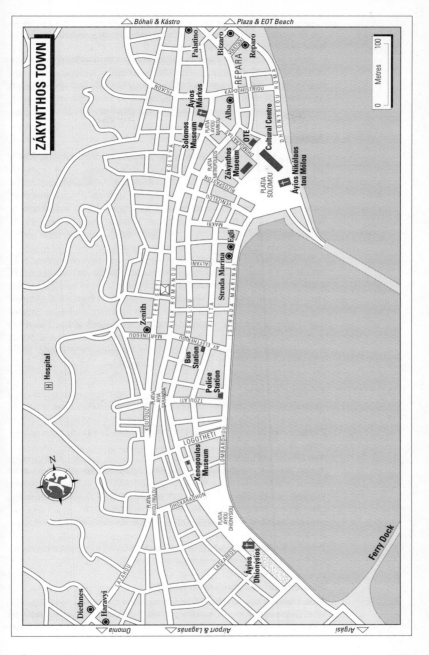

ZÁKYNTHOS TOWN

△ Bóhali & Kástro   △ Plaza & EOT Beach

- Palatíno
- Bítzaro
- Réparo
- Áyios Márkos
- Solomos Museum
- Alba
- Cultural Centre
- OTE
- Zákynthos Museum
- Áyios Nikólaos tou Mólou
- Egli
- Strada Marina
- Zenith
- Hospital
- Bus Station
- Police Station
- Xenopoulos Museum
- Áyios Dhionýsios
- Ferry Dock
- Diethnes
- Harayvi

△ Omonia   △ Airport & Laganás   △ Argási

smartest of restaurants the ambience of a racetrack. The best advice
for those seeking reasonable accommodation or a decent meal is to
head north beyond Platía Solomoú.

There is no tourist office in Zákynthos Town or indeed elsewhere
on the island. The **tourist police** (housed within the main police station on the seafront) are said to have tourism info but usually feign
ignorance. Hotels and travel businesses can help with information,
and some have free maps to supplement those on sale in the shops.

Accommodation

There is a limited range of hotels and rooms on the seafront, which
are convenient if you arrive late but hardly cheap, apart from the
Egli. Bargain-hunters are advised to seek out the small hotels at the
back of town, listed below and marked on our map. Anyone planning
to stay more than a day or so and willing to pay a little more is
advised to head for the district of Repára, just beyond Platía
Solomoú. This end of town is relatively quiet, because little traffic
has business in the suburb of Akrotíri beyond it.

Perhaps due to the earthquake and the subsequent explosion in
building, **rooms** in Zákynthos Town and outside are almost never
named. It's easy to spend half a day trekking around looking for the
elusive *"Enikiázontai Domátia"* (Rooms to Let) sign, so it's probably best to take up an offer from the room owners who meet incoming ferries in summer. Otherwise, there are rooms at the *Ypsarias
psistariá* (☎0695/42 884; ③), on Odhós Krionéri beyond Platía
Solomoú, and right on tiny Platía Ayíon Saránda (☎0695/45 194),
five minutes' walk back from the police station.

Budget hotels

Apollo, Tertséti 30 (☎0695/42 838 or 45 496). Basic modern hotel, with bathrooms and fans in all rooms. ③.

Diethnes, Ayíou Lazárou (☎0695/22 286). Double rooms only, with en-suite
baths. ③.

Egli, cnr Loútzi & Lombárdhou (☎0695/28 317). Tucked in at the side of the plush
Strada Marina, a traditional Greek family hotel offering the same views as its
smarter neighbour. All rooms with en-suite bathrooms, balconies and sea view. ③.

Haravyi, Xanthopoúlou 4 (☎0695/23 629 or 42 778). Quaint little pension
opposite the *Omonia* with small, comfy, en-suite rooms. ③.

Omonia, Xanthopoúlou 3 (☎0695/22 113). Simple, old-fashioned hotel, given
a makeover a few years ago. ③.

Pension Zenith, Martinégou 2 & Tertséti (☎0695/22 134). Small apartment
hotel with en-suite rooms; simple but adequate. ③.

Moderate to expensive hotels

Alba, Lámbrou Zíva 38 (☎0695/26 641 fax 26 642). The best mid-range deal.
Breakfast included in this small new hotel with smartly decorated and cosy
rooms. ④.

Bitzaro, Dionyssíou Róma 46 (☎0695/23 644 fax 23 493). Fairly ritzy C-class hotel in Repára area, with en-suite bathrooms, balconies and a roof terrace. ⑥.

Palatino, Kolokotróni 10 & Kolyva (☎0695/27 780 fax 45 400). Upmarket and tucked away from the seafront in the Repára area. Price includes breakfast, TV, air-conditioning. Open year-round with snazzy bar. ⑥.

Plaza, Kolokotróni 2 (☎0695/48 909, fax 45 733). Small hotel in the Repára area with en-suite bathrooms and balconies, some with sea views. ④.

Reparo, Dionyssíou Róma & Voúltsou (☎0695/23 578 fax 45 617). A friendly and modern purpose-built hotel, which has undergone an upgrade in quality and price. All rooms are en suite, with balconies and some sea views. Bar/breakfast room. ⑥.

Strada Marina, Lombárdhou, at the Platía Solomoú end (☎0695/42 761–3, fax 28 733). The largest in town, dominating the seafront: air-conditioning and TV in the rooms, 24-hour restaurant, bar, coffee shop and a rooftop pool and restaurant. Wheelchair access. ⑤.

The Town

The obvious first port of call in Zákynthos Town is **Platía Solomoú**, which was named after the island's most famous son, **Dhionysios Solomos** (1798–1857). Considered Greece's foremost poet of the modern period, Solomos wrote the *Ýmnos is tin Eleftherían* (Hymn to Liberty) which became the Greek national anthem, and was responsible for establishing demotic Greek as a literary idiom. Around the *platía* are: the cultural centre, built on the site of the destroyed opera house designed by Ziller, which doubles as a cinema; the **Library** (Mon–Wed noon–7.30pm, Thurs–Sat 7am–2.30pm), which features an interesting display of photographs of old Zákynthos; and the huge Zakynthos Museum (see below).

Museums

Zákynthos Town's two oldest museums are close to each other in Platía Solomoú and nearby Platía Ayíou Márkou. The gargantuan **Zákynthos Museum**, often referred to as the Byzantine Museum, concentrates mostly on works from that period and has a splendid collection of art rescued from churches destroyed in the seismic calamity of 1953. On display here are examples of the **Ionian School** of painting (see box p.77), though not as good as those in the churches of Lefkádha Town. Chiefly influenced by painters of the Renaissance, the school flourished on Zákynthos in the seventeenth and eighteenth centuries, and was noted for a distinctly realist approach to its religious subject matter. Saints and other figures are represented in workaday settings and in distinctly earthbound form, far removed from the sunbursts and wings beloved of earlier religious imagery. There are also works by earlier and later religious and secular artists. Apart from icons and framed paintings, there are some fantastic iconostases (altar

The Zákynthos Museum is open Tues–Sun 8am–2.30pm; 800dr.

*The Solomós
Museum is
open daily
9am–2pm;
800dr.*

*The
Xenopoulos
Museum is
open Wed–Sun
9am–1pm;
free.*

*The Maritime
Museum is
open daily
9am–2pm and
6–9pm; 800dr.*

screens) on the ground floor, while the first floor also contains
fragments of carved marble slabs from medieval churches and a
complete re-creation of the interior fresco designs from Áyios
Andhréas in Volímes. Perhaps the two most moving exhibits, however, back on the ground floor, are the intricate model of
Zákynthos Town before the catastrophic earthquake and the
accompanying giant photograph of the aftermath.

The **Solomós Museum** on Platía Ayíou Márkou is also dedicated
to other prominent Zakynthians and has recently been extended to
display more exhibits. One upstairs room is devoted solely to
Solomos and contains some of the poet's effects and manuscripts
– the collection is split between Zákynthos and Corfu, where he
spent most of his working life – and by the museum entrance there
is what is said to be part of the tree under which he sat and com-
posed the *Hymn to Liberty*. His bones rest in a casket on the
ground floor alongside those of the island's second most famous
poet, Andhreas Kalvos, and his wife. A long hall on the upper floor
contains numerous portraits of noted Zakynthians, among them
Kalvos and another acclaimed poet, Ugo Foscolo. Other noteworthy displays include an array of heraldic shields and paintings
of drama costumes.

The third museum in the centre of town is the newly created
and municipally run **Xenopoulos Museum**, tucked in tiny Odhós
Gaïta, not far from Áyios Dhionýsios church. Dedicated to the
novelist and playwright Grigoris Xenopoulos, whose works span
the first half of the twentieth century, it is in the form of a family
house, renovated and opened by the mayor in November 1998.
Exhibits include the author's personal effects, manuscripts, documents, rare editions of his books and periodicals to which he
contributed, photographs and furniture. There are also articles
belonging to his daughter, Efthalia and her sculptor husband,
Khristoforos Natsios.

The other museum worth a visit, especially for old salts, is the
Maritime Museum, some way out of town on the road up to the
Kástro. It contains a fairly comprehensive maritime history of
Greece, split into the following sections: ancient Greece;
Byzantium; the Greek revolution of 1821; the nineteenth century,
sails to steam; and the twentieth century. You are confronted by a
bewildering hotch-potch of model vessels (from triremes to hydrofoils), shields, flags, knots, medals, costumes, books, paintings,
armoury and equipment with some of the labelling in Greek only,
but there is enough to hold the attention of the most committed
landlubber for a while. Perhaps the most interesting exhibit is
equipment from the Greek naval ship *Leon*, formerly the USS
Eldridge, which reputedly took part in the infamous time-warping
Philadelphia Experiment of 1944. The ship itself is currently in the
hands of a Pireás scrap-metal company.

The Ionian School of Poetry

The Ionian School of poetry is less of a coherent school than that of painting (see box on p.77), in the sense that it had no distinctly unified style or philosophy. Rather it is a tradition of Heptanesian bards, whose writings are intrinsically linked with the blossoming of Greek thought that accompanied independence.

First and foremost is **Dhionysios Solomos**, the Dante of Zante; born in Zákynthos in 1798 and regarded as the father of modern Greek literature, he lived the last thirty years of his life in Corfu. A firm belief in the freedom of man's spirit underpins all his writings, and his *Hymn to Liberty* was adopted as the words to the Greek national anthem. He was also a great champion of the demotic language, and established it as a literary medium. His fellow Zantiot, **Andhreas Kalvos** (1792–1869), also leant heavily on the independence struggle for inspiration, but his twenty *Odes* are written in the purist literary Greek known as *katharévoussa*.

Probably the second most important nineteenth-century Ionian poet was **Aristotelis Valaoritis** (1824–79) from Lefkádha, who was also an active parliamentarian. Many of his patriotic poems are modelled on demotic klephtic songs. Lesser lights in the line were **Yerasimos Markoras** (1826–1911) from Kefalloniá, and two Ithacans, learned classicist **Lorenzo Mavilis** (1860–1912) and, more recently, leftist freedom fighter **Nikolaos Karvounis** (1880–1946). Finally, one of Greece's most highly rated poets of the twentieth century is **Angelos Sikelianos** (1884–1951) from Lefkádha. His lyrical work is firmly grounded in the demotic tradition of the previous century, but contains more contemporary philosophical preoccupations. His mammoth *Prologue to Life* adds a mystical touch to the synthesis of folkloric, naturalistic and religious themes, while his later works display a passionate belief in the beauty and harmony of the world, expressed in clear, incisive language.

Churches

Few of the town's churches survived the 1953 earthquake. **Áyios Nikólaos tou Mólou** (St Nicholas of the Quay), a former fishermen's chapel at the edge of Platía Solomoú, is the only one to have been renovated after the quake using its original stones (though the interior was restructured using modern materials). Inside are the vestments of the island's saint, Dhionýsios, patron saint of fishermen, who preached here in the sixteenth century.

More spectacular is the church of **Áyios Dhionýsios** itself, at the other end of the seafront to Platía Solomoú, lit at night like a fairground ride. Built of concrete in 1948, with a bell-tower modelled on St Mark's in Venice, it survived the earthquake more or less intact. The church contains some remarkable icons of the saint's life, as well as a magnificent sculpted silver coffin containing his relics. Recent years have seen the completion of excellent, colourful frescoes around the interior – the one depicting Creation on the back wall to the right of the entrance is particularly vivid. The marble mosaic floors are also magnificent. Interestingly, the church is formally consecrated as a monastery, so weddings, baptisms and funerals are not permitted to be held here.

Áyios Márkos, on the square of the same name, near the Solomós
Museum, is the only Catholic church on the island. It is relatively
unelaborate, both inside and out, but exudes a certain air of dignity.
A large and striking painting of St Mark receiving the gospel hangs
above the white marble altar. Among the other pictures is a dark,
ominous one of a very male-looking Ayía Paraskeví. Otherwise, there
is very little interior decoration.

The Kástro

*The Kástro is
open daily
8am–7.30pm
(2pm in
winter);
500dr.*

Zákynthos Town's only major historic site is the **Kástro**, a huge,
ruined Venetian fortress to the north of town, sited on a bluff which
was a defensive enclave from the Byzantine era onwards. Little of
the original structure remains beyond a few minor outbuildings
(mostly from the seventeenth century), some foundations and ruins
of the massive walls, but it is a remarkable piece of stone engineering, with stunning views in almost every direction. The keep,
long since overgrown by firs, now has the air of a small walled forest. It's an ideal spot for a picnic on the scented green carpet of
fallen needles or a quiet afternoon in the shade. Less than an hour's
walk from the centre of town, on the edge of the small hamlet of
Bóhali, it makes for a pleasant excursion. There are no public facilities, however, beyond the few tavernas in Bóhali, and at times the
Kástro is inundated with coach parties. If you make it up here, it is
also worth visiting the old church of Zoödhóhou Piyís, just down
the hill in Bóhali, for its vibrant frescoes and icons.

Eating and drinking

Zákynthos Town is the best place for **eating** on the island, although that isn't saying much. Travellers on a budget can snack in the cheap *psistariés, estiatória* and takeaways on and around Alex. Románou and Konstandínou. The seafront tavernas offer reasonable fare, but the smartest restaurants are in elegant Platía Ayíou Márkou, along with a couple of seriously hip and ferociously expensive music bars. The best food, however, is to be found at the trio of tavernas along the shadowy sea road beyond Platía Solomoú.

Alivizos, Dhionyssíou Róma. The first taverna along the sea road to Akrotíri offers a wide range of sophisticated staples and is very popular with Zantiots. Open later in season and, unusually, during the siesta. Live music most evenings.

Arekia, Dhionyssíou Róma. If you eat only one meal in Zákynthos Town, eat it here. This small, family-run taverna performs miracles with traditional dishes: succulent meat and fish, mouthwatering meatballs and small *tyropittákia* to die for. Jealously guarded by Zantiots, who throng for its nightly free *kandádhes* and *arékia* sessions (10pm). Open evenings only; go early at weekends.

Fioro di Levante, Platía Solomoú. Priced on a par with the smart Ayíou Márkou restaurants, but an unmissable setting for a snack or dessert.

Green Boat, Dhionyssíou Róma. Past the first two places in this list, this fish taverna offers excellent-value *pikilíes* and seating right beside the water.

Kastro, Bóhali (☎0695/23 401). A lengthy menu of island and typical Greek dishes, authentic *kandádhes* and views over the town. Worth booking ahead but not cheap.

Molos, Lombárdhou. One of the most reasonable seafront tavernas offering full meals and snacks, but the pavement seating can become busy.

Panorama, Bóhali (☎0695/28 862). Upmarket neighbour to *Kastro*, with a more sophisticated menu (and prices), but with stunning views over Zákynthos Town. Booking advisable.

Porto. At the end of the quay nearest to Platía Solomoú, this smart restaurant and bar in a two-storeyed wooden building has a wide selection of Greek and international cuisine. Expensive but popular for its fine harbour view.

Psaropoula, Lombárdhou. Next to the police station, this is probably the best of the main seafront eating houses. Excellent meat and fish, including good value *pikilíes*, a range of veggie dishes and fine barrelled wine.

Nightlife

The hub of nightlife in Zákynthos is Platía Ayíou Márkou – the most expensive place to eat or drink in town, with prices matching London's West End. A favourite with local and visiting youth is *The Base*, at the corner of the square, a bar which usually has a DJ playing anything from dance imports to Miles Davis or Philip Glass. The town has a small but energetic hard-core dance culture that's unique in the Ionian. It's based on a number of bars around Áyiou Márkou and in nearby streets, and on two record stores, *Music Magazi* on Delyssa and

*More
conventional
nightclub-
discos can be
found 4km
southeast in
Argasi – see
p.239.*

Kokos on Tertséti, which are the best places to find out about new nightclubs and one-offs (most schools of house, techno, trance, hip/trip-hop have arrived on Zákynthos). The *Jazz Café* on Tertséti has borrowed the logo and bouncing typography of the London jazz venue, but is actually a small and friendly disco-bar with a small cover charge and house/techno DJ. More sedate and appealing to rock fans is the *Ship Inn* on the seafront.

Listings

Banks and exchange Most of the main regional Greek banks are on Konstandínou, and there's a foreign exchange cash dispenser at the Ergo Bank on Dhimokratías (formerly Vass. Yioryíou and still so on some maps). A number of travel agencies, such as Konstantakos on the corner of Filitá and Kyriákou Xénou, offer "no commission" exchanges on travellers' cheques. The post office also offers exchange services. The Ergo Bank represents Western Union; there is no American Express representation on Zákynthos.

Beaches The only beach in Zákynthos Town is the municipal pebble strand beyond Platía Solomoú, which has changing rooms, toilets and showers. Entry is free if you don't use the sunbeds or umbrellas. The taverna-bar *Asteria* further along also has bathing facilities for its customers. Otherwise, the nearest beaches are south at Argási and north at Tsiliví.

Bike and car rental Sky on Dhimokratías (☎0695/26 278) and the island-wide Ionian on Mákri (☎0695/48 946 or 51 797) hire pedal bikes, as well as cars and motorbikes; Moto-Saki on Dhimokratías (☎0695/23 928) has motorbikes.

Boat trips At least ten boats circumnavigate the island, visiting spots such as the otherwise inaccessible Smuggler's (Shipwreck) Cove, daily in season; all depart from Zákynthos Town's quayside in the morning. The going rate is 2000–3000dr, depending on the season. You can pay on board or in the offices along the quay; tickets are also sold by agencies at outlying resorts, which arrange transport into town to join the cruises. One of the best is the modern MV *Pelargos*, which visits six coastal sites but the classiest vessel has to be the wooden *Dias*, which has the advantage for non-swimmers of being able to edge right into the main Blue Cave. The boat trips make much of the Blue Caves at Cape Skinári on the northernmost tip of the island but not all trips actually take you into them – and those that do often employ outboard dinghies, involving a precarious transfer from the main vessel. It is wise to check this and the exact number of stops the boat is going to make; also ensure the one you pick is going to complete the full circuit. Otherwise, be prepared for eight hours' enforced sunbathing; many just get drunk or sleep most of the trip.

Cinema In winter the theatre of the cultural centre often shows films. In summer there is an open-air cinema at the back of the municipal beach.

Email Full Internet facilities are available upstairs at *Top's* games parlour on Filitá, a few doors down from the bus station.

Hospital Above town on the continuation of Marteláou and Martinégou (☎0695/22 514–5). The outpatients and casualty departments regularly deal with tourists.

Laundry There's a tiny old-fashioned *plindírio* tucked away at the far end of Ayíou Tavoulári, between Platía Ayíou Pávlou and Platía Ayíon Saránda.

Olympic Airways Alex. Románou 16 ☎0695/28 611; airport ☎0695/28 322.

OTE Vassiléos Yioryíou (daily 7.30am–2.30pm).

Taxis Taxi ranks on Platía Solomoú and Lombárdhou by Odhós Dalváni; also available by phone ☎0695/48 400, 23 623 or 24 036.

Vice-consulate Britain, Vicky Vitsou Kitsoni, Fóskolou 5 ☎0695/48 03, fax 23 769.

Around Zákynthos Town

As the number of visitors grows, more and more accommodation appears, with newer beach resorts springing up along Zákynthos's **east coast** wherever enterprising businesspeople can bulldoze a path down to something that might pass muster as a beach. Here, as on the other Ionian islands, the east coast is green, fairly flat and protected from the open sea to the west. Unfortunately, Zákynthos's eastern beaches are sometimes prone to oil and tar pollution. Despite this, the beaches are safe and the water's fairly clean, although often at the mercy of prevailing northwesterly winds, which increase in strength in the afternoon. To the north of Zákynthos Town, villas and apartments block-booked by British tour operators make up the bulk of accommodation, especially around Tsiliví and Plános, although the new mini-resorts mentioned above tend to have more room for independent travellers. This area – on an island not noted for good walking – is also a good bet for some relatively quiet walking among small hill hamlets.

North via Akrotíri

The coast road that extends north from Zákynthos Town past the municipal beach soon becomes very attractive, once it has emerged from the drab suburbs. As it is not too busy, it can make for a fine walk the two kilometres or so up to **Akrotíri**, and it is certainly worth driving this way if you have your own transport. The road winds up beside some rocky coast, surprisingly so for the eastern side, to the small hamlet of Akrotíri, which nestles above Cape Kryonéri with its lighthouse. There is not much here, but on a hairpin bend at the pine-clad highest point, the *Balcony of Zante* taverna (☎0695/26 179; ④) commands an amazing view north and east and has an expanding number of rooms. From here the road snakes down to the more commercialized coastal plain around Tsiliví.

Tsiliví and Plános

Five kilometres north of Zákynthos Town, **TSILIVÍ** is the first real resort on this coastline, with a number of good sandy beaches offering watersports. It has now merged with the inland village of Plános, whose centre is nearly a kilometre back from the beach, to make a lively resort that is starting to attract more youngsters, though it is still way behind Laganás and even Argási. **Accommodation** options

by the sea in Tsiliví include the small plain *Hotel Anetis* (☎0695/44
590 or 28 899 fax 28 758; ④), the smart modern studios of *Filoxenia*
(☎0695/22 481; ④) or *Helen* (☎0695/ 26 953 fax 26 566; ④) and
the simpler rooms of Dhimitra Stoufi (☎0695/49 238; ③). *Moby
Dick* is the most notable of the handful of restaurants, while the
Mango Beach Bar provides light refreshments and you can catch up
on your football at the outer bar of the *Millenium Club* disco.

Most places to stay are in **PLÁNOS**, ranging from good, purpose-
built **rooms** – try *Gregory's* (☎0695/61 853; ③) or *Dolphin*
(☎0695/27 425; ④) – to smarter **hotels** such as the large
Mediterranee (☎0695/26 100–4, fax 45 464; ④–⑦) which has en-
suite rooms, a restaurant, a pool and a recently constructed
fifty–room luxury wing. Beds can also be found through *Tsilivi
Travel* (☎0695/44 194, fax 22 655, *akis-125@otenet.gr*) on the
main road into Plános. There's also a good basic **campsite**, *Zante
Camping* (☎0695/61 710, fax 63 030), 1km further on from
Plános, beyond the tiny Boúka harbour, above the beach and away
from any other settlements. An indication of the increasing tourist
presence is the fact that there are now no fewer than three Chinese
restaurants, *Passeng to Asia* also serving Indian food. Otherwise it's
the usual pot-pourri of plastic Greek tavernas, of which *The Olive
Tree* is probably the most authentic. There seems little reason to
base yourself here unless as part of a package, although it might
make a short-term base if you want to explore the northern half of
the central plain, which starts west of here.

The coast beyond Tsiliví

The coast running northwest from Tsiliví conceals a number of beaches, usually a varying admixture of sand and pebbles, which are slowly
being developed for tourism. They generally become more low-key the
further you go until you reach the distinctive kink in the coastline that
shelters the busier resort of Alykés (see p.253). First up and only a
short stroll from Plános is **Boúka** beach, a quieter but nondescript
strand with just a couple of restaurants and a few room enterprises
such as *Adamantia Studios* (☎0695/27 396; ④), back on the road.

More appealing swimming spots are to be found a few kilometres
further along. One such is **Pahýs Ámmos** – the name means "thick
sand", despite the beach comprising flat stones – which hosts the
fine *Porto Roulis psarotavérna* and has accommodation in the
shape of the good-value *Pension Petra* (☎0695/62 140; ③) and the
more upmarket, oddly named *Hotel Camelot* (☎0695/62 962, fax
61 659; ⑥). Contiguous with Pahýs Ámmos but reached by a different access road, **Dhrosiá** has a bit more sand and similar level of
development; both the *Avouras* (☎0695/61 716; ③) and *Drosia*
(☎0695/62 256, fax 62 679; ④) apartments are bright and breezy,
and sustenance is available at *Andreas* fish taverna or *Poseidon*
beach bar.

A little further on and within easy reach of the inland hamlets of
Yerakári (see below) is the beach of the same name, though some
signs refer to it as Psaroú. This lovely sandy stretch is perhaps the
finest along this section of coast, with shallow water and relatively
few visitors. There is not much in the way of facilities, but only 300m
back from it is one of the island's better campsites, *Paradise
Camping* (☎0695/61 888), hidden in thick tree cover. Almost adjacent is the tiny burgeoning resort of **Ammoúdhi**, which has a couple
of tavernas, shops and the amusingly titled bars *Last Resort* and
Camelot (again). The place is starting to attract package groups and
has some expensive studios and the more reasonable *Ruassi*
(☎0695/62 613 or 61 405; ③) and *Oasis* (☎0695/44 166 or 62
847; ④) apartments, adjacent to each other on the northwest side.

The last resort of note before the coast hooks round to Alykés is
Alikanás, which is neatly tucked into the eastern side of the headland
separating the two. There are two distinct stretches of beach: a tiny
one next to the harbour, and a longer strand below the *Shoestring*
café-bar. Otherwise no particularly attractive eating options grab the
attention, while the best bet for accommodation is the smart new
apartment block *Velendzas* (☎0695/83 561, fax 83 519; ④).

Yerakári and Tragáki

Inland from these beach resorts is a network of tiny villages that are
well worth exploring on foot or bicycle. Zákynthos Town's hellish
traffic dies away at Vanáto, and northwest of here lie some beautiful
traditional hamlets where tourism has barely begun to intrude.
Particularly recommended are the **YERAKÁRI** "trio", 10km from
Zákynthos Town and within a fifteen-minute walk of each other: hilltop **Áno** (Upper) **Yerakári**, whose Italianate campanile is visible
from miles around, neighbouring **Méso** (Middle) **Yerakári**, and
Káto (Lower) **Yerakári**. Three rather roundabout kilometres to the
east, off a minor road towards Tsiliví, is **TRAGÁKI**, which boasts
some surviving pre-earthquake architecture (Friends of the Ionian
has produced a detailed historical trail around the village). It's a
working village with courtyarded houses, a still-functioning olive
press, an ancient well and, on the outskirts, ruins of Venetian houses. Apart from a friendly *kafenío*, and two shops supplying villagers' needs, it makes absolutely no concessions to tourism. A
couple of kilometres north is **Kypséli**, another lovely hilltop village,
crowned by the attractive church of Ayía Paraskeví. The surprisingly hip *Konaki* café can provide a drink, welcome if you are walking the area.

Argási

ARGÁSI, 4km southeast of Zákynthos Town, is the closest large
resort to the island capital, with hotel complexes now climbing the
lower slopes of Mount Skopós. Commercialization is rampant, and

*Just off the
road between
Plános and
Tragáki, the
modern
Avouri
amphitheatre
hosts perfor-
mances three
times a week
in summer.
Watch for ads
or ask in
Zákynthos
Town.*

might be measured by the mildly surreal vision of an English café that proudly announces a "Greek night" every Saturday. The beach, however, is skimpy – in parts no more than a few metres wide – and there's little of note in the village beyond a once-ruined church, now rebuilt of concrete, and, hidden away near the beach (just behind the *Life's a Beach* snack bar), a tiny but beautiful Venetian chapel. All the facilities are spread along the coast road and the thoroughfare that branches off at the main T-junction.

There is little reason to base yourself here unless you're on a cheap package or want to spend time exploring the Vassilikós peninsula to the south. **Rooms** can be had at *Pension Vaso* (☎0695/44 599 or 44 207; ③) and *Andro* (☎0695/22 190; ③) on the main road entering the village, and the seafront boasts some smart hotels: the *Locanda* (☎0695/45 386 or 45 563; ⑤) and the larger *Iliessa Beach* (☎0695/45 345, fax 45 346; ④), for example, both having en-suite rooms, some with sea views, as well as pools and gardens overlooking the beach.

In the event of accident or illness, there is a 24-hour clinic on the inland road (☎0695/41 514).

Eating out in Argási is an indifferent affair, and those staying here would be better off heading into Zákynthos Town in the evening. The *Tiffany's* and *Papillon* tavernas both serve a bland mix of Greek and international food. Slightly more promising are the *Three Brothers*, which specializes in fish, and the *Big Plate*, which can offer some good vegetarian alternatives. For a complete change of scene, there's a Chinese, the *Courser*, tucked down an alley near the crossroads in the centre of town or the Thai *Hot Wok* on the coast road. Argási is also home to the island's main **discos**, most of which line the road in from Zákynthos Town, sporting hilarious facades that would not look out of place in Disneyland: *Vivlos* and *Barrage* are typical of these, while the *Caligula Club* and garish *Mykonos Town* are on the other side of the resort; entry is normally free, with prices reflected in drinks, and things rarely get going before midnight. There is no shortage of smaller bars within Argási itself, with names such as *The Wreck*, *Kiss* and *Magic Mushrooms* reflecting the attempt to create an air of decadence.

Argási is the main point of access for **Mount Skopós**, via a signposted path leaving the coast road at the first hairpin bend out of town to the south. It's a long day's hike to the summit and back, over some fairly rough terrain, and the view of the mainland and Kefalloniá to the north, while spectacular, can sometimes be misty. Up on the hill above town and signposted just to the north a more family-oriented outing can be had to the *Fun Castle* playland. The full entry of 3000dr (kids 1000dr) is not cheap but includes a drink and unlimited use of a range of facilities, while 1500dr gets you into the indoor playroom only. The adjacent zoo is separately run, and certainly does not warrant a further 3000dr ticket.

The Vassilikós peninsula

The **Vassilikós peninsula**, stretching southeast of Zákynthos Town, is the most beautiful part of the island, with untouched countryside and forest, the island's two best beaches and, for early risers, great sunrises over the Peloponnese. Most tourism in the area is through island-based companies or overseas villa companies such as Simply Ionian, and often dependent on rented transport: the KTEL **bus** from Zákynthos Town visits only four times a day, though there is a free daily private bus from Laganás to Áyios Nikólaos (see p.242). There's usually a taverna or two in walking distance of most accommodation, but otherwise you're pretty much stranded – which makes the peninsula perfect for dropouts, but not so great for those who crave company or amenities.

To add to the sense of isolation, Vassilikós, in the wake of the 1953 earthquake, is the most confusingly named area on the island. In fact, the name Vassilikós applies to the whole 14km peninsula to the southeast of Argási; the original village, Áno Vassilikós, is barely a few hundred metres of road halfway down the peninsula. However, different maps of the island attribute the name Vassilikós to various hamlets on the peninsula, and haphazard road signs only add to the confusion.

Kamínia Beach and Pórto Zóro

The road south from Argási rises up into the foothills of Mount Skopós, passing, after little over two kilometres, a signposted turnoff for the first swimming spot on the peninsula, newly-created **KAMÍNIA BEACH**, which is still not marked on most maps. A spanking new wide asphalt road leads down to the small but pretty beach, slightly wider than Argási's, which is backed by two adjacent accommodation possibilities: both are fine but the *Levantino Rooms* (☎0695/35 366; ③) is a distinctly better deal than marginally plusher *Villa Fiore* (☎0695/35 204 or 35 468; ⑤). Both establishments have bars and allow free use of their umbrellas and sunbeds to patrons, though this might be a ploy that will stop when the beach becomes better known. There is also a volleyball net set up in the slowly deepening sea.

About three kilometres further along from the Kamínia turning, another recently upgraded road winds down to **PÓRTO ZÓRO**. This is the first really nice beach on the peninsula: clean, sandy and, with a fair amount of flora, very picturesque, although it gets pretty busy. There's a canteen and a **taverna** cum bar, the *Porto Zoro* (☎0695/35 304; ④), with basic but modern **rooms** overlooking the beach, which would make Zóro an excellent place to chill out for a while.

Before the Pórto Zóro turning, a road inland leads up and over to the only two beaches on the **west side** of the peninsula, Sekánia and Dháfni, the more popular of the two, with a snack bar and taverna. Neither particularly merits the bumpy ride over partly unpaved roads, and they both attract more crowds than you might expect.

Áno Vassilikós and beaches

Back on the main road, you soon reach the small hamlet of ÁNO
VASSILIKÓS, which straggles along the road above a small beach,
which is part sand, part pebble, with deposits of sea grass. The
increasing number of **rooms**, shops, bars and restaurants here constitute the only real development on the peninsula that is not down at
sea level. If you want to stay, try cosy *Villa Anna* (☎0695/35 316;
③) or the somewhat larger *Vassilikos Apartments* (☎0695/35 280;
④). Among the **tavernas**, *O Gallos*, as the name suggests, provides
French as well as Greek cuisine, while *Dioskouri* is a more traditional, family-run place. Round the bend heading south, *O Aderefos
tou Kosta* is a popular garden taverna with range of succulent meat
dishes plus fish and numerous veggie options. A little further on the
Logos Rock Club lives up to its name by providing the hippest soundtrack on the whole peninsula.

Just to the south is the longest and one of the most commercialized beaches in this part of the island, with umbrellas stretching
almost all the way down to the end of this northeast-facing coast,
just behind Áyios Nikólaos. There are two separate access roads, the
first signposted to **Iónio Beach**; at this end of the wide strand there
is a taverna and the lushly landscaped apartment complex of Nikos
Tsirikos (☎0695/35 497; ⑤). The whole beach is more commonly
(and mystifyingly) known as **Banana**, which is how it is signposted
at the next turning, The beach has dunes and a firm, though very
narrow, strip of sand. There's nowhere to stay at this end, but
refreshment is provided by a couple of bars, including the suitably
laid-back *Relax*.

Áyios Nikólaos

About 3km from Áno Vassilikós, **ÁYIOS NIKÓLAOS** boasts the most
attractive beach on this side of the peninsula: a small stretch of sand
cleft in the middle by a rock outcrop crowned with a bar. The resort
is set in a rocky, almost desert-like landscape in a remote area of the
peninsula, and at first sight may appear to be little more than a single complex: the *Vasilikos Beach* (☎0695/24 114; ⑤), a large,
modern, if rather boxy, three-storey **hotel** set back from the beach,
with restaurant, pool and bar. Anyone staying at the hotel or using its
beach facilities (umbrellas, watersports etc) is entitled to use the free
bus service that connects with Laganás, Kalamáki and Argási several times a day. Other accommodation options include two very modern **apartment** developments with all mod cons, the *Christina*
(☎0695/35 474; ③) and *Virginia* (☎0695/35 315; ④). Among the
village eateries, the *Blue Bay* taverna cum cocktail bar offers a wide
selection of meat, fish, starters and pizza, while the *Familia* has a
similar dinner menu and particularly good omelettes for breakfast.
Down by the sea the *Plaka Beach* is a reasonable fish taverna.

Pórto Róma and Yérakas

What some maps call Vassilikós village is in fact a barely inhabited junction in the middle of nowhere, where the bus from Zákynthos Town stops and turns. Here you'll find two tavernas, the *Blue Roses Music Bar* and some houses and villas scattered in the surrounding countryside, which is lush, almost jungle-like. Lesser roads lead off to Pórto Róma on the left and Yérakas beach on the right.

The small cove of **Pórto Róma** shelters a sand and pebble beach (which occasionally suffers from oil pollution), a bar and an eponymous taverna on the cliff above, but little else. There are, however, a fair few enterprises, mostly **apartments** on or just off the road down: *Villa Kapnisi*, which rents out apartments and studios in the area around the cove (☎0695/35 331, fax 41 180; ④); *Katerina Rooms* (☎0695/35 456; ③), just off the main road; and *Mimi's Apartments* (☎ & fax 0695/35 007; ③), good-value modern units on the road that branches off to the left.

Far preferable, however, is **Yérakas**, the island's finest beach, a long lazy crescent of golden sand and shallow waters protected from the open sea and prevailing winds by low sandy cliffs. A turtle breeding ground (see box on p.244), the beach heaves during the day in high summer, but is off limits between dusk and dawn; off season, Yérakas is a stunning haven. There are two tavernas set back from the beach, of which *Gerakas* has live music in the evening, and one small snack bar on the sand, but as yet no other facilities. It is possible, however, to **stay** quite near the beach, and thus have it almost to yourself between curfew and crowds: *Liuba Apartments* (☎0695/35 372 or 35 313, fax 35 481; ④) has a field of small and basic self-catering cabins a few minutes' walk from Yérakas.

The Vassilikós peninsula

At Yérakas, look out for the booth of Archelon, the Sea Turtle Protection Society, which has information displays and a gift shop 200m from the beach.

Laganás Bay

Laganás Bay is the first glimpse of Zákynthos most tourists get from a jet coming in to land at the island's airport. **Laganás** itself is the largest single resort on the island, and the most popular, with the facilities, and problems, to match. Even in the last knockings of the season in late October, when Zákynthos can sometimes still be baking hot, Laganás continues partying around the clock while other island resorts are closing down. This is *not* a place to come for a quiet break or an early night. Its neighbouring resort to the east, **Kalamáki**, gives onto a superior section of the same beach and is much less developed – though not necessarily quieter, due to the proximity of the airport.

At nearly 9km, the beach in Laganás Bay is the longest on the island and, in spite of the crowds, one of the best. It has slightly muddy sand (firm enough for vehicles), and the sea is shallow and clear – though usually busy with bathers and pleasure craft at the

Laganás Bay

Travel agencies in Laganás and Kalamáki can arrange day-trips, including coach transfers, on the tour boats based at Zákynthos Town (see p.236).

Loggerhead sea turtles

One night in September 1995, a bomb went off in the offices of Zákynthos architect, Nikos Lykouresis, a founder of the Zakynthian Ecological Movement. No one was hurt, but the attack, believed to have been carried out by opponents of the ecology movement, took the tension between conservationists and businesspeople to a new high. The subject of the tension is the **loggerhead sea turtle**, *Caretta caretta*, which breeds on two of the main beaches on Zákynthos and elsewhere on the island besides. The turtles are an endangered species, and this is one of their largest breeding grounds in Europe.

The tensions began in the early 1980s, just when the tourism boom was taking off. Environmentalists started a campaign to protect the turtle breeding grounds where, from May to October, the females come ashore at night to lay their eggs, bury them in the sand and return to the sea. The hatchlings most frequently come out at night, burrow out and head for the water, although they can sometimes be glimpsed scuttling down the beaches in early mornings.

Protecting the turtles would, however, adversely affect business on the beach: those bars and tavernas setting out tables and chairs on the sand, the sunbed franchises who plant bayonet umbrellas in the sand, the watersports companies whose propellers proved a threat to the slow-moving animals and the discos and bars whose noise and lights would deter the females from laying and disorient the hatchlings.

The two factions, represented on one side by a coalition of ecological groups – the World Wildlife Fund, Sea Turtle Protection Society of Greece, the Zakynthian Ecological Movement and Friends of the Ionian – and by local businesses on the other, have been battling over proposals to make Laganás Bay, the main breeding ground, a protected marine park. If the conservationists win, some seafront operations will lose their businesses. The use of motorized vessels in the bay is already strictly controlled in theory, but the rules are often ignored.

No firm plan has been adopted from the three proposals, laid on the table some time back, for the future of Laganás Bay: one from the Greek

---

Laganás end. The beach between Laganás and Kalamáki is one of the biggest breeding grounds for the **loggerhead sea turtle** in Greece, where a number of strict rules are enforced. Visitors are asked not to dig up or drive over the beach, and to stay off it at night (when, in season, the turtles come ashore to lay eggs). The presence of wheel tracks and used condoms on the beach suggests that not everybody is getting the message.

There are three **islands** in Laganás Bay, none of them inhabited and only two accessible. Boat trips to **Marathoníssi**, the largest, run every few hours from stalls on the beach (around 1000dr per person). The island has a small sandy beach, part of which is a turtle breeding ground (so don't disturb any sticks you see protruding from the sand), and offers an escape from the crowds of Laganás – though it's sometimes exposed to prevailing winds and has absolutely no facilities. **Áyios Sóstis**, a diminutive rock islet near the main beach, government, which has been criticized by the Council of Europe for failing to protect the turtles; one from the environmentalists; and one from the local businesses, some of whom are coming to the realization that a marine park in one form or another is inevitable. The proposals have themselves become hostage to local government politics, as turtles don't win many votes on Zákynthos. Mounting pressure from the EU may force the government to agree to the environmentalists' demands, but that doesn't mean that the loggerheads will be safe. Previous orders to comply with court orders have been ignored, and some businesses flout basic rules of conservation on a daily basis.

Paradoxically, Greek tourism operators have discovered that a little anthropomorphism actually helps business, and the loggerhead has been pressed into the service of the merchandising industry: bars, restaurants, hotels and shops all borrow the name and image, and you can carry a memento of the imperilled reptile home on T-shirts, tea towels, paperweights, jewellery boxes, wall hangings, posters, matchboxes, decorative magnets and snowstorm shakers. It's possible that the animal itself might be killed off, only to live on as a fridge magnet.

There are a few simple things you can do to avoid disturbing the turtles' breeding habits. The World Wildlife Fund has issued the following list of **guidelines** for visitors:

1. Don't use the beaches of Laganás and Yérakas between sunset and sunrise.
2. Don't stick umbrellas in the sand in the marked nesting zones.
3. Take your rubbish away with you – it can obstruct the turtles.
4. Don't use lights near the beach at night – they can disturb the turtles, sometimes with fatal consequences.
5. Don't take any vehicle onto the protected beaches.
6. Don't dig up turtle nests – it's illegal.
7. Don't pick up the hatchlings or carry them to the water, as it's vital to their development that they reach the sea on their own.
8. Don't use speedboats in Laganás Bay – a 10kph speed limit is in force for vessels in the bay.

houses the *Cameo* discotheque, has a small pebbly beach and can be reached by a rickety wooden walkway a few hundred metres to the south of Laganás. The third island, **Peloúzo**, near the tip of the Vassilikós peninsula, is simply a large rock.

Laganás

Prior to the arrival of tourism, **LAGANÁS** was little more than a small hamlet near the mouth of a stream emptying into the bay. Now it's a massive hive of commercialism stretching for over a kilometre along the beach, and a similar distance inland along its main thoroughfare and along the Kalamáki road parallel to the beach. The bulk of accommodation here is new or purpose-built and prone to the vagaries of Greek plumbing and fittings. Bars, restaurants and snack bars are all but interchangeable, although some do go out of their way to offer alternatives to what at times can look like an unending diet of junk food. Greek has become a second language here, which is how the predominantly Anglophone visitors like it; many businesses are in fact owned or staffed by expat or retired Brits. It has the widest range of beach amenities on the island, and provides off-beach attractions such as horse-riding and ballooning. While hotels are mostly block-booked by package companies, competition has forced many of them to open their pools and grounds to outsiders – provided you use their bars or restaurants.

The resort is constructed on a simple grid plan. Roads are nameless, but you'll soon learn to navigate using familiar landmarks. The two key thoroughfares are the main drag, which runs perpendicular to the beach, and the right-hand turning nearly a kilometre back from the sea, by Dennis's Bikes, where buses turn in the direction of Kalamáki and Zákynthos Town.

Accommodation

While many of the places to stay in Laganás are monopolized by tour operators, there are still plenty of **rooms** and **apartments** to be had – although in high season it can be extremely busy, and anyone heading here should phone ahead. Accommodation is often smack in the middle of the party zone, though the southwesterly end of the resort tends to be quieter; numerous private houses offering walk-up room accommodation can be found on the road that leaves the centre of the main drag, opposite the *Time Out* bar, and curves round to the beach at the hamlet of Lithákia, at the southern end of Laganás Bay. The Union of Room-owners has an office halfway down the main drag (daily 8.30am–2pm and 5–8pm; ☎0695/51 590) and Flocas Travel (☎0695/52 802) has contacts with more upmarket rooms and apartments.

There's a basic **campsite**, or rather, a field with facilities, just a short distance southwest of Laganás – it's signposted in town, but the quickest route is to walk south along the beach for 200m to the first turn-off road, which leads up to the site. Vehicles should follow the road sign opposite the *Time Out* bar to reach the campsite about 700m on.

Hotels

Most of Laganás' **hotels** are either on the beach to the north of the main drag, or a few minutes' walk back from it. However, an increasing number now trail back towards the airport, causing some staying "in" Laganás to have to commute to the beach by bus.

Alexandros (☎0695/51 580). A small hotel, with en-suite rooms, balconies and sea views. At the quieter end of the north part of town, tucked away about 100m from the beach. ④.

Australia (☎0695/51 071–3 fax 51 857). Smallish, set back from the beach, with a pool. Jointly managed with the adjacent *Sirene*. ⑤.

Ionis (☎0695/51 141 fax 51 601). Medium-sized but very friendly hotel, away from the beach on the main drag, with en-suite rooms, balconies, a bar and pool. ⑤.

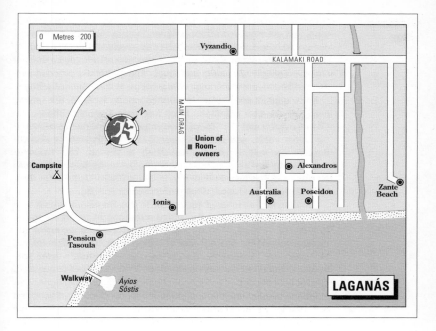

Pension Tasoula (☎0695/51 560). Between beach and campsite, a friendly place with cosy rooms and a leafy courtyard. ④.

Poseidon (☎0695/51 827–31 fax 51 199). Right on the beach and rather flashy, with a pool; air-conditioned en-suite rooms with balconies and sea views. Mostly for groups. ⑥.

Vyzandio (☎0695/51 136). On the Kalamáki road, no frills but also no package groups and probably the cheapest hotel around; basic en-suite rooms. ③.

Zante Beach (☎0695/51 130). The smartest in Laganás, set away from the party zone nearly 1km towards Kalamáki and two blocks back from the beach. En-suite rooms, balconies, restaurant, bar and pool. Very popular with north European coach parties, so unlikely to have vacancies unless booked well in advance. ⑥.

Eating and drinking

Good **food** isn't a big selling point in Laganás. Many of the seafront and main drag businesses specialize in snacks, junk food and British staples (fish and chips and fry-ups). These are, however, only versions of the original: fish will be a local white-meat, bonier, oilier but tastier than North Sea cod or haddock; and a Greek sausage (*loukániko*) doesn't taste anything like the British banger. Most restaurants are clustered around the centre of Laganás, where they compete shoulder to shoulder for passing trade. Competition keeps prices down, although the more stylish restaurants can get away with charging at least 3000dr a head, excluding drinks.

Laganás Bay

In the centre, the *Bee Garden* serves a wide range of Chinese food, and the *Pizzeria* offers pasta and pizzas made in a real pizza oven, while the *Apollo* and *Acropolis* tavernas have lengthy menus of Greek and international dishes. The latter also offers special themed Greek evenings with music and dance. The *Nefeli* is a pleasant garden taverna with a wide range of standards, just off the main drag.

For a quieter and cheaper meal than can be found in the centre, head off **on the Kalamáki road** just past Dennis's Bikes. The *Chinese Ruby* and *Taj Mahal* have comprehensive menus prepared by native chefs, and the *Hollywood Diner* offers above-average burgers, as well as imaginative salads in season. The *Taverna Zougraz*, tucked away on the right before the bridge leaving Laganás on this road, has a vast menu of pan and grilled fish and meat dishes, and also stages *kandádhes* performances at night.

Another well-advertised restaurant is the *Sarakino*, which also offers live music and has the added attraction of being set in the grounds of a ruined Venetian mansion, giving dinner the air of picnicking outside the fallen House of Usher. *Sarakino* is 2km inland, however, and accessible mainly by the restaurant's own free minibus which cruises Laganás touting for trade. Once committed, there's no escaping.

On the beach, junk food reigns supreme, but the following offer a wider range, including salads, seafood and taverna dishes: *Harbour House*, *Greek Islands*, *Blue Waves*, *Koralli* and *Blue Sea*.

There's a **bar** about every dozen metres along Laganás' main thoroughfares, with rib-tickling names such as *Ghetto*, *Kamikaze* and even *Potter's Bar*. Prices are reasonable, but the chance of enjoying a quiet drink is scarce. It's a pity to have to issue this warning, but a few unscrupulous bars in Laganás have been known to play "swap the banknote" on drunken tourists. It's advisable to double-check what you're handing over, as in some circumstances it can be impossible to negotiate. That said, Laganás is the only place you're likely to encounter this on Zákynthos. *Rescue* and *Zero's* are two of the most popular indoor discos, almost adjacent to each other on the main drag and both blessed with mercifully efficient air-conditioning but precious little taste in music.

Listings

Bike and motorbike rental Dennis's Bikes ☎0695/52 997, by the Zákynthos Town turning at the back of the main drag.

Car rental The island-wide Ionian ☎0695/51 797 or 52 114, fax 53 105 rental company has cars, jeeps and motorbikes.

Doctor There's a surgery, with English-speaking staff, on the main drag (daily 9.30am–2pm & 5–10pm; ☎0695/52 252) and Zante Medical Care has a 24-hour emergency line (☎0695/52 865).

Email Full Internet access is available at the *Cyber Saloon* café, a couple of blocks to the left of the main drag as you approach the sea from the main junction.

Exchange There are no banks in Laganás, but plenty of travel agents will change cash and travellers' cheques. The big *Eurocambio* exchange bureau is near the Kalamáki turning and there are a couple of cash dispensers further down the main drag.

Phones Besides the ubiquitous cardphones, many travel offices offer quieter metered phones, but check the tariff beforehand.

Kalamáki

KALAMÁKI is basically a baby version of Laganás, offering all the good features of the bay without the drawbacks of the main resort. It has a variety of accommodation and tavernas, and its restrained nightlife is more upmarket than that of Laganás. Just one street runs down to the sea, although a smattering of developments is springing up in lanes off it and along the Laganás road. Surprisingly, there is still very little building down at the beach. The one minus is the proximity of the airport: the drone of aircraft waiting to take off is quite audible from the centre of the village.

Accommodation

Kalamáki has a number of small, quite smart **hotels**, which are being increasingly monopolized by tour companies (the recommendations listed below keep at least some rooms for independents), as well as **rooms** owned by the proprietors of the two *Stanis* tavernas (☎0695/26 375 or 26 374; ③) towards the back of the village, and some small apartment complexes. Zakyta Holidays (☎0695/27 080), in the centre of the village, handles a wide range of rooms, apartments and villas, and can change money.

Crystal Beach (☎0695/42 788, fax 42 917). Kalamáki's largest hotel is friendly and comfortable, with an unrivalled setting overlooking the beach, at the bottom of the main street. Two restaurants and bars, and a pool. Room rates have increased sharply. ⑦.

Klelia (☎0695/27 056 or 41 288, fax 41 288). Smart, newly built forty-room hotel on the main street, but a bit soulless. ⑥.

Metaxa (☎0695/27 441–3, fax 27 445). Small, stylish building with a pool and smart rooms; excellent value. ④.

Eating and drinking

Restaurants in Kalamáki tend to be aimed at people who like to dress up for dinner, with decor and prices to match. The two *Stanis* tavernas (one situated by the road to Laganás, the other on a picturesque knoll above the beach, with its own small menagerie loose in the garden) both have extensive menus of Greek and international dishes, although the beachside version is geared more to lunches and its sibling more to evening meals. Worthwhile alternatives include *Jools' Diner*, serving English and international dishes, the *Merlis*, which mixes Greek bakes and grills with Italian cuisine, mainly pasta and meat-based dishes, and *Afrodite* taverna, with standard Euro-Greek fare at reasonable prices.

If you need to make a fast getaway, you can rent a car or motorbike at Merlis on the main road.

Laganás
Bay

Nightlife tends to begin in bars such as *Al' Sandros* or the *Moonlight*, which has live acoustic music most evenings, and gravitates towards the *Vios Club* on the hillside above the village, which has a garden with breathtaking views over the bay and islands. Tucked into the foothill below, the *Cave Bar* is a popular watering hole, and the other main disco is the *Mouses Club* at the start of the road to Laganás.

The west coast

Zákynthos's skeletal public transport service renders most of the hill villages in the west and north of the island off limits to those without transport. Local tour agencies and KTEL do offer island **coach tours** in season, varying greatly in price (KTEL has the best deal at 2000dr a head), but these are whistlestop tours with only a few breaks for meals, refreshment and sightseeing. This side of the island is well worth making the effort to visit, however, for the pre-earthquake architecture of villages such as **Kerí** and **Kiliómeno**, the sweeping coastal vistas and sunsets (most famously at **Kambí**) two of the island's oldest monasteries and the weaving centre of **Volímes**.

Kerí

Though hidden in a fold above the cliffs at the island's southernmost tip, **KERÍ** is easily accessible. The village retains a number of pre-quake, Venetian buildings, including the church of the Panayía of Kerí – who is said to have saved the island from marauding pirates by hiding it in a sea mist. Kerí is also famous for a geological quirk, a series of small tar pools mentioned by both Pliny and Herodotus, but these have mysteriously dried up in recent years. A rough path leaving the southern end of the village leads on 1km to the lighthouse, whose surrounding cliff paths afford spectacular views of the sea and tree-tufted limestone sea-arches and -stacks.

On the way there you can detour to the lake and beach of Kerí, which are actually tucked into the far southwestern corner of Laganás Bay and signposted at the modern village of Límni Keríou. The lake is an atmospheric patch of brackish, swampy water, home to reeds and a few wading birds; the beach that separates it from the sea is a good uncrowded place for a swim. The area is gradually showing signs of catching onto tourism, with a few apartments and tavernas popping up, and is also the base of one of the most reliable scuba-diving operations, the Turtle Beach Dive Centre (☎0695/48 768).

Maherádho

Some 10km west of Zákynthos Town, **MAHERÁDHO** also boasts some impressive pre-earthquake architecture, and is set in beautiful arable uplands, surrounded by terraced olive and fruit groves. The magnificent **church of Ayía Mávra** has an impressive free-standing campanile, and inside a splendid carved iconostasis and icons by Zakynthian painter Nikolaos Latsis. The town's major festival – one of the biggest on the island – is for the saint's day, which conventionally falls on the first Sunday in June. The town's other notable religious edifice, the typically Byzantine domed church of the **Panayía**, commands breathtaking views over the central plain. The interior, however, has been denuded of most of its artwork, much of it moved to Ayía Mávra.

Kiliómeno and Kambí

Ascending into the bare mountainscape of the west coast on a rough country road from Maherádho, you'll reach, after 6km, **KILIÓMENO**, the best place to see surviving pre-earthquake domestic architecture, in the form of the island's traditional two-storey, stone-built tile-roofed houses. The town was originally named after its church, **Áyios Nikólaos**, whose impressive campanile, begun over a hundred years ago, still lacks a capped roof. About six kilometres past Kiliómeno, a newly paved road loops down to the coast and back again at the village of Áyios Léon. The detour passes through farmland, cordoned off by a maze of short dry-stone walls, on its way to the jagged lavic rock of the coast. There are two points with sea access, one below an easily visible canteen, and a little further north the tiny inlet of **Pórto Limniónas**, topped by a taverna of the same name.

The main road continues climbing another 4km up into the island's highest western hills, where a turning just before Éxo Hóra leads a further 4km to the tiny clifftop hamlet of **KAMBÍ**, the destination for numerous coach tours organized to catch sunset over the sea. The village contains three cliff-top tavernas, especially built for this natural show, with extraordinary views over the 300-metre-high cliffs and western horizon, although you're likely to find yourself sharing the sunset with a sizeable crowd of fellow visitors. On an incline above the village there's an imposing concrete cross, said to have been constructed in memory of islanders killed here by nationalist soldiers during the civil war – one lurid legend says that islanders were hurled from the cliffs. An alternative history of the cross claims it was erected to commemorate those killed by the Nazis during the island's wartime occupation.

Mariés to Volímes

Five kilometres north of Kambí, following the bare mountain road north, **MARIÉS** is the only other village in the region with access to the sea. A steep, rough track leads down 7km to the small rocky cove of **Stenítis Bay**, which has a waterfront taverna and dock, while a second, paved road descends to **Pórto Vrómi**, from where small boats conduct trips to Shipwreck Bay. Mariés itself, protected in a wooded green valley, has an unusual three-aisled church dedicated to Mary Magdalene, who is said to have stopped here to preach en route to Provence. Tough hiking paths lead up onto the slopes of Mount Vrahiónas, the island's highest mountain, with views across the island and north to Kefallonía.

After this, the main mountain road veers a little further inland to reach Volímes after ten kilometres. A small detour to the east just over half way takes you to **Orthoniés**, another picturesque mountain village with a fine stone gateway, some old, squat, stone-built houses and a café. A more interesting route, however branches off east to the **Anafonítria monastery** through the eponymous village. The monastery, dating from the fourteenth century, is no longer inhabited and is currently undergoing renovation, but it is still worth going through the gateway beside the chunky square tower into the open courtyard. The main chapel is closed, but a more recent side chapel and the cemetery beyond can be visited. Food, drink and gifts are available at the nearby edge of the village.

The minor but asphalted road continues towards the coast, and within 4km reaches the area's other old holy retreat, the **monastery of Áyios Yióryios ton Kremnón**, the construction of which began in the sixteenth century. It still houses two monks and, apart from some of the original buildings, has two noteworthy features: a small chapel with some fine icons painted on wood and a peculiar round lookout tower. Close to the monastery, a newly paved road branches off to the sheer clifftop above **Shipwreck Bay**. A metal platform bracketted onto the cliff affords vertical views of the ship buried in the sand hundreds of feet below; it's quite safe, but definitely only for those with a head for heights. If you need a drink to recover, look no further than the taverna, a comforting 100m back from the edge. A footpath near the platform leads 300m over rocky scrub to the **cave of Áyios Yerásimos**, crowned by a tiny chapel.

VOLÍMES is the largest of the island's hill villages, with the exception of Katastári, and in fact comprises three smaller settlements: Káto (Lower), Méso (Middle) and Áno (Upper) Volímes, which are within a few minutes' drive of each other. Each is a small living museum of rural island architecture. **Áno Volímes**, built on a hillside surrounding the church of Ayíos Dhimítrios, is probably the best-preserved village on the entire island. Volímes is the end destination of most island tours, mainly because of its reputation for fine embroidery and farm produce, notably cheese and honey. Shops selling intricately embroidered lace and rugs of various sizes and designs, including the ubiquitous turtles, line the road of the middle village. The Women's Agrotourism Cooperative here is a self-help organization established in 1988 as part of a national, government-sponsored initiative to involve rural women in tourism; its office in Áno Volímes can organize accommodation in private homes in the villages or you can try the nearby *kafenío* (☎0695/31 322). The *Kaminaki* taverna serves good home-style cooking.

The northeast

Around twelve kilometres northwest of Zákynthos Town, the mountains that cover the whole west of the island begin to converge on the east coast. At this point the northernmost resort of any size, **Alykés**, is only a fifteen-minute walk below the sprawling mountain village of **Katastári**. Further on the peaks shelve quite abruptly, though not as precipitously as on the west coast, down to the sea, leaving only a handful of beaches. The island tapers to an end at Cape Skinári, just below which are the famous **Blue Caves**, and a little further south, **Áyios Nikólaos**, from where Zákynthos's only ferry connection with Kefalloniá departs.

Alykés

The largest beach in the region is at **ALYKÉS**, a resort that's undergoing definite development but is still quieter than Tsiliví. It's known for its salt pans (hence the name), which give the back of the village the appearance of a moonscape, while its long beach, perhaps due to a steep seabed, experiences lively surf created by the prevailing winds. The beach is actually divided into two strips by a brackish canal and the quay beside its outlet. Most of the action is on the northwestern side of this dividing waterway. Not too much **accommodation** of decent value is available to the independent traveller. The best deal by far is at the *Picadilly Hotel* (☎0695/83 606 or 83 457; ②), near the main crossroads, which has adequate en-suite rooms above a restaurant. There are quite a few **hotels** behind the beach with sea views: among these, the *Ionian Star* (☎0695/83 416, fax 83 173; ④), a small friendly place with its own restaurant and garden, the odd office-like *Aktis* (☎0695/83 956; ④), the air-conditioned *Montreal* (☎0695/83 241, fax 83 342; ⑤) and the huge, upmarket *Astoria* (☎0695/83 416 or 83 658, fax 83 173; ⑥) are worth investigating. Spring Tours (☎0695/83 035) can arrange rooms and apartments here and in nearby Katastári, the village visible on a hillside to the southwest.

The choice of **places to eat** has increased dramatically of late. Among the half-dozen or so tavernas, the *Anatolikos* is a reasonably authentic spot, the large seafront *Golden Dolphin* has a wide range of fish and meat at good prices, and the vast *Fantasia* in the village offers a variety of Euro-Greek dishes. Besides these, there are three pizzerias, the *Taj Mahal*, which also serves Indian and Chinese cuisine, and the *Bits'n'Pieces* creperie. Several much-of-a-muchness bars such as the *Sugarbush Pub* vie for the custom of the night owls. The bus system more or less gives out at Alykés, but it would make a reasonable beach base for those exploring the north with their own transport. Cars and motorbikes can be hired from Alikes rental (☎0695/83 616).

Katastári

Straddling the main road through the northeast of Zákynthos, the sprawling village of **KATASTÁRI** is the second largest settlement on the island. There is not much original architecture to admire or anything particular to divert tourists, but precisely for that reason it makes a good place to take in some real life in a contemporary island community. It would be a shame to stay in Alykés, for example, without strolling up here at least once. The most impressive, albeit modern edifice is the **church of Iperayía Theotókos**, which dominates the lower village square on the way up from Alykés. This huge rectangular brick building boasts unusual twin belfries, and a small amphitheatre has been constructed to seat people for festival activities. There's nowhere obvious to stay, but a couple of cafeterias offer a warm welcome, and the *Vlassis* taverna and *To Kendro psistariá* serve unpretentious food at giveaway prices. A post office and several functional shops complete the amenities.

North to Cape Skinári

The main road soon starts to undulate between fairly high mountainous sections and sea level – creating some major bends and hair-raising driving conditions. At 3km north of Katastári, the *Ksigia* taverna commands a bend at the top of a headland with splendid views and standard food. A little further on, the road dips to a point just above diminutive **Xíngi** beach, which is flanked by a sheer rock wall on one side and rugged coastline on the other. A short unmarked motorable track leads to a path down to the pebble beach.

Less than 2km further. the road descends again to the larger pebble beach of **Makrýs Yialós**. Here pedal boats can be hired to explore the local mini-caves and motor boats run excursions up to the Blue Caves. There's a canteen at the back of the beach, while the excellent *Pilarinos* taverna, on the hill above, rents out cheap camping plots in its shadeless grounds. The Austrian-run Red Dolphin diving centre (☎0695/93 277) is also based up on the hill. Just to the north of Makrýs Yialós you come to a pretty promontory with a small harbour and *psarotavérna*, beyond and above which there are a couple of rooms ventures; try *Klimati* (☎0695/31 225; ③) if you fancy a bit of isolation.

The Áyios Nikólaos– Pessádha ferry runs twice daily in season and takes 1hr 15min.

The next settlement is the gradually developing port of **Áyios Nikólaos**, not to be confused with the beach resort at the opposite end of the island. Note that it is sometimes referred to as Skinári, especially over on Kefalloniá, with which it is connected by the ferry to Pessádha. Perhaps tired of seeing the constant trickle of elusive tourists pour off the boat and immediately disappear towards the south, the locals have been trying to tempt people to stay by increasing the number of accommodation and dining options and occasionally grabbing visitors before they can board their vehicle. Although tourism is still low-key, the amount of building in progress suggests it may not remain so for long. At present, the best deal on rooms is at the *Panorama* (☎0695/31 013, fax 31 017; ③) as you climb to the south, while the *Blue Beach Bungalows* (☎0695/31 522–3, fax 31 524; ⑤) to the north is a huge complex with a pool and spiral waterslide that is advertised all over the island. Incredibly, some of the most expensive apartments anywhere in Greece at 70,000dr a night are to be found here at the small but exquisitely decorated and furnished *Nobelos* (☎ & fax 0695/31 1 31; ⑦), situated on a bluff above the sea. For meals, try the *La Storia* fish restaurant on the harbour or the *Xagnando* taverna above it.

As you near the northern tip of Zákynthos, the thick covering of olive and pine gives way to low-lying rocky scrub until the land peters out at **Cape Skinári**, crowned by the Korithí lighthouse. **Korithí** itself is more a scattered collection of buildings than a village, but it can claim to have one of the most charming and unique places to stay in the entire Ionian: the upper storey of an old windmill has been converted into one double room, run by the nearby *Faros* taverna (☎0695/31 132; ④). Advance booking is essential for obvious reasons. Just in front of the windmill there are steps all the way down to a section of the **Blue Caves**, but don't forget that you'll have to trudge all the way back up, so you might prefer to survey the stunning coastline from on high. The only other refreshments are at a canteen behind the windmill. You can drive to within walking distance of the lighthouse but it is not particularly spectacular. Otherwise, you can loop back round southwest towards Volímes to complete the northern circuit.

Travel details

BUSES

Zákynthos Town to: Áyios Nikólaos/Skinári (2 daily; 1hr 20min); Alykés (5 daily; 50min); Argási (12 daily; 15min); Kalamáki (11 daily; 20min); Kerí (2 daily; 50min); Laganás (18 daily; 30min); Tsiliví (11 daily; 30min); Vassilikós/Áyios Nikólaos (4 daily; 1hr); Volímes (2 daily; 1hr 30min). Services are reduced on Sundays and out of season.

There are also several daily bus connections to Athens via Kyllíni and Pátra, varying in number according to seasonal variations in ferry schedules (see below), and several services a week to Thessaloníki via Lamía, Almyrós (for Vólos), Lárisa and Kateríni. For information call KTEL (☎0695/22 255 or 42 656).

FERRIES

Áyios Nikólaos to: Pessádha on Kefalloniá (2 daily May–Sept; 1hr 15min).
Zákynthos Town to: Kyllíni (7 daily in summer, 3 daily in winter; 1hr 30min).

FLIGHTS

Zákynthos airport to: Athens on Olympic (1–2 daily; 55min).

The Contexts

The historical framework

Isolated off the west coast of Greece, perilously close to Italy, the Ionian archipelago has stood apart from the mainland and the Aegean until recent times, and its history reflects this. This section is intended just to lend some perspective to travels in the Ionian, and is weighted towards the era of the modern, post-independence nation – especially the twentieth century.

The earliest cultures

The archipelago's isolation puts it on the sidelines of the historical narrative that produced the great archeological finds at Delphi, Mycenae, Olympia and elsewhere. However, evidence in the form of tools has been found on Corfu and Kefalloniá, suggesting that the region was inhabited by Paleolithic (early Stone Age) hunter-gatherers as long ago as 70,000–50,000 BC, prior to the last great Ice Age. At this time Corfu and the other islands were still part of a dry landmass, and what is now the northern Adriatic was covered by a vast forest. These people would have originally come from the eastern Mediterranean, finding themselves "islanded" during the period 14,000–10,000 BC, when the ice thawed, raising the level of the Mediterranean by over a hundred metres. Their communities would have been agrarian and self-supporting, producing pottery and handicrafts, and worshipping earth/fertility

deities, clay figurines of which can be seen in some island museums. The development of agriculture, trade and sea travel would transform this civilization into one that learned to specialize, compete and, when it seemed advantageous, go to war.

Minoans and Mycenaeans

The Bronze Age **Minoan civilization** (2500–1100 BC) was a period of fluctuating regional dominance in the Mediterranean, based upon sea power, with vast palaces serving as centres of administration. Foremost amongst them was **Knossós** on Crete, the centre of the Minoan civilization that dominated the Aegean. Some islands in the Ionian archipelago traded with the Minoans – wood from Kefalloniá's unique fir species, *Abies cephalonica*, was used in the construction of the palace of Knossós – but on the whole they stayed apart from Minoan culture.

Also important – and closer to the Ionian – were Mycenae, Tiryns and Argos in the Peloponnese. When the Minoans went into decline, around 1400 BC, **Mycenae**, south of Corinth and 150km from what is modern-day Pátra, became the seat of power. For at least two centuries, Mycenae ruled the region – and in turn gave its name to the period – until it in turn collapsed around 1200 BC. This is a period whose history and remains are bound up with **legends**, recounted most famously by **Homer**. Mycenae was the home of Agamemnon, engineer of the **Trojan War**, which was the subject of Homer's *Iliad*, and it was the end of the Trojan War that started Odysseus' long voyage home in the *Odyssey*. Debate continues over the provenance of the *Iliad* and *Odyssey*, both in terms of their authorship – it's likely that they were originally oral epics – and whether they were journalism, fiction or both. They seem to have been based in fact, although the amount of detail accepted varies between rival authorities. They certainly reflect the prevalence of violence, revenge and war as part of the culture, instigated and aggravated by trade and territorial rivalry (one reading of the *Odyssey* casts Odysseus as little more than a pirate and opportunist). The few surviving examples of architecture from this period – sections of vast fortifications seen on Corfu, Itháki, Kefalloniá and elsewhere, and known, with Homeric felicity, as Cyclopean walls – give a measure of the level of political tension and aggression in Mycenaean Greece.

At this time, and for centuries after, Greece was a collection of small independent regions, divided by clan loyalties and geography, vying for power, and forming and dissolving alliances as the power structure shifted. These miniature states succeeded or failed depending on their level of military or economic strength; Corfu, for example, established itself as a powerful naval force, and Kefalloniá was perfectly situated to become a trading post between the east and west Mediterranean.

The Dorian and Classical eras

As the circulation of trade and population around the Mediterranean increased, so these communities had to cope with the sudden and not always welcome arrival of new peoples and businesses that might supplant their economic power. The most radical alteration to the balance of power was the influx of northern **Dorians**: their unseating of Mycenaean rule was traditionally viewed as an "invasion" but is nowadays thought to have been a fundamental shift in the region's economy, which wrought drastic changes among the palace cultures and their naval forces in the eleventh century BC.

The Dorians imported their own religion, the twelve gods of **Olympus**, supplanting the widespread cult of Dionysus – deity of wine, fruitfulness and vegetation, and originally a goddess – and other female earth/fertility deities. The Dorian era was also notable for the appearance of a "Greek" **alphabet**, which is still recognizable alongside modern Greek and which replaced the "Linear A" script discovered on Crete, and the later "Linear B" Minoan/Mycenaean script.

City-states: Sparta, Athens and Corinth

The ninth century BC saw the birth of the Greek **city-state** (*polis*). Citizens – not just royalty or aristocracy – had a hand in government and community activities, and organized commerce and leisure. Economic and territorial expansionism increased, as did overseas trade, and this would shortly create a new class of manufacturers.

The city-state was defined by those who lived in it, and each state retained an individual identity and culture. Consequently, alliances between them were always temporary and tactical. Athens and Sparta, the Dorian city-state in the southern Peloponnese, were the two most powerful, and pursued a bitter rivalry for centuries.

Sparta was founded and run according to a militaristic regime which some today describe as fascistic. Males were subject to military service between the ages of 7 and 30, and young women were also expected to excel in athletics. **Athens** was the place that developed the – at the time, limited – notion of democracy. Its literal meaning, recognizable from modern Greek, is "people power", but this only applied to "freeborn" males, and not to women or slaves. As many as 40,000 Athenians were entitled to vote at the Assembly. Not only Athens, but every city-state had its **acropolis** or "high town", where polytheistic religious activity, under the aegis of Zeus, was focused.

After Athens and Sparta, **Corinth** was the next most powerful city-state, and the one that exercised the most influence on Corfu and the Ionian islands. Corinth was both a trading centre and a powerful naval force, with strong colonialist tendencies. As well as Corfu, it settled Syracuse (on Sicily) and Lefkádha, and would later seal tactical alliances with the city-states of Kefalloniá, notably Pale and Same. Affinities between regions and city-states shifted violently when it came to war: while Corfu prospered after it was colonized by Corinth in the eighth century BC, a fierce battle between the two was one of the causes of the **Peloponnesian Wars** in 431–404 BC. Similarly, Kefalloniá's city-states all took the Athenian side during that war, only to find themselves invaded by their distrustful allies, who used the island as a power base against Corinth.

Sparta emerged as nominal victors from the Peloponnesian Wars, but the years of warfare had drained all city-states of resources and commitment to the political system. The increasingly complex world of trade was subverting the older structures, and the invention and spread of **coinage** – an innovation as radical in its time as computerization today – was expanding and streamlining commercial life. A revitalized Athens, for example, was trading as far afield as the Black Sea, and Corfu had established trade links with Egypt.

Hellenistic and Roman Greece

The most important factor in the decline of the city-states was meanwhile developing beyond their boundaries, in the northern kingdom of **Macedonia** – a territory and title still fiercely contested today.

The Macedonian empire

Based at the Macedonian capital of Pella, **Philip II** (359–336 BC) forged a strong military and unitary force, extending his territories into Thrace. He then pushed south to take the rest of Greece (including the Ionian islands), in 338 BC, defeating the Athenians and their allies at the decisive Battle of Chaironeia, just east of Delphi. On his assassination in 336 BC, Philip was succeeded by his son, **Alexander the Great**, whose extraordinary thirteen-year career extended his empire into Persia and Egypt and even parts of modern India.

These vast gains began to crumble almost immediately after the death of Alexander in 323 BC. The empire was divided up into the three Macedonian dynasties of the world, **Hellenistic**, though Corfu and the Ionian islands fell victim to a series of regional takeovers, including early incursions by the Romans.

Roman Greece

Corfu, fatefully positioned between the heel of Italy and the Greek mainland, was the first city-state seized by the **Romans**, in 229 BC. The Romans subdued the rest of Greece over some seventy years of campaigns, from 215 to 146 BC. However, Rome allowed considerable autonomy in terms of law, religion and language, and Greece and its overlords coexisted fairly peacefully for the next four centuries. While Athens and Corinth remained important cities, the emphasis of power shifted north – particularly to towns such as Salonica (Thessaloníki) along the new Via Egnatia, a military and civil road connecting Rome and Byzantium via the port of Brundisium (modern Brindisi).

The Byzantine empire and medieval Greece

The shift in power towards the north of Greece was exacerbated by the decline of the Roman empire and its division into eastern and western halves. In 330 AD Emperor Constantine moved his capital to the Greek city of Byzantium, which was transformed Constantinople (modern Istanbul), the "new Rome" and spiritual and political capital of what became the **Byzantine empire**. While the last western Roman emperor was deposed by barbarian Goths in 476 AD, the oriental portion of the empire was to be the dominant Mediterranean power for some 700 years, and only in 1453 did it collapse completely.

Christianity

Although Christianity was formally introduced during the reign of Constantine, Christian preachers had been travelling in Greece since the first century AD – Corfu is believed to have first been evangelized in 37 AD. By the end of the fourth century, Christianity was the official state religion, its liturgies (still in use in the Greek Orthodox Church), creed and New Testament all written in Greek.

In the seventh century, **Constantinople** was besieged by Persians, and later by Arabs, but the Byzantine empire held, losing only Egypt, the least "Greek" of its territories. From the ninth to the eleventh century, it enjoyed a "golden age", both spiritual and political. Intrinsic in the Orthodox Byzantine faith was a sense of religious superiority, and the emperors saw Constantinople as a "new Jerusalem" for their "chosen people". This was the start of a diplomatic and ecclesiastical conflict with the Catholic West that would have disastrous consequences in subsequent centuries. As antagonism grew, the eastern and western patriarchs mutually excommunicated each other.

From the seventh through to the eleventh century, parts of **Byzantine Greece** became a rather provincial backwater. Administration was top-heavy and imperial taxation led to semi-autonomous provinces ruled by military generals, whose land was usually taken from bankrupt peasants. This alienation of the poor primed a disaffected populace for change, almost regardless of who implemented it.

Ionian and central Greece were particular vulnerable when waves of **Slavic raiders** staged numerous sorties from the Balkans in this period. At the same time, other groups moved down into the region from **central Europe** and were assimilated peaceably. From the thirteenth century on, immigrants from **Albania** fanned out across central Greece, the Peloponnese and nearby islands.

The Crusades, the Venetians and the Ottomans

With the Byzantine empire in steady decline, the eleventh century saw dramatic rearrangements of the power structure, particularly in the western parts of Greece. The **Normans** landed first at Corfu in 1081 and occupied the rest of the Ionian over the next two years. They returned to the mainland, with papal approval, a decade later on their way to liberate Jerusalem. This was only a foretaste of regular incursions into the Ionian region by the **Crusaders** on their way to Asia Minor. Richard the Lionheart, for example, landed on Corfu in 1192, but hastily left, fearing arrest by Byzantine officials who regarded him an enemy of the Orthodox Church.

In the **Fourth Crusade** of 1204, Venetians, Franks and Germans turned their armies directly on Byzantium and sacked and occupied Constantinople. These Latin princes and their followers, seeking new lands and kingdoms, divided the best of the empire among themselves. All that remained of Byzantium were three small rival states based on Nicaea in Asia Minor, Epirus in northwestern Greece and distant Trebizond on the Black Sea.

Each of these post-imperial factions regarded itself as the rightful successor to Byzantium, and the Ionian archipelago, like the rest of Greece, passed a turbulent half-century in which they vied for power with one another as well as with the Crusaders. The islands were a part of the **Despotate of Epirus**, which had its capital at Arta on the mainland opposite Corfu. When the most powerful of the successor states, the **Empire of Nicaea**, recaptured Constantinople in 1261, the Despots of Epirus refused to recognize the revived Byzantine administration until granted considerable local autonomy.

Venice, meanwhile, had made its intentions known back in 1204, demanding the islands when the spoils of Byzantium were being shared out. In 1350 it again made an offer for the Ionian islands, but was refused. However, local lords and landowners on Corfu sensed the way power was moving in the region, and saw they would be safest with the Venetians. In 1386, Venice, taking advantage of an interregnum in the Ionians, sent an army to conquer it and was asked to "protect" the island by its leaders. Over the next century and more, Venice set its sights on subsuming the other Ionian islands and Párga – the only toehold the Venetians managed to get on the mainland – into its empire.

In the meantime, the **Ottoman empire** grew more powerful in the east. Constantinople finally fell in 1453, and a decade later most of the former Byzantine empire was in Turkish hands. Even Zákynthos was seized for a time by the Turks, as were Kefalloniá and Itháki; tiny Paxí was sacked and most of its population enslaved by the Ottoman admiral, Barbarossa. Lefkádha passed between Turkish and Venetian rule several times, before finally joining the rest of the Ionian islands under Venice in 1684.

Under what Greeks refer to as the "Dark Ages" of Ottoman rule, much of present-day Greece passed into rural provincialism, taking refuge in a self-protective form of village life that has only recently been disrupted. Taxes and discipline, occasionally backed by acts of genocide against rebel communities, were inflicted by Turkish authorities, but estates passed into the hands of local chieftains, who often had considerable independence. Greek identity was sustained by the **Orthodox Church** which, despite instances of forced conversions to the Muslim faith, was allowed to continue. Monasteries organized schools, often secretly, and became the sole guardians of Byzantine culture, although many scholars and artists emigrated west, contributing to the Renaissance.

In contrast, the Ionian islands flourished under Venice. Extensive planting of olives established an industry that continues throughout the islands today. Venice's distinctive architecture, with its signature Lion of St Mark, was transposed to the towns of Corfu, Argostóli, Lefkádha and Zákynthos. Venice sustained the lords and landowners, and brutally crushed any attempts to propose land reform. This would eventually undermine them, particularly when islanders became involved in the **Filikí Etería**, or "Friendly Society", a secret group working to build opposition against the Turks.

The struggle for independence

As the Ottoman empire itself began showing signs of unravelling, opposition to Turkish rule became widespread, exemplified by the **klephts** (brigands) of the mountains. The French Revolution of 1789 gave fresh impetus to "freedom movements" and to the *Filikí Etería*, who were recruiting on the Ionian islands as well as among exiles living abroad. Napoleon's declaration of war on Venice fired visions of independence in the Ionian, but after he had defeated the Venetians in 1797 he sent emissaries to the archipelago to establish his own authority. Nevertheless, the **French** upended the social order and freed serfs, and jubilant crowds burnt the *Libro d'Oro* (the "Golden Book" that listed those aristocrats favoured by the Venetians) in impromptu celebrations in most of the Ionian capitals. In Corfu, the French embarked on an ambitious building programme, but this was cut short by Napoleon's downfall in 1814.

Throughout the Ionian, the French were replaced by the administrators of a militarily imposed **British** protectorate. The British introduced their own judicial and education systems, and set about building roads, reservoirs and other civic projects. Despite the benefits of these innovations, British rule was marked by a high-handedness – along with a tendency to use brute force to quell dissent – that won them few friends.

The War of Independence

By 1821, the *Filikí Etería* had assembled a motley coalition of klephts and theorists, who launched their insurrection against the Turks at the monastery of **Áyia Lávra** near Kalávrita in the Peloponnese, where on March 21 the Greek banner was openly raised by the local bishop, Yermanos. Despite punitive resistance by their British rulers, the Ionian islands enthusiastically if surreptitiously supported the rebellion with money, weapons and manpower. While much of the detail of the ensuing **War of Independence** is confusing – with landowners believing they were fighting to regain their traditional privileges, and peasants seeing it as a means of improving social conditions regardless of who was in power – the Greeks, through local and fragmented guerrilla campaigns, managed to present a coherent threat to Turkish rule.

Outside Greece, prestige and publicity for the insurrection was promoted by the arrival of a thousand or so **Philhellenes**, almost half of them German, though the most important was the English poet, **Lord Byron**, who died while training Greek forces at Messolóngi in April 1824. Byron's connections with the Ionian islands, in particular Kefalloniá, conferred on him an abiding heroic status here as elsewhere in Greece.

Greek guerrilla leaders such as **Theodhoros Kolokotronis** were responsible for the most significant military victories of the war, but the death of Byron had an immense effect on pub-

lic opinion in the West. Originally, aid for the Greek struggle had come neither from Orthodox Russia, nor from the Western powers of France and Britain, ravaged by the Napoleonic Wars. Yet when Messolóngi fell again to the Turks in 1827, these three powers finally agreed to seek autonomy for parts of Greece, and sent a combined fleet to confront the Turks, then sacking the Peloponnese. After an accidental sea battle in **Navarino Bay** destroyed almost the entire Turkish fleet, and heightened aggression from Russia, Turkey was forced to accept the existence of an autonomous Greece.

In 1830 Greek independence was confirmed by the Western powers and borders were drawn. These included just 800,000 of the six million Greeks living within the Ottoman empire, and the Greek territories were for the most part the poorest of the Classical and Byzantine lands, comprising Attica, the Peloponnese and the Argo-Saronic and Cycladic islands. The rich agricultural belt of Thessaly, Epirus in the west and Macedonia in the north remained in Turkish hands. Meanwhile, the British, despite championing the cause of Greek independence on the mainland, held onto the Ionian islands until they were finally ceded to Greece on **May 21, 1864**.

The emerging state

Modern Greece began as a republic, and its first president was a Corfiot. An aristocrat and career diplomat, **Ioannis Kapodhistrias** (1776–1831) had gained an impressive reputation negotiating with the British and Russians, and won widespread support for his defence of Lefkádha against the Albanian ruler of Epirus, Ali Pasha. Kapodhistrias concentrated on creating a viable structure for the emerging Greek state in the face of diverse protagonists from the independence struggle, though his later career was marred by unpopular acts of nepotism and autocracy. Almost inevitably, he was assassinated – in 1831, by chieftains from the Máni peninsula – and perhaps equally inevitably, the Western powers who had forced the resolution of the independence issue stepped in. They created a monarchy and installed a Bavarian prince, **Otho**.

The new king proved to be autocratic and insensitive, giving official posts to fellow Germans and dismissing suggestions by the landless peasantry that the old estates be redistributed. A popular revolt forced him from the country in

1862, and the Europeans produced a new prince, this time from Denmark. Britain ceded the Ionian islands to Greece as part of this arrangement, more or less as a sweetener. **George I** proved more capable than his predecessor: he built the first railways and roads, introduced limited land reforms in the Peloponnese and oversaw the first expansion of the Greek borders.

The Megáli Idhéa and war

From the very beginning, the unquestioned motive force of Greek foreign policy was the **Megáli Idhéa** (Great Idea) of liberating Greek populations outside the country and incorporating the old territories of Byzantium into the kingdom. In 1878 **Thessaly**, along with southern Epirus, was ceded to Greece by the Turks. Less illustriously, the Greeks failed in 1897 to achieve *enosis* (union) with **Crete** by attacking Turkish forces on the mainland, and in the process virtually bankrupted the state. The island was, however, placed under a high commissioner, appointed by the great powers, and in 1913 became a part of Greece.

It was from Crete, also, that the most distinguished Greek statesman emerged. **Eleftherios Venizelos**, having led a civilian campaign for his island's liberation, was in 1910 elected as Greek prime minister. Two years later he organized an alliance of Balkan powers to fight the **Balkan Wars** (1912–13), campaigns that saw the Turks virtually driven from Europe. With Greek borders extended to include the northeast Aegean, northern Thessaly, central Epirus and parts of Macedonia, the *Megáli Idhéa* was approaching reality. At the same time, Venizelos proved himself a shrewd manipulator of domestic public opinion by revising the constitution and introducing a series of liberal social reforms.

Division, however, was to appear with the outbreak of **World War I**. Venizelos urged Greek entry on the British side, seeing in the conflict possibilities for the "liberation" of Greeks in Thrace and Asia Minor, but the new king, Constantine I, married to a sister of the German Kaiser, imposed a policy of neutrality. Eventually Venizelos set up a revolutionary government in Thessaloníki, and in 1917 Greek troops entered the war to join the French, British and Serbians in the **Macedonian campaign**. On the capitulation of Bulgaria and Ottoman Turkey, the Greeks occupied Thrace, and Venizelos presented at Versailles demands for the predominantly Greek region of Smyrna on the Asia Minor coast.

It was the beginning of one of the most disastrous episodes in modern Greek history. Venizelos was authorized to move forces into Smyrna in 1919, but by then Allied support had evaporated and in Turkey itself a new nationalist movement was taking power under Mustafa Kemal, or **Atatürk** as he came to be known. In 1920 Venizelos lost the elections and monarchist factions took over, their aspirations unmitigated by the Cretan's skill in foreign diplomacy. Greek forces were ordered to advance upon Ankara in an attempt to bring Atatürk to terms.

The so-called **Anatolian campaign** ignominiously collapsed in summer 1922, when Turkish troops forced the Greeks back to the coast and a hurried evacuation from **Smyrna**. The Turks moved in and systematically massacred whatever remained of the Armenian and Greek populations before burning most of the city to the ground.

The exchange of populations

This ensuing Treaty of Lausanne in 1923 ordered the **exchange of religious minorities** from both countries. Turkey was to accept 390,000 Muslims from Greece. Greece, mobilized for a decade and with a population of less than five million, was faced with the resettlement of over 1,300,000 Christian refugees. The *Megáli Idhéa* ceased to be a viable blueprint.

The effect on Greek society was far-reaching. The great agricultural estates of Thessaly were finally redistributed, both to Greek tenants and refugee farmers, and huge shanty towns developed around Athens, Pireás and other cities, a spur to the country's then almost nonexistent industry.

Political reaction was swift. A group of army officers assembled after the retreat from Smyrna "invited" King Constantine to abdicate and executed five of his ministers. Democracy was nominally restored with the proclamation of a republic, but for much of the next decade changes in government were brought about by factions within the armed forces. Meanwhile, among the urban refugee population, unions were being formed and the Greek **Communist Party** (KKE) was established.

By 1936 the Communist Party had enough democratic support to hold the balance of power in parliament, and would have done so had not the army and the by then restored king decided otherwise. Yiorgos (George) II had been voted in by a plebiscite held – and almost certainly manipulated – the previous year, and so presided over an increasingly factionalized parliament.

The Metaxas dictatorship

In April 1936, George II appointed a Kefallonian, **General Ioannis Metaxas**, as prime minister, despite the fact that Metaxas only had the support of six elected deputies. Immediately a series of KKE-organized strikes broke out and the king, ignoring attempts to form a broad liberal coalition, dissolved parliament without setting a date for new elections. It was a blatantly unconstitutional move and opened the way for five years of ruthless and at times absurd dictatorship.

Metaxas averted a general strike with military force and proceeded to set up a state based on fascist models of the time. Left-wing and trade union opponents were imprisoned or forced into exile, a state youth movement and secret police set up, and rigid censorship, extending even to passages of Thucydides, imposed. It was, however, at least a Greek dictatorship, and though Metaxas was sympathetic to Nazi organization he completely opposed German or Italian domination.

World War II and the civil war

The Italians tried to provoke Greece into **World War II** by torpedoing the Greek cruiser *Elli* in Tínos harbour in August 1940. The Greeks made no response. However, when Mussolini occupied Albania and, on October 28, 1940, sent an ultimatum demanding passage through Greece for his troops, Metaxas' legendary riposte to the Italian foreign minister was *"Óhi"* (No). (In fact, his response, in the mutually understood French, was *"C'est la guerre."*) The date marked the entry of Greece into the war, and Óhi Day is still celebrated as a national holiday.

Occupation and resistance

Fighting as a nation in a sudden unity of crisis, the Greeks drove Italian forces from the mainland and in the operation took control of the long-coveted and predominantly Greek-populated northern Epirus. The Ionian islands found themselves on the front line, and were taken by the Italians. The Greek army, however, lost its impetus during a harsh winter fighting in the mountains, and British backup never materialized.

In April the following year Nazi columns swept through Yugoslavia and across the Greek mainland, effectively reversing the only Axis defeat to date, and by the end of May 1941 airborne and seaborne **German invasion** forces had completed the occupation. Metaxas had died before their arrival, while King George and his new self-appointed ministers fled into exile in Cairo. Few Greeks of any political persuasion were sad to see them go.

The joint **Italian–German–Bulgarian Axis occupation** of Greece was among the bitterest experiences of the European war. Nearly half a million Greek civilians starved to death as all available food was requisitioned to feed occupying armies, and entire villages throughout the mainland and especially on Crete were burnt and slaughtered at the least hint of Resistance activity. In the Ionian, even the olive crop was sequestered, driving the olive industry underground.

The Nazis supervised the deportation to concentration camps of virtually the entire **Greek Jewish population**. This was at the time a sizeable community. Thessaloníki – where former UN and Austrian president Kurt Waldheim worked for Nazi intelligence – contained the largest Jewish population of any Balkan city, and there were significant populations in all Greek mainland towns and on many islands. Over two thousand Jews were rounded up in Corfu Town alone for transportation; fewer than a hundred returned.

With a quisling government in Athens – and an unpopular, discredited royalist group in Cairo – the focus of Greek political and military action over the next four years passed largely to the **EAM**, or National Liberation Front. By 1943 it was in virtual control of most areas of the country, working with the British on tactical operations, with its own army (**ELAS**), navy and both civil and secret police forces. On the whole, it commanded popular support, and it offered an obvious framework for the resumption of postwar government.

However, most of its membership was communist, and the British prime minister, **Churchill**, was determined to reinstate the monarchy. Even with two years of the war to run it became obvious that there could be no peaceable post-liberation regime other than an EAM-dominated republic. Accordingly, in August 1943 representatives from each of the main Resistance movements – including two non-communist groups – flew from a makeshift airstrip in Thessaly to ask for guarantees from the "government" in Cairo that the king would not return unless a plebiscite had first voted in his favour. Neither the Greek nor British authorities would consider the proposal, and the one possibility of averting civil war was lost.

The EAM contingent returned divided, as perhaps the British had intended, and a conflict broke out between those who favoured taking peaceful control of any government imposed after liberation, and the hardline Stalinist ideologues, who believed such a situation should not be allowed to develop.

In October 1943, with fears of an imminent British landing force and takeover, ELAS launched a full-scale attack upon its Greek rivals; by the following February, when a ceasefire was arranged, they had wiped out all but the EDES, a right-wing grouping suspected of collaboration with the Germans. At the same time other forces were at work, with both the British and Americans infiltrating units into Greece in order to prevent the establishment of communist government when the Germans began withdrawing their forces.

Civil war

In fact, as the Germans began to leave in October 1944, most of the EAM leadership agreed to join a British-sponsored "official" **interim government**. It quickly proved a tactical error, however, for with ninety percent of the countryside under their control the communists were given only one-third representation; the king showed no sign of renouncing his claims; and, in November, Allied forces ordered ELAS to disarm. On December 3 all pretences of civility or neutrality were dropped; the police fired on a communist demonstration in Athens and fighting broke out between ELAS and **British troops**, in the so-called **Dhekemvrianá** battle of Athens.

A truce of sorts was negotiated at Várkiza the following spring, but the agreement was never implemented. The army, police and civil service remained in right-wing hands and, while collaborators were often allowed to retain their positions, left-wing sympathizers, many of whom were not communists, were systematically excluded. The elections of 1946 were won by the right-wing parties, followed by a plebiscite in favour of the king's return. By 1947 guerrilla activity had again reached the scale of a full **civil war**.

In the interim, King George had died and been succeeded by his brother Paul (with his consort Frederika), while the **Americans** had taken over the British role, and begun putting into action the

Cold War **Truman doctrine**. In 1947 they took virtual control of Greece, their first significant postwar experiment in anti-communist intervention. Massive economic and military aid was given to a client Greek government, with a prime minister whose documents had to be countersigned by the American Mission in order to become valid.

In the mountains US "military advisers" supervised **campaigns against ELAS**, and there were mass arrests, court martials and imprisonments – a kind of "White Terror" – lasting until 1951. Over three thousand executions were recorded, including a number of Jehovah's Witnesses, "a sect proved to be under communist domination", according to US Ambassador Grady.

In the autumn of 1949, with the Yugoslav–Greek border closed after Tito's rift with Stalin, the last ELAS guerrillas finally admitted defeat, retreating into Albania from their strongholds on Mount Grámmos. Atrocities had been committed on both sides, including, from the Left, wide-scale destruction of monasteries and the dubious evacuation of children from "combat areas" (as told in Nicholas Gage's virulently anti-communist book, *Eleni*). Such errors, as well as the hopelessness of fighting an American-backed army, undoubtedly lost ELAS much support.

Reconstruction American-style: 1950–67

It was a demoralized, shattered Greece that emerged into the Western political orbit of the 1950s. It was also perforce American-dominated, enlisted into the Korean War in 1950 and NATO the following year. In domestic politics, the US Embassy – still giving the orders – installed a winner-take-all electoral system, which was to ensure victory for the Right over the next twelve years. All leftist activity was banned; those individuals who were not herded into political "re-education" camps or dispatched by firing squads, legal or vigilante, went into exile throughout Eastern Europe, to return only after 1974.

The American-backed, highly conservative **"Greek Rally"** party, led by General Papagos, won the first decisive post-civil war elections in 1952. After the general's death, the party's leadership was taken over – and to an extent liberalized – by **Konstandinos Karamanlis**. Under his rule, stability of a kind was established and some economic advances registered, particularly after the revival of Greece's traditional German trade links. However, the 1950s was also a decade that saw wholesale **depopulation of the villages** as migrants sought work in Australia, America and western Europe, or the larger Greek cities.

The main crisis in foreign policy throughout this period was **Cyprus**, where a long terrorist campaign was waged by Greeks opposing British rule, and there was the sporadic threat of a new Greek–Turkish war. A temporary and unworkable solution was forced on the island by Britain in 1960, granting independence without the possibility of self-determination or union with Greece. Much of the traditional Greek–British goodwill was destroyed by the issue, with Britain seen to be acting with regard only for its two military bases (over which it still retains sovereignty).

By 1961, unemployment, the Cyprus issue and the imposition of US nuclear bases on Greek soil were changing the political climate, and when Karamanlis was again elected there was strong suspicion of a fraud arranged by the king and army. Strikes became frequent in industry and even agriculture, and King Paul and autocratic, fascist-inclined Queen Frederika were openly attacked in parliament and at protest demonstrations. The Far Right grew uneasy about **"communist insurgence"** and, losing confidence in their own electoral influence, arranged the assassination of left-wing deputy **Grigoris Lambrakis** in Thessaloníki in May 1963. (The assassination, and its subsequent cover-up, is the subject of Vassilis Vassilikos's thriller *Z*, filmed by Costa-Gavras.) It was against this volatile background that Karamanlis resigned, lost the subsequent elections and left the country.

The new government – the first controlled from outside the Greek Right since 1935 – was formed by **Yiorgos Papandreou's** Centre Union Party, and had a decisive majority of nearly fifty seats. It was to last, however, for under two years as conservative forces rallied to thwart its progress. In this the chief protagonists were the army officers and their constitutional commander-in-chief, the new king, 23-year-old **Konstandinos (Constantine) II**.

Since power in Greece depended on a pliant military as well as a network of political appointees, Papandreou's most urgent task in order to govern securely and effectively was to reform the armed forces. His first minister of defence proved incapable of the task and, while he was investigating the right-wing plot that was thought to have rigged the 1961 election, "evidence" was produced of a leftist conspiracy connected with Papandreou's son Andhreas (himself a minister in the government).

The allegations grew to a crisis and Yiorgos Papandreou decided to assume the defence portfolio himself, a move for which the king refused to give the necessary sanction. He then resigned in order to gain approval at the polls, but the king would not order fresh elections, instead persuading members of the Centre Union – chief among them **Konstandinos Mitsotakis**, the recent Greek premier – to defect and organize a coalition government. Punctuated by strikes, resignations and mass demonstrations, this lasted for a year and a half until new elections were eventually set for May 28, 1967. They failed to take place.

The colonels' junta: 1967–74

It was a foregone conclusion that Papandreou's party would win popular support in the polls against the discredited coalition partners. And it was equally certain that there would be some sort of anti-democratic action to try and prevent them from taking power. Disturbed by the party's leftward shift, King Constantine was said to have briefed senior generals for a coup d'état, to take place ten days before the elections. However, he was caught by surprise, as was nearly everyone else, by the **coup of April 21, 1967**, staged by a group of "unknown" colonels. It was, in the words of Andhreas Papandreou, "the first successful CIA military putsch on the European continent".

The **colonels' junta**, having taken control of the means of power, was sworn in by the king and survived the half-hearted counter-coup which he subsequently attempted to organize. It was an overtly fascist regime, absurdly styling itself as the true "Revival of Greek Orthodoxy" against Western "corrupting influences", though in reality its ideology was nothing more than warmed-up dogma from the Metaxas era.

All political activity was banned, trade unions were forbidden to recruit or meet, the press was so heavily censored that many papers stopped printing, and thousands of "communists" were arrested, imprisoned and often tortured. Among them were both Papandreous, the composer Mikis Theodorakis (deemed "unfit to stand trial" after three months in custody) and Amalia Fleming (widow of Alexander). The best-known Greek actress, Melina Mercouri, was stripped of her citizenship *in absentia* and thousands of prominent Greeks joined her in exile. Culturally, the colonels put an end to popular music (closing down most of the *rembétika* clubs) and inflicted ludicrous censorship on literature and the theatre, including (as under Metaxas) a ban on production of the Classical tragedies.

The colonels lasted for seven years, opposed (especially after the first year) by the majority of the Greek people, excluded from the European Community, but propped up and given massive aid by US presidents **Lyndon Johnson** and **Richard Nixon**. To them and the CIA the junta's Greece was not an unsuitable client state; human rights considerations were considered unimportant, orders were placed for sophisticated military technology, and foreign investment on terms highly unfavourable to Greece was open to multinational corporations.

Opposition was from the beginning voiced by exiled Greeks in London, the United States and western Europe, but only in 1973 did demonstrations break out openly in Greece. On November 17 the students of **Athens Polytechnic** began an occupation of their buildings. The ruling clique lost its nerve; armoured vehicles stormed the Polytechnic gates and a still-undetermined number of students were killed. Martial law was tightened and junta chief **Colonel Papadopoulos** was replaced by the even more obnoxious and reactionary **General Ioannides**, head of the secret police.

The return to civilian rule: 1975–81

The end of the ordeal, however, came within a year as the dictatorship embarked on a disastrous political adventure in **Cyprus**. By attempting to topple the Makarios government and impose *énosis* (union) on the island, they provoked a Turkish invasion and occupation of forty percent of the Cypriot territory. The army finally mutinied and **Konstandinos Karamanlis** was invited to return from Paris to take office again. He swiftly negotiated a ceasefire (but no solution) in Cyprus, withdrew temporarily from NATO and warned that US bases would have to be removed except where they specifically served Greek interest. In November 1974 Karamanlis and his *Néa Dhimokratía* (New Democracy or ND) party was rewarded by a sizeable majority in elections, with a centrist and socialist opposition, including PASOK, a new party led by Andhreas Papandreou.

The election of *Néa Dhimokratía* was in every sense a safe conservative option, but to

Karamanlis's enduring credit it oversaw an effective and firm return to democratic stability, even legitimizing the KKE (Communist Party) for the first time in its history. Karamanlis also held a referendum on the monarchy – in which 59 percent of Greeks rejected the return of Constantine – and instituted in its place a French-style presidency, the post which he himself occupied from 1980 to 1985. Economically there were limited advances, although these were more than offset by inflationary defence spending (the result of renewed tension with Turkey), hastily negotiated entrance into the EC (as the EU was then known) and the decision to let the drachma float after decades of its being artificially fixed at thirty to the US dollar.

Crucially, though, Karamanlis failed to deliver on vital reforms in bureaucracy, social welfare and education and, though the worst figures of the junta were brought to trial, the ordinary faces of Greek political life and administration were little changed. By 1981 inflation was hovering around 25 percent, and it was estimated that tax evasion was depriving the state of one-third of its annual budget. In foreign policy the US bases had remained and it was felt that Greece, back in NATO, was still acting as little more than an American satellite. The traditional Right was demonstrably inadequate to the task at hand.

PASOK: 1981–89

Change – *allayí* – was the watchword of the election campaign which swept **Andhreas Papandreou**'s Panhellenic Socialist Movement, better known by the acronym **PASOK**, to power on October 18, 1981. The victory meant a chance for Papandreou to form the first socialist government in Greek history and break a near fifty-year monopoly of authoritarian right-wing rule. With so much at stake the campaign had been passionate even by Greek standards, and PASOK's victory was greeted with euphoria both by the generation whose political voice had been silenced by defeat in the civil war and by a large proportion of the young. They were hopes which perhaps ran naively and dangerously high.

The victory, at least, was conclusive. PASOK won 174 of the 300 parliamentary seats and the Communist KKE returned another thirteen deputies, one of whom was the composer Mikis Theodorakis. *Néa Dhimokratía* moved into unaccustomed opposition. There appeared to be no obstacle to the implementation of a radical **social-**

ist **programme**: devolution of power to local authorities, the socialization of industry (though it was never clear how this was to be different from nationalization), improvement of the social services, a purge of bureaucratic inefficiency and malpractice, the end of bribery and corruption as a way of life, an independent and dignified foreign policy following expulsion of US bases and withdrawal from NATO and the European Community.

A change of style was promised, too, replacing the country's long traditions of authoritarianism and bureaucracy with openness and dialogue. Even more radically, where Greek political parties had long been the personal followings of charismatic leaders, PASOK was to be a party of ideology and principle, dependent on no single individual member. Or so, at least, thought some of the youthful PASOK political enthusiasts.

The new era started with a bang. The wartime Resistance was officially recognized; hitherto they hadn't been allowed to take part in any celebrations, wreath-layings or other ceremonies. Peasant women were granted pensions for the first time – 3000dr a month, the same as their outraged husbands – and wages were indexed to the cost of living. In addition, civil marriage was introduced, family law reformed in favour of wives and mothers, and equal rights legislation was put on the statute book.

These popular **reformist moves** seemed to mark a break with the past, and the atmosphere had indeed changed. Greeks no longer lowered their voices to discuss politics in public places or wrapped their opposition newspaper in the respectably conservative *Kathimerini*. At first there were real fears that the climate would be too much for the military and they would once again intervene to choke a dangerous experiment in democracy, especially when Andhreas Papandreou assumed the defence portfolio himself in a move strongly reminiscent of his father's attempt to remove the king's appointee in 1965. But he went out of his way to soothe **military susceptibilities**, increasing their salaries, buying new weaponry and being super-fastidious in his attendance at military functions.

The end of the honeymoon

Nothing if not a populist, Papandreou promised a bonanza he must have known, as a skilled and experienced economist, he could not deliver. As a result he pleased nobody on the **economic** front.

He could not fairly be blamed for the inherited lack of investment, low productivity, deficiency in managerial and labour skills and other chronic problems besetting the Greek economy. On the other hand, he certainly aggravated the situation in the early days of his first government by allowing his supporters to indulge in violently anti-capitalist rhetoric, and by the prosecution and humiliation of the Tsatsos family, owners of one of Greece's few modern and profitable businesses – cement, in this case – for the illegal export of capital, something of which every Greek with any savings is guilty. These were cheap victories and were not backed by any programme of public investment, while the only "socializations" were of hopelessly lame-duck companies.

Faced with this sluggish economy, and burdened with the additional charges of (marginally) improved social benefits and wage indexing, Papandreou's government had also to cope with the effects of **world recession**, which always hit Greece with a delayed effect compared with its more advanced European partners. **Shipping**, the country's main foreign-currency earner, was devastated. Remittances from émigré workers fell off as they joined the lines of the unemployed in their host countries, and tourism receipts diminished under the dual impact of recession and Reagan's warning to Americans to stay away from insecure and terrorist-prone Athens airport.

With huge quantities of imported goods continuing to be sucked into the country in the absence of domestic production, the **foreign debt** topped £10 billion in 1986, with inflation at 25 percent and the balance of payments deficit approaching £1 billion. Greece also began to experience the social strains of **unemployment** for the first time. Not that it didn't exist before, but it had always been concealed as underemployment by the family and the rural structure of the economy – as well as by the absence of statistics.

The result of all this was that Papandreou had to eat his words. A modest spending spree, joy at the defeat of the Right, the popularity of his Greece-for-the-Greeks foreign policy and some much-needed reforms saw him through into a **second term**, with an electoral victory in June 1985 scarcely less triumphant than the first. But the complacent and, frankly, dishonest slogan was "Vote PASOK for Even Better Days". By October they had imposed a two-year wage freeze and import restrictions, abolished the wage-indexing scheme and devalued the drachma by fifteen percent.

Papandreou's fat was pulled out of the fire by none other than that former bogeyman, the **European Community**, which offered a huge two-part loan on condition that an IMF-style **austerity programme** was maintained.

The political fallout of such a classic right-wing deflation, accompanied by shameless soliciting for foreign investment, was the alienation of the communists and most of PASOK's own political constituency. Increasingly autocratic – ironic given the early ideals of PASOK as a new kind of party – Papandreou's response to **dissent** was to fire recalcitrant trade union leaders and expel some three hundred members of his own party. Assailed by strikes, the government appeared to have lost direction completely. In local elections in October 1986 it lost a lot of ground to *Néa Dhimokratía*, including the mayoralties of the three major cities, Athens, Thessaloníki and Pátra.

Papandreou assured the nation that he had taken the message to heart but all that followed was a minor government reshuffle and a panicky attempt to undo the ill-feeling caused by an incredible freeing of **rent controls** at a time when all wage-earners were feeling the pinch badly. Early in 1987 he went further and sacked all the remaining PASOK veterans in his cabinet, including his son, though it is said, probably correctly, that this was a palliative to public opinion. The new cabinet was so un-socialist that even the right-wing press called it **"centrist"**.

Similar about-turns took place in **foreign policy**. The initial anti-US, anti-NATO and anti-EC rhetoric was immensely popular, and understandably so for a people shamelessly bullied by bigger powers for the past 150 years. There was some high-profile nose-thumbing, like refusing to join EC partners in condemning Jaruzelski's Polish regime, or the Soviet downing of a Korean airliner, or Syrian involvement in terrorist bomb-planting. There were some forgettable embarrassments, too, like suggesting Gaddafi's Libya provided a suitable model for alternative socialist development, and the Mitterrand–Gaddafi–Papandreou "summit" in Crete, which an infuriated Mitterrand felt he had been inveigled into on false pretences.

Much was made of a strategic opening to the Arab world. Yasser Arafat, for example, was the first "head of state" to be received in Athens under the PASOK government. Given Greece's geographical position and historical ties, it was an imaginative and appropriate policy. But if Arab investment was hoped for, it never materialized.

In stark contrast to his early promises and rhetoric, the "realistic" policies that Papandreou pursued were far more conciliatory towards his big Western brothers. This was best exemplified by the fact that **US bases** remained in Greece, largely due to the fear that snubbing NATO would lead to Greece being exposed to Turkish aggression, still the only issue that unites the main parties to any degree. As for the once-reviled **European Community**, Greece had become an established beneficiary and its leader was hardly about to bite the hand that feeds.

Scandal

Even as late as mid-1988, despite the many betrayals of Papandreou, despite his failure to clean up the public services and do away with the system of patronage and corruption, and despite a level of popular displeasure that brought a million striking, demonstrating workers into the streets (February 1987), it seemed unlikely that PASOK would be toppled in the following year's **elections**.

This was due mainly to the lack of a credible alternative. Konstandinos Mitsotakis, a bitter personal enemy of Papandreou's since 1965, when his defection had brought down his father's government and set in train the events that culminated in the junta, was an unconvincing and unlikeable character at the helm of *Néa Dhimokratía*. Meanwhile, the liberal centre had disappeared and the main communist party, KKE, appeared trapped in a Stalinist time warp under the leadership of Harilaos Florakis. Only the *Ellinikí Aristerá* (Greek Left), formerly the European wing of the KKE, seemed to offer any sensible alternative programme, and they had a precariously small following.

So PASOK could have been in a position to win a third term by default, as it were, when a combination of spectacular **own goals**, plus perhaps a general shift to the Right, influenced by the cataclysmic events in eastern Europe, conspired against them.

First came the extraordinary cavortings of the prime minister himself. Towards the end of 1988, the 70-year-old Papandreou was flown to Britain for open-heart surgery. He took the occasion, with fear of death presumably rocking his judgement, to make public a year-long liaison with a 34-year-old Olympic Airways hostess, **Dimitra "Mimi" Liani**. The international news pictures of an old man shuffling about after a young blonde, to the public humiliation of Margaret, his American-born wife, and his family, were not popular (Papandreou later divorced Margaret and married Mimi). His integrity was further questioned when he missed several important public engagements – including a ceremony commemorating the victims of the 1987 Kalamáta earthquake – and was pictured out with Mimi, reliving his youth in nightclubs.

The real damage, however, was done by **economic scandals**. It came to light that a PASOK minister had passed off Yugoslav corn as Greek in a sale to the EC. Then, far more seriously, it emerged that a self-made con man, **Yiorgos Koskotas**, director of the **Bank of Crete**, had embezzled £120 million of deposits and, worse still, slipped though the authorities' fingers and sought asylum in the US. Certain PASOK ministers and even Papandreou himself were implicated in the scandal. Further damage was done by allegations of illegal **arms dealings** by still more government ministers.

United in disgust at this corruption, the other Left parties – KKE and *Ellinikí Aristerá* – formed a coalition, the **Synaspismós**, taking support still further from PASOK.

Three bites at the cherry

In this climate of disaffection, an inconclusive result to the **June 1989 election** was no real surprise. What was less predictable, however, was the formation of a bizarre **"catharsis" coalition** of conservatives and communists, united in the avowed intent of cleansing PASOK's increasingly Augean stables. That this coalition emerged was basically down to Papandreou. The *Synaspismós* would have formed a government with PASOK but set one condition for doing so – that Papandreou stepped down as prime minister – and the old man would have none of it. In the deal finally cobbled together between the Left and *Néa Dhimokratía*, Mitsotakis was denied the premiership, too, having to make way for his compromise party colleague, **Tzanetakis**.

During the three months that the coalition lasted, the *kathársis* turned out to be largely a question of burying the knife as deeply as possible into the ailing body of PASOK. Andhreas Papandreou and three other ministers were officially accused of involvement in the Koskotas affair – though there was no time to set up their **trial** before the Greek people returned once again to the polls. In any case, the chief witness and protagonist in the affair, Koskotas himself, was still imprisoned in America, awaiting extradition proceedings.

Contrary to the Right's hope that publicly accusing Papandreou and his cohorts of criminal behaviour would pave the way for a *Néa Dhimokratía* victory, PASOK actually made a slight recovery in the **November 1989 elections**, though the result was still inconclusive. This time the Left resolutely refused to do deals with anyone and the result was a consensus caretaker government under the neutral aegis of an academic called Zolotas, who was pushed into the prime minister's office, somewhat unwillingly it seemed, from Athens University. His only mandate was to see that the country didn't go off the rails completely while preparations were made for yet more elections. These took place in **April 1990** with the same captains at the command of their ships and with the *Synaspismós* having completed its about-turn to the extent that in the five single-seat constituencies (the other 295 seats are drawn from multiple-seat constituencies in a complicated system of reinforced proportional representation), they supported independent candidates jointly with PASOK. Greek communists are good at about-turns, though; after all, composer Mikis Theodorakis, musical torchbearer of the Left during the dark years of the junta, and formerly a KKE MP, was by now standing for *Néa Dhimokratía*.

On the night, *Néa Dhimokratía* scraped home with a majority of one, later doubled with the defection of a centrist, and **Mitsotakis** finally got to achieve his dream of becoming prime minister. The only other memorable feature of the election was the first parliamentary representation for a party of the Turkish minority in Thrace, and for the ecologists – a focus for many disaffected PASOK voters.

A return to the Right: Mitsotakis

On assuming power, Mitsotakis followed a course of **austerity measures** to try and revive the chronically ill economy. Little headway was made, though given the world recession it was hardly surprising. Greek inflation was still approaching twenty percent annually and, at nearly ten percent, unemployment remained a major problem. The latter has been exacerbated since 1990 by the arrival of thousands of impoverished **Albanians**, particularly in Epirus and the northern Ionian islands. They have formed something of an underclass, especially those who aren't ethnically Greek and are prey to vilification for all manner of ills. They have also led to the first real immigration measures in a country whose population is more used to being on the other side of such laws.

Other conservative measures introduced by Mitsotakis included laws to combat strikes and terrorism. The terrorist issue had been a perennial source of worry for Greeks since the appearance in the mid-1980s of a group called **Dhekaeftá Noemvríou** ("November 17", the date of the colonels' attack on the Polytechnic in 1973). They have killed a number of industrialists and attacked buildings of military attachés and airlines in Athens, so far without any police arrests. It hardly seemed likely that Mitsotakis's laws, however, were the solution. They stipulated that statements by the group could no longer be published, and led to one or two newspaper editors being jailed for a few days for defiance – much to everyone's embarrassment.

The **anti-strike laws** threatened severe penalties but were equally ineffectual, as breakdowns in public transport, electricity and rubbish collection all too frequently illustrated. As for the **Koskotas scandal**, the villain of the piece was eventually extradited and gave evidence for the prosecution against Papandreou and various of his ministers. The trial was televised and proved as popular as any soap opera, as indeed it should have been, given the twists of high drama – which included one of the defendants, Koutsoyiorgas, dying in court of a heart attack in front of the cameras. The case against Papandreou gradually petered out and he was officially acquitted in early 1992. The two other surviving ministers, Tsovolas and Petsos, were convicted and given short prison sentences.

The great showpiece trial thus went with a whimper rather than a bang, and did nothing to enhance Mitsotakis's position. If anything, it served to increase sympathy for Papandreou, who was felt to have been unfairly victimized. The real villain of the piece, Koskotas, was eventually convicted of major fraud and is now serving a lengthy jail sentence.

The Macedonian question

Increasingly unpopular because of the desperate austerity measures, and perceived as ineffective and out of his depth on the international scene, the last thing Mitsotakis needed was a major foreign policy headache. That is exactly what he got when, in 1991, one of the breakaway republics of the for-

mer Yugoslavia named itself **Macedonia**, thereby injuring Greek national pride and sparking off vehement protests at home and abroad. Diplomatically, the Greeks fought tooth and nail against the use of the name, but their position became increasingly isolated, and by 1993 the new country had gained official recognition, from both the EC and the UN – albeit under the convoluted title of the Former Yugoslav Republic of Macedonia (FYROM).

Salt was rubbed into Greek wounds when the FYROM started using the star of Veryína as a national symbol on their new flag. Greece still refuses to call its northerly neighbour Macedonia, instead referring to it as *Ta Skópia* (Skopje) after the capital – and you can't go far in Greece these days without coming across officially placed protestations that "Macedonia was, is, and always will be Greek and only Greek!"

The pendulum swings back

In effect, the Macedonian problem more or less directly led to Mitsotakis's political demise. In the early summer of 1993 his ambitious young foreign minister, **Andonis Samaras**, disaffected with his leader, jumped on the bandwagon of resurgent Greek nationalism to set up his own party, **Politikí Ánixi** (Political Spring), after leaving *Néa Dhimokratía*. His platform, still right-wing, was largely based on action over Macedonia and during the summer of 1993 more ND MPs broke ranks, making *Politikí Ánixi* a force to be reckoned with. When parliament was called upon to approve severe new budget proposals, it became clear that the government lacked support, and early elections were called for October 1993. Mitsotakis had also been plagued for nearly a year by accusations of phone-tapping, and had been linked with a nasty and complicated contracts scandal centred around a national company, AGET.

Many of ND's disillusioned supporters reverted directly to PASOK, and a frail-looking **Papandreou**, now well into his seventies, romped to election victory, becoming prime minister for the third time. PASOK immediately fulfilled two of its pre-election promises by removing restrictions on the reporting of statements by terrorist groups and renationalizing the Athens city bus company. The imposition of a trade embargo on Macedonia, however, landed the new government in hot water with the European Court of Justice. PASOK also set about improving the health system, and began to set the wheels in motion for Mitsotakis to be tried for his alleged misdemeanours – though all charges were mysteriously dropped in January 1995, apparently on the orders of Papandreou himself. Meanwhile, the minister of public order, Papathemelis, made the government extremely unpopular with the youth and bar/restaurant owners by reintroducing licensing laws and imposing, for the first time, minimum age requirements.

Both the major parties received a good slap in the face at the **Euroelections** of June 1994, losing ground to the smaller parties. The major winner was Samaras, whose *Politikí Ánixi* almost doubled its share of the vote, while the two left-wing parties both fared quite well.

In the spring of 1995 presidential elections were held in parliament to designate a successor to the 88-year-old Karamanlis. The winner, with support from *Politikí Ánixi* and PASOK, was **Costis Stephanopoulos**, a former lawyer with a clean-cut reputation, who had been put forward by Samaras and welcomed by Papandreou in a deal that would allow their party to see out their four-year term.

In November 1995, Greece lifted its embargo on Macedonia, opening its mutual borders to tourism and trade; in return for this, the Macedonians agreed to drop controversial clauses from their constitution and replace the offending star in their flag. Relationships were almost instantly normalized, with only the name still moot: current favourites are "New Macedonia" or "Upper Macedonia".

However, the emerging critical issue was the 76-year-old Papandreou's continued stewardship of PASOK and the country, as he clung obstinately to power despite obvious signs of dotage. Numerous senior members of PASOK became increasingly bold and vocal in their criticism, no longer fearing expulsion or the sack as in the past.

The new face of PASOK

Late in November 1995, Papandreou was stricken with severe lung and kidney infections, and rushed to intensive care at the Onassis Hospital. The country was essentially rudderless for two months, as there was no provision in the constitution for replacing an infirm prime minister. At last, in mid-January 1996, the conscious but groggy Papandreou was pressurized to sign a letter **resigning** as prime minister (though not, at that time, as leader of PASOK). The "palace clique",

consisting of Mimi Liani and entourage, were beaten off in the parliamentary replacement vote, in favour of the allegedly colourless but widely respected technocrat **Costas Simitis**, who seemed to be just what Greece needed after years of incompetent flamboyance. Upon assuming office, Simitis indicated that he wouldn't necessarily play to the gallery, as Papandreou had, with a remarkable statement:

> Greece's intransigent nationalism is an expression of the wretchedness that exists in our society. It is the root cause of the problems we have had with our Balkan neighbours and our difficult relations with Europe.

These beliefs were immediately put to the test by a tense armed face-off with Turkey over an uninhabited Dodecanese islet. Simitis eventually bowed to US and UN pressure and ordered a withdrawal of Greek naval forces.

Andhreas Papandreou finally succumbed to his illness on June 22, 1996, prompting a widespread display of national mourning; it was genuinely the **end of an era**, with only Karamanlis (who died less than two years later) and Papadopoulos (who died, still incarcerated, in June 1999) as the last remaining "dinosaurs" of postwar Greek politics. Already the **canonization** of Andreas proceeds apace, with a spate of streets renamed to honour him in provincial towns where he was always revered, but the long-term verdict of history is likely to be harsher.

Papandreou's demise was promptly followed by PASOK's summer conference, where Simitis ensured his survival as party leader by co-opting his main internal foe, Papandreou's former head of staff, Akis Tsohadzopoulos, with a promise of future high office. Following the summer congress, Simitis rode the wave of pro-PASOK sympathy caused by Papandreou's death, and called **general elections** a year early in September 1996.

The **results** were as expected: 162 seats for PASOK versus 108 for *Néa Dhimokratía*. Given that the two main parties' agendas were virtually indistinguishable, it boiled down to which was better poised to deliver results – and whether voters would be swayed by ND chief Evert's strident nationalism. The biggest surprise was the collapse of Samaras's *Politikí Ánixi*, but three leftist splinter parties did well: eleven seats for Papariga's KKE, ten for the *Synaspismós* and nine for the Democratic Social Movement (DIKKI). Evert resigned as ND leader, succeeded by Karamanlis's nephew Kostas, who is now attempting to regain the centre ground.

The current situation

Néa Dhimokratía is down but by no means out, having actually increased its strength on the mainland in the last parliamentary poll, and done well by its own standards in the closely fought October 1998 provincial/municipal polls. ND repeated its success in the June 1999 **Euroelections**, where it finished first nationwide and sent forty percent of Greece's Euro MPs to Strasbourg.

Simitis's position seems secure for the time being, though elections must be called before autumn 2000. First-term problems thus far have arisen from the economic squeeze caused by continuing **austerity measures**. In December 1996, farmers staged dramatic protests, closing off the country's main road and rail arteries for several weeks, before dismantling the blockades in time for people to travel for the Christmas holidays. Much of 1997 saw the teachers or students (or both) on strike over proposed educational reforms. And immediately after the 1998 regional elections, Simitis endorsed a stringent 1999 budget which has seen little support from within his party, let alone outside it.

That said, Simitis, by nature far more pro-European than his maverick predecessor, has devoted himself doggedly to the unenviable task of getting the Greek economy in sufficiently good shape to meet the criteria for **monetary union**. Indeed, the fact that inflation is into single figures for the first time in decades is testament to his ability as an accountant.

Increasingly amicable relations with its Balkan neighbours promise to generate jobs. **Tourism**

recovered significantly in the islands during 1999, despite NATO's spring war against Serbia, after having been in the doldrums since 1995; this was particularly encouraging to the Ionian islands and above all Corfu, where fears that the proximity of Albania in such uncertain times might adversely affect the number of visitors proved unfounded. Another improvement is that the *Eforía* or Greek Inland Revenue has made some highly publicized headway in curbing the enormous **black economy**, the largest in the EU, by requiring meticulous documentation of most transactions, and by publicly "outing" tax-dodgers.

Greece is still banking on the boost to national morale and economic prospects it received with the awarding of the 2004 **Olympic Games** to Athens, although, the new metro and airport aside, much of the work on infrastructure in the capital is still in its infancy and has been complicated by the aftermath of the earthquake which struck northern Athens on September 7, 1999, killing scores and rendering almost 100,000 homeless. It came less than a month after the devastating tremor in northwest Turkey, but ironically may have a silver lining in accelerating the **thaw in relations** between the two historical rivals. Greeks donated massive amounts of blood and foodstuffs to the Turkish victims, as well as being the first foreign rescue teams on hand in Turkey, and in turn saw Turkish disaster-relief squads among the first on the scene in Athens. Soon after, Foreign Minister Yiorgos Papandreou announced Greece had dropped its long-time opposition to EU financial aid to Turkey in the absence of a solution to the outstanding Cyprus and Aegean disputes, and further indicated that Greece would not at present oppose Turkish candidacy for accession to the EU.

Wildlife

Apart from the flora and fauna blown, washed or otherwise carried here, nature on the islands has developed from what was here over 10,000 years ago, when the icecaps melted and stranded these drowned mountains out at sea off the coastline of mainland Greece. Thanks partly to the Venetian invaders – whose extensive olive-planting programmes, at a time of general deforestation in the Mediterranean basin, bound and held much of the islands' topsoil – the Ionian islands are atypically green and fertile compared to most Greek islands.

Before the inundation at the end of the last Ice Age, great forests stretched across much of Italy, what is now the Adriatic Sea and east across the north of Greece. Extensive deforestation for fuel, building and to clear land for cultivation and grazing utterly transformed this landscape on mainland Greece, far less so on the Ionian islands. The difference can be observed on any ferry journey in the region, simply by comparing the bare brown hills of the mainland with the olive groves and pine woodlands that cover most of the eastern coastlines and lower hillsides of the islands.

Modern Greece has escaped some of the worst effects of the intensification of agriculture, but there are signs that it may be succumbing. Pesticides and chemical fertilizers are now playing a larger part in farming, controversial (and possibly carcinogenic)

olive sprays are gaining ground on Corfu and Paxí, and factory fishing threatens what is an already depleted fish stock, as well as the livelihood of independent fishing workers. Ugly and exploitative development has destroyed swaths of the country-side and coastline and, despite the eco-friendly soundbites of politicians and businessfolk, many Greeks (and, it has to be said, many visitors) regard the environment as little more than a convenient garbage dump.

Nevertheless, Greece's environment has yet to approach the state of parts of northern Europe; away from developed areas, it's still possible to find landscapes almost untouched by mankind. Rainy winters make the islands a great draw for botanists, especially in spring, and the vegetation in turn attracts ornithologists and their prey.

Flora

The Ionian archipelago follows a different biological clock from northern Europe or America, particularly noticeable in the development of its **flowers**. Despite being among the most northerly of the Greek islands, the Ionians see daffodils and crocuses in January, freesias and antirrhinums in March, and by Easter most woodlands and domestic gardens are in full bloom. Hot summers – not always guaranteed in this region – tend to blast most plant life, only for autumn rains to produce a second growth among some plants, such as dwarf cyclamen.

The best time to visit is spring, ideally around **Easter** – much of the plant life will have died back before most charter flights begin arriving in the region. By Easter, wild and cultivated carnations, geraniums, garlic, valerian and bush angelica are in flower, as is the slightly sinister bell-like datura. Country walks are likely to be scented with wild rosemary, oregano, thyme (parts of Lefkádha are smothered in this herb; beekeepers park hives in it to flavour the honey) and sage, as well as eucalyptus and myrtle, the last of which is used to line the streets in some Easter parades, giving off a heady aroma as the procession tramples over it.

The onset of **summer** brings yellow broom and, in flowering years, the tiny white star-like flowers of the olive tree. Scarlet pimpernels, anemones, camomile, campanula and love-in-a-mist abound. This is also the time that the region's two sturdiest blooms, the oleander and bougainvillea, appear. Wild orchids can materialize almost overnight. As summer progresses, new growth tends to be on the hills and lower slopes of the mountains. Hollyhocks, asphodel, pinks and grape hyacinths are common at high altitudes.

While the more mountainous islands are largely bare of **trees** at higher altitudes, the lower slopes of Lefkádha and Kefalloniá are notable for impressive stands of Aleppo pine, holm oak and, on the latter, the native Cephallonian fir (*Abies cephalonica*) – which can also be found at even lower levels, notably the beaches of Skála. The ubiquitous **olive tree** (*Olea europea*), unlike its pruned mainland relative, is allowed to grow to unmanageable sizes on the islands; some of those on Corfu and Paxí may be as much as 500 years old. As well as commonplace fruits such as apple, orange, lemon, lime, pear and cherry, figs and prickly pears are also found throughout the islands.

Birds

Despite the unwanted attention of thousands of Greek gun-owners, who seem to regard the Ionian skies as one big funfair rifle range, a great variety of **birds** breed on the islands and migrate through them. Greece is a natural stopping-off point for species that winter in Africa but breed in northern Europe. Visitors in May should catch some of the northbound swarms; the late autumn return journey is less concentrated.

After the sparrow, the **house martin** is probably the commonest bird in the Ionian, visiting in summer. As well as wheeling in great clouds over Corfu Town, it builds its mud nests in handy niches around the roofs of buildings, often under exposed eaves, where the parents can be observed feeding the young. Some canny birds simply nest in taverna awnings.

Blue tits, bullfinches, greenfinches and goldfinches are common in woodland and orchards, and in marshland and coastal dunes it's quite common to spot the avocet, bee-eater, sandpiper, grey heron, kingfisher and oystercatcher. In farmland and scrub you are also likely to glimpse the woodchat shrike, Sardinian warbler, the cirl bunting and the crested skylark. The golden oriole is one of the prettiest visitors to the islands, although if Paxí is anything to go by, its commonest habitat seems to be the deepfreeze –

islanders apparently consider them great delicacies. It's not uncommon to spot pelicans as well.

Most dramatically, there are a number of **predatory birds** common in the islands. Peregrine falcons can be spotted in more remote areas, often in pairs, usually turning endless circles on guard above a nest. Kestrels are a regular sight, hovering on thermals while hunting. Buzzards, griffons and Egyptian vultures and, in more solitary mountainous areas, the golden eagle, can also be seen, though rarely these days.

At night, you're likely to hear nightingales in less developed areas, as well as the tiny Scops owl; barn owls nest here, but are rarely seen.

Mammals

The Ionian islands share the more run-of-the-mill **mammals** common throughout Greece – rats, mice, voles, squirrels and foxes – but tend to lack the larger predators of the mainland's mountainous areas. The **jackal** is still said to be found in the remotest parts of Corfu, although with some difficulty, as it is shy and mainly nocturnal. On Kefalloniá, visitors to Mount Énos might possibly glimpse the dozen or so **wild horses** still at large on the mountain's slopes.

Hedgehogs are fairly common, and though shy will often forage in gardens. Similarly, pine martens and stone martens may also be glimpsed in fairly developed areas. At dusk, you're likely to spot an airborne mammal, the tiny pipistrelle bat.

The region's two aquatic mammals – the **dolphin** and **monk seal** – are very rare. The former can sometimes be seen, particularly around Paxí (early morning is usually the best time), when they race or play around ferries and other boats. Monk seals are rarer still, but are known to breed in caves around Paxí and other island coastlines. They are very shy, and should not be approached. As well as being endangered, the seal is easily scared away from its own habitat, although in breeding season it can also be quite protective.

Reptiles and amphibians

The summer heat and dry, rocky landscape of parts of the islands provide an ideal habitat for reptiles. Yet even **reptiles** avoid the intense heat; best times to catch them are mornings in spring, before the sun begins to bake.

Most of the islands have their own subspecies of lizard. On Corfu and Paxí, the most common is the Dalmatian algyroides, around 15cm long, with a red-brown body and dazzling blue under its lower jaw. The Balkan wall lizard, green/brown-coloured with a long tail, is seen throughout the islands, particularly Kefalloniá and Zákynthos. In the countryside south of Corfu Town, it's sometimes possible to spot the black/grey spiny agama or Rhodes dragon (this is the only place in the Ionian this resident of the Dodecanese has ever been seen).

Most dramatic of the lizards is the **Balkan green lizard**, which can be seen in open or uncultivated countryside (and sometimes the wilder gardens). This bright-green animal can grow up to half a metre in length, most of which is its tail, a crucial balance in its party-piece of running on its hind legs, from one hiding place to another. Looking like miniature tyrannosaurs, they can sometimes be spotted legging it around the gardens of the *Corfu Palace Hotel*.

A distant relative of the lizard, the **gecko**, is a common sight indoors throughout the islands, particularly at night. They cling to walls and ceilings with adhesive pads on their feet, and are both harmless and terrified of humans. Two species, the pink-tinged Turkish gecko and the brown/grey Moorish gecko, are common to the Ionian. You'll most often see them on walls or around light fittings, which attract the flies and mosquitoes on which they feed.

Tortoises can often be found on Corfu, Zákynthos and Kefalloniá. The Hermann's tortoise breeds on all three islands, and favours gentle grassy terrain. The best time to spot them is mid-morning, when they are likely to be basking between hiding places.

Two of the tortoise's smaller aquatic relatives, the European pond terrapin and stripe-necked terrapin, can be found in ponds, rivers and other freshwater environments. The European tends to be black with gold splotches, the stripe-necked grey or brown.

A somewhat larger version of the terrapin, the sea turtle, is common in the Ionian from Corfu down to Zákynthos. The **loggerhead turtle** (*Caretta caretta*) is now a protected species (see p.244), although anyone visiting Zákynthos will see that flagrant breaches of the rules regarding loggerheads are an almost daily occurrence. Like

Schrödinger's cat, it seems likely that the very act of looking at the turtles endangers them. Leatherback and green turtles also breed in the region, but are rarely sighted.

Among **snakes**, there are adders on most of the islands (if you're unfortunate enough to frighten one into biting you, note that they're not poisonous). Large – up to two metres – brown snakes are probably Montpellier snakes, a slightly poisonous snake that feeds on rats and other small mammals. Grass snakes are also quite common, and harmless. The one dangerous species is the nose-horned viper, a short snake with zigzag marks down its back, and one of the most poisonous in Europe.

In springtime, the islands are alive with frogs and toads. The **green toad** announces itself with a curious throaty noise and its remarkable bright-green and grey marbled skin. Also common is the small **tree frog**, green or brown in colour – it can alter like a chameleon – and with adhesive suckers on its feet that enable it to climb. Its mountaineering skills and love of water sometimes lead it into bathrooms, where it does similar insect-catching work to the gecko.

Insects

Grasshoppers and crickets are common in Greece, but not as prevalent as the **cicada**, whose distinctive noise typifies and evokes a Mediterranean afternoon for many visitors. Whereas the grasshopper and cricket produce their sounds by rubbing limbs together, the (male) cicada produces its rasping susurrus by rapidly vibrating cavities on either side of its body. The cicada has a green, cricket-like body, hard to find in trees and shrubs, especially as they tend to fall silent when approached.

The islands are also home to over forty species of **butterfly**, best seen in spring or early summer. Migrant butterflies that will be recognized from north European environments include the red admiral, large and small whites and the painted lady. One of the largest butterflies in Greece, the orange-yellow two-tailed pasha is a rare sighting, but remarkable; some are the size of a small bird. Cleopatras, with their large yellow wings, and the green hairstreak, a small vivid-green butterfly, can also be spotted. Most remarkable, however, are the swallowtails, with their yellow and black colouring and telltale trailing wing tips.

Books

Where separate editions exist in the UK and US, publishers are separated by a semicolon in the listing below, with the UK company given first. Where books are published in one country only, this – or the city where the publisher is based – follows the publisher's name. University Press is abbreviated as UP; o/p signifies an out-of-print – but still highly recommended – book.

Travel and general accounts

Peter Bull *It Isn't All Greek to Me* (Peter Owen, o/p); *Life's a Cucumber* (Peter Owen, o/p). British actor Bull's two books about his love affair with Greece, in particular Lákka on Paxí. Some characters are still alive on the island today, and the tiny house he built three decades ago stands on the cliffs overlooking Lákka bay.

Gerald Durrell *My Family and Other Animals* (Penguin; Viking). Very funny anecdotal memoir of Durrell's childhood on Corfu half a century ago. Excellent on the (now vanished) landscape and Durrell's passion for island fauna; big brother Larry also makes an appearance.

Lawrence Durrell *Prospero's Cell* (Faber & Faber; Penguin, o/p). The first of his islands trilogy (which includes *Reflections on a Marine Venus*, on Rhodes, and *Bitter Lemons*, on Cyprus), this has hardly been out of print since it was published in 1945. Durrell's magical diary of his time on Corfu in the year before World War II is highly recommended for visitors to the island, and mandatory for those visiting Kalámi.

Lawrence Durrell *Spirit of Place* (Faber & Faber; Penguin, o/p). Durrell's collected shorter prose pieces include recollections of Corfu and travels in the Ionian, including a return visit after the war.

Martin Garrett *Greece: A Literary Companion* (John Murray, UK). Extracts of travel writing and the classics, arranged by region. Enjoyable and frustrating in equal measure.

Edward Lear *The Corfu Years* (Denise Harvey, Athens). Superbly illustrated journals of the nonsense versifier and noted landscape painter, whose paintings and sketches of Corfu, Paxí and elsewhere offer a rare glimpse of the Ionian landscape in the nineteenth century.

Henry Miller *The Colossus of Maroussi* (Minerva; New Directions). The perfect companion volume to *Prospero's Cell*: writing in Paris in 1939, Miller was invited to holiday in Kalámi with the Durrells on the eve of World War II. Much of the book covers journeys elsewhere, but the stranger's view of Corfu (and the Durrells) is wonderfully over-the-top.

James Pettifer *The Greeks: The Land and People Since the War* (Penguin; Viking). The best introduction to contemporary Greece, its recent history, as well as politics, culture and topics such as the impact of tourism. Having worked as a reporter in Greece and the Balkans, Pettifer eschews clichés for a complex and unsparing portrait of the modern state.

Terence Spencer *Fair Greece, Sad Relic: Literary Philhellenism from Shakespeare to Byron* (Denise Harvey, Athens; Scholarly Press, US). Greece from the fall of Constantinople to the War of Independence, through the eyes of English poets, essayists and travellers.

Richard Stoneman *A Literary Companion to Greece* (J. Paul Getty Museum). Extracts from the classics, but also some more modern fare, including Kavafy's famed poem "Return to Ithaca" and Wilde on Zákynthos. Over 21 pages on the Ionian, although oddly no mention of Byron's "Childe Harold's Pilgrimage".

History and the classics

A good general history is *A Traveller's History of Greece* by **Timothy Boatswain and Colin Nicolson** (Windrush Press; Interlink), which gives a slightly dated but well-written overview of all periods

Greek. The only specific history of any of the Ionian islands in English is *Old Corfu: History and Culture* by **Nondas Stamatopoulos** (KM Typografia), an incredibly detailed, labour-of-love history of the island and town, concentrating on antiquities.

The classics

Many of the classics make excellent companion reading while travelling around Greece – not least Homer's *Odyssey*, even though its geographical links with the Ionian islands have become confused rather than confirmed over the centuries. Thucydides' *History of the Peloponnesian War* should also prove illuminating for those travelling in the Ionian islands, which were embroiled in the war. The following are all available in Penguin Classic editions:
Herodotus *The Histories*;
Homer *The Odyssey*; *The Iliad*;
Pausanias *The Guide to Greece* (2 vols);
Plutarch *The Age of Alexander*; *Plutarch on Sparta*; *The Rise and Fall of Athens*;
Thucydides *The History of the Peloponnesian War*;
Xenophon *The History of My Times*.

Ancient history

A.R. Burn *History of Greece* (Penguin). Probably the best general introduction to ancient Greece, though for fuller and more interesting analysis you'll do better with one or other of the following.

M.I. Finley *The World of Odysseus* (Penguin). Good on the interrelation of Mycenaean myth and fact.

John Kenyon Davies *Democracy and Classical Greece* (Fontana; Harvard UP). Established and accessible account of the period and its political developments.

Oswyn Murray *Early Greece* (Fontana; Harvard UP). The Greek story from the Mycenaeans and Minoans to the onset of the Classical period.

F.W. Walbank *The Hellenistic World* (Fontana; Harvard UP). Greece under the sway of the Macedonian and Roman empires.

Byzantine, medieval and Ottoman

Nicholas Cheetham *Medieval Greece* (Yale UP, o/p in US). General survey of the period and its infinite convolutions in Greece, with Frankish, Catalan, Venetian, Byzantine and Ottoman struggles for power.

John Julius Norwich *Byzantium: The Early Centuries*, *Byzantium: The Apogee* and *Byzantium: The Decline and Fall* (all Penguin; Knopf). Perhaps the main surprise for first-time travellers to Greece is the fascination with Byzantine monuments. Norwich's three-volume history of the empire is a terrific narrative account, full of deranged emperors and palace coups; a single-volume abridgement, *A Short History of Byzantium*, is also available from the same publishers.

Timothy Kallistos Ware *The Orthodox Church* (Penguin). Good introduction to what is effectively the established religion of Greece.

Modern Greece

Richard Clogg *A Concise History of Greece* (Cambridge UP). A remarkably clear and well-illustrated account of Greece from the decline of Byzantium to 1991, stressing recent decades.

Mark Mazower *Inside Hitler's Greece: The Experience of Occupation 1941–44* (Yale UP). Scholarly and well-illustrated history of Greece during the war, which demonstrates how the complete demoralization of the country and incompetence of conventional politicians led to the rise of ELAS and the onset of civil war.

C.M. Woodhouse *Modern Greece, A Short History* (Faber & Faber). Woodhouse was active in the Greek Resistance during World War II. Writing from a right-wing perspective, his history is briefer and a bit drier than Clogg's, but he is scrupulous with facts.

Archeology and art

John Beckwith *Early Christian and Byzantine Art* (Penguin; Yale UP). Illustrated study placing Byzantine art within a wider context.

John Boardman *Greek Art* (Thames & Hudson, UK). A very good concise introduction to the art of the ancient world in the "World of Art" series.

Reynold Higgins *Minoan and Mycenaean Art* (Thames & Hudson). A clear, well-illustrated roundup.

Sinclair Hood *The Arts in Prehistoric Greece* (Penguin; Yale UP). Sound introduction to the subject.

Gisela Richter *A Handbook of Greek Art* (Phaidon; Da Capo). Exhaustive survey of the visual arts of ancient Greece.

Suzanne Slesin et al. *Greek Style* (Thames & Hudson; Crown). Stunning and stylish domestic architecture and interiors, including Corfu and elsewhere in the islands.

R.R.R. Smith *Hellenic Culture* (Thames & Hudson, UK). Modern reappraisal of the art of Greece under Alexander and his successors.

Peter Warren *The Aegean Civilizations* (Phaidon Books; P Bedrick Books, o/p). Illustrated account of the Minoan and Mycenaean cultures.

Modern fiction

Louis de Bernières *Captain Corelli's Mandolin* (Minerva; *Corelli's Mandolin* Vintage). De Bernières' wonderful tragicomic epic of life on Kefalloniá during World War II and after became almost a fashion accessory among visitors to the island in recent summers. His take on historic detail has also won praise from Greek intellectuals, which should complete the recommendation. The later narrative is telescoped wildly, but the novel deserves the plaudits plastered on the cover (see box p.214).

Stratis Haviaras *When the Tree Sings* (Picador, o/p; Simon & Schuster, o/p); *The Heroic Age* (Penguin, o/p). Although unrelated to the region, these two remarkable novels are recommended for their quasi-autobiographical treatment of two periods in recent Greek history: the former a magic-realist vision of the Nazi occupation of a small Aegean island; the latter a personal history of the civil war, both seen through a boy's eyes.

Russell Hoban *The Medusa Frequency* (Picador; Harcourt Brace, o/p). While much of Hoban's avant-garde mystery takes place in the circuitry of the narrator's word processor, it also involves a journey into an underworld region which can only be accessed by a rather unusual gateway: an olive tree in the hills of Paxí.

Anne Michaels *Fugitive Pieces* (Bloomsbury; Vintage). Acclaimed Canadian poet's first novel tells tale of a Holocaust survivor rescued from Poland by a Greek archeologist after seeing his parents killed by the Nazis. Written in densely poetic prose, the story is told through diaries discovered by another descendant of the Holocaust, as the central character grows up on Zákynthos and later in Canada, where his mentor trains him to be a scholar and translator.

Specific guides

Arthur Foss *The Ionian Islands* (Faber, o/p). Published in 1969, on the cusp of the region's development, this elegant and erudite guide to the islands mixes description with a comprehensive knowledge of the archipelago's history and culture. Copies fetch fancy prices in the second-hand book market, so try your library.

Noel Rochford *Landscapes of Paxos* and *Landscapes of Corfu* (Sunflower Books, UK). Seasoned hiker Rochford has a rather dense prose style, but these are excellent pocket guides to walks around the two islands.

Hilary Whitton Paipeti *The Second Book of Corfu Walks* (Hermes Press). A more leisurely, but no less extensive, guide to walking on the island, written by a knowledgeable long-term resident. The same author has recently written a detailed account of places and events associated with the Durrell brothers in Corfu, titled *In the Footsteps of Lawrence Durrell and Gerald Durrell in Corfu (1935–39)* (Hermes Press).

Flora and fauna

Marjorie Blainey and Christopher Grey-Wilson *Mediterranean Wild Flowers* (HarperCollins, UK). Comprehensive field guide.

Anthony Huxley and William Taylor *Flowers of Greece and the Aegean* (Hogarth Press, UK). The best book for flower identification, an excellent general guide with good photographic illustrations.

David MacDonald and Priscilla Barrett *Collins Field Guide: Mammals of Britain and Europe* (HarperCollins). The best guide on the subject.

Roger Petersen, Guy Mountfort and P.A.D. Hollom *Field Guide to the Birds of Britain and Europe* (Collins; Stephen Green Press); **Herman Heinzel et al** *Collins Guide to the Birds of Britain and Europe* (Collins; Stephen Green Press). There are no specific reference books on Greek birds, but these two European guides have the best coverage.

Tom Tolman and Richard Lewington *A Field Guide to the Butterflies of Britain and Europe* (HarperCollins). A field guide that sorts out all the butterflies you're likely to see, although it's a bit detailed for the casual observer.

Language

with German second – and it is easy to see how so many visitors come back having learned only half a dozen restaurant words between them.

You can certainly get by this way, but it isn't very satisfying, and the willingness to say even a few words will upgrade your status from that of dumb *tourístas* to the honourable one of *xénos/xéni*, a word that can mean foreigner, traveller and guest all rolled into one.

So many Greeks have lived or worked abroad in America, Australia and, to a much lesser extent, Britain, that you will find someone who speaks English in the tiniest island village. Add to that the thousands attending language schools or working in the tourist industry – English is the lingua franca of most resorts,

Learning basic Greek

Greek is not an easy language for English-speakers, but it is a very beautiful one, and even a brief acquaintance will give you some idea of the debt owed to it by western European languages. On top of the usual difficulties of learning a new language, Greek presents the additional problem of an entirely separate **alphabet**. Despite initial appearances,

---

LANGUAGE-LEARNING MATERIALS

TEACH-YOURSELF GREEK COURSES

Breakthrough Greece (Pan Macmillan; book and two cassettes). Excellent, basic teach-yourself course – completely outclasses the competition.

Greek Language and People (BBC Publications, UK; book and cassette available). More limited in scope, but good for acquiring the essentials and the confidence to try them.

Anne Farmakides *A Manual of Modern Greek* (Yale UP/McGill UP; 3 vols). If you have the discipline and motivation, this is one of the best for learning proper, grammatical Greek; indeed, mastery of just the first volume will get you a long way.

PHRASEBOOKS

Greek, A Rough Guide Phrasebook (Rough Guides). For an up-to-date, accurate pocket phrase book not full of "plume de ma tante"-type expressions, look no further than Rough

Guides' very own; English-to-Greek is sensibly phonetic, though the Greek-to-English section, while transliterated, requires mastery of the Greek alphabet.

DICTIONARIES

The Oxford Dictionary of Modern Greek (Oxford University Press). A bit bulky but generally considered the best Greek–English, English–Greek dictionary.

Collins Pocket Greek Dictionary (HarperCollins). Very nearly as complete as the *Oxford* and probably better value for money.

Oxford Learner's Dictionary (Oxford University Press). If you're planning a prolonged stay, this pricey two-volume set is unbeatable for usage and vocabulary. There's also a more portable one-volume *Learner's Pocket Dictionary*.

---

this is fairly easily mastered – a skill that will help enormously if you are going to get around independently (see the box below). In addition, certain combinations of letters have unexpected results. This book's transliteration system should help you make intelligible noises, but you have to remember that the correct **stress** (marked throughout the book with an acute accent) is crucial to getting yourself understood.

Greek **grammar** is more complicated still: nouns are divided into three genders, all with different case endings in the singular and in the plural, and all adjectives and articles have to agree with these in gender, number and case. (All adjectives are arbitrarily cited in the neuter form in the following lists.) Verbs are even worse, with active verbs in several conjugations, passive ones, and passive ones used actively(!). To begin

The Greek alphabet

Greek	Transliteration	Pronounced
A, α	a	a as in father
B, β	v	v as in vet
Γ, γ	y/g	y as in yes, except before consonants and a, o or long i, when it's a throaty version of the g in gap
Δ, δ	dh	th as in then
E, ε	e	e as in get
Z, ζ	z	z sound
H, η	i	i as in ski
Θ, θ	th	th as in theme
I, ι	i	i as in ski
K, κ	k	k sound
Λ, λ	l	l sound
M, μ	m	m sound
N, ν	n	n sound
Ξ, ξ	x	x sound, never z
O, o	o	o as in box
Π, π	p	p sound
P, ρ	r	r sound
Σ, σ, ς	s	s sound
T, τ	t	t sound
Y, υ	i/y	indistinguishable from η
Φ, φ	f	f sound
X, χ	h/kh	harsh h sound, like ch in loch
Ψ, ψ	ps	ps as in lips
Ω, ω	o	o as in box, indistinguishable from o

Combinations and diphthongs

AI, αι	e	e as in get
AY, αυ	av/af	av or af, depending on following consonant
EI, ει	i	long i, exactly like η
EY, ευ	ev/ef	ev or ef, depending on following consonant
OI, οι	i	long i, identical again
OY, ου	ou	ou as in tourist
ΓΓ, γγ	ng	ng as in angle; always medial
ΓK, γκ	g/ng	g as in goat at the beginning of a word; ng in the middle
MΠ, μπ	b	b at the beginning of a word; mb in the middle
NT, ντ	d/nd	d at the beginning of a word; nd in the middle
TΣ, τσ	ts	ts as in hits
TZ, τζ	tz	j as in jam

with at least, the best thing is simply to say what you know the way you know it, and never mind the niceties. Even "Eat meat hungry" should get a result; if you worry about your mistakes, you'll never say anything.

Katharévoussa and dhimotikí

Greek may seem complicated enough in itself, but problems are multiplied when you consider that for the last century there has been an ongoing dispute between two versions of the language: *katharévoussa* and *dhimotikí*.

When Greece first achieved independence in the nineteenth century, its people were almost universally illiterate, and the language they spoke – *dhimotikí*, "demotic" or "popular" Greek – had undergone enormous change since the days of the Byzantine empire and Classical times. The vocabulary had assimilated countless borrowings from the languages of the various invaders and conquerors, namely the Turks, Venetians, Albanians and Slavs.

The finance and inspiration for the new Greek state, and its early leaders, came largely from the Greek **diaspora** – Orthodox families who had been living in the sophisticated cities of central and eastern Europe, or in Russia. With their European notions about the grandeur of Greece's past, and lofty conception of Hellenism, they set about obliterating the memory of subjugation to foreigners in every possible field. And what better way to start than by purging the language of its foreign accretions and reviving its Classical purity? They accordingly devised what was in effect a new form of the language, **katharévoussa** (literally "cleansed" Greek). The complexities of Classical grammar and syntax were reinstated, and Classical words were dusted off and resuscitated.

To the country's great detriment, *katharévoussa* became the language of the schools and the prestigious professions, government, business, the law, newspapers and academia. Everyone aspiring to membership of the elite strove to master it – even though there was no consensus on how many of the words should be pronounced.

The *katharévoussa/dhimotikí* debate was a highly contentious issue through most of the twentieth century. Writers – from Sikelianos and Seferis to Kazantzakis and Ritsos – all championed the demotic in their literature, as did the political Left in its rhetoric, while crackpot right-wing governments forcibly (re)instated *katharévoussa* at every opportunity. Most recently, the colonels' junta of 1967–74 reversed a decision of the previous government to teach in *dhimotikí* in the schools, bringing back *katharévoussa*, even on sweet wrappers, as part of their ragbag of notions about racial purity and heroic ages.

Dhimotikí returned once more after the fall of the colonels and now seems here to stay. It is used in schools, on radio and TV, by newspapers (with the exception of the extreme right-wing *Estia*) and in all official business. The only institutions that refuse to bring themselves up to date are the Church and the legal professions – so beware rental contracts.

This is not to suggest that there is now any less confusion. The Metaxas dictatorship of the 1930s changed scores of village names from Slavic to Classical forms, and these official place names still hold sway on most road signs and maps – even though the local people may use the *dhimotikí* form. Thus you may see "Plomárion" or "Innoússai" written on officially authorized maps or road signs, while everyone actually says Plomári or Inoússes.

GREEK WORDS AND PHRASES

ESSENTIALS

Yes	*Ne*	Yesterday	*Khthés*	Bad	*Kakó*
Certainly	*Málista*	Now	*Tóra*	Big	*Megálo*
No	*Óhi*	Later	*Argótera*	Small	*Mikró*
Please	*Parakaló*	Open	*Aniktó*	More	*Perissótero*
OK, agreed	*Endáxi*	Closed	*Klistó*	Less	*Ligótero*
Thank you	*Efharistó*	Day	*Méra*	A little	*Lígo*
(very much)	*(polý)*	Night	*Nýkhta*	A lot	*Polí*
I (don't)	*(Dhen)*	In the	*To proï*	Cheap	*Ftinó*
understand	*Katalavéno*	morning		Expensive	*Akrivó*
Excuse me,	*Parakaló,*	In the	*To apóyevma*	Hot	*Zestó*
do you speak	*mípos*	afternoon		Cold	*Krýo*
English?	*miláte*	In the evening	*To vrádhi*	With	*Mazí*
	angliká?	Here	*Edhó*	Without	*Horís*
Sorry/	*Signómi*	There	*Ekí*	Quickly	*Grígora*
Excuse me		This one	*Aftó*	Slowly	*Sigá*
Today	*Símera*	That one	*Ekíno*	Mr/Mrs	*Kýrios/Kyría*
Tomorrow	*Ávrio*	Good	*Kaló*	Miss	*Dhespinís*

OTHER NEEDS

To eat/drink	*Trógo/Píno*	Stamps	*Gramatósima*	Police	*Astynomía*
Bakery	*Foúrnos,*	Petrol station	*Venzinádhiko*	Doctor	*Iatrós*
	psomádhiko	Bank	*Trápeza*	Hospital	*Nosokomío*
Pharmacy	*Farmakío*	Money	*Leftá/Khrímata*		
Post office	*Tahydhromío*	Toilet	*Toualéta*		

REQUESTS AND QUESTIONS

To ask a question, it's simplest to start with the name the thing you want in an interrogative tone.

Where is the bakery?	*Parakaló, o foúrnos?*	When?	*Póte?*
Can you show	*Parakaló, o dhrómos*	Why?	*Yatí?*
me the road to…?	*yía…?*	At what time…?	*Ti óra…?*
We'd like a	*Parakaló, éna dhomátio*	What is/Which is…?	*Ti íne/Pió íne…?*
room for two	*yía dhýo átoma?*	How much	*Póso káni?*
May I have a kilo	*Parakaló, éna*	(does it cost)?	
of oranges?	*kiló portokália?*	What time does	*Ti óra aníyi?*
Where?	*Poú?*	it open?	
How?	*Pós?*	What time does	*Ti óra klíni?*
How many?	*Póssi* or *pósses?*	it close?	
How much?	*Póso?*		

ACCOMMODATION

Hotel	*Xenodhohío*	Cold water	*Krýo neró*
A room…	*Éna dhomátio…*	Can I see it?	*Boró ná to dho?*
for one/two/	*yía éna/dhýo/tría*	Can we camp here?	*Boróume na*
three people	*átoma*		*váloume tín skiní*
for one/two/	*yía mía/dhýo/trís*		*edhó?*
three nights	*vradhiés*	Campsite	*Kámping/*
with a double bed	*me megálo kreváti*		*Kataskínosi*
with a shower	*me doús*	Tent	*Skiní*
Hot water	*Zestó neró*	Youth hostel	*Ksenónas neótitos*

TALKING TO PEOPLE

Greek makes the distinction between the informal (*esí*) and formal (*esís*) second person, as French does with *tu* and *vous*. Young people, older people and country people nearly always use *esí* even with total strangers. In any event, no one will be too bothered if you get it wrong. By far the most common greeting, on meeting and parting, is *Yía sou/Yía sas* – literally "Health to you".

Hello	*Hérete*	Speak slower, please	*Parakaló, miláte*
Good morning	*Kalí méra*		*pió sigá*
Good evening	*Kalí spéra*	How do you say	*Pos léyete sta Eliniká?*
Good night	*Kalí nýkhta*	it in Greek?	
Goodbye	*Adío*	I don't know	*Dhén kséro*
How are you?	*Ti kánis?/Ti kánete?*	See you tomorrow	*Tha se dhó ávrio*
I'm fine	*Kalá íme*	Au revoir	*Kalí andámosi*
And you?	*Ke esí/esís?*	Let's go!	*Páme!*
What's your name?	*Pos se/sas léne?*	Please help me	*Parakaló, na*
My name is...	*Me léne...*		*me voïthíste*

GREEKS' GREEK

There are numerous words and phrases that you will hear constantly, even if you rarely have the chance to use them. These are a few of the most common.

Éla!	Come (literally) but also Speak to me! You don't say! etc.	*Pedhí moú*	My boy/girl, sonny, friend, etc.
Oríste?	What can I do for you?	*Maláka(s)*	Literally "wanker", but often used (don't try it!) as an informal address.
Embrós! or *Léyete!*	Standard phone responses		
Ti néa?	What's new?	*Sigá sigá*	Take your time, slow down
Ti yínete?	What's going on (here)?	*Kaló taxídhi*	Bon voyage
Étsi k'étsi	So-so	*Ópa!*	Whoops! Watch it!
Pó-pó-pó!	Expression of dismay or concern, like French "O la la!"		

ON THE MOVE

Aeroplane	*Aeropláno*	How many hours?	*Pósses óres?*
Bus	*Leoforío*	Where are you going?	*Pou pas?*
Car	*Aftokínito*	I'm going to...	*Páo stó...*
Motorbike, moped	*Mihanáki, papáki*	I want to get off at...	*Thélo ná katévo stó...*
Taxi	*Taksí*	The road to...	*Ó dhrómos yía...*
Ship/boat	*Plío/Vapóri/Karávi*	Near	*Kondá*
Bicycle	*Podhílato*	Far	*Makryá*
Hitching	*Otostóp*	Left	*Aristerá*
On foot	*Me ta pódhia*	Right	*Dheksiá*
Trail	*Monopáti*	Straight ahead	*Katefthía*
Bus station	*Praktorío leoforíon*	A ticket to...	*Éna isitírio yía...*
Bus stop	*Stási*	A return ticket	*Éna isitírio me epistrofí*
Harbour	*Limáni*	Beach	*Paralía*
What time does it leave?	*Ti óra févyi?*	Cave	*Spiliá*
		Centre (of town)	*Kéndro*
What time does it arrive?	*Ti óra ftáni?*	Church	*Eklisía*
		Sea	*Thálassa*
How many kilometres?	*Pósa hiliómetra?*	Village	*Horió*

GREEK WORDS AND PHRASES (continued)

THE TIME AND DAYS OF THE WEEK

Sunday	*Kyriakí*	One o'clock	*Mía íy óra*
Monday	*Dheftéra*	Two/three o'clock	*Dhýo/trís íy óra*
Tuesday	*Tríti*	Twenty to four	*Tésseres pará íkosi*
Wednesday	*Tetárti*	Five minutes	*Októ ke pénde*
Thursday	*Pémpti*	past eight	
Friday	*Paraskeví*	Half past eleven	*Éndheka ke misí*
Saturday	*Sávato*	In half an hour	*Se misí óra*
What time is it?	*Ti óra íne?*	In a quarter-hour	*S'éna tétarto*

MONTHS AND SEASONAL TERMS

January	*Yennári*	July	*Ioúlios*	Summer schedule	*Therinó*
February	*Fleváris*	August	*Ávgoustos*		*dhromolóyio*
March	*Mártis*	September	*Septémvris*	Winter schedule	*Himerinó*
April	*Aprílis*	October	*Októvris*		*dhromolóyio*
May	*Maïos*	November	*Noémvris*		
June	*Ioúnios*	December	*Dhekémvris*		

NUMBERS

1	*énas/mía/éna*	12	*dhódheka*	90	*eneнínda*
2	*dhýo*	13	*dhekatrís*	100	*ekató*
3	*trís/tría*	14	*dhekatésseres*	150	*ekatón penínda*
4	*tésseres/téssera*	20	*íkosi*	200	*dhyakóssies/ia*
5	*pénde*	21	*íkosi éna*	500	*pendakóssies/ia*
6	*éxi*	30	*triánda*	1000	*hílies/hília*
7	*eftá*	40	*saránda*	2000	*dhýo hiliádhes*
8	*okhtó*	50	*penínda*	1,000,000	*éna ekatomýrio*
9	*enyá*	60	*exínda*	first	*próto*
10	*dhéka*	70	*evdhomínda*	second	*dhéftero*
11	*éndheka*	80	*ogdhónda*	third	*tríto*

Glossary of words and terms

ACROPOLIS Ancient, fortified hilltop.

AGORA Market and meeting place of an ancient Greek city; also the commercial "high street" of a modern town or village.

AMPHORA Tall, narrow-necked jar for oil or wine.

ÁNO Upper; common prefix element of village names.

APÓKRIES Pre-Lentern carnival.

ARCHAIC PERIOD Late Iron Age period, from around 750 BC to the start of the Classical period in the fifth century BC.

ARÉKIA Italian-influenced folk ballads (see box p.324)

ASTIKÓ (Intra)city, municipal, local – as in phone calls and bus services.

ÁYIOS/AYÍA/ÁYII Saint or holy (m/f/plural). Common place-name prefix (abbreviated Ag or Ay), often spelled AGIOS or AGHIOS.

BYZANTINE EMPIRE Created by the division of the Roman empire in 395 AD, this, the eastern half, was ruled from Constantinople (modern Istanbul). In Greece, Byzantine culture peaked twice: in the eleventh century, and again at Mystra in the early fifteenth century.

CAPITAL The flared top, often ornamented, of a column.

CLASSICAL PERIOD Essentially from the end of the Persian Wars in the fifth century BC until the unification of Greece under Philip II of Macedon (338 BC).

CORINTHIAN Columns with capitals carved with acanthus leaves; a temple built in this order.

DHIAMERISMATA Flats or apartments, often applied to holiday rentals.

DHIMARHÍO Town hall.

DHOMÁTIA Rooms for rent in purpose-built blocks or private houses.

DORIAN Northern civilization that displaced and succeeded the Mycenaeans and Minoans through most of Greece around 1100 BC.

DORIC Minimalist, unadorned columns, dating from the Dorian period; a temple built in this order.

ESTIATÓRIO Restaurant; see "Eating and Drinking" in Basics (p.42) for fuller description.

EXOTERIKÓ International, in case of mail or phone call, literally 'outer'.

FRIEZE Band of sculptures around a temple or other building. Doric friezes consist of various tableaux of figures (METOPES) interspersed with grooved panels (TRIGLYPHS); Ionic ones have continuous bands of figures.

FROÚRIO Medieval castle; also modern military headquarters.

GARSONIÉRA/ES Studio villa/s, self-catering apartment/s.

GEOMETRIC PERIOD Post-Mycenaean Iron Age era named for the style of its pottery; begins in the early eleventh century BC with the arrival of Dorian peoples. By the eighth century BC, with the development of representational styles, it becomes known as the ARCHAIC PERIOD.

HELLENISTIC PERIOD The period following Macedonian expansion under Alexander the Great to the fall of Corinth to the Romans in 146 BC during which the eastern Mediterranean world was under Greek cultural and political hegemony.

HEPTANESE Old-fashioned term for the Ionian islands, including Kýthira.

HEROÖN Shrine or sanctuary, usually of a demigod or mortal; war memorials in modern Greece.

IERÓN Literally, "sacred" – the space between the altar screen and the apse of a church, reserved for priestly activities.

IKONOSTÁSIS Screen between the nave of a church and the altar, supporting at least three icons.

IONIC Elaborate, decorative development of the older DORIC order; Ionic temple columns are slimmer with deeper "fluted" edges, scroll-shaped capitals and ornamental bases.

IPERASTIKÓ Inter-city, long-distance – as in phone calls and bus services.

KAFENÍO Coffee house or café; in a small village the centre of communal life and probably serving as the bus stop, too.

KAÏKI (plural KAÏKIA) Caique, or medium-sized boat, traditionally wooden and used for transporting cargo and passengers; now refers mainly to island excursion boats.

KALIKANTZÁRI Hobgoblins in folklore.

KÁMBOS Fertile agricultural plateau or plain, the latter usually near a river mouth.

KANDÁDHES Distinct Ionian form of song, a hybrid of Greek folk and classical Italian (see box p.234).

KANTÍNA Shack, caravan or even a disused bus on the beach, serving just drinks and perhaps sandwiches.

KARNAVÁLI Common term for the pre-Lentern festival.

KÁSTRO Any fortified hill or a castle.

KATHOLIKÓN Central chapel of a monastery.

KÁTO Lower; common prefix element of village names.

KENDRIKÍ PLATÍA Central square.

KLEPHTS Mountain brigands, infamous for lawlessness and renowned for resistance to Turks.

KOUROS Nude Archaic or Classical statue of an idealized young man, usually portrayed with one foot slightly forward of the other.

LEOFÓROS Avenue, usually included when part of an address.

LIMÁNI Port or harbour.

LIMENARHÍO Port Authority.

MACEDONIAN EMPIRE Empire created by Philip II in the mid-fourth century BC.

MAÉSTRO Prevailing northwesterly winds, common in the Ionian in summer.

METOPE see FRIEZE

MINOAN Crete's great Bronze Age civilization, which dominated the Aegean from about 2500 to 1400 BC.

MONÍ Formal term for a monastery or convent.

MYCENAEAN Mainland civilization centred on Mycenae and the Argolid from about 1700 to 1100 BC.

NAÓS The inner sanctum of an ancient temple; also, any Orthodox Christian shrine.

NARTHEX Western vestibule of a church, reserved for catechumens and the unbaptized; typically frescoed with scenes of the Last Judgement.

NEOLITHIC Earliest era of settlement in Greece, characterized by the use of stone tools and weapons together with basic agriculture. Divided arbitrarily into Early (c 6000 BC), Middle (c 5000 BC) and Late (c 3000 BC).

NÉOS, NÉA, NÉO "New" – a common prefix to a town or village name.

NOMARHÍA The prefecture building which administers each NOMÓS.

NOMÓS Modern Greek province or county – the larger islands each constitute a separate one.

ODEION (ODHÍO) Small ancient theatre, used for musical performances, minor dramatic productions or councils.

ODHÓS Street, not usually mentioned or written in addresses.

ORCHESTRA Circular area in a theatre where the chorus would sing and dance.

PALAESTRA Gymnasium for athletics and wrestling practice.

PALEÓS, PALEÁ, PALEÓ "Old" – again a common prefix in town and village names.

PANAYÍA Virgin Mary.

PANDOPOLÍO Old-style grocer's shop.

PANIYÍRI Festival or feast – the local celebration of a holy day.

PANDOKRÁTOR Literally "The Almighty"; generally refers to the stern portrayal of Christ in Majesty frescoed or in mosaic in the dome of many Byzantine churches. Also name of Corfu's largest mountain.

PARALÍA Beach or seafront promenade.

PARAMONÍ Eve, of festival or celebration.

PEDIMENT Triangular, sculpted gable below the roof of a temple.

PERÍPTERO Street kiosk.

PINAKOTHÍKI Picture/art gallery.

PLATÍA Square, plaza.

PROTOKHRONIÁ New Year's Day.

PSAROTAVÉRNA Fish restaurant; see "Eating and Drinking" in Basics (p.43).

PSISTARIÁ Grill restaurant; see "Eating and Drinking" in Basics (p.43).

PÝRGOS Tower or bastion.

STELE Upright stone slab or column, usually inscribed; an ancient tombstone.

STOA Colonnaded walkway in Classical-era marketplace.

TAHYDHROMÍO Post office.

TAVERNA Restaurant; see "Eating and Drinking" in Basics (p.43) for fuller description.

TÉMBLON Wooden altar screen of an Orthodox church, usually ornately carved and painted and studded with icons; more or less interchangeable with IKONOSTÁSIS.

TEMENOS Sacred precinct, often used to refer to the sanctuary itself.

THEATRAL AREA Open area found in most of the Minoan palaces with seat-like steps around. Probably a type of theatre or ritual area, though this is not conclusively proven.

THOLOS Conical or beehive-shaped building, especially a Mycenaean tomb.

TILEKÁRTA Phonecard.

TRIGLYPH see FRIEZE

VÓLTA Walk or ride for pleasure, often conducted in the evening.

ZAHAROPLASTÍO Patisserie serving sweets and cakes.

ACRONYMS

ANEK *Anónymi Navtikí Etería Krítis* (Shipping Co of Crete, Ltd), which runs most ferries between Pireás and Crete, plus many to Italy.

DIKKI Democrat Social Movement, a party leftward of PASOK.

EAM National Liberation Front, the political force behind ELAS.

ELAS Popular Liberation Army, the main Resistance group during World War II and the basis of the communist army (DSE) in the civil war.

ELTA The postal service.

EOT *Ellinikós Organismós Tourismoú*, the National Tourist Organization.

FYROM Former Yugoslav Republic of Macedonia.

KKE Communist Party, unreconstructed.

KTEL National syndicate of bus companies. The term is also used to refer to bus stations.

ND Conservative (*Néa Dhimokratía*) party.

OTE Telephone company.

PASOK Socialist party (Pan-Hellenic Socialist Movement).

Index

Stay in touch with us!

ROUGH*NEWS* **is Rough Guides' free newsletter. In four issues a year we give you news, travel issues, music reviews, readers' letters and the latest dispatches from authors on the road.**

ROUGH GUIDES: Travel

Amsterdam
Andalucia
Australia

Austria
Bali & Lombok
Barcelona
Belgium &
  Luxembourg
Belize
Berlin
Brazil
Britain
Brittany &
  Normandy
Bulgaria
California
Canada
Central America
Chile
China
Corfu & the
  Ionian Islands
Corsica
Costa Rica
Crete
Croatia
Cyprus
Czech & Slovak
  Republics
Dodecanese &
  the East Aegean

Dominican
  Republic
Ecuador
Egypt
England
Europe
Florida
France
French Hotels &
  Restaurants
  1999
Germany
Goa
Greece
Greek Islands
Guatemala
Hawaii
Holland
Hong Kong &
  Macau
Hungary
India
Indonesia
Ireland
Israel & the
  Palestinian
  Territories
Italy
Jamaica
Japan
Jordan

Kenya
Lake District
Laos
London
Los Angeles
Malaysia,
  Singapore &
  Brunei
Mallorca &
  Menorca
Maya World
Mexico
Morocco
Moscow
Nepal
New England
New York
New Zealand
Norway
Pacific Northwest
Paris
Peru
Poland
Portugal
Prague
Provence & the
  Côte d'Azur
The Pyrenees
Rhodes & the
  Dodecanese
Romania

St Petersburg
San Francisco
Sardinia
Scandinavia
Scotland
Scottish
  Highlands &
  Islands
Sicily
Singapore
South Africa
South India
Southwest USA
Spain
Sweden
Switzerland
Syria

Thailand
Trinidad &
  Tobago
Tunisia
Turkey
Tuscany &
  Umbria
USA
Venice
Vienna
Vietnam
Wales
Washington DC
West Africa
Zimbabwe &
  Botswana

AVAILABLE AT ALL GOOD BOOKSHOPS

ROUGH GUIDES: Mini Guides, Travel Specials and Phrasebooks

MINI GUIDES

Antigua
Bangkok
Barbados
Big Island of
  Hawaii
Boston
Brussels
Budapest

Dublin
Edinburgh
Florence
Honolulu
Jerusalem
Lisbon
London
  Restaurants
Madrid
Maui
Melbourne
New Orleans
Rome
Seattle
St Lucia

Sydney
Tokyo
Toronto

TRAVEL SPECIALS

First-Time Asia
First-Time
  Europe
Women Travel

PHRASEBOOKS

Czech
Dutch

Egyptian Arabic
European
French
German
Greek
Hindi & Urdu
Hungarian
Indonesian
Italian
Japanese

Mandarin
  Chinese
Mexican
  Spanish
Polish
Portuguese
Russian
Spanish
Swahili
Thai
Turkish
Vietnamese

ROUGH GUIDES:
Reference and Music CDs

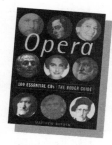

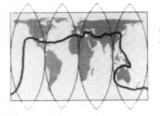
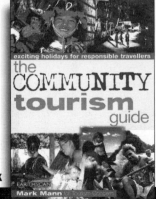